The Aesthetics of Organization

The Aesthetics of Organization

edited by

Stephen Linstead and Heather Höpfl

SAGE Publications
London • Thousand Oaks • New Delhi

SAGE Publications Ltd
6 Bonhill Street
London EC2A 4PU

SAGE Publications Inc
2455 Teller Road
Thousand Oaks, California 91320

SAGE Publications India Pvt Ltd
32, M-Block Market
Greater Kailash – I
New Delhi 110 048

British Library Cataloguing in Publication data

A catalogue record for this book is
available from the British Library

ISBN 0 7619 5322 1
ISBN 0 7619 5323 X (pbk)

Library of Congress catalog card number available

Typeset by Annette Richards
Printed and bound in Great Britain by Athenaeum Press, Gateshead

Contents

Part 4: Crafting an Aesthetic

Part 5: Aesthetics, Ethics and Identity

Part 6: Radical Aesthetics and Change

Illustrations

Notes on Contributors

Frank J. Barrett is an Associate Professor of Systems Management and Organizational Behavior at the Naval Postgraduate School in Monterey, California. He received his PhD in Organizational Behavior from Case Western Reserve University in 1990 and both his BA in International Relations (1975) and his MA in English (1977) from the University of Notre Dame. His research is in the areas of organizational change, organizational learning, generative metaphor and appreciative inquiry. In addition to numerous book chapters, he has published articles in *Organization Science, Human Relations, Journal of Applied Behavioral Science* and *Organization Dynamics*. Most recently he has written about the dynamics of jazz improvisation and possible lessons for organizational innovation and creativity. He is also an active jazz pianist.
Mailing address: Dept of Systems Management, Naval Postgraduate School, 555 Dyer Rd, Monterey, Calif. 93940, USA.
Email: fbarrett@nps.navy.mil

Pippa Carter is a Senior Lecturer in the School of Management of the University of Hull. Her research interests are in the field of Organization Theory, with particular regard to the ontological and epistemological conditions of organization, the function of management and the nature of work. These research interests are informed by the radical critique of organization theory of poststructuralism and of the modernist/critical modernist/postmodernist debate. She has published widely in this field, with 'some man' from the University of Newcastle upon Tyne.
Mailing address: The Business School, University of Hull, Hull HU6 7RX, UK.

Stewart Clegg was born in Bradford, England, but left for Australia in 1976. Since then almost all of his career has been spent in Australia, at Griffith University, University of New England, University of Western Sydney, Macarthur and latterly at UTS (University of Technology, Sydney). Stewart has published and travelled widely from Australia, including one extended trip into a metaphoric medieval purgatory. Aesthetically, he enjoys sailing, cycling, rugby football (both codes, but especially League), as well as cinema, music, theatre and politics. In terms of the latter two, he particularly laments the loss from the arena of Australian politics of its 'Placido Domingo', ex-Prime Minister Paul Keating. Nonetheless, he is well aware of the insidiousness of nostalgia as an ailment and tries to keep it at bay with physical exercise.

Mailing address: School of Management, UTS, Broadway PO Box 123, NSW 2007, Australia.
Email: s.clegg@uts.edu.au

Stephen Cummings formerly a Lecturer in Organization Theory and a Tutor in Ancient Greek History at Victoria University of Wellington, New Zealand, is currently a Lecturer in Strategy at the University of Warwick.
Mailing address: Marketing and Strategic Management, Warwick Business School, University of Warwick, Coventry CV4 7AL, UK.
Email: msmscu@razor.wbs.warwick.ac.uk

Pierre Guillet de Monthoux holds a chair in General Management at Stockholm University, where he leads the European Centre for Art and Management. ECAM is currently doing research into management of art and art-related organizations and also runs a Master of Business Art programme. Professor Guillet de Monthoux is a fellow of Åbo Academy in Finland, Witten-Herdecke University B.R.D. and Université de Sophia Antipolis, Nice, France, where he teaches managerial aesthetics. Amongst his publications on aesthetics and ethics in managerial philosophy are *Action and Existence – Art and Anarchism for Business Administration* (Accedo, 1991) and *The Moral Philosophy of Management – from Quesnay to Keynes* (M.E. Sharpe, 1993).
Mailing address: School of Business, University of Stockholm, 106 91 Stockholm, Sweden.
Email: pgm@fek.su.se

Harro Höpfl is a member of the Department of Politics and International Relations at the University of Lancaster. His principal publications are in political theory. He has written on and translated some of the political work of Calvin and Luther and has spent many years researching the early Jesuits. Harro Höpfl contributes to the MPhil in Critical Management in the Management School at Lancaster University and has published in management journals on the historical foundations of management thought.
Mailing address: Department of Politics and International Relations, Lancaster University, Lancaster, LA1 4YL, UK.
Email: h.hopfl@lancaster.ac.uk

Heather Höpfl is Professor of Organizational Psychology and Head of Department of Operations Research and Human Resource Management at Newcastle Business School, University of Northumbria at Newcastle. She is an Adjunct Professor of the University of South Australia and a Visiting Professor of the Academy of Entrepreneurship and Management in Warsaw. She has organized a number of critical management conferences over the past nine years and holds regular international seminars and workshops on developments in organisation studies. She enjoys teaching through video and novels and is committed to the radical examination of the experiential aspects of organizations.

Mailing address: Department of Operations Research and Human Resource Management, University of Northumbria at Newcastle, Ellison Building, Ellison Place, Newcastle upon Tyne, NE1 8ST, UK.
Email: heather.hopfl@unn.ac.uk

Norman Jackson is a Senior Lecturer in the School of Management of the University of Newcastle upon Tyne. After a number of years in engineering management, he gained an MA in Organizational Psychology at the University of Lancaster and a PhD from Aston University, having also studied at Manchester Business School. His research contributes to the radical critique of organization theory and reflects an interest in poststructuralism, with a touch of critical theory. He has published widely in this area, with 'some woman' from the University of Hull.
Mailing address: The School of Management, Armstrong Building, University of Newcastle, Newcastle upon Tyne NE1 7RU, UK.

Hugo Letiche is NECSI Professor of Meaning in Organization and chairs the 'Advice, Organization and Policy' major at the University for Humanist Studies, Utrecht, The Netherlands. In addition, he is a member of the visiting faculty of the Centre for Social Theory and Technology at Keele University, UK. He also teaches 'Human Relations' on the Rotterdam School of Management MBA at Erasmus University in The Netherlands. In his research, he has tried to explore the practical and theoretical limits to organizing – having published on postmodern organizational theory, emergence and complexity theory, gender and emotion. Recent articles have appeared in *Organization, Organization Studies, Personnel Review, Human Resource Development International, Emergence* and *Studies in Cultures Organizations and Societies.* Most of his publications are ethnographic essays combining close description with poststructuralist reflection.
Mailing address: Frankenslag 13 2582HB, The Hague, The Netherlands.
Email: h.letiche@uvh.nl

Stephen Linstead is Associate Director (Research) and Research Professor of Management at Sunderland Business School, University of Sunderland. He previously held the Chair of Management at the University of Wollongong, New South Wales, and has worked at Hong Kong University of Science and Technology and Lancaster University among others. Although he was born in Barnsley and still supports the Tykes, for whom his father once played, he is also an Australian citizen and has worked with a number of international corporations. He has been involved with the arts as a writer and performer since his first and only TV appearance as a singer in 1966, and has recorded and performed live and on radio sporadically since then, still hoping for his big break. Sadly, his closest brush with stardom remains the occasion when Joe Cocker accidentally urinated on his foot in the gents toilet of the 'Princess Royal' pub in Sheffield. Recent books include *Understanding Management* (Sage, 1996 – with Robert Grafton Small and Paul Jeffcutt) and *Management: A Critical Text* (Macmillan, 1999 – with Liz Fulop). He is currently Chair of the

Standing Conference on Organizational Symbolism and Corporate Culture, but still wishes he was a rock star.

Mailing address: Sunderland Business School, University of Sunderland, St Peter's Campus, St Peter's Way, Sunderland SR6 ODD, UK.
Email: stephen.linstead@sunderland.ac.uk

Brian Rusted is an Associate Dean (Interdisciplinary Programs) at the University of Calgary. He teaches Communications Studies and Canadian Studies, and has long had an interest in visual culture, architecture, cultural performance and the social organization of taste. A founding editor of the journal *Studies in Cultures, Organizations and Societies*, he maintains a conviction about the importance of ethnographic representations of cultural and organizational life. He has won awards for his creative work in writing and video.

Mailing address: Faculty of General Studies, University of Calgary, 2500 University Drive NW, Calgary, Alberta T2N 1N4, Canada.
Email: rusted@acs.ucalgary.ca

David Silverman's interests are in non-romantic qualitative methodologies, professional–client communication and conversation analysis. He is the author of 14 books. The most recent are: *Interpreting Qualitative Data* (Sage, 1993); *Discourses of Counselling* (Sage, 1997); *Harvey Sacks: Social Science and Conversation Analysis* (Polity, 1998); *Doing Qualitative Research: A Practical Handbook* (Sage, 1999). He is Professor Emeritus at Goldsmiths College, London University. He continues to argue for a rigorous, theoretically based social science which maintains a dialogue with the wider community.

Mailing address: c/o Sociology Department, Goldsmiths College, London SE14 6NW, UK.
Email: d.silverman@gold.ac.uk

Antonio Strati is Associate Professor and lectures on the sociology of organizations at the Universities of Trento and Siena, Italy. He is a founder-member of the Standing Conference on Organizational Symbolism (SCOS), and his research interests focus on symbolism, aesthetics, cognitivism and the use of grounded theory in organization studies. He is the author of *Organization and Aesthetics* (Sage, 1999) and of the textbook *Theory and Method in Organization Studies* (Sage, 2000).

Mailing address: Dipartimento di Sociologia e Ricerca Sociale, via G. Verdi 26, I-38100 Trento, Italy.
Email: antonio.strati@soc.unitn.it

Introduction

In the spring of 1999, Antonio Strati produced his impressive introduction to organizational aesthetics, *Organization and Aesthetics* (Strati, 1999). In it, he traces the various movements towards a systematic study of the aesthetics of organization over the past two decades. Notably, Strati identifies the influence of the Standing Conference on Organizational Symbolism (SCOS) and points to its contribution to the development of the field in the 1980s. The literature on organizational aesthetics has been dominated by SCOS members past and present and, in particular, by a series of writings which came from a conference on 'corporate image' organized by Vincent Dégot in Antibes, France in 1985 (Benghozi, 1987; Dean et al., 1997; Dégot, 1987; Gagliardi, 1990, 1996; Jones et al., 1988; Linstead and Grafton-Small, 1985; Ottensmeyer, 1996; Ramirez, 1987; Rusted, 1987; Strati, 1990, 1992, 1995, 1999; Turner, 1990). Strati argues that an 'Aesthetic understanding of organizational life . . . is an epistemological metaphor which problematizes the rational and analytical analysis of organizations' (Strati, 1999: 7).

Over the past twenty years the study of meaning in organizations, tacit knowledge, artefacts and cultures have all influenced the emergence of a concern for the aesthetic aspects of organization. However, it would be grossly simplistic to assume that such an interest is merely in the notion of beauty or elegance in the form, architecture or structures of organizations. Indeed, such an assumption would direct the field towards the development of an *aesthetics of organizing* with little regard for the epistemological issues with which Strati would like us to engage. It is the very fact that an aesthetic approach to organizational studies 'problematizes the rational' which makes it an important concern for organizational theorists. At the same time, a concern for the aesthetic aspects of organizing seems to be an inevitable counterpart to the privileging of appearance in organizational life. As organizations become increasingly baroque in the generation of images, texts and fetishized constructions of themselves, so a deconstructive approach rooted in a concern for the visual becomes important. Aesthetic approaches move in the spaces between the organization as regulatory (the Law) and as experience (the Body); between the cognitive and the sensory; and between the stimulus and the response. Consequently, aesthetic approaches have much to contribute to the study of organizations by working outside conventional categories and by challenging the *logic* of the organizing process.

Recent work in organization studies (Dean et al., 1997; Gagliardi, 1990, 1996; Linstead, 1994; Sandelands and Buckner, 1989; Strati, 1992) has drawn attention to the possibility of developing an aesthetics of organization as field of inquiry within organization studies. This book draws together essential foundational contributions delineating the parameters of the field. In particular, it is concerned with exploring:

- the distinction between the aesthetics of organizations and the aesthetics of organization;
- the importance of 'evocation' in organizational understanding;
- the significance of concepts drawn from postmodern thinkers dealing with what is variously termed negativity (Derrida) or the inhuman (Lyotard) – the silences, the unspoken, the unsayable, the inevitable incompletenesses, the implicit, the ambiguous, that quality which cannot be specified. These are the necessary and inescapable complement to the positive aspects of signification which are required for meaning and order to become real in the enacted organization, or which may subvert its purposes consistently;
- aesthetics as a form of emancipation/resistance;
- particular methodological problems associated with empirical investigation of the aesthetic;
- re-conceptualizations of the visual and the aural and their relevance for organizational understanding;
- the importance of recent ideas on vision, perspective and periphery for learning in organizations and pedagogical developments;
- the incorporation of theory from any of the visual or performing arts into organization studies; and
- empirical work on organizational aesthetics.

In order to address these issues the book is divided into six parts. Part 1 is concerned with *aesthetic theory* and Part 2 with *aesthetic processes*. Part 3 deals with *aesthetics and modes of analysis*, whereas Part 4 is about *crafting an aesthetic* in different contexts. The next section, Part 5, gives attention to *aesthetics, ethics and identity* and Part 6 offers a contribution to *radical aesthetics and change*.

In the spirit of criticism which derives from an examination of the 'meaningful action (of) embodied subjects', that is, of the organizational actor as a 'hybrid entity made up of non-human elements inseparable from the human person and from his/her corporeality' (Strati, 1999: 110–11), the various contributions to the book include elements of aesthetic appreciation. So, just as Strati contends that 'organizational aesthetics is not separate from the daily lives of people in organizations' (Strati, 1999: 111), neither is it possible for organizational theorists to detach themselves from the aesthetics of their own experiences, preferences, styles and judgements. We didn't insist on this when we briefed the contributors initially – it was a quality which emerged from the nature of their engagement with the project. However, it does embody the argument of the book for the restoration of experience and of corporeality into accounts of the aesthetics of organization, to acknowledge what was never lost but merely misplaced. It is apparent in reading the various contributions to the book that each contributor in their own way brings a personal aesthetic appreciation to the task of presenting their case. It was one of our more agreeable tasks as editors to note these harmonics and to give emphasis to them here.

Part 1 of the book deals with *aesthetic theory*. It is appropriate that the first chapter is from Antonio Strati, whose theoretical contributions to the development of the field have already been considerable. In the introduction to his book, *Organization and Aesthetics*, Strati speaks of the aesthetics of organizational life as 'sweetness and obsession, the feeling of pleasure and destructive desire, the source of conflict, the origin of problems of difficult solution, even in a socially constructed reality' (1999: 1). What is striking about this definition is the degree of consonance between what he is saying about the aesthetics of organizational life and Antonio Strati, the person. It is this integrity and coincidence of self-identity and expressive form which describes the possibility of a position between text and experience. In Strati's case, his commitment to empathic knowledge not only characterizes his interpretation of the space but also expresses an empathic commitment and an epistemological concern. It is precisely for this reason that a theory of organizational aesthetics has an important role to play in articulating the site of reconciliation between theory and practice.

In his chapter, Strati explores the various approaches taken by organizational scholars to the study of aesthetics and provides a valuable overview of the development of the field. A number of enquiries, he suggests, have focused on specific aspects of the organizational aesthetic, for instance the organization's internal and external image. Other studies have considered the organization's aesthetic use of decoration or embellishment, or its budget allocation for external cultural events and entertainment. Other organizational scholars, Strati included, have examined the beauty of the organization as a whole, with particular emphasis on rites and narratives about events at work, about working group and leadership styles, and about rituals of collective life identified not only as beautiful but also as of special significance for the organizational actors. In particular, this chapter highlights the 'dominance' of physical settings, and the need to give attention to aspects of setting usually neglected in organizational studies in order to illustrate the theme of aesthetics in organizations:

- the 'ideology' of corporate beauty, or rather the organization's ideology of its own beauty;
- the 'continuity' of the issue of creativity in the organizational literature on manager as artist; organization as a creative process and life; organization as play; and
- the 'diffusion' of the postmodern, or rather the overwhelming prominence that postmodern theory assigns to the aesthetic dimension.

It is difficult to read Pierre Guillet de Monthoux's chapter, 'The art management of aesthetic organizing', without an appreciation of what Turner

(1988) describes as 'connoisseurship'. Guillet de Monthoux writes with a gracious and delightful hauteur. He is deliciously urbane. The people he writes about are like old friends. He might well have had supper with them last night. Kant, of whom he writes with affectionate regard, becomes an intimate: it is as if their conversation, interrupted by this text, awaits resumption. And all this is entirely in keeping with the substance of the chapter. 'Aesthetics,' he argues, 'widens the discourse of creativity to the topic of interpretation', and this is to be found in his discussion of the ways in which organizational aesthetics can learn from art theory. Contemporary art, as reflected upon in art theory, he argues, has increasingly begun to analyze the rhetoric of the business world. Products have been used as symbols of 'poart'. Organizations are now used as business art materials. Guillet de Monthoux uses these issues to pose the question to what extent does art *in* organizations and the art *of* organizations coincide? Where, he asks, does art become the mere decoration and legitimation of what can be better understood as economic forces? To tackle this sort of question he suggests that it might be appropriate to turn to the study of political propaganda and ideological mobilization. The chapter proposes a model to explain the processes of 'totalization' and 'banalization' in a business context which is based on art theory and aesthetics.

Part 2 deals with *aesthetic processes* and begins with a chapter by Stephen Linstead – 'Ashes and madness: the play of negativity and the poetics of organization'. Linstead has a great love of language. It is hardly surprising given his subject-matter that his work should be redolent with poetic imagery, a pervading lyricism, a gentle urgency. He delights in the flow of words, gushing and spouting, transforming semantic order into a liquid prose. Here, he is concerned to explore what might be entailed in developing a poetics of organization. He begins by following a line of argument which suggests that all language carries with it a silent, implicative double, which supports and carries it and allows it to do its work. The 'postmodern' theorizing of Lyotard and Derrida, he argues, has attempted to address the unsaid and the unsayable, the sublime, the different, recognizing that life without silence is unbelievable. Beavis and Butt-head are used as an example of the power of the inarticulate, and also illustrate processes of mimesis (copying) and division which are common elements of human organizing. In organization theory, as David Levin argues, propositional language seeks to limit the effects of this 'negativity', and to construct truth only in positive terms, ingesting or expulsing inconsistent elements. Following Lévi-Strauss and Bauman, Linstead discusses this in terms of anthropoemic (incorporating) and anthropophagic (opposing) societies, and gives an organizational example of the 'proteophobia' – a fear of lack of conformity to standard – characteristic of the latter in a discussion of the mimetic management of a university. The argument then develops, drawing on the work of Heidegger, Gadamer, Levin, Iser and Caillois, into considering an alternative form of truth (aletheia) to the orthodoxy (orthotes) which is based on chance, serendipity, flashes of insight, and play.   The various processes involved in the play of negativity – agon, alea, mimesis and ilinx – are discussed, and the idea of an alternative to scientific, propositional precision – poetic precision – is put forward, drawing on the work of Georges Bataille and

J.P. Ward. Finally, the chapter considers some methodological issues for an ethnographically based poetics of organization.

Heather Höpfl's chapter, 'The aesthetics of reticence: collections and recollections', is inherently melancholic in its construction. However, it is a melancholy which is remedied by anamnesis. Like many of her writings, the chapter derives its central ideas from an experience and from an observation. In this case, the impetus for the chapter came from the sense of outrage Höpfl experienced at the predatory behaviour of another which she observed following the death of a mutual friend. In this chapter, she sets out to keep open the site of the absence and to defend it from appropriation. Accordingly, the chapter is concerned with the situated production aesthetic and with posited meaning, with loss and confiscation. It deals with the appropriation of space through collection and confinement under the guise of heterogeneity, polyvalence, carnival or plurivocity. It illustrates this idea with the construction and positing of meaning in artistic works which are produced from fragments/elements removed from their familiar context as in pastiche (an 'artistic' bricolage), for example in the photographic work of Sophie Calle. The argument uses the notion of posited (spatialized) meaning in order to consider ways in which (a) space is colonized and appropriated through the process of collection.

The posited meaning which now intrudes into the site of the absence relates to the notion of 'artistic intent' and to appropriation under the pretext of liberating heterogeneity. This process involves the appropriation of significant absence and its conversion into kitschified presence under the claim of artistic license. The meaning of the site now rests in the hands of the artist or collector who assembles and re-constructs the value of the space. It is essential, therefore, Höpfl argues, that attention is paid to the importance of critique for discernment in matters of artistic intent and production aesthetics, and that this critique forms the basis of our re-collection of these spaces.

Part 3 deals with *aesthetics and modes of analysis*. The first contribution to this part is Brian Rusted's '"Cutting a show": grounded aesthetics and entertainment organizations'. Rusted has an extremely astute, somewhat wry style and a quick and discerning eye. In a quite different way to Guillet de Monthoux, Rusted is also a connoisseur but his taste is for the well-spiced morsel and he is highly discriminating. He writes as someone who savours and delights in small, well-chosen delicacies. Rusted's work has a quality of J.D Salinger about it and there are delightful recursions throughout the text which take us back again and again to the opening scene. He tells his story with the persistence and pleasure that might be derived from unravelling a ball of knotted string and, in the end, hands over the piece of string and says, 'Can you use this for anything?' Rusted reminds us that matters of taste and judgement are also matters of power. The study of aesthetics by organizational culture researchers, he contends, has paralleled the rise of aesthetic research in Cultural Studies and, although both perspectives have common interests in culture, ritual and ideology, they have taken quite divergent paths. Typically, organizational culture researchers have stressed the normative qualities of formal organizations whereas Cultural Studies researchers stress the oppositional qualities of subcultural and leisure formations. Consequently, in this chapter, Rusted considers the influence Cultural Studies can have for the study of aesthetics in organizational settings. As such, it examines some of the more common assumptions of organizational research on aesthetics and develops these in light of ethnographic data on aesthetics which has been collected from an entertainment organization in the business of producing leisure for formal, corporate organizations.

Chapter 6 is David Silverman's 'Routine pleasures: the aesthetics of the mundane'. This is an accomplished, professional piece of writing which is concerned with the pleasure to be derived from the systematic study of organizational micro-orders – the aesthetics of the mundane or routine. Silverman is a craftsman, of course, and his style is deft. Part of his accomplishment is precisely in his elevation of the mundane to a position where its intricacies can be examined. The specific focus of the piece is on the skilful practices of both organizational members and organizational researchers. Silverman follows Garfinkel in asserting that organizational processes are to be understood as the outcome of the mundane practices through which people collaborate in reproducing a world-known-in-common, for example by inferring 'meaning' and 'intention'. Accounts of organizations depend on an aesthetic which searches for clarity in a way which is specifically opposed to kitsch.

So, Silverman advances a quasi-'modernist' position which, while acknowledging points of contact with 'postmodern' arguments, claims that organizational 'subjects' do not dissolve but are locally constituted. Consequently, Silverman calls for a search for clarity which begins with an examination of ordinary language usage. The central part of the chapter deploys studies of organizational processes which respond to this aesthetic. Inter alia, it considers studies of business meetings, human–computer interaction and work on committee meetings and professional–client interviews. Silverman is particularly concerned with how lay and scientific members constitute and resolve ambiguities. The chapter concludes with an argument that this kind of mundane aesthetic has produced a powerful, cumulative and replicable body of knowledge which is directly relevant to both central issues in organization theory and to organizational practice.

Part 4 of the book looks at *crafting an aesthetic* and deals with aesthetics in context. Chapter 7 is by Hugo Letiche, 'Observer versus audience', a study of the Netherlands Dance Theatre. Here is a chapter about dance which is full of movement. Letiche dances through his text and so it is in this chapter. What is interesting here is the movement of ideas. Letiche dances in the space between the Body and Law and creates huge perturbations and turbulences in the air. He opens up the site of performance, introduces light, illuminates dark spaces and performs. So, his chapter deals with moving bodies and performance spaces and this seems to be highly appropriate. Pursuing John Law's (1994) five criteria for ethnography – wherein research is to be symmetrical, non-reductionist, recursive, process-oriented and reflexive – Letiche examines organizing within the Nederlands Dans Theatre (NDT). Dance is treated as more of a proximal than a distal process, making its organization a special case. He describes NDT from the perspective of rehearsal, choreography, dancers, current and past performance(s) as well as the troupe's history. Via the sharply opposing principles of proximal organizing of the two NDT house choreographers Hans van Manen and Jiri Kylian, the case addresses issues of aesthetic purpose and success. Modernist openness and process is confronted with postmodern performance and success. The difference in perspective between being 'audience' and 'observer' is studied, examining how NDT's organizing determines, at once, both the researcher's and the dancer's position(s).

In Chapter 8, 'An-aesthetics', Pippa Carter and Norman Jackson take as their theme a definition of 'aesthetic' which locates it as a function of perception – the emotional response to a perceived stimulus – and argue that all organization(s) produce(s) an aesthetic which is 'designed' to elicit positive responses from all those with whom transactions, of whatever kind, take place. Carter and Jackson argue that the creation of such an aesthetic is distinct from the creation of organizational image or of legitimation, though both of these may be a part of it; that the aesthetic varies in terms of the audience; and that it is produced by varied means, both positive and negative, and ranging from seduction to coercion. What Carter and Jackson bring to this analysis is a compassion which is reflected in the seriousness of their work and their obvious empathy with the subject-matter. Carter and Jackson visited the War Cemeteries which they describe in the paper and the impact this made on them is quite clear in their writing. This is research in the empathic style which Strati proposes: rich and suffused with experience. The paper takes as an example an organization which very deliberately sets out to create an aesthetic – the Commonwealth War Graves Commission – and argues that an important element of its creation is a process of masking and denial of the experienced reality of organization, which operates to provide a conforming sense of security and, at the same time, to defer action which may threaten the status quo. This, it is suggested, is the function of aesthetics of organization.

Part 5 of the book is concerned with *aesthetics, ethics and identity*. Chapter 9, Harro Höpfl's '"Suaviter in modo, fortiter in re": appearance, reality and the early Jesuits' follows nicely from Carter and Jackson's analysis of the function of the aesthetics of organization. Höpfl brings to this chapter an elegant, intricate style with a baroque degree of elaboration and detail. Höpfl's presentation is a deliberate attempt to replicate the complexity of the subject-matter in the complexity of the argumentation. This is part of the construction of the appearance, the production aesthetic of the argument itself. Thus, he argues that self-presentation, the cultivation of appearances and even a certain theatricality as key constituents of organizational success, is not a recent invention. This chapter offers some reflections on organizational appearance, reality and rhetoric by reference to the Society of Jesus (a spectacularly successful organization) and its enemies.

In the Jesuits' analysis, falsehood and heresy had triumphed because of presentation. The successful Catholic response (the Society's mission) would therefore have to present the truth just as persuasively and attractively. The chapter explores the Society's acute sensitivity to its public face and the impression it was creating: its elaborate procedures for recruiting, training and positioning its members to ensure that the Society's 'embodiments' were presentable and persuasive; and the systematic publicity, high-profile activities, and the visibility and elegance of Jesuit edifices and emblems as the Society's corporate self-representation. Fundamental to all else was the Society's cultivation of rhetoric: the art and science of persuasive discourse, demanding both mastery of the moral substance of truth and its persuasive presentation: 'suaviter in modo, fortiter in re'.

The deliberate cultivation of appearances, however, invites a cynical, unmasking response: it had already done so in reply to the Machiavellian statecraft of manipulating appearances. The response was to unmask appearances as mere facade; reality is what is hidden behind it. The Society's many enemies similarly claimed to be able to unmask the power to control opinion, represented by Jesuits as merely a means to their spiritual ends, as in fact their real end. But ironically, unmasking was so often counterproductive: to unmask the power behind the suave facade was to affirm and confirm its reality. Höpfl uses this argument to draw parallels with modern organizations and their manipulations of corporate culture.

'Resurfacing an aesthetics of existence as an alternative approach to business ethics', by Stephen Cummings is a piece of writing which strains at the boundary of conventional understandings of organizational ethics like a dog straining at its leash. In this chapter, Cummings argues that two approaches to ethics may be discerned: codes of behaviour and forms of subjectification. Codes of behaviour here refer to systems of collective rules. Forms of subjectification, on the other hand, urge individuals to constitute themselves as subjects of moral conduct through the setting up and development of relationships with the self. Cummings suggests that this might mean, for example, relationships for self-reflection, self-examination and self-aesthetics, relationships for the decipherment of the self by oneself. It is the former approach that has been privileged with regard to the development of business ethics in recent times. In contrast, the latter has been neglected. This leads Cummings to the contention that conceiving of an organization as having a 'self' opens up the possibility of an exploration of the neglected, and, he argues, that the last works of Michel Foucault provide an excellent vein of ideas with which to approach this task. Combining Foucault's and others' ideas with this conception of organizational 'selves' provides individual organizations with an alternative ethical basis for strategic development. Consequently, this chapter puts forward the view that this alternative ethics, focused on forms of subjectification, will carry more meaning and be more efficacious than traditional collective codes within current theorizing.

Radical aesthetics and change, the subject of Part 6 of this text, offers 'Cultivating an aesthetic of unfolding: jazz improvisation as a self-organizing system'. This is another connoisseur piece. Frank Barrett writes about jazz and improvisation and, in his writing, develops and elaborates on a theme. Clearly, it is difficult for someone who is not a jazz musician to comment, but it is interesting to see how Barrett finds his ideas, enjoys them and moves from a theoretical position into a playfulness with his subject-matter which is reminiscent of Linstead in Chapter 3. Barrett puts forward the view that, given the shift to a post-industrial society, it has been argued that there is a need for a new model of management that acknowledges the management of complexity and knowledge creation as a central task of organizing. There is a need for organizational members at all levels to think, plan, innovate, process information and that this requires a different metaphor or model for understanding the process of organizing. It seems that what is called for is a model of diverse specialists living in a chaotic, turbulent environment, making fast, irreversible decisions, highly interdependent on one another to interpret equivocal information, dedicated to innovation and novelty. Barrett explores Karl Weick's suggestion that the jazz band be studied as a prototype organization. Consequently, this chapter explores the nature of jazz improvisation and proposes that managers do what, in fact, many jazz players do: fabricate and invent novel responses without a prescribed plan and without certainty of outcomes, discovering the future that their action creates as it unfolds. Barrett then discusses some of the characteristics of jazz improvisation and argues for an aesthetic of surrender and attunement, asking:

> what would our organizations look like if managers and executives were encouraged to recapture a poetic wisdom, to be suspicious of past successes, to create provocative learning relationships, to see affirmative engagement as a core task, to value wonder over suspicion, surrender over defensiveness, listening and attunement over self promotion?

In his book *The Ideology of the Aesthetic*, Eagleton (1990) poses a great many reasons why a study of aesthetics should be given serious attention. Not least he confirms the location of the various movements at work in this book in saying that 'the general tendency of this current of thought can be seen as a steady undermining of the mind in the name of the body', and he goes on to argue that the 'very emergence of the aesthetic marks . . . a certain crisis of traditional reason and a potentially liberating . . . trend of thought'. However, Eagleton counsels that while 'there is in the aesthetic an ideal of compassionate community, of altruism and natural affection, . . . which represents a threat to rationalism . . . the political consequences of this are ambivalent' (1990: 60). As Strati puts it, this requires that we also look at work experiences which are 'felt to be ugly, tragic, grotesque or in execrable taste' (1999: 111): a transgressive radical aesthetic at work between the body and the law. 'The law,' Eagleton says, 'is male, but hegemony is a woman; this transvestite law, which decks itself out in female drapery is in danger of having its phallus exposed' (1990: 58).

Our final chapter looks at how an 'ugly' and 'tragic' locality was rejuvenated as a practising social, political and spiritual community – which incidentally contained real transvestites who exposed the metaphorical ones. The Pelourinho district of Salvador, Bahia, in north-eastern Brazil was, until recently, more famous for its *travestis*, or transvestites, than anything else – but it held within it a huge potential for existing cultural innovation to provide a means for regeneration. Stewart Clegg, in '"*The Rhythm of the Saints*": cultural resistance, popular music and collectivist organization in Salvador, Bahia in Brazil', based on fieldwork in Pelourinho, discusses the regeneration of the area. Once a centre of the Portuguese slave trade, the area was well-to-do bourgeois, with fine buildings, but as the trade and wealth disappeared it became the seedy red-light district of the town famous for drugs, prostitution and transvestism. The government supported a transformation of the area in the late 1980s, centred around the world-famous drum school featured in Paul Simon's album of the same name, and creating an original aesthetic of African, Latin and Southern European influences. Now a successful tourist attraction as well as a thriving community, the chapter examines the nature of the transformation and the role aesthetics played in its success.

In sum, then, we hope that this book will contribute to an understanding of the aesthetics of organization by lifting (or at least rustling) the skirts of more conventional organization and management theories to show them for what they are – phallic manifestations capable only of reproduction in text: law without body. The aesthetic then must function to heal the rift between experience and ways of apprehending the world, to reunite 'humanity with a world which seems to have turned its back on it' (Eagleton, 1990: 66). This book is our collective contribution to this process.

Stephen Linstead and Heather Höpfl
Sunderland and Newcastle upon Tyne

References

Benghozi, P.J. (ed.) (1987) *Art and Organization*, Special Issue of *Dragon*, 2 (4).

Dean, J.W., Ramirez, R. and Ottensmeyer, E. (1997) 'An aesthetic perspective on organizations', in C. Cooper and S. Jackson (eds), *Creating Tomorrow's Organizations: A Handbook for Future Research in Organizational Behaviour*. Chichester: Wiley. pp. 419–37.

Dégot, V. (1987) 'Portrait of the manager as an artist', *Dragon*, 2 (4): 13–50.

Eagleton, T. (1990) *The Ideology of the Aesthetic*. Oxford: Blackwell.

Gagliardi, P. (ed.) (1990) *Symbols and Artifacts: Views of the Corporate Landscape*. Berlin: de Gruyter.

Gagliardi, P. (1996) 'Exploring the aesthetic side of organizational life', in S.R. Clegg, C. Hardy, and W.R. Nord (eds), *Handbook of Organization Studies*. London: Sage. pp. 565–80.

Grafton-Small, R. and Linstead, S.A. (1985) 'Bricks and bricolage: deconstructing corporate image in stone and story', *Dragon*, 1, 1: 8–27.

Jones, M., Moore, M. and Snyder, R.C. (eds) (1988) *Inside Organizations: Understanding the Human Dimension*. Newbury Park, CA: Sage.

Linstead, S.A. (1994) 'Objectivity, reflexivity and fiction: humanity, inhumanity and the science of the social', *Human Relations*, 47 (11): 1321–46.

Ottensmeyer, E. (1996) 'Too strong to stop, too sweet to lose: aesthetics as a way to know organizations', *Organization*, 3 (2): 189–94.

Ramirez, R. (1987) 'An aesthetic theory of social organization', *Dragon*, 2 (4): 51–63.

Rusted, B. (1987) 'It's not called show art! Aesthetic decisions as organizational practice', *Dragon*, 2 (4): 127–36.

Sandelands, L.E. and Buckner, G.C. (1989) 'Of art and work: aesthetic experience and the psychology of work feelings', in L.L. Cummings and B.M. Staw (eds), *Research on Organizational Behaviour*, Vol. 11. Greenwich, CT: JAI Press. 105–31.

Strati, A. (1990) 'Aesthetics and organizational skill', in B.A. Turner (ed.), *Organizational Symbolism*. Berlin: de Gruyter. pp. 207–22.

Strati, A. (1992) 'Aesthetic understanding of organizational life', *Academy of Management Review*, 17 (3): 568–81.

Strati, A. (1995) 'Aesthetics and organization without walls', *Studies in Cultures, Organizations and Societies*, 1 (1): 83–105.

Strati, A. (1999) *Organization and Aesthetics*. London: Sage.

Turner, B.A. (1988) 'Connoisseurship in the study of organizational cultures', in A. Bryman (ed.), *Doing Research in Organization*. London: Routledge. pp. 108–22.

Turner, B.A. (ed.) (1990) *Organizational Symbolism*. Berlin: de Gruyter.

PART 1

AESTHETIC THEORY

1

The Aesthetic Approach in Organization Studies[1]

Antonio Strati

The underlying assumption of the aesthetic approach to the study of organizations is that, although an organization is indeed a social and collective construct (Berger and Luckman, 1966; Knorr Cetina, 1981; Latour and Woolgar, 1979; Schütz, 1962–66), it is not an exclusively cognitive one but derives from the knowledge-creating faculties of all the human senses (Strati, 1996a).

This assumption has a number of consequences. First, the organization is considered as the product of specific processes whereby it is invented, negotiated and redefined by using the entire complex of the knowledge-creating faculties of both organizational actors and organization scholars. Second, within the organization flourish personal idiosyncrasies, specific modes of interpreting events, different views of what to do and when to do it, and the ceaseless negotiation of values, symbols and organizational practices: these refer also to aesthetics. Accordingly, the aesthetic approach (Strati, 1992, 1999):

1   *shifts the focus of organizational analysis* from dynamics for which explanations can be given – or at least for which actor rationales can be reconstructed *a posteriori* – to dynamics more closely bound up with forms of tacit knowledge (Polanyi, 1962, 1966). The network of the sensory and

perceptive faculties of both organizational actors and organization scholars produces knowledge that is not entirely verbal, nor entirely sayable. Other languages intervene, from visual to gestural, and other knowledge-creating processes, from intuitive to evocative.

2   *alters the scholar's attention rules* as s/he conducts empirical and theoretical inquiry. As well as the ratiocinative and abstractive capacities of the subjects who identify with an organization, the aesthetic approach takes account of their ability to see, hear, smell, touch and taste and their aesthetic judgement, which is otherwise implicit and hidden by the abstractive capacities. Also these human faculties have power on organizational life, and they influence the negotiation of both the organization's day-to-day practices and its ultimate meaning. The scholar's attention rules focus on the capacity of all the human senses to produce organizational knowledge, starting with his or her own perceptive and sensory abilities.

3   *highlights the heuristic shortcomings* of those studies and theories of organization which rely on the causal explanation of organization phenomena; which rely on the myth of the rationality of organizations; and which propound an objective and universal interpretative key to organizational life.

These are the themes that I shall investigate in this chapter. I begin by stressing that the qualifier 'aesthetic' is attached to this approach in order to highlight its diversity from those based on cognitivism and rationality. I shall then illustrate the categories best suited to both empirical and theoretical exploration of organizational routine. These are categories derived from the philosophy of art, and they furnish the aesthetic approach with routes to the understanding of organizational life. The chapter concludes with a brief description of the emerging strand of organization studies devoted to aesthetics, and of the specific contemporary contribution made by the aesthetic approach to the empirical and theoretical study of organizations.

Aesthetics as *ars analogi rationis*

The beginnings of a theory of aesthetics can be traced to the philosophical works of Alexander Gottlieb Baumgarten (1735, 1750) and Giambattista Vico (1725). These authors provide the first outlines of aesthetics, and their ideas shed extraordinary light on the meaning of the qualificatory term 'aesthetic' attached to this approach to organizational studies, and on its distinctiveness with respect to other approaches.

For both Baumgarten and Vico aesthetics is a specific mode of knowing distinct from intellectual and rational knowledge. Since its origins, therefore, aesthetics has been distinctively heuristic in nature (Zecchi and Franzini, 1995: 257) rather than representative of the object of analysis. This constitutes the theoretical starting-point of the aesthetic understanding of organizational life. But exactly what sort of knowledge is aesthetic knowledge?

Baumgarten (1750–8) writes that aesthetics is the science of sensible knowledge distinct from intellectual and scientific knowledge; a modality of knowledge which, though inferior, is nevertheless autonomous and ineluctable. Indeed, there is no philosopher, observes Baumgarten (1735), who does not remain even temporarily trapped by confused and obscure knowledge, in which meanings are not clearly distinguishable, either one from the other or in their constitutive parts. There is no philosopher who does not pass through this form of comprehension of surrounding reality before achieving the scientific knowledge yielded by the capacities of abstraction and ratiocination. Rational intelligence has always some reference to sensible knowledge, some nexus with a *sensitiva idea*. However, the fact that philosophers cannot achieve intellectual and abstract knowledge without prior aesthetic knowledge does not imply that the latter is merely a level or stage of the former. On the contrary, aesthetics operates alternatively to and in parallel with higher gnoseology: it is *ars analogi rationis* (Baumgarten, 1750–8). As such, as art is analogue to reason, it raises a metaphysical-baroque challenge against the analytical rationality that seeks after the truth.

This challenge is of crucial importance for the aesthetic approach to the study of organizations. And it is even more forcefully posited by Giambattista Vico. It is indeed in his antithesis between aesthetic thought and rational thought that the aesthetic approach finds its *raison d'être*. With his project for a new science, Vico (1725) deliberately sets himself in conflict with Cartesian philosophy. There is wisdom that is not rational but poetic, he writes, and it is rooted in those relations which are not 'reasoned' but nevertheless bind us to surrounding reality.

The relations to which Vico refers are those that are sensed and imagined. How can they be represented? By means of logical poetry. Which implies that logic is not entirely embodied in *logos*, that it does not exclusively pertain to Cartesian rationality. Logic, observes Vico, pertains also to mythical thought, meaning that the poetic fable, like the mythic narrative, and like the mute gesture, are expressions of a logic, of poetic logic. This logic has no grounding in the Cartesian rational order but nonetheless communicates spiritual meanings. Hieroglyphics, gestural language, myth and metaphor are its forms of knowing. It is these poetic operations that enable us to conserve the concreteness of our relationship with things and with the original meaning of the world: a relationship which Cartesian rationality is unable to sustain.

If we are not to lose this contact with the world, this concrete relationship with reality, it is not sufficient for aesthetic knowledge to flank Cartesian rational thought. Here Vico diverges from Baumgarten, for he maintains that there are not two distinct and independent forms of knowledge that coexist because they relate to different spheres of action. There is a conflict between the two gnoseologies whereby the force of myth and poetic logic imbues the *logos*.

Accordingly, the aesthetic understanding is not only distinct from cognitively based knowledge of organization, it stands in antithesis to it: it disputes such knowledge and seeks to pervade it with its wisdom. The aesthetic approach emphasizes that rational analysis neglects extremely important aspects of quotidian organizational practices, and also that it must necessarily do so, given that it is unable either to grasp these aspects or to understand their meaning for the organization. Yet if these neglected aspects are of such importance, and if approaches to organizational study based on analytical methods are unable to handle them, what plausibility attaches to the descriptions that they propound of organizational phenomena?

Obviously, the antithesis is radical, but without the presumption that the aesthetic approach can provide either a more authentic or a more complete interpretation of organizational life. Rather, the organizational knowledge thus obtained is partial, fragmented and modest. It bears no resemblance to the generalizable, universal and objective knowledge yielded by approaches that use analytical methods. Nor does it claim to be part of a paradigm seeking to achieve supremacy among organizational theories. On the contrary, to adopt this approach implies expressing resistance and opposition to the pre-eminence of any specific tradition of organization study over others, and assailing the dominion of rational cognition in organization theory. This is done by focusing organizational inquiry on those aspects that can be understood by deploying the heuristic capabilities of all the senses, rather than that of intellectual reasoning alone.

The implications of all this will be explored in the sections that follow. I shall begin by examining the aesthetic characterization of the approach, reflecting on whether it signifies art, emotion or the passive contemplation of organizational events. I shall then consider the criteria available to the researcher who employs this approach, showing that aesthetic categories prove to be useful tools for this purpose.

Aesthetics and contemplation

The etymology of the lexical root *aisth*, from ancient Greek, and especially the verb *aisthànomai,* conveys the heuristic action of aesthetics: feeling through physical perceptions. Aesthetics, however, is not merely receptive: that is to say, it does not involve action by a knowing subject essentially characterized by passivity to surrounding reality. The verb *aisthànomai* denotes, in fact, the stimulation of the abilities related to feeling.

This is an important specification which rules out any equivalence between the aesthetic approach and the passive reception of organizational life. Aesthetics is an aid to observation, notes Odo Marquard (1989), and as such it is antithetical to *anaesthetica,* which is a means of putting people to sleep; an outcome, according to Marquard, that aesthetics can also achieve. How? By transforming sensitivity into insensitivity, and art into somnolence by aesthetizing reality.

Researchers who analyze organizational life using the aesthetic approach, therefore, must begin by arousing and refining their own sensory and perceptive faculties.

Aesthetics and art

Aesthetic understanding should not be confused with artistic understanding. Such confusion easily arises, however, because aesthetics has its roots also in the theory of art and not only in philosophy.

An example may give an idea of this delicate but important boundary between the aesthetic approach and artistic understanding. Imagine that you are in a workshop and are repelled by its smells. This is a qualitative datum of organizational analysis collected by a sensory faculty: it is, that is to say, a datum appropriate to the aesthetic approach.

Smell sheds light on an aspect that organizational literature habitually ignores, given that it considers odour only insofar as it signals health risks in a work environment, or adds a picturesque detail to the description of a workshop. The aesthetic approach, by contrast, regards the disgust provoked by the smells in the workshop as a matter for inquiry. Is the distaste of the researcher also felt by those who work there? Or have they got used to it? Do the smells identify the workshop for them, their working conditions, the content of their work? Are the smells an initiation test for newcomers? Do they evoke nostalgia for people who no longer work there? Outside the workshop, do smells carried with them signal workshop personnel to other members of the organization?

Numerous and diverse paths of analysis open up, all of them yielding knowledge on the everyday activities of the organization. As will be noted, none of this involves the artistic understanding of organizational life. Having physically felt, with one's senses and in the course of one's research, repugnance at these smells means that:

1   A particular sensory and perceptive faculty was activated in order to know the organization aesthetically.
2   The researcher's attention focused on a problem of day-to-day organizational life, specifically on organizational phenomena provoking a feeling of repugnance.
3   S/he used an aesthetic not an artistic sensibility to do so. The aesthetic sense that recoiled at the workshop smells did not require the researcher to possess artistic talent. Nor did s/he need the baggage of artistic and philosophical knowledge possessed by an art critic or a philosopher to feel such repugnance.

4   The researcher used an aesthetic category, given that the feeling of repugnance is one such category: namely, as we shall see, the category of ugliness.

The etymology of the words 'aesthetics' and 'art' further clarify the non-equivalence between the two concepts. The term 'art' derives from the Latin *ars*. The origin of 'art' in ancient Greek is *techne*, not *aisth*. Etymologically, 'art' signifies 'transforming raw materials with ability and intelligence', and this is very different from 'knowing on the basis of sensible perceptions', which is the meaning of 'aesthetics'.

Aesthetics and emotion

Even more subtle than the misconceived equivalence of aesthetics to art is its relationship to emotion.

The emotions yield knowledge on organizational life. Anger and bitterness, boredom, disappointment, fear, anxiety, joy, enthusiasm, passion: these are all emotions tied to ethical codes, rights and obligations, and values specific to collectivities which operate in organizational contexts (Sims, Fineman and Gabriel, 1993). Emotion also marks out a possible course of inquiry for the researcher. Verbal and written emphasis, embarrassment, outbursts and confidences, as well as interruptions, evasiveness and sudden changes of subject, are forms of emotional behaviour which highlight organizational events, personal experiences and fantasies and provide the researcher with empirical material on which to work. Moreover, emotion is at odds both with the myth of rationality in organizational analysis (Putnam and Mumby, 1993) and with the cognitivist paradigm in organization studies (Fineman, 1996).

However, the fact still remains, as Renato Barilli (1995: 16) points out, that aesthetic feeling relates not so much to the heart and the sentiments as to the senses, that is, to the network of physical perceptions. Seeing, hearing, feeling, tasting and smelling are actions which provoke emotions in both organizational actors and the researcher.

It is on this broad range of perception-yielding perceptions that the principles and ambits of the aesthetic approach rest. The emotions aroused by the sensory and perceptive faculties provide the aesthetic approach with important materials for empirical and theoretical analysis. In other words, they constitute a set of organizational phenomena that the aesthetic approach finds congenial but which do not distinguish it from other approaches to the organization.

This concludes my introductory remarks on the significance of the qualifier 'aesthetic' attached to this approach to the study of organizations. We have seen that it evinces an antithesis between the epistemological options available to those who seek organizational knowledge or who construct theories of organizations. In short, researchers who use the aesthetic approach activate the entire complex of their sensory and perceptive faculties. This means, for example, that a researcher will judge the fact that a joke by a shop-floor worker is 'relished' by his or her workmates to be a qualitative datum that warrants analysis: for taste is a category of aesthetics. The same applies to a 'comic' situation or to one described as 'grotesque'. These are qualitatively rich data for researchers who use this approach, since both the comic and the grotesque are aesthetic categories. That is to say, these are the categories which distinguish this approach from others. They are accordingly examined in the next section.

The categories of aesthetics and organizational understanding

The aesthetic categories constitute a set of criteria which provide the scholar of organization with useful guidelines. They define lines of analysis which further highlight the fact that the aesthetic approach seeks to acquire understanding about organizations that differs from rational and scientific knowledge.

Consider, for example, the presentation of a strategic decision for appraisal by the management of an organization. A certain grace in its presentation, the adding of something exceptional or amusing, the creation of an aura of heroic enterprise around it, the arousal of awe in the listeners, may prove important in the ensuing decision process. First of all, it lightens the atmosphere and throws the decision to be taken into relief: an important aspect, this, but one which does not concern the aesthetic approach, which instead becomes necessary when the researcher wishes to examine:

1   the capacity to make oneself felt, to speak to the heart of people, to arouse their enthusiasm, to touch their feelings, to sensitize them;
2   the subtle sense of pleasure, as well as of satisfaction, that the taking of a decision may arouse in those concerned; for them, it may be a beautiful decision;
3   the fact that pleasure and satisfaction are not felt by all the decision-makers. In the eyes of those who have opposed it, the decision may be kitschy and tasteless;
4   the specific organizational setting in which the decision process unfolds.

This setting is distinguished by odours, gestures, voices, the glances and the sensations of the persons who interact in the construction of the decision process and of the decision taken. But these are odours, gestures and voices that do not occur in a vacuum. The room itself in which the meeting is held makes them more complicated, because they mix with the smell of the paint, the noise of chairs being shifted and of pages being leafed through, with the artificial glow of the overhead projector. The artificial lighting also affects the sensations of the decision-makers by placing them in a temporal situation devoid of the sense of an unfolding day typical of natural light.

The aesthetic approach highlights the fact that the researcher can avoid committing the cognitive and rational error of ignoring the bodies of the people involved in the decision process and only considering their minds. In other words, if one wishes to understand what happened at the meeting it is not sufficient to examine the different rationalities present and the different issues at stake. Aesthetic categories, in this context, represent a useful aid to the organizational researcher. They direct his or her attention to the elements that more thoroughly account for the complex experience of the decision-makers.

Each of the aesthetic categories which I discuss below, apart from grace, relate to the entire range of the sensory and perceptive faculties – to seeing, hearing, smelling, touching and tasting. They traditionally constitute a repertoire of notions with which to address and to analyze the arts. They also represent an important set of concepts for the aesthetic understanding of organizational life, as I now seek to show, basing my discussion on a review by Raffaele Milani (1991).

Beauty

As undoubtedly the principal aesthetic category, beauty has been given a variety of definitions (Bodei, 1995; Vattimo, 1981; Zecchi, 1990): luminosity, symmetry, proportion, capacity to attract and deceive, persuasive force, manifestation of hidden natural laws, harmony, beatitude, freedom, and others besides. Beauty has been described as an absolute principle which flanks truth and goodness, or as a category akin to goodness or, again, as truth.

Beauty consequently pertains to numerous areas of inquiry, from ethics to gnoseology, from Western philosophy with its Greek and Latin matrix to Eastern thought with its Buddhist influence. In the end, as Raffaele Milani (1991: 68) points out, the beautiful arises from the contemplation of a fact or an object, or a form of behaviour, and is simultaneously able to yield a particular form of knowledge profoundly rooted in the history of civilizations.

Beauty is also a category of especial importance for the study of organizations. It permits exploration of the bonds that tie people to the organizations for which they work, to their work environments, to the materials that they use and transform. It lays bare the forms of organizational structuring based on sentiment and on perception of the beautiful, and it highlights the conflictual dynamics related to the definition of organizational beauty that arise between corporations and the various occupational and professional communities that work for them.

The sublime

The sublime has been a matter of philosophical controversy since the first century BC, when treatises and counter-treatises set out the principal features of this aesthetic category: the inspiration of great thoughts and the echo of a great soul; the *pathos* which unites the work and its reader.

Although distinct from beauty, the sublime always interacts with it, or merges with it. It is the product of nobility of soul wedded to purity, majesty and sacredness. It arises in those moments of rapture or euphoria when the personality seemingly disintegrates; it involves the mysterious pleasure aroused by contemplation of tragic events or representations of terror and anguish. Whereas the beautiful evokes serenity and harmony, the sublime excites pleasure mixed with pain; a state of mind which, according to Kant, pertains to the personality in its non-logical, emotional aspect. The sublime is the joy that fills the soul in the presence of whatever is truly such, almost as if the soul itself has created it.

In organizations this category evinces the *pathos* of the material and non-material organizational artefacts that embody the organization's memories. The sublime, in fact, is the aesthetic category with which one observes the emotional knowledge of the purity, the grandeur, and the tragedy of such artefacts, possessed by participants in organizational life almost as if they themselves have generated their beauty, magnificence or horror.

The ugly

The aesthetic category of ugliness denotes what is asymmetrical and ill-proportioned, whatever disfigures form. It is therefore a category which stands in relation to the beautiful (Rosenkranz, 1853). This is not because the beautiful requires the ugly for its definition. The beautiful is an absolute, whereas ugliness is possible only in relation to the beautiful and finds its measure, not in itself, but in beauty. Ugliness is therefore a relative concept. It poses a threat to the beautiful and must therefore be eliminated.

Although always the subject of philosophical reflection, the category of ugliness attracted especial attention from the mid-nineteenth century onwards, following industrialization and against the background of the moral and physical disfigurement that it produced. It denotes the pathology of the modern world, the malaise that reveals the existence of a greater internal evil, the disruptive and dangerous passions, whatever arouses repugnance, and whatever results from hatred, from contempt.

Kitsch and camp are concepts which belong to the category of the ugly. Kitsch was born with industrialization and with the urbanization associated with it. It represents the alienation of bourgeois society, the state of being determined by things rather than determining them, the celebration of the mundane, the mixing of the bogus and the mediocre with bad taste. Camp instead highlights the calculated posture of self-seduction in the excessive, the unnatural and the artificial. Together with kitsch it highlights the spurious, the profane, the grace realized in banality, the constructed and simpering artifice.

In the study of organizations, the category of ugliness sheds light on the features that distinguish an organization as mundane, fake and bereft of an aura of sacredness. It concerns ugly work environments, jobs that are ugly because of their content, of ugly relations with the boss or with colleagues, and ugly experiences in everyday organizational life. In other words, ugliness is the absence of beauty: it is whatever in the daily routine of an organization should be erased. Ugliness, moreover, is the category which more than others generalizes the aesthetic in the life of organizations. The fashion industry provides the most blatant example: it is a manifestation neither of the sacred nor of the ideal grandeur of the sublime, nor of the virtue of grace.

The comic

The category of the comic concerns both action deliberately taken to provoke laughter and to be ridiculous, and the different forms of laughter. Comedy springs from an unexpected release from fear. Comedy is what the category of ugliness eventually becomes (Rosenkranz, 1853); a category which, as we have seen, initially relates to the beautiful. But whereas beauty is the exclusion of ugliness, comicality fraternizes with it; it dispels the repugnance provoked by ugliness and transforms ugliness into comedy, thereby evidencing its paltriness with respect to beauty.

The comic comprises a variety of notions: grotesqueness, caricature, irony, wit and humour. The relationship between the category of ugliness and those of the beautiful and the sublime is the basis of caricature. In it, ugliness reaches its apogée in the gross and vicious distortion of the subject: the beautiful becomes travesty, the sublime is reduced to emphasis and vulgarity, the gracious to whimsy. It is on the metamorphosis of the ugly that the notions of grotesque, humorous and satirical rest. Humour springs from reflection that seeks to dispel social fictions by dramatizing their components. Humour is the absurd, the paradoxical, nonsensical, satirical. Related to satire, but less aggressive, is the simulation–dissimulation of irony.

The comic is part and parcel of everyday organizational life. Joking about situations and events, poking fun at superiors or inferiors or colleagues, lightening a heavy atmosphere with a wisecrack that makes oneself or others look ridiculous: these are all forms of behaviour to do with the category of the comic. There are, moreover, situations in organizations which are structured by comedy. It is a common ritual for the chairman of a meeting to open proceedings with a humorous remark. Speakers on official occasions often begin with a witticism; and so too do those who intervene to ridicule them. Other forms of comicality in organizations are jokes about one's occupational community, or about those who do not belong to it, or wisecracks about the professionalism of women at work; sarcasm at the abilities and dedication of those considered extraneous to the organization, to the temporal cadences of work; sneers at the work traditions of different ethnic groups or of workers from distant and poorer regions.

The gracious

The gracious concerns the visual and aural pleasure aroused by people and things. As regards people, grace relates to action based on spontaneity and virtue. More generally, grace is at once loveliness and charm.

Grace is an important category in the study of organizations. It is embodied in the smile of the air hostess, where it is functional to the airline's customer relations; in the care devoted to making the beds in a hotel; in the offering of chocolates and newspapers to passengers on high-speed trains; in a policeman's dealing with citizens; in the provision of a service by a public agency. Grace, graciousness, ingratiation, pleasantness, are all components of this category of aesthetics, which more than the others is able to evince aspects and elements of the quality of everyday life in organizational settings. Grace elicits gentleness: a category which communicates insights and emotions which are sweet and tender, and which surprise and enchant.

Grace also evokes elegance, which is stylization and precision. The category 'elegance' applies to the demeanour of subjects in an organization: whether they are characterized by spontaneity or inner discipline. 'Elegant' can be used to describe the quality of work done, an example being 'elegant' mathematical models which are simple and effective in execution and organized into coherent chains of reasoning.

The picturesque and the agogic categories

Gombrich (1982) wrote that the picturesque indicates that the normal relationship of recognition and evocation has been reversed so that picturesque effects appear in the world around us. This is a reversal whereby the spectacle of nature evokes a favourite painting, or a workaday event unexpectedly but happily reminds us of a film that we have especially enjoyed. The picturesque, in fact, is a category which conveys us into the realm of the bizarre, the odd, the capricious, but also of the ludic and the amusing; the realm, that is, of games. But not in the general sense, since, as Johann Christoph Friedrich Schiller (1795) writes, this is a game played with beauty which does not constrict human experience, either internally or externally, but renders it complete.

As a notion inhering in the picturesque, game-playing creates nothing that is real: it does not produce facts and objects, it does not work towards a pre-defined end. It instead represents, knowingly imitates, demonstrates. It does so by relying on the 'as if' and on the invention that sustains it (Milani, 1991:

205). The 'as if' lies at the basis of much fantasizing and projecting in organizations, just as game-playing underpins work cultures and symbols.

The agogic categories are those grounded in movement and rhythm: *adagio, andante, presto* and *prestissimo* in music and dance, or the rhythm of a painting, but also the alternation of peak and slack times in everyday work. Rhythm inheres in dance and music, but also in the wave-like flow of customers through a shop, so that it is sometimes full and sometimes empty. In other words, rhythm is the tempo with which the keys of a piano are struck, but also those on a computer keyboard. It is the rhythm at which a *corps de ballet* dances but also the rate at which a factory department works. Consequently, the rhythm established for an organization's means of production, among work colleagues, in the organization's output is not merely a matter of how many goods are produced or services delivered in a given period of time. It is, like the rhythm and colours of a painting, not solely a quantitative and economic fact.

The tragic

Tragedy springs from the impermanence of human happiness, from fear of the unknown and the apparently inevitable. It arises from an inner threat, psychological and never quelled, from the fact that even in an ethically ordered world unexpected events occur to plunge it into chaos. The tragic is a very different category from the beautiful. It stands closer to the sublime in the mysterious pleasure of pain and its representation.

For Plato, tragedy was the dynamism of the passions. Aristotle, who laid the foundations of tragedy, assigned to catharsis the task of purging the emotions of pity and fear, and of celebrating good's victory over evil. Since these early definitions were first formulated, a luminous figure has emerged from the dynamic of innocence, guilt, duty, myth and world-views: the hero.

In organization studies the category of the tragic highlights the omnipresence of the heroic: the leader who stakes everything against the odds; the work group that works tirelessly to rescue the organization from exceptional difficulties; the rank-and-file operatives who strike against management's refusal to improve working conditions for themselves and their children; the workers who defend their company against a hostile take-over; and so on.

The sacred

The sacred is the aesthetic category which emphasizes that the reality and fiction of human experience are not rationally distinct. In its various forms, sacredness relates to the unsayable and the unseeable, to the magical and the inviolable, to dreams and premonition, to the exceptional and the divine.

The sacred is the representation of the invisible through the visible features of divinity; and as such it is a vital aspect of the artistic iconographies of numerous cultures (Eliade, 1952). Sacredness is also the reverence and worship that the uniqueness of works of art aroused before their technical reproduction became possible (Benjamin, 1936). The sacred, therefore, is not morally determined, but derives from a relationship with the divine and its power. It always conveys an element of magic and returns the sensible objects to origins which, though not celestial, nevertheless lie over and above the human faculties.

The sacred arises from the fantastic and legendary phenomena that represent whatever is marvellous, unusual, irresistible, memorable and inexplicable. It belongs to the oneiric realm where the archetypicality and mysterious expressive freedom of dreams reside. This is indeed immaterial, fleeting, incoherent, made up of symbols and enigmas, but it describes humanness and represents it.

What light does this category shed on organizations? It tells us that, although there are sacred places, sacred objects and actions invested with sacredness, they stem not from rational motivation but from the relationship between reality and fiction in human experience. Consider the imaginary territories that belong symbolically to organizational actors and on which no-one must trespass, an example being professional competence. An organization as a whole may become sacred. Its closure would arouse the sense among those who have established a cultural relationship with it that something unique and fine has been lost.

The study of organizational aesthetics

The aesthetic categories show that there are organizational phenomena to which the aesthetic approach pays particularly close attention, but that it is not alone in doing so. The aesthetic approach, in fact, is a way of studying organizations that has arisen in the 1990s by drawing on other approaches to organizational study: organizational symbolism and the cultural analysis of organizations (Jones, 1996; Turner, 1992) and the dramaturgic approach (Mangham and Overington, 1987).

Consider the aesthetic categories of the sacred, the tragic, the gracious and the picturesque. One notes that the investment of some event or some feature of an organization with sacredness – because it is deemed unique by the people who work for it or because it is tied to some specific organizational mythology – is a phenomenon investigated by scholars of organizational symbols and cultures. The same applies when the symbolic approach highlights action 'as if' or action as 'game'. If one then considers style – the mode of display adopted by those who belong to a particular organization, or dressing and acting according to canons that reinforce the organizational identity – together with research and study conducted by the organizational symbolism, one also notes the contributions made by the dramaturgic approach.

I will now conduct a more specific discussion of the context of research and theory in which the aesthetic approach was born and developed, and then briefly illustrate the ideas yielded by research that has used the approach. The aesthetic understanding of organizational life, in fact, belongs within the more general framework constituted by studies of the aesthetics of organization in the second half of the 1980s. I shall also refer to the theories arising from study of artistic organizations and from the recent revival of interest in the relations between art and the social order. Finally, analysis of the visual is also an important referent for the aesthetic, especially as regards the problematics that it highlights in the comprehension of visual cultures and in the visual description of social phenomena. I begin with the latter.

Analysis of the visual

Analysis of the visual involves principally the study of the photographic image and research carried out using photography. Gregory Bateson and Margaret Mead conducted 'the first saturated photographic research in another culture, the results of which were published in *Balinese Character* (1942)', comment John Collier and Malcolm Collier (1967: 12) in their manual on photography as a research method in anthropology. Ethnographic research based on visual material uses other media as well, however. Ethnographic films in Finland date back to the First World War, and videotape is also used in ethnographic and sociological research. Nevertheless, it is mainly anthropology and sociology that rely on the visual in the analysis of social phenomena. These disciplines suggest different methods of analysis:

1   *Visual anthropology* considers the image to be both an instrument of documentation and its source. The intention is to gain insight into the cultures of the collectivities under examination. Information is gathered both on and off the film, and the researcher learns to see through 'native eyes'. Visual anthropology collects visual material like the snapshots in family photograph albums in order to study changes in the way that the family describes itself (Chalfen, 1991). Or, as we have seen, it directly produces visual material in order to record social action and the places in which it occurs.

2   *Visual sociology* tends to interfere deliberately with the collectivities with which it comes into contact. Visual material is still the means to explore reflexive relations among the creation of visual imagery, its perception and social structures (Hill, 1984). But ever since the studies published in the *American Journal of Sociology* between 1910 and 1915 on housing in Chicago, one notes the endeavour of visual sociology to denounce injustices, the marginalization of social groups or their deprivation. Thus

visual material is collected and produced in order to heighten awareness or to mobilize participation, or to re-experience social events, or even as self-analysis.

The methodological issues raised by the analysis of the visual (Henny, 1986; Mattioli, 1991; Wagner, 1979) are therefore both subtle and important to the aesthetic approach. They highlight that understanding organizational life on the basis of aesthetically produced documents is a delicate and complex matter, whether they are produced by the organizational actors or whether they are an artefact created by the researcher.

Study of the arts

Studying art yields insights into the relationships between meanings and social order if it is not confined to analysis of the social and material conditions of art alone; if, that is, 'art's independent meanings and their special status' (Blau, 1988: 270) are not ignored, trivialized or denied. With reference to sociological studies, Judith Blau identifies four principal reactions to the aesthetic status of art:

1   *Acceptance* that although art is part of aesthetics it is incidental to research. Consequently, art publics and their differences are studied in educational terms, artists themselves in terms of their demographic features, cultural institutions in terms of organizational forms.
2   *Recognition* that although art may arise from specific practices, it displays unique and distinctive features. Analysis therefore concentrates on the ethical social implications of art: whether it promotes social integration or whether it perpetuates social class differences. This tradition of study rests on the premise that aesthetic qualities are able to improve or to impair social life.
3   *The assumption* that art is merely a social definition. Consequently, it is the institutional processes operating in those areas of society conventionally defined as 'artistic' which are studied.
4   *The presumption* that art has its own ontological status. Thus the researcher examines the conditions under which different arts develop, and how their differing qualities give rise to social meanings and influence collective actions and broad-gauge institutional practices.

Once again, of principal significance for understanding of the aesthetic approach to organizations are questions of methodology. Especially important is the difference between the aesthetic approach and the first three traditions of study of the arts, which have made significant contributions to organizational study (Becker, 1982; DiMaggio, 1986; Peterson, 1976). The qualification 'aesthetic' to the approach, in fact, constitutes a specific form of understanding organizations, whereas 'when art worlds are viewed most particularly as peopled worlds, art becomes a vehicle for studying social arrangements of all kinds, or of any kind. But art values and products become largely irrelevant' (Blau, 1988: 272).

Organizational analysis of aesthetics

The study of aesthetics in organizations is a new strand of organizational analysis which originated in the mid-1980s. It arose as part of the assault waged in those years against the positivist and rational paradigm then predominant in organization theory and research (Martin and Frost, 1996; Zey-Ferrel and Aiken, 1981). It shared both its aims, methodology and subject of study with these radical positions: their aim because it was the organization that aesthetic approach sought to understand; their methodology because it conducted qualitative analysis of organization; and their subject of study because it analyzed nuances and impalpable elements instead of strong causal relations. In this latter respect, the offensive was directed principally against the pervasiveness of cognitivism in the study of organizations, and against rational explanation 'at all costs' (Gagliardi, 1996; Pfeffer, 1982; Strati, 1998).

Certain issues have been of particular importance for the development of this strand of organizational analysis:

a   the images that diffuse internally and externally to the organization and relate to events of importance for organizational identity and for identification with the organization by its members (Bolognini, 1986; Buie, 1996; Costa, 1986; Schneider and Powley, 1986; Stern, 1988);

b   the physical space of the organization. Research and design have highlighted the overt and covert aspects of the corporate image and of the organizational control exercised through the architecture (Berg and Kreiner, 1990; Carter and Jackson, in this volume; Doxtater, 1990; Grafton-Small and Linstead, 1985; Witkin, 1987);

c   the miscellaneous set of artefacts that constitute the organization's corporate landscape. Such artefacts embody the organization's symbols and meaning systems without recourse to conceptual and abstract knowledge. This is because this knowledge is always preceded by sensory experience that intellectual reflection is frequently unable to grasp or to express (Gagliardi, 1990, 1996);

d   aspects less closely tied to the physical-spatial or visual, like the metaphor of manager as artist (Dégot, 1987), the beauty of social organization (Ramirez, 1991), the idea that work comprises an essential aesthetic element (White, 1996), the phenomenological philosophy of the eye and strategic visions of the organization (Guillet de Monthoux, 1996);

e   organizational management that can learn from art more as artistic form than as artistic content (Bjorkegren, 1993); which must celebrate art values rather than mere corporate ones when sponsoring entertainment for corporate ceremonies (Rusted, 1988); and which must bring art patronage closer to the ideal of proactive participation alongside art promotions in the public arena (Jacobson, 1996).

As we shall see, the aesthetic approach encompasses all these organizational topics, but always from the standpoint that I have described.

The aesthetic understanding of organizational life

The aesthetic approach I will now describe developed from an empirical study of the organizational cultures and symbols of three Italian university departments. Further studies followed which were based on research conducted in manufacturing industry and in artistic production. Again based on field research are studies on the knowledge of an organization yielded by analysis of its artefacts and on the contribution by visual cultures to the production of metaphors of organization. These various works have a number of features in common:

a   They give priority to the aesthetic category of beauty: the beauty of the organization *tout court*; the beauty of the organization that no longer exists and which nostalgia and myth enhance; the beauty of materials and the sense of profound pleasure felt by those who work with them; the beauty of being free from the duty to perform useful work and to make useful things. However, beauty is not the only aesthetic category used in analysis of organizational phenomena, since it sets in motion many others, beginning with the sacredness that inheres in the organization by virtue of its uniqueness.

b   They have the same empirical and theoretical purpose. The aesthetic approach is valid if it is able to produce new grounded organizational knowledge and to generate new concepts of organization. Examples of these are the conclusion that the physical space of an organization is not an empty container; that the aesthetic experience is the glue that holds an organization 'without walls' together, which delimits it and defines it; that the metaphor of organization as hypertext highlights the particularist and pagan organizational knowledge which always has a producing subject, internally to the organization as well; that, by contrast, the metaphor of the photograph conveys the organizational knowledge which views the organization as the reality which confronts it, and which is subject-less, incremental and imbued with sacredness.

c   They view the aesthetic experience of organizational life as predicated on the concept of the elusiveness of the object of knowledge. This entails that the aesthetic datum cannot be separated from its *pathos* for organizational actors and for the researcher, and also that the aesthetic nature of organizational experience cannot be grasped by objective observation. It signifies, moreover, that an organization is not an artistic object that can be analyzed *ad infinitum*, perhaps drawing on art studies. Instead, following John Dewey (1929, 1951), an organization is an ongoing phenomenon which cannot be crystallized into dualistic and static forms, or into abstract theoretical forms which neglect its distinctive features of temporariness, mutability and precariousness.

d   They require empathetic understanding by the reader. By evoking knowledge, and by relying on the concept of plausibility, they involve the reader in a process of both seeing and not seeing the organization studied, and they place him/her in a situation that s/he finds plausible.

The aesthetic approach is based on an underlying epistemological option, which I have mentioned on several occasions in this chapter when discussing the importance of knowledge tied to mythical thinking instead of analytical-intellectual procedure; the crucial nature of knowledge arising from intuition and evocation; and the fact that the aesthetic approach problematizes the organizational knowledge acquired using analytical methods. However, a further important issue should be borne in mind, one which I have stressed elsewhere (Strati, 1996b: 217, 1999: 50–3): epistemological options, too, have an aesthetic foundation. As Thomas Kuhn (1962) writes, the choice of a paradigm is not always based on arguments for or against, since its aesthetic quality may have a decisive bearing on its selection.

Conclusions

The aesthetic approach, like the strand of studies of aesthetics in organizations, emphasizes the importance of people's sensory and perceptive faculties in the analysis of the organizational phenomena that they generate. Consequently, the approach insists on the shortcomings of organizational theories based exclusively on analytical methods and, in particular, on cognitivism and rationality.

The qualifier 'aesthetic', in fact, denotes that the approach takes account of all the human senses. It indicates, in other words, that an organization is beautiful or ugly; that beautiful or ugly work goes on within it; that some colleagues may have beautiful personalities, others not; that the organization's members work with elegance and pleasure. It also indicates the odours smelt, the noises heard and the surfaces touched in an organization. These phenomena are all of value for organizational analysis: they embody in not yet rationalized, still sensory form, the culture and symbols of everyday life in an organization and thus yield rich and unusual qualitative data.

The aesthetic approach occupies a distinctive place in the recently formed strand of studies of organizational aesthetics. It stems to a certain extent from Max Weber's thought on sociological methods of inquiry (Weber, 1922).

Weber points out that in order to understand social action it is necessary to grasp both the subjective sense of the people responsible for it and the orientation imposed on such action by the attitudes of others. However, there are two different methods available for the interpretation of meaningful social action. One of them is the intellectual approach, whereby interpretation is based on rational evidence. The other method gathers evidence by emotionally or artistically reliving the social action, which it does by virtue of the imagination's sympathetic penetration. It is on the latter form of knowledge that the aesthetic approach to organizations is based. However, as Schwartz and Jacobs (1979) observe, Weber regarded empathetic understanding as a secondary concern, while in his view, and still today for organization studies, the principal goal is the causal explanation of social action. The aesthetic approach, by contrast, reverses the relation and gives priority to the empathetic form of understanding in organization studies.

The undeniable contribution that both the aesthetic approach and the strand of studies on organizational aesthetics give to the theories of organization is to highlight that, almost a century after their beginnings, organizational studies have changed both thematically and methodologically. The certainty has faded that there exists a limited and pre-established number of objects of analysis which should be prioritized because they lead directly to the principal features and problems of an organization. Nor is it certain that there is a specific number of truly reliable methodologies for organizational analysis, since only these are scientific while the others yield only fiction or journalism. Some decades after the foundation of the discipline, these certainties – that organizational knowledge is valid because it concerns 'true' organizational issues and that it is scientific and rational – have given way to paradigmatic fragmentation and a plurality of approaches.

It is therefore important that researchers should seek to understand organizational life without looking for a rational explanation of organizational phenomena at any cost. The aesthetic approach prompts the organization scholar to develop new awareness of organizational life rather than devise new ways to rationalize it. It does so by focusing on matters that the organizational literature until recently regarded as of little relevance to the life of organizations. The study of aesthetics highlights the limits of this convention in theories of organization and shows how they can be overcome. It starts, like Yaron Ezrahi (1990: 136), by denying the 'truth' whereby it is 'as if machines, like the working class and the lower middle class, were themselves classified as belonging in the domain of low material culture and the fine arts socially associated with upper-class culture were enlisted to the mission of investing them with some of the virtues of upper-class taste'.

Note

1 This chapter was written with the help of a grant by the Consiglio Nazionale delle Ricerche (Prot. n. 150911, 19/12/1996) for a period of study at the

Wissenschaftszentrum Berlin fur Sozialforschung - Research Group 'Metropolitan City Studies' directed by Bernward Joerges.

References

Barilli, Renato (1995) *Corso di estetica*. (1st edn 1989). Bologna: Il Mulino. (English translation: *Course on Aesthetics*. Minneapolis, MN: University of Minnesota Press, 1994).

Bateson, Gregory and Mead, Margaret (1942) *Balinese Character: A Photographic Analysis*. New York: New York Academy of Science.

Baumgarten, Alexander Gottlieb (1735) *Meditationes philosophicae de nonnullis ad poema pertinentibus*. Halle in Magdeburgo: Grunert.

Baumgarten, Alexander Gottlieb (1750–8) *Aesthetica I–II*. Frankfurt am Oder: Kleyb (photostat: Olms: Hildesheim, 1986).

Becker, Howard S. (1982) *Art Worlds*. Berkeley, CA: University of California Press.

Benjamin, Walter (1936) 'Das Kunstwerk im Zeitalter seiner technischen Reproduzierbarkeit', in *Zeitschrift fur Sozialforschung*, Paris. (English translation: 'The work of art in the age of mechanical reproduction', in Walter Benjamin, *Illuminations*, ed. Hannah Arendt. New York: Harcourt Brace, 1968, pp.219–66).

Berg, Per Olof and Kreiner, Kristian (1990) 'Corporate Architecture: Turning Physical Settings into Symbolic Resources', in P. Gagliardi (ed.), *Symbols and Artifacts*. Berlin: de Gruyter. pp. 41–67.

Berger, Peter and Luckman, Thomas (1966) *The Social Construction of Reality*. New York: Anchor Books.

Bjorkegren, Dag (1993) 'What can Organization and Management Theory Learn from Art?', in J. Hassard and M. Parker (eds), *Postmodernism and Organizations*. London: Sage. pp. 101–13.

Blau, Judith R. (1988) 'Study of the Arts: A Reappraisal', *Annual Review of Sociology*, 14: 269–92.

Bodei, Remo (1995) *Le forme del bello*. Bologna: Il Mulino.

Bolognini, Bruno (1986) 'Images as Identifying Objects and as Organizational Integrators in Two Firms', *Dragon*, 3: 61–75.

Buie, Sarah (1996) 'Market as Mandala: The Erotic Space of Commerce', *Organization*, 3 (2): 225–32.

Chalfen, Richard (1991) *Turning Leaves: The Photograph Collections of Two Japanese American Families*. Albuquerque, NM: University of New Mexico Press.

Collier, John and Collier, Malcom (1967) *Visual Anthropology*. Albuquerque, NM: University of New Mexico Press.

Costa, Joan (1986) 'Toward a Signaletic Symbology of Identity in Corporate Communication', *Dragon*, 5: 5–16.

Dégot, Vincent (1987) 'Portrait of the Manager as an Artist', *Dragon*, 2 (4): 13–50.

Dewey, John (1929) *Quest for Certainty*. New York: Open Court.

Dewey, John (1951) *Reconstruction in Philosophy*. New York: Holt.

DiMaggio, Paul J. (ed.) (1986) *Nonprofit Enterprise in the Arts*. New York: Oxford University Press.

Doxtater, Dennis (1990) 'Meaning of the Workplace: Using Ideas of Ritual Space in Design', in P. Gagliardi (ed.), *Symbols and Artifacts*. Berlin: de Gruyter. pp.107–27.

Eliade, Mircea (1952) *Images et symboles: essais sur le symbolisme magico-religieux.* Paris: Gallimard.

Ezrahi, Yaron (1990) *The Descent of Icarus. Science and the Transformation of Contemporary Democracy.* Cambridge, MA: Harvard University Press.

Fineman, Stephen (1996) 'Emotion and Organizing', in S.R. Clegg, C. Hardy and W. Nord (eds), *Handbook of Organization Studies.* London: Sage. pp. 543–64.

Gagliardi, Pasquale (1990) 'Artifacts as Pathways and Remains of Organizational Life', in P. Gagliardi (ed.), *Symbols and Artifacts.* Berlin: de Gruyter. pp. 3–38.

Gagliardi, Pasquale (1996) 'Exploring the Aesthetic Side of Organizational Life', in S.R. Clegg, C. Hardy and W.R. Nord (eds), *Handbook of Organization Studies.* London: Sage. pp. 565–80.

Gombrich, Ernst (1982) *The Image and the Eye. Further Studies in the Psychology of Pictorial Representation.* Oxford: Phaidon.

Grafton-Small, Robert and Linstead, Stephen (1985) 'Bricks and Bricolage: Deconstructing Corporate Image in Stone and Story', *Dragon,* 1, 1: 8–27.

Guillet de Monthoux, Pierre (1996) 'The Theatre of War: Art, Organization and the Aesthetics of Strategy', *Studies in Cultures, Organizations and Societies,* 2 (1): 147–60.

Henny, Leonard (ed.) (1986) 'Theory and Practice in Visual Sociology', *Special Issue of Current Sociology,* 3 (34).

Hill, Michael (1984) *Exploring Visual Sociology.* Monticello, IL: Vance Bibliographies.

Jacobson, Marjory (1996) 'Art and Business in a Brave New World', *Organization,* 3 (2): 243–8.

Jones, Michael Owen (1996) *Studying Organizational Symbolism.* Thousand Oaks, CA: Sage.

Knorr Cetina, Karin (1981) *The Manufacture of Knowledge: An Essay on the Constructivist and Contextual Nature of Science.* Oxford: Pergamon Press.

Kuhn, Thomas (1962) *The Structure of Scientific Revolutions.* Chicago: University of Chicago Press.

Latour, Bruno and Woolgar, Steve (1979) *Laboratory Life: The Social Construction of Scientific Facts.* Los Angeles, CA: Sage.

Mangham, Iain L. and Overington, Michael A. (1987) *Organizations as Theatre.* Chichester: Wiley.

Marquard, Odo (1989) *Aesthetica und Anaesthetica. Philosophische Überlegungen.* Paderborn: Schoningh.

Martin, Joanne and Frost, Peter (1996) 'The Organizational Culture War Games: a Struggle for Intellectual Dominance', in S.R. Clegg, C. Hardy and W.R. Nord (eds), *Handbook of Organization Studies.* London: Sage. pp. 599–621.

Mattioli, Francesco (1991) *Sociologia Visuale.* Turin: Nuova ERI.

Milani, Raffaele (1991) *Le categorie estetiche.* Parma: Pratiche Editrice.

Peterson, Richard (1976) *The Production of Culture.* Beverly Hills, CA: Sage.

Pfeffer, Jeffrey (1982) *Organizations and Organization Theory.* Marshfield, MA: Pitman.

Polanyi, Michael (1962) (1st edn 1958) *Personal Knowledge.* London: Routledge and Kegan Paul.

Polanyi, Michael (1966) *The Tacit Dimension.* Garden City, NY: Doubleday.

Putnam, Linda and Mumby, Dennis (1993) 'Organizations, Emotions and the Myth of Rationality', in S. Fineman (ed.), *Emotion in Organization.* London: Sage. pp.36–57.

Ramirez, Rafael (1991) *The Beauty of Social Organization*. Munich: Accedo.

Rosenkranz, Karl (1853) *Aesthetik des Hasslichen*. Koenigsberg: Borntraeger.

Rusted, Brian (1988) 'Corporate Rhetoric Versus Social Action: Identifying Contradictions in a Service Organization', in M.Owen Jones, M.D. Moore and R.C. Snyder (eds), *Inside Organizations. Understanding the Human Dimension*. Newbury Park, CA: Sage. pp. 333–42.

Schiller, Johann Christoph Friedrich (1795) *Vom Erhabenen: zu weitern Ausfuehrung einiger Kantischen Ideen; Ueber das Pathetische; Ueber das Erhabene*. Berlin: Hempel.

Schneider, Susan and Powley, Ellen (1986) 'The Role of Images in Changing Corporate Culture: The Case of A.T.&T.', *Dragon*, 2: 5–44.

Schütz, Alfred (1962–6) *Collected Papers I–III*. The Hague: Nijhoff.

Schwartz, Howard and Jacobs, Jerri (1979) *Qualitative Sociology. A Method to the Madness*. New York: Free Press.

Sims, David, Fineman, Stephen and Gabriel, Yiannis (1993) *Organizing and Organizations*. London: Sage.

Stern, Stephen (1988) 'Symbolic Representation of Organizational Identity: The Role of Emblem at the Garrett Corporation', in M. Owen Jones, M.D. Moore and R.C. Snyder (eds), *Inside Organizations. Understanding the Human Dimension*. Newbury Park, CA: Sage. pp. 281–95.

Strati, Antonio (1992) 'Aesthetic Understanding of Organizational Life', *Academy of Management Review*, 17 (3): 568–81.

Strati, Antonio (1996a) *Sociologia dell'organizzazione. Paradigmi teorici e metodi di ricerca*. Rome: La Nuova Italia Scientifica. (English translation: *Theory and Method in Organization Studies*. London: Sage, 2000).

Strati, Antonio (1996b) 'Organization Viewed through the Lens of Aesthetics', *Organization*, 3 (2): 209–18.

Strati, Antonio (1998) '(Mis)Understanding Cognition in Organization Studies', *Scandinavian Journal of Management*, 14 (4): 309–29.

Strati, Antonio (1999) *Organization and Aesthetics*. London: Sage.

Turner, Barry (1992) 'The Symbolic Understanding of Organizations', in M. Reed and M. Hughes (eds), *Rethinking Organization*. London: Sage. pp. 46–66.

Vattimo, Gianni (1981) 'Estetica', in *Enciclopedia di filosofia*. Milan: Garzanti. pp. 274–8.

Vico, Giambattista (1725) *Principi di una scienza nuova*. Naples: Mosca. 3rd edn 1744. (English translation: *The New Science of Giambattista Vico*, ed. T.G. Bergin and M.H. Fisch. Ithaca, NY: Cornell University Press, 1968).

Wagner, Jon (ed.) (1979) *Images of Information*. Beverly Hills, CA: Sage.

Weber, Max (1922) *Wirtschaft und Gesellschaft. Grundriß der verstehenden Soziologie*. Tübingen: Mohr. (English translation: *Economy and Society: An Outline of Interpretive Sociology 1–11*. Berkeley, CA: University of California Press, 1978).

White, David A. (1996) '"It's Working Beautifully!" Philosophical Reflections on Aesthetics and Organization Theory', *Organization*, 3 (2): 195–208.

Witkin, Robert (1987) 'The Aesthetic Imperative of a Rational-Technical Machinery', *Dragon*, 2 (4): 109–26.

Zecchi, Stefano (1990) *La bellezza*. Turin: Bollati Boringhieri.

Zecchi, Stefano and Franzini, Elio (eds) (1995) *Storia dell'estetica*. Bologna: Il Mulino.

Zey-Ferrel, Mary and Aiken, Mike (eds) (1981) *Complex Organizations: Critical Perspectives*. Glenview, IL: Scott, Foresman.

2

The Art Management of Aesthetic Organizing[1]

Pierre Guillet de Monthoux

Introduction – *kunst ist kapital*

If the German artist Joseph Beuys, who sadly left us at the beginning of the 1980s, was right in claiming that art is tomorrow's capital it seems reasonable to consider aesthetics its new organization theory. In this chapter I will attempt such a Beuysian reinterpretation of some ideas from art theory and aesthetic philosophy. Beuys not only performed his art in a multitude of events; he also preached his art-based and aesthetics-rooted theory of social organization wherever he exhibited, from huge art shows like the Kassel Documenta to small avant-garde galleries like René Block's in Berlin and New York. He prophesied that a new kind of art was about to reorganize our world, no longer an art defined by its surrounding institutions. A century earlier art escaped academies, cathedrals, castles and museums and in the guise of marginal avant-gardism it hovered homeless for a while. Now, Beuys sensed, it again seemed determined to land and let a new world be organized out of its auratic energy. Beuys kept repeating that we needed a new enlarged concept of art to grasp what was to happen. Let us follow the master from Düsseldorf and stumble three minute steps towards such a redefinition. First I will use some aesthetic theory to outline some aspects of aesthetic organizing. Then I will use two cases to touch upon how this form of organizing might be managed, and finally combine it all in a model for reflecting on aesthetic organizing.

Aesthetic organizing – structures

Aesthetic processes – Kantian transcendence and Dantian transfiguration

If asked, I think Immanuel Kant would be prone to define art management as a kind of gardening. What Kant definitely shares with romantic philosophers is a conception of art as a piece of divine nature. An overwhelming number of Kant's examples of the beautiful and sublime are naturalia such as flowers or waterfalls. He definitely prefers roses in a vase to flowers depicted on a canvas. Instead of admiring sculptures or Stillebens he prefers the beauty of crimson lobsters on a nicely dressed dinner-table. To Kant, art makes us marvel before God's creation. The romantics were to carry this conception of art to completion by suggesting that natural science learn from art. Schlegel for instance talked about literary criticism as an experimental science by which readers were inspired to look upon poetry as a 'so-called research . . . an experiment in history' (Benjamin, 1973: 60). Aesthetics, which had been made fashionable by Baumgarten's treatise of 1750 as the sense-logic of truth, soon became looked upon as a method for the scientific investigation of the natural world as facts and figures would never by themselves add up to an understanding of God's nature. In the same vein the young Hegel, sharing Tübingen digs with Hölderlin and Schelling, noted that philosophizing takes as much '*ästhetische Kraft*' as writing poetry and that those who only see '*Tabelle und Register*' without art never can aspire to truth (Hegel, 1986: 263). To Kant it was already obvious that a scientist needed an artist's imagination in patching together the fruits of observation. Aesthetics was the road to grasp an art which, even if mediated through an artist's talent, always was a creation of divine inspiration.

The third Kantian critique sets out to research the power of creation in a '*Kritik der Urteilskraf*' accessible in English under the somewhat feeble title of *The Critique of Judgement*. Kant turns aesthetics into a theory of energy by which we can tackle the power of art. In this critique we find in the bud the ideas of genius that romantics were later, pretty unKantianly, to blow up to heroic proportions. There is clearly an immense difference between, say, a Fichtean idea of human creativity and Kant's aesthetic geniality. Creativity to Kant is a matter of divine grace, a deistic quasi-mystery, the mastering or managing of which it would be sheer heresy to attempt. After respectfully recognizing the mystery of creativity in his book he therefore centres upon its worldly interpretation.

At this stage enters Kant's contribution to aesthetic organizing. He notes that art attracts us and has a very special organizing property. Our admiration of art has the strange property of transporting us from our private individuality into a space of public human community. In its worldly aspect art must therefore be regarded as a most powerful '*res publica*'. It indeed operates in such a bizarre antinomous way that Kant devotes a whole complex book to rescue this aesthetic mystery from the heavy files of unsolved miracles of irrationality. Let us recall the famous antinomy.

How can we explain that art fuses us together when taste, what we usually call our experience of art, clearly is a subjective phenomenon usually causing not unity but distinction? When we say that 'everyone has his own taste' it is 'only another way of saying that the determining ground of this judgement is merely subjective . . . and that the judgement has no right to the necessary agreement of others' (Kant, 1952: 205). Indeed judgement is always made by individuals. But still we constantly try to convince others of the universality of our taste by the endless and indecisive disputes typical of art worlds. We, Kant insists, encounter many everyday examples of organizations which only seem to hold together thanks to this mysterious aesthetic judgement. Unlike other more precise determinations, those judgements have not been arrived at by presenting convincing discursive logical arguments. Nevertheless, aesthetic organizing in human affairs is so powerful that, Kant seems to imply, we must assume the existence of universality to be at play in aesthetic matters too. But here it is not a universality we can account for by objective proofs based on concepts. Aesthetic organizing works instead by contention and conflict. Kant's enlightened theoretical ambition, what he calls his 'rationalizing judgement', leads him to pin-point aesthetic organizing as a dialectic where

> *1. Thesis* The judgement of taste is not based upon concepts; for if it were it would be open to dispute (decision by means of proofs).
> *2. Antithesis.* The judgement of taste is based on concepts; for otherwise, despite diversity of judgement, there could be no room even for the contention in the matter (a claim to the necessary agreement of others with this judgement). (Kant, 1952: 206)

Regardless of whether we like Kant's rationalism or not, somewhat paradoxically it gives us good arguments for not discarding aesthetic organizing from the scientific truth-seeking agenda. In today's organizational studies Rafael Ramirez' book *The Beauty of Social Organization* (1991) adapts a Kantian line of thought by borrowing Susan Langer's neo-Kantian distinctions between 'discursive' and 'presentational' logic. Ramirez also refers to systems romantic Gregory Bateson's view of aesthetic organizing as 'patterns that connect'. Ramirez' book examines cases of organizations kept together by that glue of aesthetic judgement. His Mexican museum and two music festivals, in France and Scotland, are somewhat prosaic compared to Kant's preoccupation with the organization of the whole human '*Gattung*': that is, mankind. When a nightly wanderer, as on a Caspar David Friedrich canvas, encounters the sublime force of a waterfall in some dark forest it endows him with a feeling of cosmic unity. His subjective experience becomes a trampoline catapulting his single little self to the objective horizon of all mankind. Kant makes us aware of the trampoline effect – what he calls the aesthetic dialectics – but when on the verge of saying something about the very essence of its powers he almost bashfully only remarks that 'its determining ground lies, perhaps, in the concept of what may be regarded as the supersensible substrate of humanity, (Kant, 1952: 208). These are careful words uttered on the threshold of the temple of God, the almighty ruler of our own nature. For Kant nature is, strictly speaking, the only art work worthy of our entire admiration. Theories of aesthetic organizing based on culture have therefore often taken Kant as their negative point of departure. In *Truth and*

Method (1994) Hans Georg Gadamer explores the limitations of Kant's aesthetics. He notes that Kant's third critique consists of two parts. After the first part on aesthetics the Königsberg philosopher embarked on a second part on teleological judgement where he argues that nature has a purpose of its own, a teleology, approachable through transcendental philosophical investigations. Gadamer concludes that Kant is more interested in using his ideas on aesthetics for understanding nature than the human affairs of culture (1994: 54). This explains the paradox that Kant and his followers discuss aesthetics whilst leaving out art from their inquiries. Ramirez too, regardless of the fact that he studies artistic organizations such as museums and festivals, likewise claims that aesthetic organizing can be understood without paying attention to art. To Gadamer it is obviously a fixation on nature that brings about this neglect of art and culture in Kantian thinking on aesthetic organizing. In consequence Gadamer suggests that we barter the word 'culture' for the German concept of '*Bildung*' launched by Wilhelm von Humboldt. *Bildung* is not used by Kant who focuses on the cultivation of the individual's own capacities and talents. While 'culture' easily tends towards ideas of cognition, learning and even training '*Bildung*' refers to both the Latin '*formatio*' and German word for 'image', *Bild*. In the context of aesthetics *Bildung* would be preferable because as Gadamer says 'the word *Bildung* evokes the ancient mystical tradition according to which man carries in his soul the image of God, after whom he is fashioned, and which man must cultivate in himself' (1994: 11).

By shifting from Kantian nature-culture to Humboldtian *Bildung*, however, we risk going from what art philosopher Thierry de Duve (1996) has called an 'aesthetics without art' towards something like 'art without aesthetics'. To the Kantian interest in the judgement and taste of the individual subject today's art philosophers have added a fascination with objects. Kant values unique art-experiences as a carrier of human universals, what Bateson calls the 'patterns that connect'. In contemporary aesthetics this direction of search, from the private subjective experience into public objective *sensus-cummunis*, often seems completely reversed. While yesterday's Kantians wandered in the wilderness of landscape we and our art philosophers find ourselves submerged and glutted by cultural artificiality. Everyday life, at least in the West, is like swimming in a sea of symbols branded by hallmarks of public meaning. In the field of organizational studies we find numerous studies of how objects and symbols are manufactured to build and maintain spheres of public meanings. In a world where the 'public' is omnipresent in both politics and economy the 'private' becomes the object of desire. This is what Thierry de Duve seems to imply when saying that Kant has to be reconsidered after Marcel Duchamp made art out of a most public object: a urinal. In the ready-made world of universal publicity the private has to be reconquered and this seems to be what so called postmodern art is about. Arthur Danto, the New York philosopher who spends much time wondering how everyday urinals, neckties, Brillo boxes and Campbell soup cans can be considered art, has given this aesthetic process a name. Kant had aesthetics investigate the *transcendence* by which art transfers us from the special to the general and universal but today Danto reflects on how contemporary art reinvents the private, special and particular going from our mass-fabricated serial world of commodities. He called this the '*transfiguration* of the commonplace' (1981).

Aesthetic fields: Schillerian play between form and matter

Both aesthetic processes of transcendence and transfiguration, the Kantian cementation of a *sensus-communis* by means of judgement as well as the aesthetic conquest of individuation, have spatial dimensions. Any project of aesthetic philosophy implies an aesthetic field to which Kant's third Critique functions as an intellectual fortification. It seems that Kant so forcefully demarcated this field that Gadamer and others have felt a need to loosen up its borderline fortifications. Since 1790, the year of publication of *Kritik der Urteilskraft*, the field has been subject to openings and closures, to careful narrowing down and bold expansions.

The enlightened gardening and cultivation of judgement can only thrive on this aesthetic field which Kant, like a proud explorer, locates as an island of natural art between the two continents of 'pure' and 'practical reason' which he had mapped in his previous Critiques of 1781 and 1785. In the first Critique where he treats our knowledge of nature Kant epistemologically emancipates us into enlightened egos. In the second he reflects on the goodness of our conduct in free social interaction. He argues that it takes two different approaches to reflect on either knowledge or freedom. Both epistemology and ethics, the two Kantian approaches, concern us all. As humans we are both '*homo phenomenon*' and '*homo noumenon*', both physical creatures and, at the same time, ethical beings gifted with the very unique human ability to philosophize and reflect on our own actions. Kant and the philosophy of enlightenment specially insisted on this human condition: our privilege of freedom and its duty, self-legislation. The two first Critiques provide us with a complex and intricate dualistic system. The two realms have to be connected. Man must, in order to remain a human being, both accept his physicality and assume the responsibility that freedom implies. Still, Kant insists, different laws of nature and codes of conduct apply. By using legal terminology he emphasizes the sharp formal distinction between pure and practical reason by saying that they belong to different 'jurisdictions' because 'the concept of freedom determines nothing in respect of theoretical cognition of nature, and the concept of nature likewise nothing in respect of the practical laws of freedom (Kant, 1952: 37). If pure reason takes over we forget about ethics and our freedom. If the logic of practical reason conquers the realm of pure reason we end up with the kind of madness called rationalism. Human existence presupposes connections between the two, but still they must be kept from blurring, invading and dominating each other. To Kant the third Critique seemed to open up a possibility to manage this dualism.

Here again one comes to think of the management of modern organizations. Industry has had its engineers, Fayols and Taylors aspiring to a 'science' of management and administration. Economics has its Williamsons proposing organizational wisdom based on political economy and its ethical foundations. In the everyday management of organizations technical standards and rules compete with moral maxims and principles of efficiency. Kant would, had he been a management guru, have proposed a third possibility – aesthetics. He would ask both economists and engineers to relax their firm respective convictions to master the world by ethics or science. It might be somewhat odd to envisage Kant in the role of such a management guru but it is far easier with one of his aesthetic vulgarizers: Friedrich Schiller.

In letters *On the Aesthetic Education of Man* (1982) the poet Schiller in 1793 accounts for the third Critique by giving an art entrepreneur's version of the aesthetic philosopher's brand new book. Schiller's letters, in contrast to Kant's treatise, offer a combination of aesthetic thinking and art management ideas. As any modern management guru, Schiller uses his literary charm to package Kant's aesthetics into a handy tripartite model. On the one hand, he says, there is '*Stoff*', materiality and on the other '*Form*'. Both matter and form exert considerable attraction for us poor human beings. The category of '*Stoff*' stands for the earthy, natural, animal. '*Form*' belongs to the realm of thought, logic, dream and system. Schiller dramatically re-stages the Kantian dichotomy as a tragic Scylla-Charybdis threat. If we succumb to the material temptation we end up hooked on '*Stoff*', lose our humanity and become dull barbarians. To escape into '*Form*' is hardly better. It means withdrawal into daydreaming about logically possible worlds, turning us first into utopians and, God beware, if we are granted some worldly power it might transform any daydreamer into a tyrant, pressing his mad mental blueprints on his fellow men by brute force. Schiller, who was himself appointed an honorary citizen by Danton in Paris, had a very special managerial formalism in mind: Robespierre's use of Madame Guillotine in service of his Jacobin utopia. The dilemma of dualism, here in its old philosophical guise of 'polarity', cannot be resolved by choice between the two forces or drives. Instead of choice, Schiller evokes another idea of modern philosophy later to become a panacea to the social sciences: equilibrium. But, as in economic models, this equilibrium

> remains no more than an Idea, which can never be fully realized in actuality . . .
> and the utmost that experience can achieve will consist of an oscillation
> between the two principles in which now reality, now form, will predominate.
> (Schiller, 1982: 111)

Schiller thus presents aesthetics as a philosophy helping and educating man to develop the faculty of blending Form and Matter in such oscillation or, to use Schiller's far more expressive German key concept, *Schwung*. *Schwung* results from a third innate drive – what Schiller calls the 'play-drive'. *Play* is our saviour from dualism and Schiller concludes that man is 'only fully a human being when he plays' (1982: 107). Schiller moreover promises that the drive of play will be philosophically capable of 'bearing the whole edifice of art' since it is by means of art that we can awaken our slumbering play-drive. The beautiful and sublime, melting and energetic beauty as the poet called them, force us to realize that form and reality matter equally. A Winkelmannian antique marble statue imposes both its 'life' and internally fixed 'materiality' on the onlooker. In reading Kant, Schiller discovers an artist's organizational mission: to make art which will inspire his fellow men to play, to become an art manager with *Schwung*.

Aesthetic actions – creation and interpretation

Kant mapped the aesthetic field and Schiller saw its opportunity for art. But what kind of activity or action is art? Kant stated that

> Art is further distinguished from handicraft. The first is called free, the other may be called industrial art. We look on the former as something which could only prove final (be a success) as play, i.e. an occupation which is agreeable on its own account; but on the second as labour, i.e. a business, which on its own account is disagreeable (drudgery), and is only attractive by means of what it results in (e.g. the pay) and which is consequently is capable of being a compulsory imposition. (1952: 164)

Kant's distinction between 'pay' and 'play' is rooted in his idea of art as a spiritual matter distinguished by *Geist*. Kant wanted to limit the scope of mechanical world-views, like the Newtonian approach of David Hume for instance, otherwise tending to abort human action of all its intentionality by reducing it to a scientific, causal, billiard-ball phenomenon. Here Kant argues that art should not be considered an instrumental action. This makes it distinct from both commerce and work, and is perhaps why its value cannot be fully accounted for by economic theories of exchange- or use-value. Still art can be present in the worlds of craft and industry as Adam Smith had pointed out when noting that we buy wares and vote for political solutions because they 'charm' us (1979: 183). Utility alone cannot explain why manufacturers expand their sales, Smith concludes. Success in markets does not entirely depend on buyers paying for useful tools but also on inventing new funny toys for people to play with. To Smith this playfulness, this Schillerian organizational quality of real art, has great importance for economic growth.

When talking about art it has become pretty commonplace to embark on the theme of 'creativity'. Aesthetics, however, widens the discourse of creativity to the topic of interpretation. Kant's transcendental focus seems to be preoccupied with our interpretations of God's creation. Schiller, much more than Kant, put an emphasis on the task of man as artist in triggering playful interpretations. The first focuses on the action of the spectating interpreter while the second takes the creative agent more into account. Almost two centuries later Gadamer adds another aspect and reorients the meaning of action in aesthetic play in order to 'free this concept of the subjective meaning that it has in Kant and Schiller' (Gadamer, 1994: 101). While Kantianism seems to concentrate on 'interpreting creation' the aesthetic hermeneutics of Gadamer is more interested in 'creating interpretation'. To Kant creation was a datum, something God given. To Schiller it becomes more of a matter of fact, something man made. But aesthetic philosophy bothers little about discovering the universally new or inventing novelty which seem to be the constant blind-alleys into which so called creativity-research runs. Aesthetic action is fundamentally geared towards onlookers like theatre spectators or concert-hall audiences. In 1750 Alexander Baumgarten had defined aesthetics as a *'scientia cognitionis sensitivae'* (1988: 3). Kant, as we have seen, opposed the definition of aesthetics as a branch of cognitive science. First, he only found two senses worthy of aesthetic interest: vision and audition. Secondly, he discarded their physiological aspects from the agenda of aesthetic philosophy. What mattered to aesthetics was not the physiological function of the senses, or their behaviour, but the making sense of what was seen or heard. Today's aesthetics points to many cases, of which the Duchamp ready-mades have become archetypical, where we cannot visually decide if an object is art or not. Reception, rather than perception, becomes relevant from an aesthetic point of view.

But much interpretation remains uncovered by the term 'reception'. Besides bringing home a piece of art, experiencing its beauty or sublimity as a gift offered to us, it might engage us in reflection. This is precisely what happens to Kant and other aesthetic philosophers. Reflection seems far more active than reception. Reflection is intellectual while reception often has more emotional traits. But we have to be careful with over-intellectualizing reflection. 'There is no science of the beautiful, only Critique', says Kant (1952: 165).

In a similar analytical mode we might discern different actions on the 'creative' side of art. Kant on the one hand recognized the quasi-mystical powers of creative geniuses but, on the other, he admits that there are 'mechanisms' the mastering of which prevents the soul in art becoming 'bodiless and evanescent'(1952: 164). A poet must master language, a painter drawing and a singer must read music. Creation is based on the technical actions by which art is executed. Beside execution we have notation that also takes technical skills for the score, script or sketch to be operational.

Aesthetic organization – the Gadamerian Kreis

Aesthetic philosophy renders a feel for an aesthetic *field* of *play* for two aesthetic processes of *transcendence* and *transfiguration* carried out by conjunct *creation/interpretation* in different actions as *reception, reflection, execution* and *notation*. But who are the players?

When aesthetic philosophy defends the specificity of its aesthetic field it consequently reminds us that art cannot be produced as regular goods and services. It comes about in organizations which Gadamer calls *Kreise*. Gadamer focuses on the emergence of poetry and how texts are animated into art. Having his roots in traditional scriptural hermeneutics he naturally fetches images from the realm of religious organization where the auratic quality is brought about in the cultic actions of a congregation. This has little resemblance to chains of production. It is rather a circular or rounded process. Aesthetic organizing cannot, at least if we opt for Gadamer's idea of the play in a *Kreis*, be treated as some kind of manufacturing. Nor should it be reduced to a social system of only human interaction. To Gadamer a *Kreis* is a kind of a melting pot. In its centre the 'word' emerges as a concrete work-of-art that, so to speak, proves its art status by a powerful concreteness holding together its very own circle. The reading of a text or playing of a drama is, to Gadamer, of course taking place in a social setting with special rules, norms or conventions. Some sociologists of art have developed institutional theories to grasp how art is made by investigating such normative management of art-worlds. But these functional aspects of organizing can never get to the heart of the matter. Nor is it, as we have mentioned above, of any use to engage in psychological studies of personal subjective needs or individual motives for playing because plays on the aesthetic field should not be confused with 'game-playing' or some psychological '*Spielbedürfnis*'. Heidegger's disciple Gadamer postulates that if we want aesthetically to understand art-work as '*das ins-Dasein-treten der Dichtung selbst*' we have to philosophically confront the '*ins-Dasein-treten*' itself instead of escaping to sociology or cognitive psychology.

Another contemporary philosopher, the Frenchman Gérard Genette (1994), casts doubt on regarding art works as objects of human work. Maybe we should drop the word 'work' for the French '*oeuvre*'. To '*oeuvrer*' is rather to 'create' while the French word for work, '*travail*' has as little place in aesthetic vocabulary as the German word '*Arbeit*'. To Genette an art work like a poem or a novel can never be located in the objective text. To do so would leave aesthetics for magics. Genette also criticizes the postmoderns who identify art creation with 'writing'. He also attacks the American Nelson Goodman whom he accuses of maintaining in *Languages of Art* (1969) that

> la forme literaire est le texte ecrit, et l'on se souvient peut-etre de la devotion scripturale pseudo-derridienne des annees soixante-dix, ou l'oeuvre destitueé au profit du Texte, celui-ci se voyait identifiés a l'Ecriture opposé a la Parole a peu prés comme le Bien au Mal. (Genette, 1994: 110–1)

Genette calls this Goodmanian approach 'pseudo'-Derridean in homage to Derrida whom he never would blame, as he blames Goodman, for reducing literary art-making into linguistic techniques of denotation or representation. Although they attack different enemies both Genette and Gadamer converge on an important point. Art is itself an actor. Art only exists when it works. If we want to take aesthetic organization seriously we therefore have to grant art the status of agency. An aesthetic organizing perspective cannot tolerate regarding art as objects like a Mona-Lisa-picture or a Don-Quixote-novel. But, of course, art as an agent is, like most humans, vague, elusive and multifaceted.

An *Oeuvre* – a Work of Art – says Genette is more than the sum of its immanent manifestations. A drama like *Hamlet* is printed in a book. It however only dwells partly in a notated script and partly in the executed script – i.e. the staged play. The *Symphonie Fantastique* partly hides in the score as well as in its realization – the concert. A plan for an art work and its execution both carry the *Oeuvre*. Genette, as opposed to Goodman, claims that you can never define and catch it completely in a printed text or score. The *Oeuvre* as an agent has to be brought out in between its manifestations. This complex exercise might encompass both archeological hindsight and, what Goodman calls, 'projections' of new meaning. From an aesthetic perspective Genette emphasizes that an art work therefore should never be mistaken for its manifestations. The examination of books and scores can never fulfil the requirements of an aesthetic investigation of a Balzac novel or a Beethoven symphony. The very point of aesthetic organizing is to turn art into one of several agents.

If we follow the Kantian track as developed in Gadamer and Genette we will come to regard art works as something as dynamic as human action. We now abandon a materialistic Mona Lisa idea of art as framed canvas painted by someone famous, reminding us of something. The Mona Lisa idea sees art as a durable – not to say eternal – good possessing intrinsic value or qualities. This view of art might be fairly suitable for some institutions like museums or other conservatories. However, it neglects the role of organizing in making art work. And it has little to do with aesthetic philosophy. Perhaps the reason why organizational scholars like Ramirez overlook art is that they are blinded by this narrow Mona Lisa paradigm of art?

If we leave painting or poetry for the performing arts it, of course, becomes easier to envisage art as aesthetic organizing. The more we learn about its history the more limited seems the idea of art as an intimate dialogue between some genial artist and his admirer. Creation and interpretation involve numerous agents whose aesthetic organizings the history of the performing arts makes us follow over time, from the 'salon', where all the action was shared amongst a party of cultured art lovers, to the industrialized showbiz performances of professional actors. In the salon, the avant-garde soirée or the hippie happening, participants mixed spectation and acting. In the bourgeois salon or the courtly theatre practically everyone possessed the skills to sing a score or take a part in a play. Frequently the King, in honour of whom a play was performed, himself appeared on stage. The noblemen of the court were often playwrights or conducted rehearsals as eloquent and witty connoisseurs. The development of bourgeois mass audiences brought about copyright reforms protecting creative writers specializing in notation. Execution was handled by increasingly industrialized actors. To this split of roles between agents backstage came a similar differentiation frontstage with increasingly amateur audiences supplied with reviews by critics of the press. Out of such aesthetic 'field stories' we might add meat to the bones of a simple model with some agents positioned in an aesthetic *Kreis* where art resides in its midst:

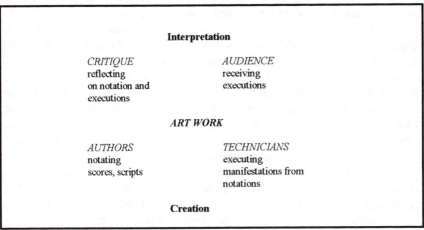

Figure 2.1 *Art Organization as a Gadamerian* Kreis

Art management – strategies

Kreis-keeping

Organizing, understood in an aesthetic philosophical mood, is a delicate matter that can be demonstrated 'Wittgensteinianly' without explicit definitions, known 'Anscombianly' without observation or 'Langerianly' presented beyond concepts of discursive logic. Didn't Kant himself allude to this when stating that in matters of art no science would be possible only critique? Let us skip the idea of science with its flavour of planning and perfection and explore the managerial meaning of this criticism.

   As so many earn their everyday livelihood helping art to come about, there are good reasons to examine such 'art management'. In the field mapped by aesthetic philosophy the actions of different agents bring about aesthetic processes. Most aesthetic reference works, however, caution us to refrain from treating such actions as recipes, rules or standard techniques for goal achievement. This is not to deny that making art implies many sorts of instrumentality. But mastering spelling, carving stone or mixing colours does not make the poet, sculptor or painter. Artistry is hardly identical to learning methods or manners and, accordingly, the art management we are looking for will not be a new form of a scientific management.

If we look at what art administrators and managers do, it often seems like a kind of safeguarding: like curating in the sense of carefully keeping ideals alive. If we listen to aestheticists we soon will find that 'ideals' of art manifest themselves more 'really' than our everyday materialistic or rationalistic conceptions of 'idealism' would allow. The ideal of art could, for instance, take a concrete form of a nicely orchestrated *Kreis*. Then art management would, perhaps, imply the fostering of a Kantian faculty to judge whether such a *Kreis* slips out of order. To manage here will be to maintain aesthetic quality, although it cannot be reduced to quantitative terms suitable for more regular forms of managerial control. Art management would then mean to foresee and forestall the disintegration of Kreises already in existence.

Those who naturally qualify as 'art managers' display a kind of human ecological behaviour that can be characteristic of critical management on the individual level. It mostly seems that they manage by refraining from action. Artists, for instance, actively manage their careers by avoiding people, places and situations. They break away from customs and patterns. They are more like sensitive Picassos quickly divorcing yesterday's conquest than managers pushing towards tomorrow's goals. Jasper Johns is said to have systematically dropped doing something as soon as he caught a glimpse of similar work. By similar negative actions critics try to decontextualize events in order to make them stand out as centres of new *Kreises*. When two world wars turned the famous gallerist Kahnweiler into the role of a critic by putting an end to his business he wrote essays that argued the case of a very special 'cubist' art by vehemently denying all its links to other art forms. For all its pathetic attempts or pretentious failures, for all examples of art mismanagement resulting in 'the kitschy' or 'the arty', there seems, likewise, only to be negative remedies of critical escape or rejection. While management scholars often portray their heroes, the managers, as constructivist visionaries the art historians rather present their avant-garde entrepreneurs as moody opportunists mysteriously mastering the timing of escapes and divorces to perfection. But this individual avant-garde behaviour is difficult to decode any further. It is as if irrationality, such as that inspired by a Marcel Duchamp ready-made or a John Cage event, must be the dead-end verdict when we remain on the biographical level of individual art world tactics. What about approaching those mysteries from the point-of-view of aesthetic organizing, instead of an individual action? Can we better grasp art management by looking at how *Kreises* are strategically handled? Let us test this idea using two cases from contemporary art.

Bonk Business Inc.

In 1993 a Finnish corporation called Bonk Business Inc. celebrated its centenary and in 1995 it went public in Sweden. The presentation was followed by several employment ads in Stockholm papers searching for at least five hundred young hostesses, and announcing the intentions of Bonk to make a friendly take-over of Volvo Cars. Bonk was introduced to the Swedish audience by a fancy Swedish advertising agency called 'Paradise'. Those who were lucky to get hold of a copy of the company history could enjoy the speech delivered by the company founder Pär Bonk on the occasion of the first issue of company shares in 1893:

> Behold, my papa, fisherman Bönken, did realize his vision of greasing the wheels of industry with anchovies. He built a factory to transform the viscosity of the fish into various oils. He lubricated the sawmills of Kainu and rolling mills of Routsinpythää and Tallintehdas. He shipped his lubricants and other anchovy products to every corner of Finland and Europe, and even to the New World – to America. It is anchovies that have greased the machines on which our well-being depends. (Gullichsen and Stanley, 1993: 12,14)

The company history is introduced by Alvar Gullichsen, its young dynamic product development manager. We understand that this is the jubilee of an industrial success story with which all Finns feel at home. Bonk Business is rooted in the firm belief

> that our founder Pär Bonk came to this world to ignite an inextinguishable fire of creativity that would solve the world's problems before the end of the millennium . . . (it is) the story of simple Finnish folk who founded a multi-global enterprise for the benefit of mankind. (Gullichsen and Stanley, 1993: 7)

The 'little handy volume' was published to inform the public 'who we are and from whence we have come' so that everyone could join in and make a contribution to a 'great future ahead'. The stage is set: a self-made entrepreneur from a humble background, a useful and simple product, plus a populist pathos of industrial progress to wealth through hard honest work.

Pär Bonk, the legendary founder of the company, miraculously materialized on the drawing pad of the young art student Alvar during a Björneborg jazz festival. According to Gullichsen and his partner, film and music producer Richard Stanley, it started not unlike an economic enterprise – as a lazy hangover idea at the Gullichsen summer residence on the Baltic Sea. Alvar's mother had just found an old Swedish anchovy tin which induced a heated debate between Gullichsen and his English brother-in-law. Subsequently Alvar and Richard developed sculptures called 'Raba Hiffs' into what became samples of Bonk Business Inc. product lines. This, in turn, became the start of Bonk's modern success in marketing so-called 'defunctioned' machines, beloved for just being nice to look at while consuming no energy, needing no repairs and demanding no skills to operate.

Alvar Gullichsen explains that Bonk Business Inc. is a showcase of Finnish economic growth and a text book example of both product development and advertising history. In a TV documentary of the Bonk case we can follow Gullichsen and his team approaching other managers, offering them the opportunity to sponsor and support the Bonk jubilee and inscribe themselves in the project by adding their own example to the Bonk story. As Stanley now puts it Bonk has developed into a kind of 'movement' to which both people and firms join and contribute. This may explain the support from 'Paradise'. Bonk has also been approached by artists like Finnish poet Bo Carpelan who contributed the incredibly kitsch poems of the unknown relative and amateur poet Amelie Bonk to the family heritage. Many photographers who feel like working in a 'Bonkish' fashion propose pictures. Apart from the collection of

2.1 *Bonk Celebrates its Centenary*

old Bonk machines and products, a small industry has grown around Bonk featuring videos, records, souvenirs and clothing. Many who have read about Bonk, and even those who have been to their jubilee exhibitions in Björneborg and later in Stockholm, have serious doubts. It this a real case of successful management or is it a case of postmodern business art?

No doubt these Raba Hiff Machines were improvements on both Duchamp's ready-mades and Jean Tinguely's do-nothing machines. The fact that the business press wrote about them indicated that more businesses than Bonk had their toys masquerading as efficient tools of the market place. Bonk only seemed to present what many a money-making postmodern industrialist had been long since doing.

Although Alvar Gullichsen is a successful painter he nevertheless grew up as an heir of a large industrialist family. His grandmother Marie Gullichsen was the leading lady in most Helsinki cultural salons and a close friend to artists like the famous architect Aalto, also christened Alvar. Her grandson is a shareholder of the family corporation Ahlström. The young capitalist grew up in complete familiarity with modern art. A friend draws a portrait of Alvar as an artist-entrepreneur:

> Alvar is unlike most artists who complain and consume gallons of cheap red wine puking up their bitterness against all that moves. Actually I have a bit of a problem seeing him as a traditional artist – he resembles more one of those young managers in a computer business. (Gullichsen and Stanley, 1993)

Alvar is outspoken about his background and clarifies the self-financing of Bonk Business in a TV interview:

> Without an inherited fortune and a regular dividend there would never have been any Bonk Business. However I have never ever been in doubt of my own ability to create value. I have evidence enough of my own creativity so I just keep doing what I am interested in. Doing singular, strange, mystical, funny and fantastic things. The most rewarding part of the Bonk experience has been to build machines, to screw the branded steelplate to a machine and incorporate it into the Bonk Business family. (Gullichsen and Stanley, 1993)

On the Bonk stage Alvar Gullichsen acts out the role of the artist-capitalist under his own name while Richard Stanley features in the Bonk publications as Kompressor Sven Triloquist, Director of Repackaging.

In the team there is a Bonk photographer, a Bonk machine-builder and a copy-editor. The creativity around Bonk Business is however not completely free-wheeling. Bonk Business is a family firm trying to maintain old-time spirit and enthusiasm, although a growing number of new generation shareholders tend to get less and less involved with the business. For some curious reason Bonk seems to share this problem with the Ahlstrom group. The way real business copes, i.e. by reanimating its spirits with a corporate identity campaign, is not far away from that of which the successful Björneborg and Stockholm historical Bonk Business show are good cases. This strange parallelism also concerns technology. When Ahlstrom launched a new miracle technology furnace for burning waste Bonk presented its Black Hole Suction Technology to an amazed art world. As in any corporation we can go to the 'Festschrift' and explore each generation's contribution to the Bonk dynastic growth.

From old Bönken's son Pär (1853–1908), to grandson Pärre (1885–1943) and young Barry Bonk (1933–), and from old Bönken's garrum lubricant produced out of Baltic anchovy, the mechanical inventions of Pär and the electro-mechanical gear of Pärre to Barry's consumer hits like Doc. Lithium's

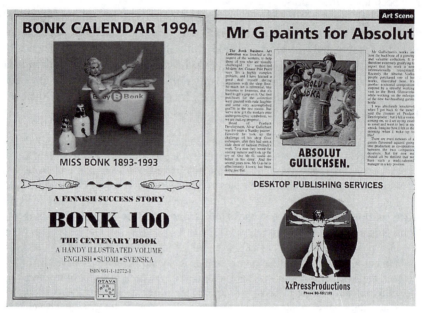

2.2 *Gullichsen takes Centre Stage*

Pet Pump and the Raba Hiff defunct contraptions, the Bonk Business exhibitions are full of typical trade show avalanches of strange industrial products such as tinned tele-foam for remote cleaning or Toblerone-like packaged Bermuda Triangles. Both are the fruit of a new department: the Bonk Repacking Division founded on the marketing theory of 'parasitic relationship' of which Philip Kotler would be proud. It is explained in a Bonk brochure as a

> so called 'synergy' method of manufacturing meaning that the original supplier . . . has all the problems of manufacturing and distribution, from materials, factories, staff, contract expenses, bulk shipping, insurance and other wasteful expenses. The marketing company's basic expense . . . is in designing of the label and . . . even the specially trained and highly paid gluemeisters costs can be minimized. Repackaging is the recycling of old ideas in new guises. An environment-friendly strategy leading to greater profits.

Some 100,000 bewildered museum-goers have strolled through the large Bonk shows in Finland and Sweden. They have partaken of company prints and products and watched several performances with Gullichsen and Stanley delivering lectures on Bonk Business Inc. philosophy. A TV series, based on the amazing newly discovered Bonk film archives that contain really revolutionary unknown Eisenstein advertising footage for Bonk's early Soviet marketing, is under production and both Germany and France are lining up for more shows. Still both Gullichsen and Stanley convincingly insist that this is no parody of industry and that they honestly 'love this old machinery and advertising'. They claim that the real target for their performances is art. Gullichsen and Stanley love good old archaic industry with its concrete hardware engineering. But Bonk's new postmodern stuff, the defunctioned and repacked products, performs what any art object does – it just advertises itself as having economic value, as being a good deal for the buyers. Stanley concludes:

> Art has changed a lot in our time. Like rock and roll there is behind the frontstage a huge concealed commercial machinery. People do not see this. Art is today like a business corporation. Take for instance the big Finnish corporation Nokia. People see its advertising and products but have never seen the factories. Today even regular business has turned invisible. Like art, making it has become a black box to people. Bonk Business makes them see the inside of the box again. But now it's imagination. (Gullichsen and Stanley, 1993)

Christo Corporation

Bonk Business Inc. both monetarily and mentally thrives on being an old-fashioned self-financed family firm. It's a nostalgic piece of private art. Christo Corporation headed by Christo Javacheff, born and educated in socialist Bulgaria, is the opposite. Javacheff like Gullichsen has an academic art education. But while the latter staged Duchampian puns in his family circle the former was ordered out on *kolchoses* to help farmers along the Orient Express tracks hide their poverty from the eyes of Western tourists with theatrical tricks and settings. Those communist Patomkin illusions were Christo's very first land art installations. If Gullichsen is a child of the private sphere of enterprise and art, Javacheff is a product of official political art. As a young stateless refugee he earned his livelihood as a street caricaturist. Instead of an advertising man like Stanley, Javacheff professionally teamed up with a French general's daughter who co-signs his art work. Christo presents his wife, art manager and CEO of the Christo Corporation in a TV interview:

> Jeanne Claude is my lover, the president and treasurer of Christo Corporation. She can make my dream possible through the strong relations she builds up. She manages the continuous cash flow we need to pay our workers. She is really a manager, more practical, controlling and realistic than me. She sees both the big chances and the many, many small details.

In late June 1995 the latest of the Christo and Jeanne Claude wrappings was performed on the Berlin Reichstag building. The days before the opening this was like a building site. Fences and enclosures with 'stay out' signs surrounded the house on which ex-DDR building workers climbed like mountaineers. The site was guarded by an army of young guides who helped visitors with information about the installation. The press centre round the corner was constantly crowded and those who were lucky could catch a glimpse of the two Javacheffs inspecting the preparations like arty rock stars.

The project had started in 1971 as a postcard from Berlin gallerist and Christo's friend Michael Cullen urging him to wrap its depicted building. What Christo calls the 'software phase' took an exceptional 22 years – far more than for any other wrapping project. During these years several lobbying campaigns were launched. The final one started in 1986 with a Berlin real estate developer, Roland Specker, collecting a list of 70,000 signatures from Berliners wanting the Christo project. During 1993 the artist's team personally visited 180 Bundestag members to prepare for the final vote which took place on 25 February 1994 in Bonn.

2.3 *The Reichstag Wrapped*

A 70-minute long debate, broadcast live, ended with 292 votes for and 223 against lending the Reichstag to the artists for a limited period. For every excess day a fee of 10,000 DM was established in the contract signed between the Bundestag and the Christo GmbH, the German joint stock company especially founded to carry out the project under the supervision of Christo's New York-based corporation.

In contrast to Bonk, Christo operates completely in the public sphere. His projects like Valley Curtain, Running Fence, Surrounded Island or Pont Neuf mostly concern communities. In Berlin the project became the subject of a national political debate that split political parties. Those against pretended that they were saving the symbolic face of the nation. Who could guarantee that this was not a huge joke, a satirical attack on a monument representing national values from Bismarck onwards? Those who, like, probably, Helmut Kohl himself, feared that the artists were pulling the nation's leg were countered by the friends of the project. Hadn't Christo worked for 22 years on this wrapping? That seemed to be guarantee enough of its seriousness. Opportunistic politicians who frequently deceived their voters should learn from such a visionary. Didn't Christo promise to recycle the wrapping materials as lining for roadbuilding? And, as a final and probably decisive argument, this event would be a symbol of the reunified Germany, a spectacular launch for a new Germany which would be totally free of expense for German taxpayers. To all Bundestag members Christo of course made his managerial principles crystal clear:

> We pay with our own money. We finance it by the sales of our preparatory original works of art. This is all linked to the idea of freedom. Everything in this project is about aesthetics including the finances. No strings attached when we finance this way. . . . to keep the project pure and demonstrate its incredible presence. In that way there is no justification or the moralization you usually find in public art. The project is one of pure poetical inspiration.

Revealing his Marxist schooling and a sense for local monetary ecology, Christo adds that

> We are very economical as to how we spend the 26 million in the community, on salaries and materials for hardware. This has nothing to do with the case when artists sell a picture for 100 million. Such an art prize is a total mystification simply because the picture has cost less than 100 dollars in canvas, colour or framing . . .

During the whole event prints, catalogues, books, videos and limited edition preparatory works were sold from special sales points. Freshly printed postcards showing the development of wrapping preparations were sold by salespeople scattered around the Reichstag in front of which the representatives from the television and press were posted.

Some pirate postcard salesmen apart, the whole area was kept clean from commercial advertising. When Springer attempted to build a pavilion near the Reichstag, Christo threatened to cancel his installation if the construction was not immediately stopped. The suppliers to the project were not allowed to make any kind of advertising on the site. This would, if the project is seen as an *art* project and not a *construction* project, have been out of place since they were not sponsors but sold their goods and services to the Verhüllter Reichstags GmbH, the German subsidiary of Christo Corporation, for regularly negotiated market prices. The self-financing allows the Christos to control their project and let 'pure aesthetics' rule its realization. Thus by turning their own artwork into a private incorporated business Christo and Jeanne Claude paradoxically avoid its commercialization.

2.4 *Practice Wrapping*

Threats to aesthetic organizing

The realization of contemporary art work takes much managerial effort. Bonk and Christo offer good examples of such complex aesthetic organizing with a multitude of agents cooperating to achieve a Bonk show or Reichstag wrapping. On the tactical level much of this work hardly differs from the tasks necessary to manage a trade fair or a building site. As in any performing art, they draw upon skills such as technical drawing, logistics, insurance, financing, lobbying, personnel management and press relations. Apart from *auteurs* such as Christo Javacheff and Alvar Gullichsen there are agents such as Roland Specker, Jeanne-Claude Javacheff and Richard Stanley handling a number of technical creative aspects such as the selection and purchase of materials, hiring of construction workers, copy-editing of text material, etc. In the Bonk case the Paradise advertising agency was an active partner and in the

Christo case many firms worked both as suppliers of the wrappings and as publishers of prints, books and videos associated with the projects. For Christo the hardware side of the wrapping is like any engineering project. When reminded of their considerable cost he remarks that they cost much less than other aesthetic enterprises such as Hollywood pictures or architect-designed skyscrapers. But apart from the tactical planning and realization, which Christo calls the hardware phase, there is a 'software phase' of aesthetic organizing that has to be managed. What does this aspect strategic art management mean?

For Christo the work in the software phase is about convincing potential agents to join the project for 'aesthetic reasons'. In the case of the Reichstag, the Pont Neuf or Valley Curtain the strategic art management process had to persuade agents such as communities, landowners, the press, the critics and cooperating technicians of the aesthetic value of the projects. When this fails, such as in the attempt to wrap the Champs Elysées in Paris, Christo never blames technicalities but his and Jeanne Claude's 'lack of intelligence and sensitivity'. The 22 years preceding the Berlin project are full of examples of strategic management involving subtle aesthetic rhetorical persuasion both through personal contact and the mass media.

In the subtext of the public debate on the Reichstag project can be perceived an imminent threat: a threat with which Christo's strategic art management had to cope. Let us call it 'totalization'. Christo's art has, indirectly through his own background, roots in official monumental art. In Berlin Christo dared to propose an art work involving a political monument in this country with both leftist and rightist past of totalitarianism. Nazis and communists had both made ample ideological use of art. Art was instrumentalized for propaganda by officials often, like many Nazi leaders, considering themselves to be artists. Christo's proposal clearly ran the risk of being taken for either an Albert Speerish installation or a satire on the monumentality of Nürnberg parades. In the aftermath of dictatorship, aesthetics and art have been locked away in the poison cupboard. When postmodern philosophy revived an interest in aesthetics political philosophers showed considerable scepticism. To Frankfurtian Jürgen Habermas a democratic dialogue could have little to do with art. The enlargement of art, as Joseph Beuys dared to suggest, was seen as a dangerous antidemocratic act. Hadn't Hitlerism thrived on the greasy broth of romanticism spiced with transcendental metaphysics? What could prevent art, especially public and monumental art, from turning into a transcendentalist tool for concocting new swastikas or red stars? A deeply felt and well-documented fear for such organizational symbolism had therefore to be countered by the Christo campaign. The following words by Peter Conradi of the SPD bear witness to the existence of an art management with that strategic purpose:

> The very long preparation and the public debate of their meaning are integral parts of Christo's projects. During 22 years Christo has spoken with innumerable politicians, journalists, artists, critics and citizens about the

wrapping of the Reichstag building. I am impressed by the stubbornness and
visionary power to make possible what seems impossible. This is a political, as
well as a democratic artistic action. It is not elitist since it involves people. I
wish we politicians had such stamina, vision, endurance and in our campaigns.[2]

For Christo the strategic management directed against suspicions of
totalitarian tendencies rested primarily on his almost populist urge to dialogue.
Again and again he denies that he wants to make new symbols. Metaphysics is
banned for demystification. He presents himself as a man wanting to
communicate with fellow men:

> I am an artist, and this means that I embody . . . an urgency and priority. To
> realize how important it is to make such things. Creativity simply means to
> establish this tremendous priority and focus . . . the project of the Reichstag has
> to translate a broader idea of art . . . related to the people . . . the project makes
> the people see, rediscover ordinary routine surroundings . . . when behind the
> door of a museum they say 'this is art' . . . in the street, in town . . . they start to
> think . . . 'it is art?' – 'no, this can't be art?' . . . this is the most important...but
> I have no control of what they really see . . .the projects are always bigger than
> my own imagination.

While some enthusiastic politicians call the installation a 'peaceful creative
scission in the history of the building very different from the Reichstag fire half
a century ago' or a way to bring out 'pure form under the soft drapery', Christo
himself emphasizes the temporary, ephemeral nature of his installation. For
Christo it is a homage to the present and brief:

> I enjoy it when it is realized. I spend time on the site and experience the real
> thing that exists for such a brief period of time. The brief period of a few days
> is an example of this extraordinary freedom . . . this humility, the project will
> soon be gone, like our child, our life . . . they are very uplifting projects,
> optimistic, full of energy. They have all the dynamics of the cloth, that normal
> sculptures do not have.

The threats for Bonk Business are hardly those of cementing some new
anti-democratic values. Bonk on the contrary balances on the edge of populism
and its paradoxical tone resembles a humorous advertising campaign. Instead
of countering totalitarian suspicion Bonk has to cope with the opposite threat
that may be called *banalization*. In cultural criticism we find many analyses of
the banality of the media and mass consumption. The most influential banality-
analysis is probably Adorno's media criticism of popular showbusiness based
on the Marxian diagnosis of capitalist forms of social reproduction. Richard
Stanley's presentation of Bonk does not hide the banal tendency of the project:
'This is not great art. Bonk is for people to enjoy like a football match or going
swimming. It's a joke and meant to be fun.' But Stanley immediately adds:

You know it is a joke but at the same time you want it to be real. And one of the great things of democracy is to be fooled whilst being aware and knowing you are being fooled. Bonk makes people aware of how things are while fooling them. It makes them wake up and watch things more carefully. Is this a piece of sculpture or just a useless, defunct, machine?

Totalization as a sort of version of transcendence run amok. Banalization can be envisaged as an extreme form of transfiguration where everyday phenomena are catapulted into our private sphere without any individuation taking place. Totalitarian art tends to be pretentiously mystical or even 'arty' while the banalization ends up in ridiculed 'kitschness'. Christo, fearing the transcendental pretentiousness of museums or the symbolism of eternal values emphasizes the ephemeral and fleeting. Bonk claims to have turned down a take-over offer from a big soft drinks multinational and keeps one foot firmly anchored in the museum world so as not to drift away into the Coney Islands or Disneylands of commercial marketplaces.

Beyond Beuys – conclusions

If we combine the strategic issues with the structures of the aesthetic organizing model two destructive forces become visible. First there is the force of *Totalization* that threatens to take over aesthetic organizations and turn them into political instruments of which we have so many fearful examples in our time. In terms of the model totalization can be depicted as imploding forces →← which seem to pull the agents into the centre. Art turns into a kind of evil maelstrom sucking free agents into its powerfield. It's not difficult to give very concrete examples of that destruction. Political revolts and revolutions are often initiated by aesthetic positive powers. There is a hope for a new avant-garde society or even an aesthetic state (Chytry, 1989). On the left, this was the period when Chagall went back to Vitebsk to run a Bolshevik art school, when Kandinski resettled in Moscow or Tatlin projected his monuments to the revolution. On the right, it was when Jünger welcomed a Stahlgewitter, Heidegger had hopes for Graeco-German counterpower to technology or Nolde and Barlach regarded themselves as friends of the expressionist novelist Goebbels. But springtimes are awfully short (Guillet de Monthoux, 1983) and soon the agents become more and more locked up by their own creation.

Art in the middle of the model implodes, as indicated by the bold arrows, into a *Gesamtkunstwerk* (Groys, 1992) and the early rebels are either imprisoned or exiled as the *Kulturbolsjeviks* of the 1920s (Golomstock, 1990). This implies the end of authorship. Art itself, i.e. the state or political system, is given full authority and critics, technicians and audiences are firmly turned into its puppets. This is what happened to the Brechts and Lukaczs – after a lucid creative period of reflection they took on the uniforms of censoring commissars of the *Gesamtkunstwerk*. The artists themselves stop signing their

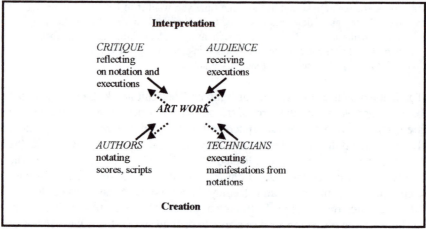

Figure 2.2 *Aesthetic disorganizing by totalitarian implosion or banalized explosion*

creations as free individuals. They turn into monks of holy state-orders manufacturing icons of its metaphysical power according to accurate standards. In a totalitarian context art leaves experimentation and ambiguity for symbolic perfection. Technicians supply the tools of symbolic domination and, finally, the audience loses its role as receiving spectators. Much like the audience of a participatory show, like the Bread and Puppet Theatre described by Paul Jeffcutt (1996), the public is dragged onto the stage. This is the final stage of a totalitarian tragedy. Art becomes a parade whose whole purpose is to propel an audience into the most total of all participations: war. The '*totale Mobilmachung*' of Ernst Jünger goes from sublime fiction to brutal fact by means of the Conradian Wagnerianism of an *Apocalypse Now*.

Banalization as an opposing threat to aesthetic organizing has more to do with corporate business culture than the organizational symbolism at work in a totalitarian *Gesamtkunstwerk*. The banalizing forces, shown by the dotted arrows in figure 2:2, work in opposite directions to the totalizing ones. Art in the centre fades out or even explodes leaving the agents playing interactive sociological games. Beuys wanted to enlarge the concept of art but in banalization it is blown so wide open that art itself no longer exists. 'Anything is art' means the death of art. What remains is culture of a kind that Adornists have been deploring for several decades. Artists from Schwitters, who named his version of Dada 'Merz' after Kom-merz, to Warhol, with his ironical celebrity-cult, have attacked this banalization. In its extreme, banalization leads to an empty nihilism. Original art sources are watered down like Grim Gebrüder monsters in sweet pastel Disney pyjamas. Everything becomes a matter of personal taste and we end up with a degenerative idea of art as a question of the utmost subjectivity. Leftist cultural criticism blames this all on the capitalist market but liberals like Georg Simmel or Max Weber, to whom society itself ultimately had to be understood as an art work, turned against such a de-aesthetization of culture.

I think Georg Simmel, who started by writing on Raphael and ended with Rembrandt, could more inspire further investigation into ways to manage aesthetic organizations than Max Weber, who mostly stuck to religious analogies. As I have tried to show, a new field of organizational as well as managerial aesthetics *must* go back to art as its empirical domain. In the last century social scientists learnt from literature as their main source for social analysis (Czarniawska-Joerges and Guillet de Monthoux, 1994). It is, therefore, no coincidence that the two art cases here mentioned are so closely connected to the business world. It might well be that tomorrow's economic organization will be managed in order to operate primarily in aesthetic fields. Bonk Business and the Christo Corporation are just two examples of such new emerging enterprises. Whilst bewildered economists and confused management scholars lacking aesthetic education and interest in art call them 'virtual enterprises', 'experience industries', 'immaterial firms' or 'imaginary organizations', art critics, inspired by Warhol's Factory, have already registered a much more appropriate name of 'business art business' (Parmesani, 1993). It thus seems that the managers of successful firms of the future will be less preoccupied with profits or employment than with aesthetics and art.

Notes

1 Paula Brinbaum, Dominique Bouchet, Idolina Conde, Ivar Björkman, Ken Friedman, Romain Laufer, Wolfgang Welsch, Karin Pott, Ekkehart Kappler, Bengt Kristensson-Uggla, Erik Kruse, Rafael Ramirez, Antonio Strati, Gunnar Olsson, Claus Otto Scharmer and Hans Weil have inspired this chapter with their comments and remarks.
2 Deutscher Bundestag Druck, 12 Wahlperiode, 211 Stizung, Bonn, Friday 25 February 1994.

References

Baumgarten, Alexander (1988) *Theoretische Ästhetik*. Hamburg: Felix Meiner Verlag.
Benjamin, Walter (1973) *Der Begriff der Kunstkritik in der deutschen Romantik*. Frankfurt am Main: Suhrkamp.
Chytry, Josef (1989) *The Aesthetic State*. Berkeley, CA: California University Press.
Czarniawska-Joerges, Barbara and Guillet de Monthoux, Pierre (eds) (1994) *Good Novels, Better Management*. London: Harwood Academic Press.
Danto, Arthur (1981) *The Transfiguration of the Commonplace*. Cambridge, MA: Harvard University Press.
de Duve, Thierry (1996) *Kant after Duchamp*. Cambridge, MA: MIT Press.
Gadamer, Hans-Georg (1994) *Truth and Method*. New York: Continuum.
Genette, Gérard (1994) *L'oeuvre de l'art*. Paris: Seuil.
Golomstock, Igor (1990) *Totalitarian Art*. London: Collins Harvill.
Goodman, Nelson (1969) *Languages of Art*. London: Oxford University Press.

Groys, Boris (1992) *Staline oeuvre d'art totale*. Nimes: Jacqueline Chambon.

Guillet de Monthoux, Pierre (1983) *Action and Existence*. Chichester: John Wiley.

Gullichsen, Alvar and Stanley, Richard (1993) *Bonk 100, a Finnish Success Story*. Helsinki: Otava Publishing Company.

Hegel, Georg F. (1986) *Werke in 20 Bänder. Band 1*. Frankfurt am Main: Suhrkamp.

Jeffcutt, Paul (1996) 'The organization of performance and the perfomance of organization', in Paul Jeffcutt, Robert Grafton Small and Stephen Linstead (eds), *Organization and Theatre*, Special Issue of *Studies in Cultures, Organizations and Societies*, 2 (1): 95-110.

Kant, Immanuel (1952) *The Critique of Judgement*. Oxford: Clarendon Press.

Parmesani, Loredana (ed.) (1993) *Business Art Business*. Milan: Flash Art Books.

Ramirez, Rafael (1991) *The Beauty of Social Organization*. Munich: Accedo.

Schiller, Friedrich (1982) *On the Aesthetic Education of Man*. Oxford: Clarendon Press.

Smith, Adam (1979) *The Theory of Moral Sentiments*. Oxford: Clarendon Press.

PART 2

AESTHETIC PROCESSES

3

Ashes and Madness: The Play of Negativity and the Poetics of Organization

Stephen Linstead

Whatever given meaning I start from, I exhaust it . . . or finally I fall into non-sense.
> . . . But how can we remain, dissolved, in non-sense? It cannot be done. Any non-sense must inevitably open up onto some kind of meaning . . . leaving an after-taste of ashes and madness.[1]

Philosophy ought really to be written only as a poetic composition.[2]

Introduction

This chapter explores what might be entailed in developing a poetics of organization. It begins by following a line of argument which suggests that all language carries with it a silent, implicative double, which supports it, carries it and allows it to do its work. The 'postmodern' theorizing of Lyotard and Derrida in particular has attempted to address this important area of the unsaid and the unsayable, the sublime, the différend, recognizing that the life without silence is unlivable. Beavis and Butt-head are used as an example of the power of the inarticulate, and also illustrate processes of mimesis (copying) and division which are common elements of human organizing. In organization theory, as David M. Levin argues, propositional language seeks to limit the effects of this 'negativity', and to construct truth only in positive terms, ingesting or expulsing inconsistent elements. Following Lévi-Strauss and Bauman, this is discussed in terms of anthropoemic (incorporating) and anthropophagic (opposing) societies, and an organizational example of 'proteophobia' – a fear of lack of conformity to standard. The argument develops drawing on the work of Heidegger, Gadamer, Levin, Iser and Caillois into considering an alternative form of truth (aletheia) to programmed orthodoxy (orthotes) which is based on chance, serendipity, flashes of insight, and play. The various processes involved in the play of negativity – agon, alea, mimesis and ilinx – are discussed, and the idea of an alternative to scientific, propositional precision, poetic precision, is put forward drawing on the work of J.P. Ward and Georges Bataille. Finally, the chapter considers some methodological issues for an ethnographically based poetics of organization.

Negativity, mimesis and the différend

Thought begins in astonishment. (Plato, Thaetatus, 155d, quoted in Rella, 1994: 83)

Huh huh huh huh huh huh huh. (Butt-head in Judge et al., 1993, no pagination)

Heh heh heh heh heh m heh heh. (Beavis, ibid.)

Beavis and Butt-head divide the world into that which sucks, and that which kicks ass or is cool. Following Lévi-Strauss (1966) we know that this kind of mental operation can be considered to be a fundamental property of mind, but also that this kind of division is both arbitrary and difficult to establish. Indeed, it is characteristic of Beavis and Butt-head's experience that their attempts to classify the object world – the world of others – and themselves invariably detumesce and fall flat. They are not actually members of Todd's gang 'They're our friends, even though they don't know it . . .' (Judge et al., 1993) – and are taken advantage of by the gang just as they in turn take advantage of the hapless Stewart Stevenson – 'They let us hang with them. Except like if we have to drive somewhere, we have to ride in the trunk. They told us it's the law' (Judge et al., 1993). They have no understanding of humour, perpetually telling non-jokes which reinscribe well-known stories with key ingredients missing, or inappropriate ones added. They are obsessed with bodies – their own, small animals, females – yet are hopeless in dealing with any process except destruction. They live in a world of fantasy and horror, a curiously mundane gothic. Yet they struggle on, despite the permeability of categories, as in this discussion of the relative pugilistic merits of Jon Bon Jovi and a blade of grass:

Bon Jovi would scream at the grass.

But that would make the grass mad.

Yeah so then it would like have to kick his ass.

Uh, but if like Bon Jovi and Richie Sambora jumped the grass while it was sleeping, they might have a chance.

The grass would still kick their asses.

Yeah. (Judge et al., 1993)

Beavis and Butt-head remain, as we can see from the above, uncomfortable with rationality and inarticulate in the face of experience. Their trademark sniggers say nothing, and yet say it all. Yet somewhere in there is an echo, a recognition of something that is at play in all communication – the silence, the unspeakable, the unarticulable. Negativity.

Yet Beavis and Butt-head as text do have an impact on reality.[3] Real people have their lives altered irreparably by these characters. I have sat open-mouthed through an episode of The Oprah Winfrey Show in which 'victims' and their parents or friends, people who attempted the pranks that Beavis and Butt-head get up to, confessed the damage they had caused. These included two seven-year-old children who burnt down their home after watching an episode of the MTV cartoon at their babysitter's house, and a 17-year-old who lay on the freeway and was crushed by a truck. These and similar events caused so much concern that the show was banned in some countries, while others were forced to show it only late at night, and a recent Beavis and Butt-head book contains the disclaimer:

> Beavis and Butt-head are not role models. They're not even human. They're cartoons. Some of the things they do would cause a real person to get hurt, expelled, arrested, possibly deported. To put it another way: Don't try this at home. (Judge et al., 1993)

What is so compelling about these abject characters? It may be that the part-fantasy, part-reality world that they inhabit is closer to the world we carry round in our heads, the images which guide our actions, than we care to admit. It may be that the everyday life we experience, as opposed to that which happens, is more like the half-cartoon world of Roger Rabbit, where toons (fantasies) are relegated to second-class status in the world of reason, but still constantly stand up and stake their claim to equity. But equally I think it is their struggle to divide up the world into neat categories, their recognition of the ambiguity and interpenetration of these categories, and their inarticulacy in the face not only of complexity, but even simplicity, that strikes a chord. In the pursuit of 'cool', they are pursuing their own sort of 'quality', their own quest for excellence. The process of copying, of mimesis, is a fundamental process in human learning and understanding, including the establishment of standards of behaviour and criteria for knowledge. It is a part of the developmental process through which we learn first how to survive, then discover who we are by imitating, then bricolating and innovating with the behaviour and symbols of others. It turns the principle of undifferentiation into an imperative for survival – and a phenomenally successful one – until entry into the symbolic world of the Other, and embarkation on the long path to adulthood, asserts differentiation, division and closure as the touchstones of social life. That the mimetic process is compulsive is one reason for its efficacy in the early stages of human development, in that we don't have to think about strategies until thinking skills are themselves well developed. But the persistence of mimesis in its compulsive qualities also has a downside, as can be illustrated by the lengths to which real people – real adults – have taken their imitation of the cartoon to the point of their own extinction. Just like Tom Peters and Bob Waterman (1982) and their many adherents in the organizational world, Beavis and Butt-head have their categories of excellent and not excellent and they look for the simple keys to success. But unlike the airport lounge organization theorists, they at least begin to acknowledge that their copies are merely simulacra (i.e. fantasized copies to which there is no properly corresponding original – see Baudrillard, 1983), and that the world is resistant to this kind of activity, frequently leaving us speech-less.

Robert M. Pirsig (1974) makes a similar point in *Zen and the Art of Motorcycle Maintenance*. He argues that views of the world can be divided into two categories, classic and romantic. The classic is concerned with form, with abstraction, with underlying principles and with reason. The romantic is associated with experience, surface form, feelings, immediate responses and the aesthetic. But this division cannot be sustained. As Pirsig demonstrates, the classic itself has its own aesthetic, which constitutes an emotional attachment to 'reason' and the form/appearance of rational processes/structures. Interestingly, Pirsig uses Plato's Socratic dialogues to demonstrate how (Plato's) Socrates cleverly exploits his power as interlocutor to force his dialectical opponents to construct their arguments in his terms, a point which Derrida and Barthes were also making at the same time but in a different language. This reinscribed aesthetic here is recognizable as being both ideological and political – a discursive relation of power/knowledge, to follow Foucault.

The aesthetic response is therefore a complex one. At its root it consists of a distancing between subject and object, an opening up to the object as object, the experience of the appearance of the object without regard to significance, meaning, interest or cause and effect. On the morning I first drafted this piece I was delayed in traffic on the road to Sydney. The day was perfect: sunny, warm but still morning fresh, the colours of sky and leaf and flower bright as only antipodean colours can be. The scent of burnt gum wafted across the air. Immersed in the delight of being, I found myself dawdling along in the inside lane being overtaken by everyone else, even missing lights at the change, heedless of the Randwick appointment I should have been rushing to keep. This unself-consciousness is characteristic of the aesthetic response (Linstead,

1994; Sandelands and Buckner, 1989: 120).[4] Indeed many works of art are designed to exploit this gulf, this différend between aesthetic experience and conventional significance (Lyotard, 1988). This response is pre-conscious; it is beyond words; it is under the boundary or limen of consciousness. This limen is the site of difference:

> the limen . . . the border understood not as an exclusion but as the potential for transit between subject and subject, between subjects and things. A subject, in a word, capable of relating to alterity without mythologizing it. (Rella, 1994: 6)

However, as Derrida observes, consciousness is not itself originary and unmediated but consists of a fitting in of experience to a pattern or trace of previous orderings of experiences, previous responses. Consciousness is thus second-hand, deflected, historical and interested in the object which is inserted into consciousness. Where preconscious responses create conflictual feelings with regard to conscious understanding, they become banished but nevertheless remain, an emotional counterpart to the logical or linguistic supplement whose absent presence is necessary for the positive functions of language to occur. Just as language does violence to other language when achieving its positive project, and yet cannot escape its own incompleteness, its remainder (Lecercle, 1993), it has an emotional doppelganger.

Whenever we use language in its conventional form we are inescapably trapped into perspectives, biases, distortions and representations without which there would be no knowable world, which for all intents and purposes are the world as we know it, but which are indeed not the world as it is. Language is thus false to its object (a betrayal by misrepresentation) and yet gives itself away when subjected to scrutiny (betrayal by confession). The first of these betrayals (that of différance) is not avoidable (although positive science might argue that it is) and is both inevitable and necessary as we have said earlier. The second betrayal, that addressed by deconstruction, is more difficult to unravel but this nevertheless becomes an obligation. It is not however, a nihilistic obligation but an affirmative one, and although there are several forms of linguistic betrayal which we might adopt, they are not all equally commensurable or substitutable. Postmodern ethics would argue that it is our responsibility to choose the better form of betrayal, of giving in to necessity, of bowing to the inevitable. Let us remind ourselves of Derrida's words:

> But if no-one can escape this necessity, and if no-one is therefore responsible for giving in to it, however little he may do so, this does not mean that all the ways of giving in to it are of equal pertinence. The quality and fecundity of a discourse are perhaps measured by the critical rigour with which this relation to . . . history . . . and to related concepts is thought. Here it is a question both of a critical relation to the language of the social sciences and a critical responsibility of the discourse itself. It is a question of explicitly and systematically posing the status of a discourse which borrows from a heritage the resources necessary for the de-construction of that heritage itself. (1978: 282)

Proteophobia

Let us now take another look at what that symbolic heritage might contain in the way of how extreme difference, or strangeness, is handled. Claude Lévi-Strauss (1955/1989) argues that primitive societies deal with strangeness in a way which differs from that of civilized societies. Difference means danger, therefore strangers are dangerous. Primitive 'anthropophagic' societies devour, ingest and consume strangers to absorb their special magic and power into themselves. Civilized 'anthropoemic' societies reject them, cast them out, drive them away, exclude them. As Bauman (1993: 165–7) argues, Lévi-Strauss, perhaps seduced by nostalgia and a fondness for the crispness of the binary divide (see also Derrida, 1978: 278–93), fails to fully acknowledge that these processes are inseparable. They are indispensable twin mechanisms of social spacing, in every society and at every level.

These social spacing strategies however, when metaphorically extended from societies which physically ingest the other, can be seen also to be psychological strategies. They are the means by which our sense of self is manufactured and positioned, subject and object differentiated, waste defined and rejected, order inserted into the system. Yet in so doing, they produce an in-between category, neither one nor the other, neither filth nor purity which is not rejected yet is not acceptable either. The abject irritates the system until it can be recategorized, the boundaries re-drawn, and the horrid abomination either reconstructed or rejected fully. Autopoetic or self-creating systems, as all human systems are, which are in the process of genesis or change are particularly vulnerable to anomalous phenomena. The anxious antipathy towards ambiguity which this produces Bauman calls proteophobia.

> The term refers to the apprehension aroused by the presence of multiform, allotropic phenomena which stubbornly defy clarity-addicted knowledge, elide assignment and sap the familiar classificatory grids. Proteophobia refers therefore to the dislike of situations in which one feels lost, confused, disempowered. Obviously, such situations are the productive waste of cognitive spacing: we do not know how to go on in certain circumstances because the rules of conduct which define for us the meaning of 'knowing how to go on' do not cover them. (Bauman, 1993: 164)

This struggle to know how to go on in the face of a situation which breaks new ground and may challenge old rules is primarily conducted through linguistic attempts to redefine the situation and arrest its movement. Yet attempts to create an unambiguous aesthetic of mastery in language inevitably fall prey to language's inescapable slipperiness. This can be illustrated by the look at a recently opened *Asia-Pacific Institute of Technology*. Physically the Institute is of a very striking design, and after its founding in the early 1990s quickly became one of the top ten most popular tourist sights in an area known as a tourist centre. Yet in policy and practice also the President often seemed to regard it as an aesthetic object for self-contemplation. The Institute had opened the doors of its spectacular new site almost three years before the words quoted below were written. As most staff contracts were therefore about to be renewed or otherwise, the President had decided to write to all staff on the subject of appointments and promotions, to explain the policies that were being operationalized. The following extracts are taken from his letter circulated to all academic staff:

a) We went after the best, in the belief that first rate people would bring first rate people. It worked . . . [the process] seems to be serving the Institute reasonably well.

b) The criteria and procedures for academic review have been determined by the Senate; the policy papers are available to all faculty. What I wish to write about is my understanding of the background and spirit behind these policies.

c) The quality of teaching is never easy to measure. Student evaluations and peer opinions are collected. We observe how our colleagues work with students who come to their offices for assistance. We see how they guide and inspire students in extra-curricular activities. Such data are at best semi-quantitative; some can be subjective.

d) The quality of research is easier to measure if only because certain time-honoured yardsticks have been established among the world's leading research Universities. . . . In each field and speciality, the leading departments/groups around the world have defined for us an 'absolute' standard . . . the question to ask when one of our own is under review is : 'How favourably does he/she measure against that standard?'

e) . . . academic judgement rests primarily with members of the faculty, who will act with professional competence, high expectations, fairness, and understanding.

f) Some candidates will be found to have delivered a good performance, but in one way or another fallen short of the Institute's very high expectations. If the indications are that the candidate is likely to be able to overcome his/her temporary difficulties, a new contract will be extended.

g) In some cases, serious doubts may arise as to whether the very high expectations of the Institute will ever be satisfied. Such candidates may well have fulfilled their responsibilities reasonably well, and would be able to meet normal standards. But in order for (the Institute) to stand among the world's top research universities, normal standards are not enough . . .

h) [On personal professorial chairs]: The test to pass becomes 'Would such a candidate be appointable to a professorship in a top-ranking University in his/her particular discipline and speciality?' Whether this person is the world's best candidate at the time is not at issue, but whether he/she qualifies . . .

i) It may be said that in an open competition one goes by relative standards, relative in the sense that the vacancy would be filled by the very best candidate

relative to all other competitors. Through internal promotion, however, absolute
standards are used, in that the standards are fixed by external bodies: leading
departments in the candidate's speciality. One can meet absolute standards
without being the very best available in the world. Thus, in the present context,
absolute standards are easier to meet than relative standards . . .

I have chosen this sample, which is indicative of the tone of the whole
paper (some 2,500-3000 words) as they seem to me to illustrate the President's
proteophobia. He does not know how to go on, he does not like not knowing
how to go on, and therefore he speaks most assuredly about how to go on. The
language and tone of the piece is propositional, concerned with standards and
criteria, and is apparently very confident in its assertion that the Institute is
mimetically recruiting 'the best' in all its fields of activity. Quote a) is typical
of the bullish rhetoric that the 'best' can be unequivocally determined and
successfully attracted, and also carries with it the assumption that a collection
of individual stars is necessarily a good team. This, in a Confucian culture
where the ability to fit into a social group is what determines the sense of self-
worth rather than individual accomplishment, stands out as anomalous (Bond,
1990; Westwood, 1992). Furthermore, it was the rumbling disquiet amongst a
significant minority of the staff that *guangxi* (connections), family and social
acceptability were of paramount importance in the reality of appointments in
the University which had prompted the President's letter – and of course the
letter implies at least some recognition of 'trouble' through its own necessity.
Key senior academics (including two Deans and one Pro-Vice-Chancellor) had
left because of a lack of real input into the policy process (often despite formal
inputs being made); there was extensive informal criticism of internal politics
(although it was regarded as career suicide to voice this formally and most staff
were also very guarded privately); there was a perceived bias towards a certain
ethnic group of appointees (who were not locals and could not speak the native
tongue) and to US-trained PhDs – an unusual irony in a country where
'localization' was the dominant postcolonial administrative initiative. In all of
the review process the candidate was not interviewed, and in any case, none of
the staff involved had any formal training in appraisal.

The President talks about 'the background and spirit' of the policies, quote
b), in a sense acknowledging their inevitable imperfection and the possibility
that interpretation is necessary to make the policies meaningful – in other
words, they do not speak for themselves. Within a paternalistic culture such as
the one in which the Institute was located, issues such as these would be
resolved by the wise intervention of the sagacious patriarch, as head of the
'family'. This is exactly what the President is doing by means of his letter –
speaking both to and for the criteria – yet ironically he seems compelled to
insist that the basic principles of natural science are guiding his words,
assuming in several places throughout the text that both 'absolute' and
'relative' criteria do in fact speak for themselves, through the actions of the
decision-makers.

In discussing the evaluation of teaching, quote c), however, he raises a controversial issue: 'we observe how our colleagues work with students who come to their offices for assistance.' This raises a very serious question: who are (or is?) the 'we' carrying out this surveillance? On what occasions and with what frequency? How can this 'we' possibly appraise what takes place behind the doors of someone else's office? How do they record and re-present their impressions? Does the candidate know that this is happening? And is this indicative of a process of informal appraisal that takes place constantly on other issues, not related to teaching? In this sense, are the department to become their own policemen? (Smith and Wilkinson, 1996). It would seem that for this process to work, all candidates would need to manage their relationships with their colleagues very consciously (see Sewell, 1998). In a system which it would appear relies to a considerable extent on tacit knowledge and implicit processes, the President nevertheless expresses a politic preference for quantitative criteria and apologizes for potentially 'subjective' views.

The President represents a system which is, first, new and, second, mandated by its government to be 'world-class'. The President himself was not appointed from a world-class university, albeit a good one, and quite how impressive was his track record as a scholar rather than as an administrator was the subject of some debate in his field. The Institute immediately therefore took the route of trying to establish its identity-criteria by mimesis – copying those criteria from other institutions which it felt were consistent with its vision, or fantasies, and it seemed uninterested in engaging in any sort of debate with established paradigms, current standards, or being path-breaking or original in any of its systems. As the outgoing Pro-Vice-Chancellor (Research) remarked privately: 'It's a three year-old institution trying hard to be three-hundred.' It appeared to be unable or unwilling to cope with ideas and approaches which were either emergent or critical as these might threaten to divert it from its mission – to be a bastion of normal science. This was even further interpreted to mean in the North American tradition – over 90 per cent of staff PhDs were from 'top' US universities.

With his comment on research, quote d), the President indicates his concern with absolute standards or Bauman's 'clarity-addicted knowledge' and again ironically reveals the paper to be an attempt to establish an illusion of clarity about the decisions which are made. The following comment, quote e), however, almost contradicts this avowed belief in allowing that the process relies on such intangibles as 'professional competence' (of academic staff – i.e. scholars – although they had no strictly professional training in recruitment or appraisal) 'high expectations, fairness and understanding'. There is no indication that this is any more than a belief, a good intention, a wish or at worst simply rhetoric, and there is no mechanism offered to check whether 'fairness and understanding' have been achieved. Again, the unhappy permeability of 'absolute' standards appears to be creeping back into the system. In a system that appears to be obsessed with monitoring all the activities within its compass, it seems ironic that the processes of evaluation themselves are not reflexively monitored.

The following two comments, quote f) and quote g), construct the commitment to 'very high expectations' and to normal standards as being inadequate. Yet it seems that how standards are established is entirely relative and not at all absolute – it is always comparative against other persons and performances even when outside comparisons are made. In any recruitment process there are few unassailable pre-given standards – the candidate for internal promotion is usually assessed hypothetically against someone the assessor knows, and sometimes for the internal consistency of their own work where the assessor is competent to judge. This explicitly occurred during the process of appointments in the Institute as reported by panel members, where panels repeatedly conjured up names that they considered 'acceptable' and invited comparison with candidates. Of course, in fields where multi-disciplinarity also entails incommensurable paradigmatic approaches, this assessment procedure can become highly problematic for an original, radical or path-breaking candidate in an emerging field (see Martin and Frost, 1996). In this institution, disciplines were 'normalized' and the irony of the President's statement about standards is that it appears to have been made in order to create a legitimating space in which cultural and paradigmatic criteria could continue to be implicitly applied without contestation. After the field had been delimited in such a restricted way, the espoused criteria of 'normal' and 'high' probably were capable of quantitative expression on a scale of normal – more normal. Through condensation, a diversity of issues are rendered expressible and capable of consideration only in terms of a single criterion – 'quality' – which successfully masks other forces at work.

Throughout the paper the President expresses a commitment to standards which his own writing reveals are permeable and highly suspect, and in fact are community-determined – a community in which considerable power is vested in the top of the hierarchy. They are also subject to doubt and controversy – for example, in the case of what would happen where the assessors do not agree. The President seems to imply that such disagreements do not occur, which is contrary to what experience would suggest, unless participants in the system actively seek to avoid disagreement, not voicing opinions until they know how the powerful think. This also confirms emphatically what our reading has been suggesting: that between his words, silenced but very active, something else – some significant interpretive activity – has to take place in order to suppress those unavoidable implications of the text that would interfere with the passage of these words into reality, for mimetic method to generate proteophobic community. As if to underscore the fragility of the edifice of the President's text, its dark side was illuminated when shortly after the issue of the letter, it became known that almost one-third of the existing staff were not to have their contracts renewed.

Negativity: the silent double

> The modern coinage negativity, or some equivalent means of eschewing indicative terminology, becomes inevitable when we consider the implications, omissions, or cancellations that are necessarily part of any writing or speaking. These lacunae indicate that practically all formulations (written or spoken) contain a tacit dimension, so that each manifest text has a kind of latent double. Thus, unlike negation, which must be distinguished from negativity, this inherent doubling in language defies verbalization. It forms the unwritten and unwritable – unsaid and unsayable – base of the utterance. But *it does not therefore negate the formulations of the text or saying*. (Budick and Iser, 1987: xii, emphasis added)

The President's text, like all texts, contains a mixture of the unsaid (unsaid either by implicit or explicit choice made on the basis of interest, which is the object of ideological critique; or by unconscious suppression, which is the object of critical analysis, and the first focus of deconstruction) and the unsayable (that which is beyond explicit expression, like something always just out of visual focus or at too low or high a frequency for audibility, yet which affects that which takes place in the expressible frame – the ultimate yet unfocusable focus of deconstruction). The fact that the President's text has a silent, implicative 'double' does not necessarily negate his words, it only works alongside them. There is also a sense in which this doubling cannot be deduced from the text, nor in fact from the outside world. It works more as a process that marks a threshold in ways of knowing, acting and speaking – negation would cross that threshold with a contrary position to the text, resurfacing the unsaid as opposition, whilst negativity can create spaces in which that crossing can occur, but is not necessitated. It could be considered to be the underside of the text.

There is a sense of negativity which relates not just to the silent spacing of the text, but to aesthetic and even ethnographic response. That is the ability or 'negative capability' to become a non-positive, non-indicative, non-assertive space, in the sense of the Platonic *khora*, where experience is allowed to come to bear (the function of the chorus in Greek theatre was to bear witness). This can be expressed in the sense of increased sensibility, or as a listening act rather than the controlling and constructing gaze implied by the emphasis on visual interpretation in reading experience.

> The hermeneutical experience also has its logical consequence: that of uninterrupted listening. A thing does not present itself to the hermeneutical experience without its own special effort, namely that of 'being negative towards itself'. (Gadamer, 1975: 422)

The assertive approach, whether to experience or text, is an attempt to determine significance in a way which resonates with Bauman's anthropophagic approach where difference is incorporated and reconstructed, and in effect denied. Difference, as in the President's letter, thus becomes expressible only in terms of a continuum of good or bad rather than as object and other, through a suppression of diversity. The other side of this assertiveness is where difference is not denied but repressed, banished. Difference is other and hence to be defended against. Gadamer argues for an approach to difference which is not assertive but passive, thought which with Vattimo's (1988) approval would be weak, which opens itself up to difference. For Heidegger, these two styles were approaches to truth, the one operating through correspondence or correctness to form and orthodoxy (orthotes); the other through openness, moments of insight, chance and serendipity, uncovering nuances, implications, hints and subtle nudges (aletheia). The two are connected, in science as well as art, but it is not sufficient to suggest that the aleatory is merely a preparatory moment for orthodoxy:

> We must acknowledge the fact that aletheia, unconcealment, in the sense of the opening of presence, was originally only expressed as orthotes, as the correctness of representation and statement. But then the assertion about the essential transformation of truth, that is, from unconcealment to correctness, is also untenable. (Heidegger, 1962: 187; see also 1971: 51–61)

Following from this, we can become alert to the situation that the silent double, the underside of the text, carries with it its own form of truth – aletheia, or the aleatory truth of negativity. We might then be concerned with distinguishing between those forms of language that seek to become open to incursions of negativity, and those which tend to suppress it. By analogy, as we move to consider the underside of organization, we would need to consider methodologies which similarly allow chance, surprise and flashes of insight their legitimate place. In taking this consideration further, let us look at the distinction between propositional and poetic discourse, and the workings of play in understanding.

Propositions and poetry

The receptive, passive approach to truth which I have outlined requires that truth be approached, not through interrogation, but through listening. Although he emphasizes the importance of 'saying' in order to explore and uncover, Heidegger also regards 'listening' as important to the development of this alternative, aleatory approach:

> The more poetic a poet is – the freer (that is, the more open and ready for the unforeseen) his saying – the greater is the purity with which he submits what he says to an ever more painstaking listening, and the further what he says is from the mere propositional statement that is dealt with solely in regard to its correctness and incorrectness. (Heidegger, 1962: 216)

Poeticizing, following Levin's reading of Heidegger, is this process of the pursuit of aletheia. It is therefore imperative that this process is not controlled and restricted by the rules of propositional discourse: 'when the truth that belongs to propositional discourse is allowed to regulate our poeticizing, it brings the play of sounds and meanings, the interplay of words and experiencing, to a stop' (Levin, 1988: 433). So the truth which this poetic approach pursues is carried in the sound, rhythm and patterning of the words, the images they carry with them, the tension at play between the words and experience, the multiple levels of meaning that surround them. It is a multiplex truth which cannot be reduced to its propositional content. Levin, following Gadamer (1975), attempts to more clearly draw this distinction between poetic discourse and propositional discourse:

> In propositional assertion words state: they propose meanings; they set them down and make them stand; they are positioned in a fixed way, corresponding to a correspondingly fixed state of affairs. In poetic discourse, words work in a different way, they play, they resonate freely, they breathe . . . in poetic discourse . . . words can defy logical connectivity to open up hermeneutical fields for the coming forth of new meanings. Poetizing discourse is therefore not deriviative from some paradigmatic propositional discourse. Rather it is the contrary which is true . . . Propositional discourse derives from an original poetizing: it is constituted by transformation from a discourse in which words are poetizing into a discourse in which words are assigned clear, fixed meanings. (Levin, 1988: 437)

Propositional discourse relies on establishing fixity of meaning, where poetizing discourse consists of flow, play, and connectivity. We might be reminded here of Kristeva's 'semiotic', the indeterminate flux that underlies the semantic connectivity of the 'symbolic'; or Barthes' comment that 'denotation is the last of connotation' – which is to say that fixed meaning is not the originary source of language, but its social achievement. Indeed, Ward (1979: 89, emphasis added) argues 'the language of poetry is almost definable as *that which cannot be used in ordinary discourse* or in the affirmation of social organizations'.[5]

Play in language: the split signifier

Nevertheless, even when it is at its most propositional, any text rests upon a series of gaps which open up – at the empirical level between the author and experience (the authorial eye), at the textual level between the author and their words (the authorial 'I'), between the words themselves and between the words used and those not used, between the text and the reader, and between the reader and the reader's experience (which relation a text may disrupt). These gaps, however, are not stable, and consequently are in play against each other, constantly shifting and moving, frequently at multiple levels, causing meaning to slide this way and that (Iser, 1987: 325–9). The distance between the propositional and the poetic is, consequently, frequently blurred and breached.

Iser's primary concern is to translate some anthropological concepts drawn from the work of Bateson (1981) and Caillois (1961), which relate to the ways in which animals and humans signal the gaps between 'reality' and present performance and thus create a 'play space', into the analysis of literary texts. Bateson, for example, noted that otters would playfully nip each other's ears. This nip, he noted, does not denote the bite for which it would normally stand (for example, as a warning or attack) but the bite *itself* is fictional – the otters 'are usually communicating about something which does not exist'. In other words, the 'fight' is not a fight, but a performance, and their actions are not representational, but performative play, governed not by rules of correspondance but by a play framework. Crucially, the signifier/signified distinction (which is maintained in conventional representation) is not simply dissolved into a world of free floating signifiers (as poststructuralist argumentation might have it, taken to its extreme) which might occur in dreaming or daydreaming, but the signifier is split. On the one hand, the split signifier exploits its previously code-governed determinacy within a framework of the 'as if': on the other it becomes free to release new meanings and implications, to overstep its limits (Iser, 1993: 249). It does not mean what it denotes, yet this in itself acts as a denotation, 'bringing into existence something that does not exist', allowing the conventionally unimaginable to be imagined (Iser, 1993: 248). A rather dramatic and elaborated human example of the workings of the split signifier would be consensual sado-masochism as discussed by James Miller in his biography of Michel Foucault. Here whips, chains and acts of physical violence are not simply cruelty and abuse, but a symbolic means to develop both the trusting relation on which the s-m play frame is based and the intensity of physical sensation – the 'limit-experience' – on which individual personal growth may be founded (Miller, 1993).

The split signifier then introduces a reflexive dimension into referentiality (i.e. I do not mean what I say) but also an improvisational one (i.e. I mean more than I say and say more than I mean). The play frame holds the split signifier – just – from running away into the untrammelled play of delirium (Lecercle, 1985). Yet as I have argued elsewhere on the relations between objectivity, reflexivity and fictionality, even ostensive reference is itself a language-game in which the degree of play is artificially limited, or suppressed, by convention, but from which play is not absent (Linstead, 1994). As Ward (1979: 9) argues, 'speech bleeds and is unbounded at its edges'. It is this space which deconstruction exploits, the rustle of negativity from which otherness can emerge.

Modes of playing: *agon, alea, mimesis* and *ilinx*

> . . . it is the game itself that plays, in that it draws the players into itself and thus itself becomes that actual subjectum of the playing . . . Someone who understands is always already drawn into an event through which meaning asserts itself. So it is well grounded for us to use the concept of play for the

hermeneutical phenomenon as for the experience of the beautiful. When we understand a text, what is meaningful in it charms us just as the beautiful charms us. It has asserted itself and charmed us before we can come to ourselves and be in a position to test the claim to meaning that it makes. (Gadamer, 1975: 446)

Just as propositional language may slide into the poetic when in play, even when fully improvisational meaning follows some rules of intelligibility which give relative stability, which may, as Gadamer argues, acquire an aesthetic significance of their own. They may even be persuasive because the form in which they are presented is familiar and attractive, regardless of their content. For example, some of the seductive power of Hitler's speeches can be felt if the emotive signifiers – such as Jew – are replaced by more innocuous ones. What we know was not a rational argument nevertheless in many passages successfully imitates such argument and appears reasonable when the signifiers that retrospectively alert us to its full significance are removed. These highly influential rules of intelligibility, Iser (1993: 258–9, 337n18) argues, are founded on various combinations of what Caillois (1961: 4, 44, 67) regarded as four fundamental anthropological dispositions. These dispositions set limits to the more generalized processes of play at work within texts, aiming towards 'results' as a temporary resolution of the deeper existential aporia to which they are responses. Consequently four major types of games can be distinguished.

In its pure form, *agon* is contest, but a contest in which the rules are set up so as to artificially create equality of chances which give a precise value to the winner's triumph (e.g. boxers are not allowed to use weapons or assistants, and are matched for weight, horses may be matched for age and handicapped by weights according to form). *Alea* is chance, and winners do not defeat adversaries, but fate. Dice games and many, but not all, card games are of this nature. *Mimicry* is illusion, role-playing, games in which the participants assume characters in an imaginary milieu, and persuade others to accept this for the period of the game. *Ilinx* is harder to define, but I would suggest that rather than Caillois' definition of it as 'the pursuit of vertigo', a whirling dizziness caused by the temporary destruction of the stability of perception, we might more usefully label it 'carnival' – in the original sense of a space in which the only rule is that all the rules are there to be broken. Abandon, orgy, raving, all would be part of ilinx, as would unremitting irony and absurdity.

- In agon, contest, the player desires to win by merit under conditions of regulation, by relying only on themselves (or the team) and their efforts.

- In alea, chance, the player desires to win by luck, by anxious submission to fate, relying on everything except themself and powers that are elusive.

- In mimicry, illusion, the player desires to be another personality and succeeds by creating an acceptable imaginary universe.

- In ilinx, carnival, the player desires ecstasy, unboundedness, and freedom from constraint, and does this by confounding bodily equilibrium, ordinary perception, and conscience.

We might further add that each of these prototypical dispositions pursues a characteristic form of 'truth': agon seeks 'objective' truth through the control of variability and the application of rules; alea seeks revelatory truth through serendipity; mimicry seeks understanding, the truth of the other through insight; ilinx seeks improvised truth through rejecting knowledge, counter-memory, breaking rules to allow for revelation. Each also implies particular perspectives on knowledge and power. Agonistic knowledge is based on individual skill and competence, is canonical but can be challenged in particular ways, and power is very much behavioural (to the victor, the spoils). Aleatory knowledge is serendipitous, and power is always outside the individual. Mimetic knowledge is dramatic knowledge, knowledge of the other (real or imagined), power being gained through an extension of the repertoire of the mimic and the ability to create verisimilitude – conditions for the consciousness of others. Knowledge from ilinx is revelatory, a result of going beyond the limits of the present: power may be both absolute and anarchic, supreme or subversive, depending on the dynamics of self-indulgence and self-abandonment followed. Each mode also has features which we might regard as positive or negative. Agon seeks to overcome difference and produces incremental development in particular ways, such that surprises are generally limited to single events and are within a range, and a clear sense of individual responsibility for performance. On the other hand, difference may be increased, specific variables may be manipulated, individual flair may be squeezed out and the victors may be able to manipulate the rules to achieve hegemony, and domination of others. Alea produces a joyful relation to the world when successful, but equally powerful feelings of disillusionment. Although it intensifies difference, whether successful or unsuccessful, victors and vanquished alike are powerless, and have no responsibility for their achievements. Mimicry encourages imagination and can increase emotional and cognitive range, leading to greater understanding of others, but it may lead to loss of self-identity, a loosening of a grip on reality, and the co-optation or colonization of others. Ilinx offers a powerful release, self-discovery, a redrawing of boundaries and a discovery of unimagined limits and inexpressible experience. On the other hand, it may result in anarchy, loss of self-identity, a breaking of limits that results in harm and disaster, and chaos. Even the reversals of carnival in misrule have to be time-bounded.

In texts, and I am arguing in human organization more generally, of which texts are a part and an exemplar, these prototypes combine, merge, and dominate each other in different ways. Iser (1993: 259-73) explores in some detail the ways in which the various games may combine, and particularly the effects of combination on the differences between results-oriented games (agon, alea) and process-oriented games (mimicry, ilinx). For our purposes here it is not necessary to present his arguments in detail, but we can return to our consideration of the President's letter to identify some of them in play. What dominant game was the President playing in writing what he did? I read it as primarily a combination of agon and mimicry. Agon because the theme of the letter is that some are better than others, and that there are rules for determining how the game should be played. Indeed, the degree to which the letter signals its own status relative to the game is unusual, yet it continues to attempt to suppress the split signifier – the outcomes of the game are meant to reflect a reality. The fact that the rules are not well understood or obvious, and that there is an unvoiced opposition to which the President's letter is both anticipation and reply, lends the subversive shadow of ilinx to the piece, but nevertheless it is about 'the best', the 'world-class' the winners and by implication, the losers (some of whom were, of course, among the addressees). Mimicry not solely because the University was trying to mimic the best in the world, or at least, elicit a model, or a simulacrum, from these Universities to which it could conform, but because the President was establishing a role for himself and the University, and was creating the parts for the supporting players in doing so. He had to be credible in his evocation of the partially imaginary universe he was creating, and credible in his portrayal of the part he was writing for himself in it, in order to persuade both the winners and the losers – and in this case it was mainly the losers he was worried about – to accept and take up the parts written for them. It is, however, most important for him to attempt to exclude wherever possible elements of alea (chance) and ilinx (anarchy) which would undermine his portrayal of a measurable world in which quality was unequivocal – yet he is unable to be absolute even in that, and does concede to some subjectivity. In his failure, however, he might remind us of Bateson's observation that life is 'a game whose purpose is to discover the rules, which rules are always changing, and always undiscoverable' (Bateson, 1981: 19).

Bringing poetry into play

Of course, despite our arguments that language is unstable, leaky and intertextual, it is also functional, though our view of functionality taken here recognizes the overlapping, blurring and multiplicity of functions. This perspective, however, is not inconsistent with the arguments of structural linguist Roman Jakobson, who argued that language had six functions which were not necessarily disaggregable. Language emphasizing the *emotive* function – e.g. 'Woe is me!' – would draw attention to the speaker's emotional state. The *conative* function addresses itself to the emotive response required from the listener, and 'buttonholes' them: 'Look here!', 'Pay attention!', 'Kiss me quick!' The *referential* orientates to the conveying of contextual information in an objective way: 'At the third stroke, it will be 4:29 precisely'. The *phatic* inclines towards establishing or maintaining contact: 'How are you?', 'Lovely weather we're having, isn't it?', or in a written text, such phrases as 'However . . . ', 'On the other hand' which lubricate communication. The *metalingual* orientates itself toward the code, often checking that the same one is in use by speaker and hearer, addresser and addressee – in the words of the Monty Python sketch 'Nudge, nudge, wink, wink, say no more, know what I mean?' The *poetic* or *aesthetic* function is orientated towards the message itself, its qualities treated for their own sake: 'it's not what you say, it's the way that you say it'. In the piece by the President which we discussed earlier, despite the emphasis on the referential, the President exploits both the emotive and conative, and much of his discourse is metalingual, being about the code itself although attempting to appear transparent. The poetic function is relevant too, since the form of the message, which was very well written,[6] is also an important part of what it conveys.

Yet Jakobson does not consider in this typology the aspect of the poetic function which, when it becomes the dominant purpose of the discourse, creates *poetry* – the fact that it is reflexive and focuses on language itself to the extent that it insulates itself from actual discourse, in the adoption of poetic diction, rhythm, etc. As Ward (1979: 91) observes 'in what one . . . has to call "poetry" it is the arrangement of the language itself which renders it distant from social interaction'. In doing so, it does more than merely attempt mellifluity, it seeks to extend language beyond itself, to say what language cannot say, to explore its limits in the face of experience. Paradoxically, whilst it entails a highly disciplined approach to the use of language in achieving a precision of effect in response to affect, it also entails a surrendering to wherever language might run on to, an improvised negativity which can create both exhilarating openings of appreciation and understanding as much as the banal cul-de-sacs of kitsch. Often the sole purpose of poetry is to challenge assumptions about meaning and disrupt convention, to disturb rather than comfort. Even when the experience it is trying to reflect is troubling, it does not stop at trying to convey the richness of that trouble, which is where most anthropological poetry seems trapped, but to trouble language itself.

Georges Bataille: the sacred hatred of poetry

Up to this point, we have identified poetry with play, with a movement which reveals the incomplete closures of propositional and representational language, and which is also a small part of the ways in which even these languages achieve their effects. We have also looked at the four major aspects of play, especially idealized in games, which occupy a space between the regulated language of propositions and the less restricted imagery of poetry. We have also considered how language which appears propositional may in fact depend on poetic or aesthetic features to carry its argument, rests upon inexpressible elements, and can embody the types of approach to play typical of gaming.

What I want to do now is briefly turn to poetry itself and consider what poetry sets itself to achieve in 'troubling' language.

Georges Bataille, who died in 1962, was not only sensitive to, but driven by, his realization that poetry must trouble language, indeed do violence to it. Bataille might be seen as one of the founding fathers of literary anthropology, as many of the ideas above appear, in one form or another, in his work. He was a maverick or *dilettante* intellectual who consistently crossed disciplinary boundaries, writing on anthropology, literature, economics, art, music and pornography and in the form of essays, poems and novels. His work influenced the 'postmodern' writers – Baudrillard in particular, as well as Lyotard, Derrida and Foucault – though not always directly and often through inversion. Bataille's readings of Hegel, Heidegger and Nietzsche are somewhat idiosyncratic; yet his development of Durkheim and Mauss had a significant impact on the development of the symbolic understanding of the sociology of consumption (Featherstone, 1991: 21–2).[7] These influences are often drawn from Bataille's radical critique of the economics of exchange which was based on his own construction of the idea of the 'sacred', the transformative power of transgression, and the importance of sacrifice, yet they fail to fully explore the significance of these concepts which are also abundant in Bataille's other writings, and with a somewhat different emphasis to that normally taken.

For Bataille, the question which troubled Foucault – 'what does it mean to be human?' – could only be answered through the collective – to be human is to be social, and independence is an illusion. Bataille's concerns were more focused on how we remain human, how we sustain our sense of humanity. What was essential for Bataille was to face up to the inevitabilities of one's social and existential reality – a problem not of being but of socialization, of becoming not through immanence but through communication. Yet what was critical for Bataille was the quality of this communication, and he distinguished between homogeneity and heterogeneity as the two main dimensions of social cohesion. All societies, he argued, display an impulse towards social homogeneity but this is usually resisted through the adoption, or the reality, of a heterogeneous structuring. However, where a society strives to bring all sides of its being into alignment, such as with modern capitalism, where an economics of utilitarianism is used to justify the reduction of social identity to that of social role, homogeneity dominates. As a result, true communication, which depends on communal effusion, becomes restricted, destroying creativity and collective effervesence and replacing them with calculation and purposiveness, work and the rule of law. In a heterogeneous society, structures and arrangements would be flexible enough to allow social roles to emerge from individual inclinations. Where a homogeneous society restricted itself to function, it concentrated its attention only on those things at its heart, ignoring or censuring those things at the margin. A heterogeneous society, however, had to take account of both core and margin.

Alongside this, Bataille adapts Durkheim's concept of the sacred and the profane. The sacred, for Bataille, was the unifying element of society, where people offer themselves up to the values of that society in *sacrifice*. The sacred is 'the forbidden element of society that exists at the margin where different realities meet' (Richardson, 1994: 34). The sacred is whatever is beyond the limits of the profane, which is glimpsed through the sacrificial act but not contained by it. A heterogeneous society, characterized by its responsiveness to different realities, gives attention to those intersections where evidence of other realities breaks through to, or wounds, the present reality. The sacred other is revealed in 'bodily exhalations (blood, sweat, tears, shit); extreme emotions (laughter, anger, drunkenness, ecstasy); socially useless activity (poetry, games, crime, eroticism) all of which take the form of a heterology that homogeneous society would like to expel' (Richardson, 1994: 36).

Poetry then, is a form of socially useless activity which may reveal the sacred. For Bataille, the essence of existence was paradoxical, stemming from the individual's awareness of their own incompleteness, signalled by the existence of and need to engage with, the other. Simultaneously striving to achieve and assert its own independence and singularity, the individual also desires to achieve continuity with that which is beyond it – which would of course destroy its uniqueness. We are therefore always driven towards what would destroy us, an urge toward the impossible, in a condition of anguish. Our essential motivation is to go beyond our limits, to court our own destruction, to attain the *impossible* state of overflowing, of repletion (Richardson, 1994: 38). In relation to language, then, the impossible was always incommunicable, always what was beyond expression, the inadequacy of communication which redoubled upon our sense of singularity, of isolation. In relation to knowledge, every knowledge brings with it its own form of ignorance because it moves away from non-knowledge, or un-knowing. The rational accumulation of knowledge is not only false, but arrogant. The task of poetry then was to break down the limits of language through revealing them, smashing through them for a moment only to reassert them (which was how Bataille saw the relation between transgression and taboo).

The experience of writing is an experience of loss – an intense awareness of the irreducible element of experience. The object of language, being unobtainable, functions as a remainder, a residue – that which language has to leave behind because it cannot encompass it. The aesthetic confronts these limits of being and finds itself poised on the edge of

> a booby trap opening up between our feet as we stand on it . . . A pit of instability and vertigo into which we are plunged, it is a tumultuous process which constantly leads to explosion. But since the ceaseless explosions constantly exhaust it, it can only continue on one condition: that among the beings which it engenders, those whose explosive force is exhausted should leave room for new beings, joining the game with new vigour. (Bataille, cited in Lala, 1995: 113)

Life then is a constant expenditure of self, a constant exhaustion of being, but an exuberant, excessive exhaustion. Poetry needs to *hate* – both in the sense of confronting those emotions and experiences which 'beautiful' or lyric poetry suppresses, such as horror, violence and death, and in the sense of subverting language itself – because otherwise it must remain trapped in the everyday, confined in the banal. The hatred of poetry then is fuelled by impossibility, which is both its means and its unattainable object, the non-sense which gives it a meaning beyond reason, knowledge or logic. In addressing and surrendering to the impossible, becoming lost in its madness, the poet ceases to be, dies momentarily and is reborn. It is this renewal which Bataille seeks, which is why his seeming obsession with death and dying is an affirmative one rather than a nihilistic one – and which resonates with the non-positive, non-restrictive or suppressive sense of negativity which I have presented earlier. It is the possibility of the occasional breaching of the limits of the everyday which leads Bataille in his attempts to find ways of remaining on the margin, in touch with the sacred, on the edge of madness, insight and rebirth through the *wounds* which are afforded by the poetic moment.

The poetic moment

Bataille employs poetry as one of a number of modes of expression, which he frequently mixes, as part of his project of coming to terms with negativity, and creates a rather special status for it, even when he is most frustrated by it. As Lala argues: 'Using new bases for aesthetics and for knowledge, Bataille's thought takes an experience of writing driven by the impossible and by the hatred of poetry, and develops the substance of an anthropology' (1995: 115). What I want to do now is to consider whether poetry, in addressing both the nature and limits of language and the inexpressibility of experience, which is clearly beyond the scope of normal interactional and purposive discourse, can have any place in the sociological or anthropological study of social and organised life, even if it has only a limited place in that life itself. Does poetry, for example, express anything important about that life? Does, or can it, express part of the researcher's experience of the research setting that other forms of account cannot capture? Is there such a thing as precision in poetry, and what is it? I will then consider the implications of this for method; the recent arguments for anthropological poetics or poetic anthropology, and their possible consequences for ethnographies of organizations.

Section VII of Alfred, Lord Tennyson's elegy, *In Memoriam*, is a passage where the poet, having alighted on the doorstep of his deceased friend's home, experiences a sudden realization that his friend is not going to answer the door, and will never again answer the door, and with this 'unlocking' comes simultaneous awareness of the merging of past and future in the present, of possession, mutability, and loss. Here it is:

> Dark house, by which once more I stand
> Here in the long unlovely street
> Doors, where my heart was used to beat

So quickly, waiting for a hand,

A hand that can be clasp'd no more –
Behold me, for I cannot sleep,
And like a guilty thing I creep
At earliest morning to the door.

He is not here; but far away
The noise of life begins again,
And ghastly thro' the drizzling rain
On the bald street breaks the blank day.

The economy of Tennyson's words here is directly proportional to the significance of the insight – the fact that it happened in a moment gives it the momentum to open up other evocations, to become a nodal point where several intertextual vectors, recollections and envisionings, intercross. Distinct from the aesthetic moment, which I have discussed elsewhere (Linstead, 1994) as the moment of dislocation from the social dimensions of experience, where the observer attends to the objective qualities and form of the object as object and forgets its significance, the poetic moment is a merging of object and significance in which the former opens up the latter.[8] It is this dual sense of 'moment' that defines it as specifically poetic – it is the poetic treatment of the moment that does not simply describe it accurately, but selects specific features of the experience to be treated in such a way as to be defining of it, to strip away noise and release the power of evocation. So although the poet is not seeking to be specific and precise in the same way that scientific language seeks accuracy and generalizability, poetry does nevertheless have qualities of specificity, precision, accuracy and general applicability, but these need to be thought of in terms of silence as much as of expression, of the merging of hermeneutic horizons as much as in the definition of one perspective. These may often rest on a technical approach to language that could be called 'scientific', as Gadamer (1975) argues, but science and scientific method are here defined as a special case of artistic method, a tool which helps to increase the power of art and accordingly of hermeneutic understanding within its material context, rather than the ultimate refinement of understanding for which the affective and subjective are a resource. As Bataille confessed, these modes of precision may be mixed: 'I am not a scientist, in the sense that what I am talking about is indirect experience, not objective material, but as soon as I talk objectively I do so with the inevitable rigour of the scientist' (1987: 33).

There are clear differences in what the accurate treatment of the poetic moment might accomplish and what systematic argument developing from measured observation and logical premises habitually achieves. Poetic insight is aleatory, often enigmatic, often fragmentary, and often atopic in that it involves a sense of dis-location from its setting – think of Eliot's passage in 'Little Gidding':

We shall not cease from exploration

And the end of all our exploring
Will be to arrive where we started
And know the place for the first time.

What we may encounter in the unnameable, then, may well be what we term beauty, but in the sense that Tennyson's sadness is beautiful, or Wilfred Owen's tragic poems of the western front have beautiful pity. As Dostoevsky remarked, "'beauty is a terrible and frightening thing, because it is indefinable and one cannot define it, because God has given us nothing but enigmas'" (in Rella, 1994: 121). Yet despite its enigmatic qualities, there is clear development in poetry, and in the works of a poet, which are not only visible in the epic or didactic works. We learn more about the human dimensions of war from the poetry of Wilfred Owen (who did so much with Tennyson's legacy) for example, than in even cumulated biographical accounts and letters of several thousand more words, yet the powerful humanity and spirituality of Owen's horrifically realistic work speaks of far more than the unpleasantnesses taking place in northern France at the beginning of the twentieth century (Stallworthy, 1990). What Owen does is gaze upon that which revolts and traumatizes him, and embraces it as part of human activity – albeit a horrifying part and one which would ultimately kill him – but he constantly strives to engage with it as it is, without glorification, mythologizing or denial. As such this gaze is inclusive in the way that Bataille's gaze would be, in a way which achieves insight through embracing horror and passing through it. It is an attitude to existence which has to be hungry for experience, resilient to its arduous demands, and bountifully energetic.

Can, and should, this kind of all-embracing, aleatory, fragmentary development be incorporated into the research process? Does the breaking down of disciplinary boundaries within the conceptual compass of the humanities and social sciences extend to a merging of methodologies across these fields into this 'gaze'? If it does, is there any kind of organizing or even emergent logic to this process, or is it really no more or less than 'anything goes'? What, if any, are our options?

Ethnography and poetry: towards an organizational poetics?

For Franco Rella, the arts and social sciences partake of the same substance, because social science is in essence a *tragic* endeavour, as it has to incorporate 'the tragic awareness that the truth can never be contained within a system or an idea, but the erratic movement of a search: in the *quete* of an enigma' (1994: 84). Performative approaches and propositional language and their associated methodologies merely court *hubris*, as they deny the impossibility of their project, as we noted above. Language may encircle its object, but tighten the cord and it slips the knot every time – all we have are angles, shots, cuts, near misses, facets, perspectives, shadows, errors, glowing embers, fragments, laughter. It is of course Georges Bataille, who, Rella argues, in writing which is both itself enigmatic and recognizes the enigmatic nature of everyday life, recognizes this and produces a body of work which is fragmented and yet linked – not logical, yet possessing of a different kind of logic, a logic of the fragment (Rella, 1994: 83). It is such a fragmentary logic which, I would argue, ought to be typical of postmodern approaches to social investigation, wary as they must be of metanarrative and author-ity, suspicious of representational strategies, reflexive about their own subjectivity and its complicity in their texts, and alert to the multiplicity of local knowledges (Gottschalk, 1998: 208). Yet across the social sciences, few attempts to radicalise the forms in which social investigation finds its expression have been attempted outside of social anthropology, and even there, this has not been unproblematic. Denzin (1997: 199–228) discusses ethnographic poetics as one of a number of 'narratives of the self' in which the ethnographer's gaze turns inward, including dramas, novels, autoethnography, autobiographies, memoirs, reflexive fiction, parallel texts, and what Marcus (1994) has called 'messy texts'. Denzin's review of the history of poetic writing in both social anthropology and sociology is instructive and his analysis of the common criticisms levelled at such writing (1997: 216, 253, 285) encompasses critique from both positivists and poststructuralists – including the charge of the lack of a public method by which to assess validity (Kunda, 1993) and that the proper business of ethnography is to describe a social world accurately and with validity (Van Maanen, 1995: 23) from two organizational ethnographers. Denzin usefully discusses different forms of reflexivity found in the new writing, and moves on to consider reading tactics active in the construction of such texts in what he calls the 'sixth moment' of ethnography – its contemporary phase in which ethnography is moving through self-deconstruction to re-engage with radical democratic practice (1997: 287).

Two aspects in particular of Denzin's discussion are relevant to our purposes here. One is that the messy texts which blur and sample genres are not attempts to capture experience more fully or comprehensively, as no text can do everything at once. What they do demonstrate is a 'writerly self' that 'spills over into the world being described . . . with a particular hubris that is neither insolent nor arrogant. The poetic self is simply willing to put itself on the line and to take risks'. The texts are multi-voiced not in the sense that they encompass many speakers using their own words (a common and literal narrowing of the interpretation of plurivocity) but because they shift perspective quickly and easily, which is what poetry allows them to do, seeing a situation simultaneously from different angles. This passionate engagement of the self with the world – without attempting to dominate it – is characteristic of poetic sensibility. Secondly, there is the dimension which we have seen in Tennyson, the ability of the poetic to glimpse the sublime, which Stanley Diamond avers is what interests him the most about poetry:

> the way in which the pain and the fatality of existence can be the context for the
> most marvellous symbolic constructions of the human spirit. The constructions,
> let us say language, explode the context in ways that are mysterious. The

symbol becomes substantial . . . The context from which it is hatched crumbles. Now that is the achievement. (Stanley Diamond, quoted in Rose, 1991: 227, cited in Denzin, 1997: 213)

Whether it ever rises to the heights which Diamond's work certainly does on occasion reach, where the poetic dimension of language has been most engaged in social science, whether in fiction or in ethnographic poetry or one of the more messy hybrid forms, it is possible to discern five broad categories of usage:

a) As an encapsulation of the aesthetic dimensions of the ethnographic situation – creating a richer account

When producing accounts of organizations, the reporting constraints and customary analytical paradigms frequently lead to the suppression of much of the phenomena experienced (e.g. the phenomenon of humour, which has still been addressed by only a handful of researchers). Organizational settings, themselves being pre-programmed even when contested, easily associate with other programmatic styles of interpretation and communication in ways which 'leave the culture and self sucked dry of meaning' (Prattis, 1985: 108). Poetic approaches restore some of the more aesthetic dimensions of the field experience missing from frameworks which privilege cognition and structural features – poetry being a different form of observation (Rose, 1983).

b) As a form of self-expression of the ethnographer's feelings and responses to the setting left out of the ethnographic account

An extension of the first, here the focus is less on rich description of the context and more on the accurate communication of the fieldworker's responses to that context – such as culture shock – which may be important devices in helping the fieldworker to cope (Prattis, 1985: 113; Flores, 1982: 17). What emerges here is of course what we always knew but discounted from relevance, that anthropology is always an emotional experience, that the ethnographer is an important part of the ethnography, and that feelings and responses change over time. These accounts tend to chart an evolving emotional landscape, a sort of subtext beneath the ethnography, and may well be the contents of personal field journals kept by the ethnographer alongside their fieldnotes, but never published. The focus here could be said to be the invigoration of the ethnographer's silenced voice.

c) As a form self-exploration in coming to terms with aspects of the self revealed in the encounter with the other

A rather deeper excursus than is perhaps implied in the previous type of account, where the ethnographer here is concerned not just with expressing and recording their feelings, but coming to terms with the psychodynamics of the encounter with the subjects in the field. The object here begins to extend beyond the field encounter towards a deeper level of encounter with 'truth' and 'selfhood', an encounter achieved more by listening as by speaking. Here the ethnographer does not just 'take something away' from the field experience – an aesthetic experience for example – which can be almost collected and contemplated away from the field, but is actually changed by the experience. The field becomes part of the ethnographer's self – self and other merge as the other speaks within the self. As Prattis paraphrases Marcoux (1977), 'strangeness is a major component of critical consciousness and it does not lie out there, in other cultures, but is incorporated within ourselves' (Prattis, 1985: 109).

d) As a 'voice' which echoes across several works, charting the development of the authorial 'self' over time

Not common, but such collections as Eisenberg (1998) which draw from poetic works evoked by field experience over time and across a number of different settings and moods, which may form a sort of narrative, which may be longitudinally developmental, or which may simply reveal the swirling of the self in a variety of experiential currents. What may be happening here is what Rose (1983) notes, in relation to the poetry of Stanley Diamond (1982), as 'poetic observation' – an exploration of where the self 'resides in relation to his experience and to the poem [form], where the subjects of the poem exist in relation to the poet and where the reader stands in relation to subjects author (observer) and text'.[9] Here these relations are explored as they shift over time, and as the writer speaks not just about the state of a particular field setting, or of the writer's state of mind, but to their own social/cultural setting, in the here and now of the reader. Here poetics may also begin to realize ways in which it is politicized.

e) As a code switching between levels of meaning

Fieldwork can be seen as a process of phenomenologically switching between one code of meaning and another code. In anthropology this has traditionally been constructed as the distinction between the 'emic' and the 'etic', the difference between being involved with and capturing the detail of the field setting in the terms of the 'other' and stepping back and out and theorizing the situation at a more generalizable level. But there are obvious contradictions between being both in and out of a situation in this way which theory suppresses. Furthermore, the 'other' operates on several heterogeneous layers of meaning through a multi-phased consciousness and collapsing these into just one, as any field researcher knows, is impossible – even when more than one perspective is taken something is necessarily left out, something else privileged. Heterogeneity is always untranslatable into codes other than itself. Ethnographers themselves also are hardly without implication in the process, their own overcodings of their experience leading them inevitably to prefer some kinds of data above others, some stories above others, some kinds of respondent above others, some kinds of theoretical analysis above others, some kinds of representational genre above others. Poetry, or poetic language, for Flores (1982) is a hermeneutic tool; an intermediary code; a means of switching between codes, particularly between the interiority of the personal and the exteriority of the analytic, the 'state of nature and the state of mind' (Ridington, cited in Prattis, 1985: 108); a means of bringing the sensitivity and awareness of the knower into the account; and a means of developing a methodology of understanding. This attempt to catch the ambiguities and contradictions of the field homologically can be taken further – not switching between codes but dissolving codes, merging them, making them complementary so that movement between them becomes seamless, a fragmented flow rather than a switching. Bataille's work as a whole illustrates this fluidity of sensibility – my own more modest attempt at something of this nature can be found in Linstead (1998).

Finally, if we consider the options left open to us in trying to work with the poetic dimensions of language in bringing our own experiences and those of organizational participants into a theorized relation, we would seem to have a continuum of options:

a) preserve the basis of qualitative social science but recognize the limitations of propositional language

Here the field would remain much as it is, although we would proceed with a greater vigilance against the tendencies of language to slip into positivism, import functionalist considerations by the back door, suppress disturbing alternatives and reify its own concepts.

b) as a) but include other forms of language in the presentation of data (e.g. widening the range of 'voices' incorporated to include non-verbal symbolic systems)

Here a wider range of voices of participants might be a starting point for inclusion, but non-linguistic artefacts as well as poetry, dance, music, art, would be studied for their social significance – i.e. what they convey about those who make and use them rather than simply for their aesthetic significance, which was also the focus of the anthropologists with whom Bataille was associated through the journal *Documents* (see also Flores, 1985).

c) as b) but include other forms of language in the analysis of data (e.g. telling scientific 'stories')

A more radical step, if we begin to include poetic language not as data to be subjected to rational and propositional language in analysis, but as part of the analysis itself. Here we begin to *think poetically* alongside more accustomed modes of analysis, perhaps in a literary anthropology.

d) reposition the 'scientific' element as one of a number of means to an end – that of understanding the other in context (e.g. organizational analysis as an art form – a Gadamerian hermeneutic position)

Inevitably, we will come to consider the relative importance and positioning of those elements of the social sciences, especially the study of organized life, which most preserve the 'scientific' element of analysis, respective to those which broaden the bandwidth of analytic sensibility.

e) as d) but recognizing that the end is unattainable, because of the unsayable (a broadly postmodern position)

In other words, by subordinating 'scientific analysis' to that of 'artistic' analysis, we are not completing or perfecting a more comprehensive mode of analysis, although it may be more inclusive of the variety of experience, because of the limitations of language and what it does not and cannot say. Here a deeper understanding of the nature of the *poetic* – in Bataille's sense what is beyond words – emerges.

f) use context, means and the encounter with the other as a springboard for attaining marginality – glimpsing non-sense, encountering the un-nameable (e.g. Bataille's literary anthropology)

Here the poetic impulse to engage with the unsayable takes us outside the bounds of poetic language, positioning us on the margins of the profane and the sacred, exposing us to risk and reward, enabling us to glimpse, however fleetingly, what may lie beyond analysis. A poetic rather than a literary anthropology, but bringing us closer to the sense of commitment and sacrifice, the *hatred* of limitation and empty decorousness, that is the poetic for Bataille.

g) proceed only *through poetic language and fragmentary logic, but in an inclusive way (an option which Bataille implied, but did not take)*

This is a further and even more erratic step into the unknown – to proceed only by the emerging logics of excess, of exuberance; to push language to its limits along with experience; to rule no experience out of our compass; to accept no limits to the economy of thought; to poeticize and theorize and dramatize and metaphorize as we analyze; to proceed through atopy, enigma, silence and laughter. Perhaps this could genuinely be called an anthropological poetics – a methodology of understanding (Linstead, 1993; Linstead et al., 1996; Prattis, 1985: 108). The ear of the poet and the eye of the ethnographer come together to create a gaze which, unlike the disciplining gaze of surveillance which as

Foucault notes works through the mechanics of propositional discourse, is a gaze of inclusiveness, not containment, which is shaped by the object of its vision rather than dominating it:

> Beauty is in the exuberance of this gaze, which *negates nothing and embraces everything in its trajectory*: it is the real overthrow of the decrees of an economy tied to the production of things, and to their simple, desperate and mortal consumption. The beauty that this gaze finds in the real, in things and in other gazes, can truly be the chance for the salvation that the world of ephemeral things awaits from us, we, as Rilke wrote, the most ephemeral. (Rella, 1994: 106, emphasis added)

From the economics of the transaction to an economics of energy; from the cold light/dark of rationality to the white heat of excess – poetics has its own precision, the precision of negativity and non-sense, which offers to open up the field of organization studies to the broader field of human understanding.

Notes

1 From Georges Bataille (1962) *L'impossible*. Paris: Editions de Minuit, p. 129, cited in Marie Christine Lala (1995) 'The hatred of poetry', trans. Peter Collier, in Carolyn Bailey Gill (ed.), *Georges Bataille: Writing the Sacred*, London: Routledge. p. 110. The translation here is significant – an alternative translation of the same extracts presents the ideas with far less impact or clarity:

   > If I start from any meaning, I exhaust it . . . or eventually I fall upon meaninglessness.
   >   . . . But how to stop there, dissolved, at meaninglessness? That can't be done. A piece of meaninglessness, and nothing more, opens onto some meaning or other . . . Leaving an aftertaste of ashes, of dementia. (Georges Bataille (1991) *The Impossible*, trans. Robert Hurley. San Francisco: City Lights. p. 109)

2 Ludwig Wittgenstein (1984) *Culture and Value*, ed. G.H von Wright, trans. Peter Winch, Chicago: Chicago University Press, p. 483, cited in Wolfgang Welsch (1997) *Undoing Aesthetics*, London: Sage, p. 59, n. 97.

3 Welsch (1997: 130–1) similarly notes that not only do texts impact on 'reality', understood as 'living conditions external to the work' – understood through *interventionary hermeneutics* – but they unavoidably draw on semantic features of that context to become meaningful in the first place – *contextual hermeneutics* – and in the process change these features through internally interacting interpretative elements in the work itself – *work hermeneutics*. The task of engaging with all of these aesthetic features is that of *interpretative hermeneutics*, here understood in a sense of interpenetration of work and context more in resonance with postmodernism, especially the mood of Derrida's well-known view that 'there is nothing outside the text'.

4 The reverse is also true. On a previous occasion I was so concerned with the significance of the appointment for which I was late that my awareness of the world outside my fantasm dissolved, including the speedometer reading of 180 kph and the police car waiting on the central reservation to enforce the legal limit of 120 kph. I was soon reconcretized by flashing blue lights and a fine of over A$600.

5 Prattis (1985: 110) agrees that 'poetic language is almost an "otherness" of language, distinct from everyday forms of communication'. Hartman (1981: xxi)

similarly asks 'Is not literary language the name we give to a diction whose frame of reference is such that the words stand out as words (even as sounds) rather than being, at once, assimilable meanings?'

6   The Institute was very sensitive to the linguistic quality and correctness of its public productions, and employed technical journalists to help all its staff with their output.

7   One problem with identifying Bataille's influence is that it is widespread but fragmentary, and is often not cited where it is most felt. George Ritzer (1998), for example, in his introduction to Baudrillard's *The Consumer Society* notes the influence of Durkheim but not that of Bataille, even when he identifies themes in this early book which Baudrillard was to develop in his later works such as *Symbolic Exchange and Death*, which were among Bataille's core themes. Ritzer is not entirely to blame of course, for Baudrillard (1998) does not mention Bataille directly once in the book, despite his obvious and considerable influence.

8   Rorty (1991: 88) notes the poetic moment as a more epochal mood that may occur simultaneously across many different areas of culture – 'the moment when things are not going well' – where the way in which things are represented becomes an issue, old words garner new senses, neologisms are coined, new sensibilities emerge.

9   Eisenberg (1998: 197) considers his poetry 'a map of my heart in the world. Each one encodes a feeling or insight that emerged in the middle of a thousand commitments, decisions, dilemmas, and things to do. In this sense there is no isomorphic relationship between a poem and a client, a person, or even an experience.'

References

Bataille, Georges (1987) *Eroticism*. San Francisco: City Lights.

Bataille, Georges (1991) *The Impossible*. San Francisco: City Lights.

Bateson, Gregory (1981) *Steps to an Ecology of Mind*. New York: Chandler.

Baudrillard, Jean (1983) *Simulations*. New York: Semiotext(e).

Baudrillard, Jean (1998) *The Consumer Society: Myths and Structures*. London: Sage.

Bauman, Zigmunt (1993) *Postmodern Ethics*. Oxford: Blackwell.

Bond, Michael Harris (1990) *The Psychology of the Chinese People*. Oxford: Oxford University Press.

Budick, Sanford and Iser, Wolfgang (eds) (1987) *Languages of the Unsayable: The Play of Negativity in Literature and Literary Theory*. Stanford, CA: Stanford University Press.

Caillois, Roger (1961) *Man, Play and Games*, trans. Meyer Barash. Glencoe, NY: Free Press.

Denzin, Norman (1997) *Interpretive Ethnography: Ethnographic Practice for the 21st Century*. Thousand Oaks, CA: Sage.

Derrida, Jacques (1978) *Writing and Difference*. London: Routledge and Kegan Paul.

Diamond, Stanley (1982) *Totems*. Barrytown, NY: Open Book/Station Hill.

Eisenberg, Eric (1998) 'From anxiety to possibility: poems 1987–1997', in Anna Banks and Stephen Banks (eds), *Fiction and Social Research: By Ice or Fire*. Walnut Creek, CA: Alta Mira. pp. 195–205.

Featherstone, Mike (1991) *Consumer Culture and Postmodernism*. London: Sage.

Flores, Toni (1982) 'Field poetry', *Anthropology and Humanism Quarterly*, 7 (1) March.

Flores, Toni (1985) 'The anthropology of aesthetics', *Dialectical Anthropology*, 10: 27–41.

Gadamer, Hans-Georg (1975) *Truth and Method*. London: Sheed and Ward.

Gill, Carolyn Bailey (ed.) (1995) *Georges Bataille: Writing the Sacred*. London: Routledge.

Gottschalk, Simon (1998) 'Postmodern sensibilities and ethnographic possibilities', in Anna Banks and Stephen Banks (eds), *Fiction and Social Research: By Ice or Fire*, Walnut Creek, CA: Alta Mira. pp. 205–33.

Hartman, Geoffrey (1981) *Saving the Text: Literature, Derrida, Philosophy*. Baltimore, OH: Johns Hopkins University Press.

Heidegger, Martin (1962) *Being and Time*. New York: Harper and Row.

Heidegger, Martin (1971) *Poetry, Language, Thought*, trans. Albert Hofstadter. New York: Harper and Row.

Iser, Wolfgang (1987) 'The play of the text', in Sanford Budick and Wolfgang Iser (eds), *Languages of the Unsayable: The Play of Negativity in Literature and Literary Theory*. Stanford, CA: Stanford University Press. pp. 325–39.

Iser, Wolfgang (1993) *The Fictive and the Imaginary: Charting Literary Anthropology*. Baltimore, OH: Johns Hopkins Press.

Judge, Mike, Marcil, Chris and Johnson, Sam (1993) *This Book Sucks . . .* New York: Pocket Books.

Kunda, Gideon (1993) 'Writing about reading' (review essay), *Reading Ethnographic Research* by Martyn Hammersley and *Reading Ethnography* by David Johnson, *Contemporary Sociology*, 22, 13–15.

Lala, Marie-Christine (1995) 'The hatred of poetry in Georges Bataille's writing and thought', in Carolyn Bailey Gill (ed.), *Georges Bataille: Writing the Sacred*. London: Routledge. pp. 105–16.

Lecercle, Jean-Jacques (1985) *Philosophy Through the Looking-Glass: Language, Nonsense, Desire*. London: Hutchinson.

Lecercle, Jean-Jacques (1993) *The Violence of Language*. London: Routledge.

Lévi-Strauss, Claude (1955/1989) *Tristes Tropiques*. London: Penguin.

Lévi-Strauss, Claude (1966) *The Savage Mind*. London: Penguin.

Levin, David Michael (1988) *The Opening of Vision: Nihilism and the Postmodern Situation*. London: Routledge.

Linstead, Stephen (1993) 'From postmodern anthropology to deconstructive ethnography', *Human Relations*, 46 (1): 97–120.

Linstead, Stephen (1994) 'Objectivity, reflexivity and fiction: humanity, inhumanity and the science of the social', *Human Relations*, 47 (11): 1321–46.

Linstead, Stephen (1998) 'The dishcloth of Minerva: absence, presence and metatheory in the everyday practice of research', in Anna Banks and Stephen Banks (eds), *Fiction and Social Research: By Ice or Fire*. Walnut Creek, CA: Alta Mira. pp. 235–53.

Linstead, Stephen, Grafton Small, Robert and Jeffcutt, Paul (eds) (1996) *Understanding Management*. London: Sage.

Lyotard, Jean-François (1988) *The Differend: Phrases in Dispute*. Minneapolis, MN: University of Minnesota Press.

Marcoux, M. (1977) 'The relationship between poetry, philosophy and the anthropological imagination', paper presented to the N.E.A.A., March.

Marcus, George (1994) 'What comes (just) after "post"? The case of ethnography', in Y. Lincoln and N. Denzin (eds), *The Handbook of Qualitative Research*. Thousand Oaks, CA: Sage. pp. 563–74.

Martin, Joanne and Frost, Peter (1996) 'The organizational culture war games: a struggle for intellectual dominance', in Stewart Clegg, Cynthia Hardy and Walter Nord (eds), *The Handbook of Organization Studies*. London: Sage. pp. 599–621.

Miller, James (1993) *The Passion of Michel Foucault*. New York: Simon and Schuster.

Peters, Thomas and Waterman, Robert (1982) *In Search of Excellence*. New York: Harper and Row.

Pirsig, Robert M. (1974) *Zen and the Art of Motorcycle Maintenance*. London: Corgi.

Prattis, J. Iain (1985) 'Anthropological poetics: reflections on a new perspective', *Dialectical Anthropology*, 10: 107–17.

Rella, Franco (1994) *The Myth of the Other: Lacan, Deleuze, Foucault, Bataille*. New York: Maisonneuve Press.

Richardson, Michael (1994) *Georges Bataille*. London: Routledge.

Ritzer, George (1998) 'Introduction' to Jean Baudrillard, *The Consumer Society: Myths and Structures*. London: Sage. pp. 1–24.

Rorty, Richard (1991) *Essays on Heidegger and Others: Philosophical Papers Vol. 2*. Cambridge: Cambridge University Press.

Rose, Dan (1983) 'In search of experience: the anthropological poetics of Stanley Diamond', *American Anthropologist*, 85 (2): 345–55, June.

Rose, Dan (1991) 'In search of experience: the anthropological poetics of Stanley Diamond', in I. Brady (ed.), *Anthropological Poetics*. Savage, MD: Rowan and Littlefield, 219–33.

Sandelands, Lloyd and Buckner, Georgina C. (1989) 'Of art and work: aesthetic experience and the psychology of work feelings', in Larry L. Cummings and Barry M. Staw (eds), *Research in Organizational Behaviour, Vol. 11*, Greenwich, CN: JAI Press. 105–31.

Sewell, Graham (1998) 'The discipline of teams: the control of team-based industrial work through electronic and peer surveillance', *Administrative Science Quarterly*, 43 (2): 397–429.

Smith, Steve and Wilkinson, Barry (1996) 'We are our own policemen!: organizing without conflict', in Stephen Linstead, Robert Grafton Small and Paul Jeffcutt (eds), *Understanding Management*. London: Sage. pp. 130–44.

Stallworthy, Jon (1990) *The Poems of Wilfred Owen*. London: Chatto and Windus.

Van Maanen, John (1995) 'An end to innocence', in John Van Maanen (ed.), *Representation in Ethnography*. Thousand Oaks, CA: Sage. pp. 1–35.

Vattimo, Gianni (1988) *The End of Modernity*. Oxford: Polity.

Ward, J.P. (1979) 'The poem's defiance of sociology', *Sociology*, 13 (1): 89–102.

Welsch, Wolfgang (1997) *Undoing Aesthetics*. London: Sage.

Westwood, Robert (1992) *Organizational Behaviour: A Southeast Asian Perspective*. Hong Kong: Longmans.

Wittgenstein, Ludwig (1984) *Culture and Value*, ed. G.H von Wright, trans. Peter Winch. Chicago: Chicago University Press

4

The Aesthetics of Reticence: Collections and Recollections

Heather Höpfl

Remembrances and resentments

In 1971, I returned from university to my home town in the north west of England. Runcorn, though those who know it now as a sprawling over-spill town for Liverpool will find it hard to believe this, was built on an old river crossing at the narrow point of the River Mersey where Ethelfleda had built a fort to protect the river from invasion by the Danes in the ninth century. Rum Cofa is mentioned in the Doomsday Book. In the eighteenth century it boasted a spa and prospered from the river traffic that passed up the Mersey. The Bridgwater Canal was built in 1761 and the old town of Runcorn lay between the river and the canal. The Runcorn of my childhood was a small place with a population of just over 20,000. On the High Street was a magnificent emporium. It smelt of coffee, exotic teas and smoked bacon. Church Street was a bustling main street with Marcel Modes for dresses for important occasions such as the Whit Walks, birthdays and Christmas. Robinson's Haberdashery store had aerial runways that criss-crossed the shop carrying cash and receipts between sales assistant and the cash office. The Co-op Cafe did tea and toasted tea-cakes and had waitresses in black and white uniforms and a starched white cap tied low across the forehead. Home and Colonial sold provisions from across the Empire and Handley and Beck (Chandlers) sold everything one could imagine in hardware from an enameled tundish to a garden gate. The fruiterers, florists and fishmongers sold their wares from marble slabs which opened on to the street and the Army and Navy Stores did a roaring trade in forces surplus clothing which factory workers wore as their own type of uniform. On Sunday I went to Sunday school and wore white ironed gloves. This was the world that I left in 1967 to go to Bristol and I saw little of Runcorn or its changes until 1971 when I came back with some time to spare.

Where I had attended primary school in the old Victorian building with the air-raid shelters standing in the yard; where I had learned something of the nastiness and viciousness of children and their intolerance of difference; where I discovered the insensitivities of teachers – I had once had to stand on the teacher's table while she raised my skirt to show the class that I was wearing an old dress which I had grown out of as a blouse under my skirt; and, where 'good discipline' was synonymous with a terrible repression, now stood a bus station – 'modern' in the most offensive style of sixties nastiness of glass and concrete: cheap and serviceable to match the impoverished lives of the local people. Not only had my school gone but also Bethesda Congregationalist Church. Bus shelters now stood where my friend, Ann Ramsden, attended three times on Sunday for morning service, Sunday school and evensong. The dusty old museum with its grand charm had also gone. Church Street was altered beyond recognition. It was wider and made up of two-storey, flat-roofed buildings selling electrical goods, car accessories and food. There were at least three new supermarkets in the new buildings. Overall, the impression was of the suburban ribbon development of a large city but this was a small town and its heart had been ripped out.

Without the physical edifice of the school it was difficult to confront my resentments about what went on there. It was impossible to stand in front of a busy and ugly bus station and to reflect on the tyrannical regime which had been inflicted on the hundreds of school-children who had previously gathered on that site for the purposes of their 'education'. A few years earlier I had visited Toul in north-east France. During my visit, I had been taken to see a wall in the old town where a number of local people had been shot by the invading Germans. The wall bore the scars of the bullets and it had been left as it was as a reminder of the loss and pain inflicted on the town. I do not know if the bullet holes are still there now, some thirty years later, or if those who died are still remembered. I suspect not – at least, in the case of the wall. The absence of the school, the red-brick repository of so many things that I needed to address, was a deprivation. And, somehow the intensity with which I might have squared my experiences against the building, to have stood face-to-face with it and, I might have hoped, to assign my experiences to its keeping, was left with me. The school had gone without trace and, contrary to the notion of cleansing or eradication, I found my emotions were now homeless. The space into which they could have been projected was now occupied and, moreover, occupied in such a way as to prevent any engagement with the history of the site. It seemed too soon. I was not prepared for the substitution. The change in the surface landscape reduced my history to experiences which no longer had a location in space and physical reality. As I looked at the buses coming and going, I turned to my friend from Bristol and said, 'I used to go to school here'. 'Here?' He looked at me questioningly. 'Well, all this wasn't here then.'

Death of a sales representative

The argument presented in this chapter is concerned with the occupation of a space and the usurpation of that space and its consequences. In practice, this is an everyday experience from the person who finds their neighbour's car parked in 'my space', to the person who finds themself supplanted in the affections of a partner by someone who, in effect, 'takes their place'. To take this argument further, however, I will resort to a rather ordinary example which came from the curious information given to me by the Microsoft grammar checker. Recently, I was preparing an article for publication and, as I tried to run the grammar checker, I was given the following correction by the machine's politically correct grammarian. 'Salesman', I was informed is a gender-specific term and I should consider 'salesperson', 'sales clerk' or 'sales representative'. Unfortunately, in this case, the salesperson in question was Arthur Miller's Willy Loman, the purveyor of the life-lie. Miller's *Death of a Salesman* would, if I adopted the term I was urged to favour, become 'Death of a Sales Representative'. Of course, I was not *obliged* to change anything but worse was to follow. 'King', I was told was also a gender-specific term that I might consider changing to 'monarch', 'ruler' or 'sovereign'. Well, I might, but this time the story I was relating in the text was drawn from Italo Calvino's fairy stories: a tale about a king who has lost a precious ring. The term 'king' is gender specific because the text calls for a gender specific term. The king is old and forgetful, whimsical. His character comes with the baggage of his role in the text. The fairy tale creates a vivid image of an old man with the mannerisms of an old man. He is a king with all the imagery that the term carries. Monarch is feeble by comparison. Later in the text I had improperly used the word 'man': 'a man comes to the castle'. The grammar checker invited me to consider changing this to refer to an 'individual', 'person', 'human being' or whatever. But, this is Italo Calvino's story and not mine and 'a man comes to the castle'. As I worked my way through the text, being encouraged to trade 'wife' for 'spouse' and being roundly upbraided for quoting the word 'whore' from Diderot – 'Sexist expression. Replace with *prostitute* if that is the intended meaning' – I began to experience considerable irritation with the persistent invitation to correct (Latin, from *cor* (as *com* before *r* – with) + *regere*, lead straight, direct). Every pronouncement of the grammar checker became a struggle over propriety and every 'Ignore' command I issued a defiance. I could only stand deficient in the light of the invitation to accept a more appropriate term or phrase. *I stood corrected.* Well, of course, this example might offend. It might well offend those who see the regulation of language as a necessary hygiene. It might equally offend those who see this example as a hyperbolic overreaction to a harmless piece of software which I am not obliged to use anyway.

My purpose in this example is to draw attention to the status of whatever might be construed as 'the original' and to examine the regulatory function of what is posited or imposed. In order to do this, I need to refer again to the notion of cancellation and crossing out. The original is cancelled and something '*other*' is offered. However, the *other* seeks to perform a curious arrogation. It is offered as the 'correct', the 'proper', and stands in the place of the original. However, the cancellation of the original is not without cost. The original is *de facto* apposite as the choice of the author. This is lost in the impoverished substitution. 'Death of a Sales Representative' is not the same as *Death of a Salesman*. It is not nearly so poetic but, more importantly, it is not what Miller intended. Calvino speaks of a 'king' because he wants his readers to imagine a 'king' not a monarch. His king is not a sexless monarch but an old man. The power of the assertion about Diderot's 'whore' is diluted by the substitution of the word 'prostitute'. Moreover, the substitution cannot be effected without making a travesty of the original translation which dates back to the eighteenth century. Of course, this is not quite true. It *can* be done and a modern translator might chose to regulate Diderot's language to avoid 'sexist expressions' but this requires an arrogant disregard for the original. Consequently, it is necessary to focus on such presumption and to look for its source in the *mode of production*.

Organized consumption and the construction of meaning

In recent years, considerable emphasis has been given to the place of consumption and, in particular, the role of signification in the construction of meaning. Baudrillard (1975, 1993), for example, argues that the way in which things are signified is far more important for the construction of meaning than *mode of production*. What is communicated by the product or products is more important for the construction of meaning than the way in which they were produced. It is the product and its signification which becomes the primary mediator of meaning under corporate capitalism.

This chapter seeks to explore the nature of '*the thing produced*' through an examination of loss and melancholy, production aesthetics and the construction and theoretical significance of the allegory. In particular, the production aesthetics claimed for the work of the photographer Sophie Calle are used to illustrate some of the key themes addressed in this chapter. Consequently, the primary concern of the chapter is with cancellation and the appropriation of a place, with the effects of such appropriation and, ultimately, with the loss of collectivity. The first example drawn from my primary school experiences serves to illustrate the effects of the dislocation of experience from place. The second illustration, though more banal, serves to demonstrate the ordering of a space, to examine the power to define. These examples provide two dimensions to be explored specifically through the writings of Walter Benjamin (1977) on allegory and Sophie Calle's photographic exhibitions which have been critically acclaimed for their liberating heterogeneity. The extent to which these claims are reasonable is subjected to scrutiny. Then, these two related concepts are drawn together through the related themes of melancholy and appropriation in order to examine the way in which the production aesthetics of organizations are disempowering. Against the discursive celebration of difference, the paper proposes an *aesthetic of reticence*.

The aesthetics of production

The mode of production of '*the work of art*' is clearly important: in intent, in the product itself and in its meaning. Artists of the various media have been concerned to address these issues in relation to their own work – the functions of art, the role of the museum, the nature of representation and so forth. Indeed, more than this, Crimp (1982), in his piece 'Appropriating appropriation', reproaches himself over the production of, in this case, *postmodern* art in order to address the relationship between appropriation and aesthetics (see also Crimp, 1980a, 1980b). Despite parallels which might be drawn with the aestheticization of organizations, these issues have rarely been aired in the context of organizational theorizing *per se*. Yet, following Baudrillard (1993) and Featherstone (1991), there are important contributions to be made to an understanding of the role of aesthetics in organizations and, indeed, in the aestheticization of everyday life.

The most obvious reason for choosing to look at the production of the work of art is to do with the types of explanations which are attached to its intentions and its interpretations. A more significant issue for this argument is concerned with the cancellation of the space: the substitution of one set of intentions for another. The functionalist architectural nightmare of the bus station cancelled what had occupied the site before. For me, it cancelled the memories, few joys, many anxieties and the varied experiences which attached to the site. In the example of the grammar checker, this issue of cancellation is taken further in that the status of the original in relation to the status of the proposed substitution is brought into question. Here the question is to do with regulation through the power to define. In the first instance, there is a loss which through being detached from a particular location also becomes detached from a location in time. There is a loss of place and a loss of history: a spatio-temporal dislocation. In the second illustration, the issue is to do with the *power to define* what is appropriate to a site and hinges on a hierarchical arrangement of such power. I am subjected to what amounts to a *moral imperative* to accept the authoritative alternatives suggested by the apparently neutral arbiter, the machine.

Melancholia and arrogation

There is a sense in which my reflections on my inability to consign my assorted memories of my primary school days might be regarded as melancholic. I am saying that the loss of the physical building in some sense deprived me of a location for feelings which, thus deprived of cathexis, became nebulous and undischarged. This distortion is a characteristic of melancholia and one which serves to illustrate a number of points about organizations, not least the distortions which occur in relation to discontinuities, shifting locations, substitutes and, most importantly, the power to define the function and meaning of a site.

Freud theorized melancholia as the reaction to the loss of a loved object, where the lost object is withdrawn from consciousness, and as a state which necessitates internal work which produces inhibition. 'In mourning it is the world which has become poor and empty; in melancholia it is the ego itself' (Freud, 1984: 254). In melancholia, the ego is presented as worthless, morally inferior, subject to self-reproach. There is no interest in living, in eating or sleeping. Freud observes that the many self-accusations that melancholics typically call upon themselves, appear rarely to describe the patient but, more obviously, someone else whom the patient loves, has loved or should love. The reproaches which attach to the object have been shifted onto the patient's own ego or, as Freud elegantly puts it, 'the shadow of the object fell upon the ego' (Freud, 1984: 258) and the object loss was transformed or *introjected* into an ego loss. It is precisely this form of reasoning which individuals who have been made redundant appear to rehearse to themselves. Whereas on one level they may know themselves to be the victims of economic forces, management stratagems, misinformation or lies, the experience of redundancy is commonly felt extremely personally. The reproaches which might more properly be addressed to the organization find expression in the personal experience of ego loss. There is evidence of a lack of self-worth. What is properly the failing of the firm is understood as a personal failing although this may be apparent only in destructive behaviour rather than in the content of conversation.

Moreover, Freud argues that where the love of the object is expressed as a narcissistic identification (as, to continue the example, might be the case with the loss of a job), the ego seeks to incorporate the object into itself. Yet at the same time there is ambivalence and conflict about this process of incorporation. The disliked, resented, dispiriting, degrading aspects of a job, for example, might be conciliated in order to allow the individual to remember and embrace the memory of the lost job with affection and fondness. The significance of this is and the parallels which should be looked for in organizational life are as follows. *First*, that melancholy is related to loss, often to a perceived deficiency or failure in the Other which results, reflexively, in self-reproach so that the melancholic individual may perceive themselves to be the occasion of such failure. *Second*, that melancholy is, in its course, *self-destructive*.

Allegory is melancholic

We can develop this argument through an analysis of Benjamin's (1977) conception of allegory and, in particular, of the conception of allegory as melancholic. The concept of allegory is important to the extent that, by its focus on incoherent fragmentation, it draws attention to a particular problem of production aesthetics and, as Featherstone (1991: 23) has argued, aesthetic consumption. Here the intention is to focus on the *production* of allegory and, by implication, to give emphasis to production aesthetics. Benjamin's development of the concept of allegory is explored in his study of Baroque drama (Benjamin, 1977). Allegory, for these purposes is understood to be an extended metaphor, the description of one thing under the image of another, a description which is designed to convey a different meaning from that which is being explicitly expressed. These definitional characterizations of allegory have important implications for the construction of 'the work of art' and for organizational aesthetics. In allegory, the allegorist takes an 'element out of the totality of the life context, isolating it, depriving it of its function' (Bürger, 1984: 69). The allegorist joins the isolated reality fragments and thereby creates meaning. The constructed meaning is thus 'posited meaning' (Bürger, 1984: 69) since 'it does not derive from the original context of the fragments' (Bürger, 1984: 69).

> If the object becomes allegorical *under the gaze of melancholy* [italics added], if melancholy causes life to flow out of it and it remains behind dead but eternally secure, then it is exposed to the allegorists, it is unconditionally in his [sic] power. That is now quite incapable of emanating any meaning or significance of its own; such significance as it has, it acquires from the allegorist. (Benjamin, 1977: 183–4)

The producer and the thing produced are deficient, exhibit loss, are melancholic. If one of the functions of organizations is to create allegories in order to give coherence to their purposes and rationalizations, so the particular conjunction of fragments are inherently melancholic. The only meanings which such fragments retain are those which are posited by the organization itself: of course, usually by management in the production of such allegories. What the organization defines as 'within', whether it be the construction of its own history, the management of its past, the attributes of members which are desired or such like, is by capture and appropriation within this scheme of reasoning, rendered melancholic since such a construction is founded on a loss, is mortified by capture and is subject to the construction of the allegorist. Since the allegorists themselves are 'within' they too are mortified by the construction. Such is the role of melancholy in the production aesthetics of allegory. Allegory figures significantly in the aesthetics of organizing. The point is that, while it is the case that allegory is open to multiple interpretations, it is the authorship of the allegory which gives meaning to the particular assemblage of fragments. The ability to find other experiences outside of the organization is limited by the power of the allegorist to define the meaning of the fragments.

Saprophytic consumption

The exhibition of loss and the saprophytic consumption of the allegorist deserves further attention. A saprophytic organism feeds on dead matter. In the mortification of the fragments from which the allegory of organizational life is constructed or, put another way, in the way in which mere attributes of the individual come to be valued by the organization, the fragments/attributes are derived of their purpose and are mortified. Hence, the term saprophytic consumption is used to apply to the continued appropriation of the mortified fragments. Like arms or legs disconnected from the body and unable to function apart from it, the appropriated attributes of individuals in work organizations function like so many amputations. Here the link between the production of 'the work of art' and its appropriative process should become more apparent. Owens (1980) draws on Benjamin's conception of allegory to make the persuasive assertion that postmodern art thrives on 'appropriation, site specificity, impermanence, accumulation, discursivity, hybridization' (Owens, 1980: 75, quoted in Bertens, 1995: 90). So too, then, can the production of the aesthetics of organizing be argued to bear precisely these characteristics as means by which the appropriation of attributes can be made to seem orderly and rational and to give apparent coherence via the positing of meaning and the regulation of the fragments.

How this relates to the aesthetics of organizations is most clearly illustrated through the work of the French-born artist/photographer Sophie Calle. This is by no means to single out Calle for particular criticism nor even to attempt to do justice to her artistic intentions. The production of her work is used here as a device to manipulate the theoretical framework in which her work, by virtue of its particular mode of production, is located. Indeed, precisely the same standpoint could be used from which to criticize this chapter itself since, in many respects, it conforms to the same aesthetic impulse both in its mode of production and in its appropriations. Calle's work appears to offer an inversion of the dominant mode for the apprehension of art. However, it might also be seen as a means by which the status quo emphatically reinforces itself and, significantly, it might be seen as an appropriation. Here an attempt is made to make transparent the nature of the appropriation and in reversal to appropriate the work of the artist in the service of this contrary line of argument. The production of this particular style of work invites this response and, if the work itself is in turn considered as a site of consumption, it poses the question of who is in control of the production aesthetics.

Re-membrance

Phelan (1993: 146) relates the story of Calle's involvement in a project where she was photographing the galleries of the Isabella Stewart Gardner Museum in Boston, USA. Phelan describes how, in 1990, several valuable paintings were stolen from the gallery and Calle began to interview visitors and members of the public asking them to describe the stolen paintings. The interviews were then transcribed and the transcriptions placed next to her photographs of the gallery. The production imperative which guided this course of action was the idea that the descriptions and memories of the missing work, in some sense, gave the paintings a continued 'presence' and this, according to Phelan, 'gestures toward a notion of the interactive exchange between the art object and the viewer' (1993: 146). The paintings were re-membered in the photographs and the text, preserved in captured memories and re-placed in the gallery in order to give them some presence in their physical absence. Phelan sees this as liberating and a challenge to the rhetoric of the objectives of museums and galleries where works of art appear to be 'under house arrest' (1993: 146) and she goes on to argue that the memories and descriptions become performative expression within the representational context of the museum. The descriptions, Phelan argues, become the supplement of the stolen work and, therefore, implicitly, in the run of her argument, restore the polysemic voices of the representations.

The melancholic production aesthetic

On the other hand, it might be said that the descriptions and memories become the re-presentations of the loss and, therefore, in their own aesthetic tensions must carry the melancholy of their function. That is to say, not to become or acquire status in their own right but only ever to stand in relation to the loss: to be defined in relation to the absence which they now come to represent. This is extremely problematic. Phelan argues that the fact the descriptions varied widely supports the view that the interaction between the art object and the spectator is performative and, therefore, resists the claims to validity and accuracy which she rightly attributes to the discourse of reproduction. This argument has some appeal in terms of its claim to a liberating heterogeneity. It appears to challenge the hegemony of art experts to define and categorize works of art and to select, interpret and present art for consumption and to make the production of the work of art a participative process. In this process, Phelan argues, 'the disappearance of the object is fundamental to performance; it rehearses and repeats the disappearance of the subject who longs always to be remembered' (1993: 147). This line of argument suggests that to be kept out of the picture is inherently melancholic. However, in Calle's production aesthetic, to be restored to the picture is always and only defined in terms of loss and, moreover and significantly, it is not the loss which originally occasioned the melancholy but a more superficial absence which recalls rather than recovers the original loss and which tacitly bears the melancholy of this impoverished substitution. It is necessary to be clear here that the impoverishment of the substitution is not in terms of the relative worth of the work of art and its recollection in memory and description but rather in the relationship of one to the other. That is to say, the production of the latter is an act of recovery. The description stands in relation to the original work and in all its creative richness cannot logically take precedence over the original and, therefore, is defined in terms of its relationship and captured by that definition.

It is more securely located in its subordination and implicit veneration of the lost object by the attempt to work within the definition of the original. The apparent liberation of heterogeneity and participation is a delusion and, worse, is an appropriation which invites the abused to parade the scars of their appropriation, indeed, their very mortification for consumption. Hence, the producers are both consumed in the process of consumption and consumed again as dead matter in the allegorical construction of their labours.

The mortification of recollections

The fact that the framing of the lost object by text is characterized by heterogeneity is itself paradoxical. That is to say, when the original is lost and replaced by individual pieces which in themselves are original, if only as recollection, but the work is then appropriated by text, that this is done in the name of liberation, creativity and the celebration of heterogeneity. The opposite is in fact true. The very diversity which promises participation is, in fact, the cause of paralysis. The fragments are rendered powerless by the claims of the authorial voice and neutralized under the promise of inversion. These fragments can not invoke the power of their collectivity. The gathering together of fragments is a mode of production which deprives the fragments of meaning while claiming the opposite and, in fact, posits its own. In doing so it usurps the power of the collectivity and substitutes fragmented recollections. The very possibility of inversion is captured. There is no sting (Canetti, 1987; Cooper, 1983, 1990; Linstead and Chan, 1994). The reversal cannot be performed. The fragments cannot rid themselves of the asymmetry (Linstead and Chan, 1994: 11) of the mode of their production and their mortification into a captured form. In this sense, death, indeed, has no sting. The supplement, conceived of in this way, does not achieve the over-turning of the privileged position of the original work of art, as Phelan (1993) has argued, but remains now more firmly secured into a position of subordination. Moreover, it is now regulated by absence as opposed to presence: the absent 'original' as form, the absent 'author' as artist. There is no explicit commonality in interpretations, indeed, the nature of the form precludes or disdains collective interpretation; there is no commentary on the process of production since this is irrelevant to the production of the work; difference is exalted and the power of difference to subvert is paradoxically eradicated by dispersion.

The affirmation of mere reproduction

In the romantic conception of the collaborative production of 'the work of art' what appears to be a celebration of difference is, in fact, an affirmation of reproduction. Of course, the apparently liberating heterogeneity of the descriptions appears to repudiate the notion of a 'valid' reception of the original work and, in the reconstruction and re-presentation of both text and photographs, of the need for any notion of 'accuracy' in reconstruction. There is only the definitional validity which arises from the relativity of the standpoint of each contributor. Consequently, there appears to be a completely different aesthetic impetus in Calle's work to that of re-production of 'the work of art' and reproduction in general. Reproduction, in the conventional sense of the term, requires accuracy, precision and skill in order to replace loss or absence with sameness and, in this sense, the reproducible object allows for creativity only in relation to the ingenuity which might be brought to bear on the process of reproduction. Thus, variation and imagination are free to work in the process of reproduction but only to the extent that they ensure the perfection of the reproduction as copy. The aesthetic is always captured within the form. In other words, creativity is always subordinated to the process of production. On the basis of this, it might be argued that the contributors to Calle's exhibition are induced to celebrate their varied recollections and memories in the construction of an elaborate simulacrum of the lost object. While superficially they are invited to contribute to difference, they are in fact invited to reproduce the work of art within the framing of the form. In other words, they are invited to endorse the reproduction of the signification and, more literally, their contributions are to be organized to fit into the framing of the 'original', are to be squeezed into a defined (and hierophantic) space.

Sentimentality and the kitschification of difference

The power of the reproduction is now more insistently exercised by an absence, (the absent original, the absent author) and so comes to exercise its hold over the contributions as differences. These, in absentia, perform the culminating act of the reproduction by the regulation of difference. The recollections of memories of absence provided by the contributors are characterized by the heterogeneity of the texts. These may vary considerably in their attempts to recall the lost object, may be elegant or clumsy, may be detailed or impressionistic, may seek accuracy or favour figurative interpretations. The act of recollection or *anamnesis* here is an act of affirmation which can only be performed from a position of implicit subservience. Even a critical or dismissive text can only be constructed by first acknowledging the position of the lost object. Calle, it seems, works out of melancholy and not mourning (Freud, 1984: 258). For Calle, the 'work' of art is in the *conception* of what is presented. Thus, whereas in reproduction (of the work), the uniqueness of the work of art is deprived of its power by replication and consequent kitschification as, for example, in the mass reproduction of the work of L.S. Lowry in the 1960s, in the production aesthetics of the work of art as conception and not artefact, that is, with the emphasis on the process of production and not on the product *per se*, Calle succeeds in achieving a higher order of reproduction in which it is those who contribute to the work who are deprived of power and whose contributions are kitschified by sentimentality and a romantic view of the celebration of difference.

Appropriation and the cancellation of the collectivity

In the case of the photographs and texts, there is an appropriation of the recollections of the individual contributors and a violation of the privacy (cf. Baudrillard, 1983) of the relationship between the individual and the lost artefact which, in being captured and consumed in the process of construction of 'the work of art', is made available for consumption. Moreover, the individual contributor is subjected to the illusion of collaboration in the conception of 'the work of art' whereas it is clear that the contributions are merely elements within the artistic conception of, for want of a better term, the author of the work, and only gain the status of an entity within 'the work of art', that is, have any intrinsic worth, when they are processed, ordered and presented by the 'author/artist'. There is clearly a hierarchy of interpretation at work in which the 'artist's' meanings take precedence. The construction of the work is based on asymmetrical relations. The subject is restored to the picture not in the sense of recovering the loss of the subject but precisely in the sense of reproducing subjection.

The mausoleum and the museum

In 1991, Calle took her ideas further in her contribution to the *Dislocations* exhibition at the Museum of Modern Art in New York where she asked curators, guards and restorers to describe the paintings that were on loan from the permanent collection (Phelan, 1993: 147). However, this time she went further than she had in Boston and asked the contributors to draw small pictures of their memories of the paintings. She then arranged the texts and pictures according to the dimensions of the space normally occupied by the paintings and called her piece 'Ghosts'. If a museum is a mausoleum to art then it is perhaps fitting that ghosts should haunt its corridors. Calle's work was dispersed throughout the permanent collection: a collection which contained re-collections of its missing parts. Absence is acknowledged and brought within the physical present but absence cannot speak for itself in this conception – it is irreducibly appropriated in the service of a particular 'work of art'. This is not the merging of the author into the cultural product as discussed by Lash (1990). However, it is certainly a highly specific part of the process of the aestheticization of daily life (Featherstone, 1991: 102) although, in saying this it is important to acknowledge that Featherstone himself does not see this process as leading to the death of the subject whereas the argument presented here clearly does. This reflects the way in which the production aesthetics are created and, following Benjamin (1977), here the emphasis is on the melancholic impetus to produce and, significantly in the case of the aestheticization of everyday life, on the desire for the lost object.

In many senses, Calle's work could be argued to be inherently melancholic and yet, in the apparent emancipation that it offers, this is not acknowledged. Phelan's enthusiasm for Calle's work and her view of it as subversive seems strangely unreflexive when she argues that 'she (Calle) offers the words of others about other works of art under her own artistic signature . . . (and) subverts the goal of museum display. She exposes what the museum does not have and cannot offer and uses that absence to generate her own work' (Phelan, 1993: 147). It is interesting to note that, whatever Calle's intentions, it is the claim to authorship which is praised here. On the one hand, it is quite easy to see that Calle's work might be readily received as exciting and interesting and its conception is quite delightful in many ways. The idea has appeal and it is not difficult to see why the exhibition might command some critical acclaim. However, in terms of its dynamics, it requires careful scrutiny.

On authority and the power to posit meanings

Using Benjamin's conceptualization of allegory, it is the case that in allegory, the allegorist takes an element out of the totality of the life context, isolating it and depriving it of its meaning. In the allegorical project of assembling accounts and memories of works of art there is a coincidence of artistic intent and the appropriation of the space once occupied by the original. The melancholy of the producer, the allegorist, impels the closure of the space once occupied by the original by the deletion of the original and the insertion of the 'accounts' which are memories and recollections detached from their contexts and the lives of their authors and captured and forced into a coherence of posited meanings under the pretext of a liberating heterogeneity. The space which represents the lost object and which could remain as a significant absence, which could be mourned, which could define itself through loss and removal, rather is colonized, captured and kitschified by a narcissism which protects itself from the threat of recognition by its claim to be 'a work of art'.

The primary concern here is with authority and the regulation of the site of what Phelan argues is performative expression (1993: 146). In practice, there are many sites of performance and experiences of recollection. However, the site of such expression is regulated by the metaphorical and metonymic movements which sustain the production of order. It is this regulation and ordering of the site of performance, here the space of the work of art, which Derrida (1978) considers in his essay on Artaud, 'The Theatre of Cruelty and the closure of representation' (see Bürger, 1984). The regulatory function of text, temporality and tropes, of absence defining presence, and of subordination, governs the possibility of performance. Authority over performance sites derives from the initiator, the creator, the author, and originates in a verbal fiat which initiates and then regulates the text. In this case, the author constructs an allegory of recollections and experiences such that the contributions themselves are trivialized by the schematization. Experiences, albeit that these too are constructed, are translated into consumable constructed performances.

Arrogance and appropriation

The allegorist joins the isolated fragments, the memories and recollections, and thereby, even where the author signals entry to the work, the author imposes an authoritative meaning if only in the trajectory of the intention. In this case, the allegorist usurps the already heterogeneous reception of the original work and replaces it with the intentions, interpretations and narcissism of the author. Such posited meanings do not derive from the original context of the fragments but from the representational intentions of the author. Looked at in this way, the *Ghosts* exhibition, where the collections of drawings and text were specifically designed to occupy the defined spaces of the original works, rather than liberating, seems to have involved a two-stage appropriation: first, the appropriation of the memories and work of the individuals who were invited to contribute to the exhibition; and, secondly, the appropriation of the space of the original work. This latter point is important since it is not even necessary to get as far as the absent object before the travesty of the usurpation becomes apparent. The significance of the appropriation attaches to the arrogation of the space. The original is replaced and its place is taken, confiscated, so that it can neither remain as an absence in its own right nor can it depart.

In Benjamin's terms, the allegorist is unable to mourn the loss and let the object depart and the inherent melancholy of this situation ensures that the space and what comes to occupy it will not only be dead but will remain secure and unconditionally in the power of the allegorist. Consequently, the space, the absence, is no longer capable of emanating any meaning or significance of its own. Likewise the fragments of meanings, memories and recollections brought in to occupy the space are deprived of meaning. The significance of the space and of the production which comes to occupy the space, are at the mercy of the allegorist. The transgression of what was, by the overwriting of the space, the defacement of the space, produces a simulacrum which, in moving from production to reception, transgresses the viewer by depriving the viewing subject of meaning on the pretext of offering meaning in abundance. However, this example serves to draw attention to issues which have a far wider range of significance. Whereas Phelan sees Calle's 'accounts' as the supplement to the absent works of art, it is more consistent with our argument and with Owens' (1980) position to view the 'accounts' as the supplement to the authority of the privileged and posited meaning which the author (Calle herself) gives to 'the work of art'.

The invitation to delight in public humiliation

In Benjamin's conception of allegory there are two production aesthetic concepts. The first of these is primarily concerned with the material itself and with the removal of an element from its context. The second concept is concerned with the way in which meaning is posited in the fragments. These production concepts are complemented by an interpretation of the processes and production of the reception of the work (Bürger, 1984: 69). Benjamin views the producer of the allegory as melancholic and the recipient as pessimistic and speaks of 'the profound fascination of the sick man with the isolated and insignificant which is succeeded by the disappointed abandonment of the exhausted emblem' (1977: 83–4). In this context, the insistent occupation of an empty space deprives the viewer/other of the power and freedom to interpret, or simply to be in relation to, absence, impoverishes and ultimately disappoints. What is presented as the creative new work is, in fact, mere reproduction. However, as was stated earlier, reproduction permits difference and ingenuity only insofar as it serves the reproduction of output. In this example, the 'work of art' is a reproduction to the extent that what is reproduced is the means of controlling production and the appropriation of what is rightly the production of others. The allegorist as producer of such copy deprives the work of its nature: the contributions have nothing which is their own and yet, in the nature of the thing, must delight in their public humiliation, in the celebration of their abuse, even their death in the service of the production (Sievers, 1994). The contributors are made to feel that the appropriation of their individual contributions is worthy of celebration. They are applauded for their contributions to 'the work'. However, these small pieces – some less competent, less insightful, less intelligent than others – are exhibited for public consumption. Likewise, employees who must perform their roles within the overall performance of the organization may be required to exhibit themselves in various ways for the appraisal and consumption of the customer. They are humiliated in their exhibition of their service for the consumption of others in such a way which is all the more degrading because it is a public demonstration of their worth.

Heterogeneity is made into an emblem of participation in order to distract from the power of commonality and commonality itself is made to sound banal. The power of common interest is rendered commonplace. There is a pernicious and seductive inversion at work in this substitution which exalts difference in order to regulate by more precise classification, in which the aesthetics of order and ordering has primacy over and explicitly ridicules an aesthetics of experience. Hence form and function (of people and things) are valued to the extent that they are in the service of production and, as a consequence, they come to bear the inevitable shadows of instrumentality and transience.

The loss of the collectivity

The most significant aspect of this discussion lies in the notion that allegory results in mortification and that the production aesthetics of allegory are inherently melancholic. The consequence of this assertion is the identification of loss as being the loss of the collectivity. In the pursuit of what is paraded as liberating heterogeneity is the loss of the notion of commonality. What is held in common is, in fact, appropriated in the service of the author/artist or, as the argument runs here, in the service of the allegorist. The celebration of difference serves to destroy the collectivity and to reinforce the power of the artist. Phelan's 'clever girl' appraisal of Calle is a case in point. It is not the individuals who make up her work who are praised but rather her skill in giving voice to their heterogeneity. Yet their work is only unified in the meaning that it has for Calle. Individually they might take pride in their contribution and enjoy seeing their work exhibited. However, their contributions only have meaning in the context of that provided by Calle. They are given a place within a collectivity and then locked there without remission by the meanings which are assigned to them. The only rationale for their being located in proximity is Calle's and the only comfort they can find is in the identification of similarity and dissimilarity. Beyond this the contributions have no status other than that of fragments because that is all they are and as such they have no reason for collective purpose, identification or, indeed, action. They can only come together as those who share a place in the construction of another. Within the construction they have no other commonality, no reason, no direction, no purpose other than that assigned to them. There is no collectivity because none is permitted within such framing.

On reticence and restitution of the collectivity

Organizations produce allegories in order to create meaning, to give coherence, to impose order. The celebration of difference – be it at the level of the 'employee of the month' or the provision of policies on diversity and equal opportunities – conceals the imperative of the organization towards the construction of the allegorical form and the positing of its own ideology. The more obsessively the coherence of meaning which is pursued the more transparent the melancholy of the organization. The paradoxical celebration of difference, whether of standing in the hierarchy or of social mix or of wealth of opportunity, belies the homogenization imposed by the allegorical framing and, since the framing is one of a subjected commonality, removes the possibility of a radical awareness of collectivity. When organizations celebrate difference they celebrate with funerary rites. The aesthetics of performance are all about what is concealed in the pursuit of performance: *Totentanz*. The organizational member is dislocated in spatio-temporal terms and can never confront the site/source of their anguish. The school has become a bus station.

The means of living has become the *raison d'etre*. The site of production is regulated by the moral imperative to accept the 'correct' interpretation of the allegory. Any variation from the 'correct' interpretation is regarded as deviant, militant. The organization member is invited to make the corrections which will be approved of by the 'checker' and defiance is not well regarded.

The site of production, the site of the construction of allegory, is the site at which extravagance proliferates and overwhelms. As the end of the twentieth century approaches, there is an increasing preoccupation with the elaborate production and proliferation of excess, of apparently liberating heterogeneity, of the pursuit of the sublime, of the aestheticization of daily life. Matter fills up all space. Choice is a bewildering illusion which reduces the actor to speechlessness. Matter presides over the construction space: proliferates, colonizes, conquers and, ultimately, mortifies the contributors. Resistance becomes impossible in the face of overabundant, excessive, intricate construction yet, in the spurious rhetoric of aesthetics, the claim is made that the space is multi-vocal. Production aesthetics when translated into the aesthetics of organized production, that is when applied to organized work, demonstrate an elegant falsehood, a gross misrepresentation. The final defence against proliferating meanings and colonizing materiality is, perhaps, resistance to classification, an unwillingness to engage: an *aesthetics of reticence*.

References

Baudrillard, J. (1975) *The Mirror of Production*. St Louis, MO: Telos Press.

Baudrillard, J. (1983) *Simulations*. New York: Semiotext(e).

Baudrillard, J. (1993) *Symbolic Exchange and Death*. London: Sage.

Benjamin, W. (1977) *The Origin of German Tragic Drama*. London: NLB.

Bertens, H. (1995) *The Idea of the Postmodern: a History*. London: Routledge.

Bürger, P. (1984) *Theory of the Avant-Garde*. Manchester: Manchester University Press.

Canetti, E. (1987) *Crowds and Power*. London: Penguin.

Cooper, R. (1983) 'The other: a model of human structuring' in G. Morgan (ed.), *Beyond Method: Strategies for Social Research*. London: Sage. pp. 202–18.

Cooper, R. (1990) 'Canetti's Sting', *SCOS Notework*, 9 (2/3): 45–53.

Crimp, D. (1980a) 'On the museum's ruins', *October*, 13: 41–59.

Crimp, D. (1980b) 'The photographic activity of postmodernism', *October*, 15: 91–101.

Crimp, D. (1982) 'Appropriating appropriation', in P. Marincola (ed.), *Image Scavengers: Photography*. Philadelphia, NJ: Institute of Contemporary Art/University of Pennsylvania Press. pp. 27–34.

de Man, P. (1986) *The Resistance to Theory*. Manchester: Manchester University Press.

Derrida, J. (1978) *Writing and Differences*. Chicago: University of Chicago Press.

Featherstone, M. (1991) *Consumer Culture and Postmodernism*. London: Sage.

Freud, S. (1984) *On Metapsychology*. Harmondsworth: Penguin.

Lash, S. (1990) *Sociology of Postmodernism*. London: Routledge.

Linstead, S.A. and Chan, A. (1994) 'The sting of organization: command, reciprocity and change management', *Journal of Organizational Change Management*, 7 (5): 4–19.

Miller, D. (1989) 'The limits of dominance', in D. Miller, M. Rowlands and C. Tilley (eds.), *Domination and Resistance*. London: Unwin Hyman Ltd.

Owens, C. (1980) 'The allegorical impulse: toward a theory of postmodernism', Part I, *October*, 12: 67–86 and Part II, *October*, 13: 59–80.

Phelan, P. (1993) *Unmarked: The Politics of Performance*. London: Routledge.

Sievers, B. (1993) *Work, Death and Life Itself: Essays on Management and Organization*. Berlin: Walter de Gruyter.

PART 3

AESTHETICS AND MODES OF ANALYSIS

5

'Cutting a Show': Grounded Aesthetics and Entertainment Organizations

Brian Rusted

> Separation, simplicity, silent norms of pertinence: this one depoliticizing strain
> is of considerable force, since it is capitalized on by professions, institutions,
> discourses and a massively reinforced consistency of specialized fields. (Said,
> 1983: 146)

Introduction

There is a woman standing by a cubicle door in an office tower somewhere in
the Loop, Chicago's downtown business district. The washroom is pristine,
anonymous in the way office tower washrooms are: free of clutter and devoid
of personal artefacts or signifiers of identity. The woman is 'using' the
facilities in a novel, ingenious and perhaps unorthodox way: she is speaking,
relieving herself of words. There are no apparent interlocutors. Wearing a pant
suit – that unfortunate, leisure hybrid of polyester and the work ethic – she
addresses the wall, the mirror, the porcelain fixtures. She carries a large
handbag with her which perhaps is slung over one shoulder, perhaps resting on
the countertop beside the sink. A tissue is tucked into her sleeve. She has white
hair, is in the advance of years, of retirement age, perhaps older.

The woman is speaking, not just out of relief but also to rehearse. She is
making an account of her actions for the past year. Conjunctive, additive (Ong,

1982), biblical, one after the other, she parades a series of events for which she claims a transitive responsibility. 'I booked Norm Krone's orchestra three times for shows; I got a dozen cold calls from people needing trios for social dates; I hired eight novelty acts for children's parties, and used some close-up magicians and four comedians for fundraisers, I had referrals . . .' She is rehearsing an annual report. Her discourse is sprinkled with names, places, and entertainment jargon. She talks like an old-time theatrical booking agent, a commodities trader in the entertainment market, a broker in a tower of song and dance.

This woman is isolated, without an audience, and apparently without organizational affiliation, and yet her words suggest a very complex and well-ordered knowledge: they have sequence, hierarchy, variety, category and type, and they imply events, occasions, alliances, and networks. Whether performance, or rehearsal, the conversation suggests particular aesthetic and organizational knowledge.

Betty's talk captivates me, puzzles me. I carry around her words like a snapshot in a wallet, displaying it at every available opportunity, mulling it over, struggling to find significance. It is a tenuous, fleeting moment, one that betrays both a distinctive set of aesthetic meanings (e.g. novelty acts, close-up magicians, and so forth) and a very particular set of actions. That is, she uses these meanings, does or makes something with them (shows, society dates, parties, fundraisers, and so forth). Her conversation is a moment of work-life when aesthetics and organization are superimposed. Her conversation offers a view of what Paul Willis calls 'symbolic work' (Willis, 1990), the way social groups ' "handle" the raw material of their social and material existence' (in Clarke et al., 1976: 10), a view that sees organizational formations and their aesthetics in 'their relation to the dominant culture – the overall disposition of cultural power in the society as a whole' (Clarke et al., 1976: 13).

This conversation in a Chicago office bathroom attracts me because of its aesthetic richness and the seductive possibility that reading these aesthetic categories will provide access to her organizational world. It also lets me understand a crucial difference in how Organizational Culture research and Cultural Studies think about aesthetics. Although both fields have developed in tandem over the last two or three decades, they rarely overlap despite mutual interests in culture, subculture, symbol, ritual, style and aesthetics. Certainly organizational researchers have expressed an interest in ideology (Clegg, 1989) but not specifically in terms of aesthetics. This chapter will consider the implications such difference has for the cultural analysis of aesthetic practices in organizations.

Aesthetics in organizational culture research

> To acquire a position of authority within the field is, however, to be involved internally in the formation of a canon, which usually turns out to be a blocking device for methodological and disciplinary self-questioning. (Said, 1983: 149)

When Raymond Williams published *Keywords* in 1976, he suggested that the book had its origin in a post-war feeling that people were speaking a different language than they were before the war. The book attempted to map broad changes in language usage, particularly in relation to class and social formations. In many instances, he did not start with a particular word, but with 'what can be called a cluster, a particular set of what came to seem interrelated words and references . . .' (Williams, 1976: 22). The first word that he considered was 'aesthetic'.

Williams traces the word back through its invented German use in relation to art and beauty, to its Greek origins in describing the sensuous perception of material things. He concedes that the word today has this connotative association with art and beauty, and often, now, visual appearance generally (i.e. aesthetics). The word, he says, 'is a key formation in a group of meanings which at once emphasized and isolated SUBJECTIVE (q.v.) sense-activity as the basis of art and beauty as distinct from "social" or "cultural" interpretation' (Williams, 1976: 32). Williams identifies this trajectory in the use of the word, yet editorializes about its damaging consequences: the separation of art from society.

Given that Williams identifies this change of meanings with the post-war period, it is not surprising to find the British social anthropologist Edmund Leach making a defence of aesthetics in the early in 1950s. His study of Burmese political systems is predicated on the importance of aesthetics to social organization. Despite the tendency for cultural researchers to dismiss aesthetic activity as so many 'frills' in favour of the more 'functionally essential' actions of social life, Leach makes the claim that aesthetics forms the basis of social communication within groups and 'to understand the ethical rules of a society, it is aesthetics that we must study' (1954: 12).

Organizational Culture research on aesthetics often places a similar stress on the importance of aesthetics given the rational, technical and functional hegemony of most corporations. Despite such *topoi*, the tension between a subjective treatment of aesthetic activity and its cultural treatment remains. Often the cultural treatment is elided or disguised in the effort to read as aesthetic everyday behaviour not commonly associated with Art, or with the effort to validate an aesthetic consideration of the sensuous in light of the dominant rational-technical rhetoric of the corporate workplace. The consequence is the valorization of the subjective and sensuous approach to aesthetics and the subsequent marginalization of aesthetics in social organization. This strategy is often reinforced by the appeal to pre-World War II views on aesthetics, influenced by Kant in some instances (White, 1996), Langer in others (Ramirez, 1996).

Witkin's analysis (1990) of the 'room at Unilever' is a case in point. His objective in reclaiming aesthetic discourse and reintegrating it into organizational life begins with pointing out how aesthetics has been trivialized because it emphasizes the sensuous: 'It is the separation of the sensuous aspect of aesthetic experience from knowing and understanding that has led to the trivialization of the aesthetic domain' (1990: 327). In a rhetorical move not dissimilar to the one he tries to unmask, Witkin acknowledges the contributions of Cultural Studies scholars yet trivializes them in the same breath. Their work concentrates on youth, leisure and consumption, topics we 'must overcome if we are to realize more clearly the important role played by aesthetic factors throughout society' (1990: 328).

In an earlier article dealing with the concept of 'style' (which is identified more frequently as the site for aesthetic, symbolic work in Cultural Studies, cf. Clarke, 1976; Hebdige, 1979), Witkin makes the same dismissal of the Cultural Studies research. The emphasis on leisure rather than work disqualifies Cultural Studies research from serious consideration by those interested in aesthetics and organizations (Witkin, 1989: 4).

This dismissal of Cultural Studies has four decisive outcomes for Organizational Culture research. First, it mystifies the nature of aesthetics. Perhaps this recalls the work of the anthropologist Robert Armstrong, who saw aesthetic experience as an 'affecting presence' that is both 'complex and elusive to study' given its three natures –'physical, social and affecting' (1971: 34). Witkin sees the working of aesthetic experience in a similar manner: 'The value structure of an organization, manifest at the level of social interaction and of the physical artifacts which mediate such interaction, calls out a presence in the actor that is the locus of its continued recreation' (Witkin, 1990: 330). Second, the Organizational Culture researcher is granted the status of connoisseur. Choice of subject, description and analysis are driven entirely by the researcher's expertise and the formalist emphasis on and reduction of the 'room at Unilever' to 'an absence of real colour . . . unrelieved, rectilinear planes . . . the strong vertical and horizontal lines . . .' (Witkin, 1990: 334). Such a New Critical strategy in interpretation requires refined and specialized attention to textual form separated from the contingencies of everyday life.

Third, the researcher avoids engaging aesthetic practices as lived responses to power. In terms of the particular analysis of the material culture of Unilever, this means that the aesthetic significance of the artefacts at Unilever is located *in* the artefacts themselves rather than in the actions (or meanings) of particular people (designers or users of this room). Rhetorically, the artefacts are presented as active agents: 'By such means, the room at Unilever, and rooms like it everywhere, successfully achieve, at an aesthetic level, the separation of head from body, or rationality from sensuous values . . .' (Witkin, 1990: 337).

Finally, the tactic of dismissing Cultural Studies for its emphasis on leisure and consumption results in a rigid and uninvestigated use of the term *organization*. For Witkin this is clear: 'an organization is a rational-technical machinery' (1989: 191), or 'The present paper develops a view of the aesthetic imperative inherent in the ideal-typical modern organization. I have in mind, here, the kinds of large formal organizations that many of us are familiar with in our daily lives . . .' (1990: 325). A further consequence of this tactic is the displacement it perpetuates regarding the complicity modern organizations have with consumption. As Judith Barry has noted: 'The intense investment corporations have in the production of pleasure for the labour force could serve as the basis of a kind of logic for consumption' (Barry 1987: 261).

In Strati's treatments of aesthetics and organizational life, tactics similar to Witkin's appear (1989, 1992, 1995, 1996). He does not refer directly to the contributions of a Cultural Studies approach to aesthetics and organization but he does make a blanket dismissal, in this instance motivated by its well-knownness rather than a preoccupation with youth, leisure, or consumption:

> I will omit, assuming them to be already well known, certain themes of structural functional analysis (e.g. aesthetics as a symbolic resource in the organizational success, aesthetics as a code for structuring communicative processes, or aesthetics as a norm for the organization's functioning). (Strati, 1992: 578)

Such a process of distillation leaves him with the familiar, mysterious residue. His perspective involves the legitimation of the aesthetic treatment of material not often associated with art practice: 'There is no painting to examine and re-examine; there is no music to listen to; the original aesthetic object is absent' (1992: 580). From almost the first sentence, the approach he outlines locates itself in mystification: 'This subject of study is rather a mysterious one. I certainly cannot draw upon clear-cut definitions of the aesthetic feeling, nor on any personal convictions on the matter' (1989: 207); 'The aesthetic experience of organizational life, which relates both to the entire organization in abstract and to its specific events, activities, and products, evades reiteration and analytical examination unlike a beautiful picture or a beautiful piece of music' (1995: 85); or 'The more aesthetics becomes a form of organizational knowledge, the more it is cryptic and difficult to grasp' (1996: 209).

The researcher is again granted the position of connoisseur, in this instance because the beauty of the organization 'is not self-evident' (Strati, 1995: 84), and because it requires a 'process of evocation' (1995: 85) to summon it forth for analysis. The praxis of this research is also divorced from any discussion of hegemony in the context of organizational life. The research objective is the enlargement of organizational life, one that sees aesthetics as a feature pervading organizational life rather than an approach that compartmentalizes aesthetics 'into organizational products or into the various boxes in which organizational life is conducted and studied' (1992: 569).

However, Strati does work to expand the concept of organization to which aesthetics can be applied. His notion of an 'organization without walls' (1995) is an attempt to grapple with the role of aesthetics in work settings that are not bounded by the spatial-geographic limitations of a rational-technical workplace. He asserts that this is a new and novel concept for organizational studies (1995: 84), but this admission in itself points out how the rejection of Cultural Studies research has narrowed Organizational Culture research.

The discussion of aesthetics in such expanded organizational settings was well established by the 1950s (Powdermaker, 1950; Leach, 1954), and it certainly becomes one of the challenges of conducting contemporary ethnography (MacCannell, 1976; Dorst, 1989). Howard Becker's influence on the study of aesthetics and organization (Becker, 1974, 1980, 1982), derived in part from the work of Arthur Danto (1964), offers a clear lineage for Cultural Studies researchers (Hall and Jefferson, 1976; Becker and McCall, 1990). Even the discussion of political neutrality in aesthetics has been a longstanding feature of Cultural Studies (Bird, 1979). The exclusion of Cultural Studies perspectives from Organizational Culture research has meant two decades must elapse before this approach is appropriated and permitted to expand the concept of organizations at work for Organizational Culture researchers.

The point here is not to undermine the importance and contribution of aesthetics in Organizational Culture research. Rather, it is to identify the limitations of erasing any affinity between Organizational and Cultural Studies research. The remainder of the paper attempts a retrieval of Cultural Studies first through a discussion of ethnographies of folk aesthetics and then a consideration of critical approaches to aesthetics and popular culture.

Folk culture and organizational aesthetics

> . . . the workplace is usually a part of an organization . . . the workplace is not an isolated social setting but is an integral part of a larger phenomenon . . .
> (Jones, 1987b: 149)

Now some might feel that the real issue surrounding the scene of Betty talking to herself in the office bathroom is entirely methodological: what on earth was I doing conducting research in a women's washroom of a Chicago office tower? At what point is participant observation overtaken by voyeurism? Whatever merit such questions might have in general, they do not divert me here. I was not in the bathroom, I did not hear this woman talking, I did not even overhear her talking.

Her conversation was reported. It was relayed as part of an account of events in the women's washroom. It was then (and is now) a representation, a performance. It was this other conversation in which I participated.

Kathy, one of the secretaries in the entertainment production company comes back to the office after a trip to the washroom and says, 'Guess what? Betty's in the bathroom talking to herself!' Those of us within earshot feed on this anecdote, peck it apart for the gristle of detail and nuance. As good gossip (Paine, 1967), it carries much evaluative material about the organizational actors, us included: we are young and immune to the afflictions and aberrations of age; the lack of long-term involvement with the company gives us some ironic detachment when talking about those higher up and in longstanding. Kathy's discovery is evidence in a cautionary tale – look what can happen if you take this job too seriously: you end up talking to yourself in the can.

Kathy's performance of this conversation is symbolic work. It permits her to articulate a contradictory commitment to the organization. The performance suggests both the pressure of her hierarchical position (as it does for Betty) and her distance from particular traditions and aesthetic conventions (while simultaneously suggesting Betty's proximity). Such a performance suggests that the organizational boundary which makes sense of Betty's aesthetics is not placed productively at the perimeter of the workplace she and Kathy occupy. Neither is it simply placed around an 'organization without walls' or an 'artworld'. These are convenient, spatial metaphors which help contain the ethnographic present. The organizational boundary for Betty's aesthetics is temporal and suggests a depth and diversity of cultural traditions that extend beyond the immediate social networks of current practitioners that share her sense of grounded aesthetics. To site her aesthetics in the place of her work is to miss their articulation with 'the larger phenomena' of dominant culture.

At the conclusion of a discussion on the politics of Cultural Studies, John Fiske takes some time out to distinguish popular culture from folk culture. Popular culture is 'culture understood as the production and circulation of meanings and pleasures, and of the popular as an intransigent, oppositional, scandalous set of forces' (1989: 177). For several pages, folk culture is straw for his argument because it 'is the product of a comparatively stable, traditional social order, in which social differences are not conflictual, and that is therefore characterized by social consensus rather than social conflict' (1989: 169). In the end he diminishes their differences, even concedes that 'there are, or have been, folk cultures of oppositional industrial groups' (1989: 171). Although neither Fiske nor Organizational Culture researchers reference any folklore scholarship on aesthetics, his comments suggest accidentally that they may have some contribution to make, in understanding both the temporal organization of aesthetics, and the conflicted relations such aesthetics have within a spatially limited group and without.

Research by Michael Owen Jones now provides nearly three decades of thought on the relationship between aesthetics, work, and folk cultural context. Jones has helped clarify the use of terminology with a review of the distinctions between 'the aesthetic', 'aesthetic attitude', 'aesthetic response', 'aesthetic judgement' and 'taste' (1987a), and he has provided several important demonstrations of how the ethnographic approach to folk aesthetics can be applied in the study of worklife and organizations (1987b and 1987c). He has also re-read classic management theory with an ethnographer's eye and worked to expand the notion of 'organization' that operates in our field (1987b).

Folklorists continue to research aesthetics, work and organization (see for instance Dewhurst, 1984, 1988), and Jones's influence continues to be felt. Such work provides a firm basis for the consideration of ethnographic approaches to aesthetics in addition to offering alternative settings to the youth and leisure focus that Organizational Culture researchers feel taints Cultural Studies.

In the description of the field site for a study of aesthetics in North Carolina, John Forrest claims that 'no one has attempted an ethnography of all of the aesthetics of a community' (1988: 34). Whatever arrogance might cling to such a statement, his work does signal the very distinctive and virtually unacknowledged contribution which Folklore continues to make to the study of aesthetics. His objective is to try and ground aesthetics in the context of everyday life, although in this instance rural and traditional practices rather than urban, youth consumption. Forrest is able to mix both the aesthetics of the domestic and leisure sphere with those of the secular workplace, and the sacred. Paralleling Cultural Studies projects in this area, Forrest recognizes that aesthetics plays a role in 'social networks and relationships' (1988: 35), and as his research unfolds, it is clear that aesthetics is in the service of distinct factions within the community. It is not merely an opportunity to demonstrate his connoisseurship, or the imagined stability of the community; it is a resource for social action within the community.

Forrest's approach to aesthetics is still hampered by the tensions that Williams outlined more than a dozen years before. Forrest wants to essentialize aesthetics as a subjective state of appreciation. He dismisses the symbolic, semiotic, communicational approaches to the subject and falls back on Armstrong's view of aesthetics as an affecting presence (Forrest, 1988: 32). His sense is that to do otherwise will tempt the researcher with the content of the art object, and lure her away from the social relations which maintain the traditions of performance and interpretation. Why he does not see the later direction as also communicational is not made clear.

What he sought in this research was a sense of aesthetics in action, that is, a sense of how the aesthetic categories that characterized aspects of everyday life were used by residents to negotiate their place in the world, especially so when under pressure to change. The spirit of this project is shared by Leslie Prosterman's study of everyday aesthetics associated with festivals and fairs in the American midwest. She spent nearly three years documenting these major ceremonial events in the life of small communities and going 'from region to region, town to town, café to café, farm to farm' (Prosterman, 1995: 7) for in-depth, formal interviews with participants. The result is a thorough description of the aesthetic criteria used to produce goods for county fairs with a clear demonstration as to how these 'criteria also facilitate social life by providing a basis of evaluation and a set of rules for personal interaction' (1995: 166).

Both Forrest and Prosterman struggle with the connotations of the term aesthetics – how can an ethnographic researcher interested in everyday life understand a concept commonly associated with elite practices? On the one hand they want to resist institutional hierarchies that separate high from low culture, while on the other they want to invoke the legitimations that art and aesthetics convey. They are seeking a place for folk aesthetic practices that is outside the conventional, temporal siting of art and aesthetics (Phillipson, 1996). Prosterman's response, in part is to understand everyday practices as having a lineage descended from elite practices of earlier times. However unsatisfying such cultural devolution might be, she rightly points out that the terms Art and Aesthetics have symbolic capital in our society: those whose practices are excluded by these categories 'become shut out from what is popularly called the cultural life of our nation' (Prosterman, 1995: 186). Seeing everyday aesthetics in this sense is redemptive, however laboured the juxtaposition of art and life might be.

In a more urban application of ethnography to aesthetics, Gary Alan Fine develops a similar analysis of restaurant kitchens. The very fact that the products of this form of work are to be judged (by producers and consumers alike) 'on their sensory qualities' (Fine, 1996: 13) is enough reason to invoke aesthetics in his analysis. The basis of his analysis involves the aesthetics of culinary work, what makes it good in the eyes of practitioners and how it is constrained by the economics and organizational setting of restaurants. Although he admits that the culinary world is not a commonly recognized artworld, the relevance of aesthetics and talk about aesthetics is not diminished.

While these approaches to aesthetics demonstrate both the process and significance of researching aesthetics in organizational forms as complex as a community, a restaurant, or regional institutions like county fairs, Prosterman provides a further dimension. She explores the historical determination of aesthetics. 'The weight of tradition and the number of people who have participated in related action in other periods give sanction to the present' (1995: 42). This is an important elaboration on the relation of aesthetics to social organization, one which distinguishes it from most sociological and organizational approaches. Not only can aesthetic practices be considered in terms of their contribution to the articulation of difference and identity in contemporary contexts, much as Fiske views popular culture, they can also be seen in terms of their re-articulation, appropriation, and critique of historical contexts. The combination of these two perspectives – a thorough treatment of the ethnographic present and an appreciation of historical integration or transformation – form the broader basis of the contribution Cultural Studies makes to aesthetics.

Popular culture and organizational aesthetics

> Artistic work lasts when it has an organizational basis that preserves and protects it. (Becker, 1982: 350)

Later in the day, I will see Betty, after she has left the bathroom and returned to the office. For more than forty years she has worked for this small, family-owned company in the business of entertainment production. Although she would likely be forced to retire if she was employed by a more formally structured organization, here she works on at her own pace, continuing to bring in business from both longstanding clients and new contacts. The percentage of her commissions turned back to the company ensure her office space and company resources.

She has come to work today because her original boss and CEO of the company is visiting to meet personally with one of the firm's oldest clients. This is his only account now and his ceremonial appearance is not lost on Betty. At one time Betty was the only other employee in the company, and Arthur's visit is an opportunity for her to demonstrate that she is still making a contribution to the organization's profitability. She will look for an opportunity during the day to perform the report for Arthur which she has rehearsed in the company's washroom.

Although earlier formulations of aesthetics in Cultural Studies often focus on style in youth subcultures (Clarke, 1976; Hebdige, 1979), later work clarifies one of the underlying polemics of the aesthetic approach to culture. As Ian Hunter says, it treats aesthetics as ethics, 'an autonomous set of techniques and practices by which individuals continuously problematize their experience and conduct themselves as the subjects of an aesthetic existence' (1992: 358). Paul Willis's research on the symbolic work of everyday culture is positioned as a critique of the 'hyperinstitutionalization' of art in everyday life (1990). His thesis is that the received concepts of art and aesthetics are completely separated from the contexts of everyday life, and the popular resources commonly used to create shared meanings.

> The fundamental project is to present and understand the creative symbolic elements of ordinary life, an important part of which is certainly the role and use of popular representations, but understood through their use in – not reflection of – the everyday. (Willis, 1990: 6)

This perspective is a productive development of an earlier effort to link aesthetics with ideology more often associated with Frankfurt School critical theory (Adorno, 1984; Chaplin, 1994; Slater, 1978). On the surface, Willis's view is similar to that held by Organizational Culture researchers dealing with aesthetics: aesthetics must be brought to bear on any reading of everyday life, particularly life in the workplace. The emphasis Willis places on *use* is one of the important features of the Cultural Studies approach to aesthetics, and one that distinguishes it from the indictment that Cultural Studies is only concerned with consumption. The fabrication of identity and meaning is a product of 'symbolic work . . . the application of human capacities to and through, on and with symbolic resources and raw materials . . .' (Willis, 1990: 10). The interpretive basis of this approach to the study of such symbolic work is an appreciation of what Willis calls *grounded aesthetics*, 'a process whereby meanings are attributed to symbols and practices and where symbols and practices are selected, reselected, highlighted and recomposed to resonate further appropriated and particularized meanings' (1990: 21).

On the surface too, this approach bears a resemblance to the use of aesthetics in Folk Culture research. Certainly there is a common disdain for elite culture and a sense of how it operates to exclude the everyday symbolic work of people. There is also a shared sense of how aesthetics contributes to the construction of a sense of identity and place. The difference is in the absence of an explicit concern with aesthetics and ideology. Both Folklorists and Organizational Culture researchers seem to bracket their research sites so that a relation between aesthetics in the community or organization and hegemonic forces outside it is not engaged (see Greenhill, 1995). This is the decisive contribution of Cultural Studies: 'Meanings alternative to those preferred by the dominant culture, generated within the experience and consciousness of a suppressed social group, may be brought to the surface and so transform the original discourse' (Clarke, 1976: 178). To return to Witkin's rejection of Cultural Studies mentioned earlier, it now seems to lie not with the preoccupation with leisure and consumption, but rather with Cultural Studies' focus on oppositional social forms.

> What happens is not the creation of objects and meanings from nothing, but rather the *transformation and rearrangement* of what is given (and 'borrowed') into a pattern which carries a new meaning, its *translation* to a new context and its *adaptation*. (Clarke, 1976: 178)

The challenge for Organizational Research is to bring the same spirit of rigour and analysis to the study of aesthetics in hegemonic forms. The emphasis Willis and others place on the aesthetic *use* of symbolic resources is a distinct advance on the views of consumption and culture industry descended from the Frankfurt critique. It also highlights the way Organizational Culture researchers replace a consideration of the aesthetic practices of actors in an organization with their own connoisseurship (Kuhn, 1996).

Betty's occupation as an entertainment producer required a long-term apprenticeship to gain the grounded aesthetics appropriate to her business. An indication of the complexity of this can be gained from a consideration of the range of aesthetic choices available to her. In the company office there is a vertical file with over 1500 'one sheet' biographies of entertainers and acts looking for work. Less than a third of these have been summarized for ready and routine substitution into proposals for clients. In a given year, the company might use 300 entertainers and acts so the grounded aesthetics of selection and ordering are central to the practice of a producer like Betty. Not only did this mean knowing the varieties of acts from which one could chose; it also meant knowing how to pitch the act in the sales performance before a client:

> You have to be able to pick out some things that would catch a client's imagination so that they would really like to see that act, and it's hard to say somebody is a singer. It doesn't mean a thing. You have to be able to know, I often say when I go to a client now, 'I'm going to tell you about a singer and I know that anybody's reaction is: before that woman or that gal opens her mouth you're shaking in your boots wondering what kind of a voice is going to come out. But this girl has a voice that is so true and clear as a bell and beautiful, and she uses it the way a musician uses an instrument. She gets the soft tones, and the exciting tones, and she just seems to reach out from that stage and that

audience is in her arms . . .' So when you sell like that, I didn't say, 'Yes, she has a nice voice and she can sing.'

Of the hundreds of entertainers hired by this company over 60 per cent were musical groups. It is possible theoretically to divide these groups into numerous categories such as orchestras, trios, pianists and so forth yet none of these categories can be considered homogeneous. Aesthetic skill here involves the knowledge of myriad differences between the individuals in any one category. Orchestras and orchestra leaders provide a case in point.

There are more than fifty orchestra leaders listed in the Chicago Association of Professional Orchestra Leaders. About a dozen of these get routine use by Betty's company. Within this category, it is possible to see these leaders in one of three ways: as *dance* orchestras, as *show* orchestras or as *society* orchestras. The most desirable are in the dance and show classifications.

Dick Judson, a longtime orchestra leader explains that when he first began as a leader, he concentrated on society work, '. . . mainly playing society parties, a lot of debutante parties where families would spend lots of money to introduce their daughters to society, and lots of just family dinner parties and dances'. By starting to do 'club dates' or 'jobbing dates', Judson moved away from this society classification. As a dance orchestra, the work would be similar to that of a society orchestra – dinner dances – but the audiences would be larger, more diverse and frequently have corporate or industry affiliation. There is a status hierarchy carried by these categories and often musicians must trade their needs for creative status for the commercial demands of the job. The society work and jobbing dates are viewed as 'commercial' work (Stebbins, 1968; see also Faulkner, 1971). Musicians in general, leaders in particular might find 'pride and self-respect in being able to 'cut' any kind of music' (Becker, 1953: 92). Skill in the performance of the job replaces the concern of the implied hierarchical difference in types of music. Joe Vito, another Chicago orchestra leader, explains this in terms of the show orchestra classification: '. . . where there is an act, where you have to back the act, and you have to have the background to be able to conduct the band for whatever act is on the show: a magician, a singer, a dancer.' An orchestra leader's ability to 'cut a show' is the most highly regarded by entertainment producers. There is no need to hire two orchestras – one for the show after a dinner, another for the dance which follows. The leader's skill at reading music and hiring musicians who can, reduces the cost of rehearsal time prior to the date. To hire across these categories held the direst of consequences:

> Some orchestras were strictly dance orchestras which could play a socko dance, but they would be lost, it would be torture if the act was trying to tell them how to play their show . . . They couldn't read the act's music and the act was sweating blood, and a 'No, no! The drumbeat comes here!'

Each entertainment producer like Betty has a sense of which orchestra leaders they feel are better able to 'cut a show' and they contract accordingly. This sense of taste or 'manifest preference' (Bourdieu, 1980) is not grounded solely in personal or subjective values: the conventional categories for understanding orchestras and their leaders, and for selecting them produces and reproduces the collective, shared identity that allows this organization to perpetuate itself. The everyday performance of taste in this context also produces a network of social relations, hierarchies of privilege and reciprocal loyalties between producers, their clients and the contracted entertainers (Becker, 1953; Rusted, 1988).

The symbolic work of such grounded aesthetics 'places identities in larger wholes' and realizes 'the structured collectivity of individuals as well as their differences' (Willis, 1990: 12). An organizational approach to aesthetics does not simply see aesthetics as a necessary and integral part of organizational life: 'Instead it treats aesthetic judgements as characteristic phenomena of collective activity' (Becker, 1982: 39).

Grounded aesthetics and organizations

> The history of a popular genre can usefully concern itself with the ways its dominant features were positioned within prevailing community taste, with ways its materials excite and regulate audience response, and with ways it transgresses or observes the boundaries of good taste and social propriety. (Jenkins, 1992: 22)

Returning to the office after lunch, I will meet Kathy on her way out. She makes a horrible grimace of disgust as she passes me in the hall, not stopping to explain. I wonder aloud, 'What's Kathy's problem?' Everyone feels for her, and Nancy explains 'Oh, she's just P.O.'d because Arthur ran out of Poligrip and he needs to get his dentures in before he makes his presentation to the Cummins people. He sent Kathy out to get him some more Poligrip. Like this is in her job description!'

Without his dentures, Arthur will invite me into the meeting to observe how he makes his presentation to Cummins. He is Betty's mentor. All I can think about is the litany of contracts she rehearsed in the bathroom, and the fact that Kathy never returned with the Poligrip.

The sales pitch is the central cultural performance of an entertainment producer. Structured with substitutable motifs and formulaic phrases, the performance articulates the narrative flow of the event being sold.

> You had to be able to sell the type of acts that you were so enthusiastic about that you couldn't say, 'Now here's a nice little singer, she's a pretty little girl with a nice talent.' You got to be able to sell like gangbusters so that, I used to say, 'I just left a meeting: they can't wait! I don't think they can live another day until they have that show.'

Betty admits to learning these performance skills by watching Arthur in his sales presentations.

> When I first went out with him to go to see how to sell a show, I was so impressed with how he described his act and how he laid out the balance of the show – 'you build the show and you put this act on first and then the next act is in a little contrast, and then you bring it up again, and build until the last act is just, you could just find your audience getting to their feet to say, 'Bravo!' because it is such a well balanced and good show.' And so he had this way of selling.

When she began working in the late 1930s, the company was merely 'a theatrical booking agency . . . we weren't called producers or anything'. They were one of a panoply of organizations distinguished only on the basis of the acts they represented, comparable to other forms of 'brokerage' (Rose, 1995: 8). There were agents who 'specialized in circus type acts, some who booked nightclubs', theatrical agents, general agents 'who would book anything and everything', and the large organizations like Music Corporation of America (MCA) or General Artists Corporation (GAC) that booked big bands for radio. As the company's office manager, Don, recalled, their company was one of many 'little William Morrises'.

> They were, you know, it was good solid entertainment, these were people who were really direct from the vaudeville circuit, and when vaudeville died, this is what they really went into . . . and we used a great many of them, you know, magicians and comedians, vocalists, dancers of all types, tap dancing and ballet type of thing, or we put a little show together.

In Albert McLean's study of *American Vaudeville as Ritual*, he makes the point that these agents and producers were at the heart of whatever success vaudeville had. Even though the content of shows would change, the agents and producers would ritualize the flow of entertainment in a fashion very close to that described by Betty and Don:

> The rhythm consisted of a series of controlled accelerations toward climaxes of excitement; the mood derived from the comic effect of vivid contrasts . . . The audience, largely unaware of managerial strategy, only knew that the peak of the show would be reached with a celebrity performer well along in the bill. (McLean, 1965: 93)

The basis of this aesthetic performance goes back to variety entertainment forms in the nineteenth century, the minstrel show, the circus and so on. Benjamin Keith whose own start was in the circus is often credited with inventing vaudeville when he began to put his idea of 'continuous performance' to work in his own theatre (Keith, 1898: 15). The flow of acts in this continuous performance was explicitly part of the 'psychology' of the industry (Gottlieb, 1916).

The variety in vaudeville's entertainment meant that these impresarios could create wide appeal for 'the vast numbers of city folk' who were unable to afford legitimate theatre (Nasaw, 1993: 27). The entertainment was seen as 'genial subversion' (Snyder, 1989: 161) that provided a symbolic means of redress for diverse and often disenfranchised peoples moving into and making American cities. Vaudeville was 'the compelling esthetic experience' (McLean 1965: 10) that made sense of this dislocation for city folk. The structure of the program both reflected and appealed to these needs: 'The program as a whole offered no consistent message; individual acts might offer conflicting or competing messages. In the end, what vaudeville communicated was the pleasure of infinite diversity in infinite combinations' (Jenkins, 1992: 63).

The end of vaudeville is usually tied to the appearance of radio and talking motion pictures. Keith himself became involved in radio entertainment as the 'K' in RKO (Snyder, 1989: 159). The fact that the aesthetic practices formulated in that era continue to be practised in the world of industrial club dates and corporate entertainment is lost on most historians. Although the audiences and settings may have changed, McLean's reading of the symbolic significance of this performance genre is still applicable more than sixty years later: 'It offered, in symbolic terms, the sweet fruits of success neither as reward nor as a promise, but as an accessible right for all those participating in the new life of the cities' (McLean, 1965: 11).

Conclusion

> The important fact, then, is not a mere descriptive inventory – which may have the negative effect of freezing popular culture into some timeless descriptive mold – but the relations of power which are constantly punctuating and dividing the domain of culture into its preferred and residual categories (Hall, 1981: 247).

Jameson has suggested that *pastiche* is one of the defining tropes of late capitalism. It is the characteristic form of expression of 'a world in which stylistic innovation is no longer possible, all that is left is to imitate dead styles' (1983: 115). Its prevalence signals 'the disappearance of a sense of history, the way in which our entire contemporary social system has little by little begun to lose its capacity to retain its own past' (Jameson, 1983: 125). In at least one sense, this chapter shares this view of pastiche: by the time the vaudeville style of entertainment is recombined by Betty's company and sold to corporate and industrial audiences, it evinces a certain morbidity.

As Kaja Silverman has noted, such reworking of dead styles is also a means of inserting the performer or practitioner 'into a complex network of cultural and historical references' (1986: 150; see also McCracken, 1988). This would involve not just an appreciation of style, but also a consideration of the organizational context of lived, aesthetic practices. Despite the quite profound change in performance context and the social use of this popular style, the grounded aesthetics of entertainment producers like Betty preserve a sense of continuity and tradition. One goal of this chapter has been to demonstrate this continuity.

The aesthetics of such symbolic work often points out the banal centre of Cultural Studies: the repeated emphasis on the fabrication of resistant subjectivity and oppositional politics (Morris, 1990; Hartley, 1992). When vaudeville's emphasis on 'infinite diversity and infinite combination' is taken up in the middle of this century by corporate consumers, it suggests a change in the political valence of this style of entertainment. Vaudeville's early subversion is overshadowed by the later commercial interests of showmanship and technical skill and what might be considered the more hegemonic motives of corporate users (employee loyalty, increased efficiency, commitment, etc.). In the private world of corporate leisure (Barry, 1987), such consumption could be seen as a resistant effort to preserve a sense of taste and standards separate from and critical of the more dissipated and diverse expressions of dominant, mainstream popular culture. Such an observation does strain the metaphor and point up the banality of this as political theory.

There is unquestionably a sense in which power has inflected these aesthetic practices throughout this century. In different periods, their expression has been diverse and contradictory, and they continue to have an ambivalent relationship with the dominant culture. Questions of power however are not exclusively about the subjects of study. Another goal of this chapter has been the implications of the researchers' choices when conceptualizing aesthetics in organizations. Their choices have very particular consequences for how organizations and their members are conceived.

I have tried to consider the place of aesthetics in the study of organizations and to suggest affinities with Cultural Studies. I have tried to give examples of ethnographic contributions to a critical and historical view of aesthetic practice. The ability to identify the nature, practice and inheritance of aesthetic categories evident in the workplace is no guarantee of opposition or resistance. It might offer insight into how that hegemony continues to be reproduced, and it might signal our complicity as researchers in such a hegemonic process. Losing sight of this, the rhetoric of mystification and connoisseurship naturalizes and privileges both the position of the researcher and certain formal views of organizations.

Cautionary tales, gossip, the manufacture of a transient sense of community among disaffected employees, all are worthy features of Betty's washroom report, but they do not circumscribe her conversation completely. Aesthetics, says bell hooks, 'is a way of inhabiting space' (1990: 104), and Betty's rehearsal of the aesthetic sacra of her profession is her way of inhabiting the complex and contradictory relations her aesthetics have with history and with power. Listening to her talk is a means for organizational researchers to inhabit ours.

References

Adorno, Theodor (1984) *Aesthetic Theory*. London: Routledge and Kegan Paul.

Armstrong, Robert Plant (1971) *The Affecting Presence: An Essay in Humanistic Anthropology*. Urbana, IL: University of Illinois Press.

Barry, Judith (1987) 'Pleasure/leisure and the ideology of corporate convention space', in Lorne Falk and Barbara Fischer (eds), *The Event Horizon: Essays on Hope, Sexuality, Social Space and Media(tion) in Art*. Toronto: Coach House Press.

Becker, Howard (1953) 'The culture and career of the dance musician', *Human Organization*, 12 (1), (reprinted in Charles Nanry (ed.), *American Music: From Storyville to Woodstock*. New Brunswick, NJ: Transaction Books, 1972).

Becker, Howard (1974) 'Art as collective action', *American Sociological Review*, 39 (4), December.

Becker, Howard (1980) 'Aesthetics, aestheticians, and critics', *Studies in Visual Communication*, 6 (1), spring.

Becker, Howard (1982) *Art Worlds*. Berkeley, CA: University of California Press.

Becker, Howard and McCall, Michal (eds) (1990) *Symbolic Interaction and Cultural Studies*. Chicago: University of Chicago Press.

Bird, Elizabeth (1979) 'Aesthetic neutrality and the sociology of art', in Michèle Barrett, Phillip Corrigan, Annette Kuhn and Janet Wolff (eds), *Ideology and Cultural Production*. New York: St. Martin's Press.

Bourdieu, Pierre (1980) 'Aristocracy of culture', *Media, Culture and Society*, 2 (2).

Chaplin, Elizabeth (1994) *Sociology and Visual Representation*. London: Routledge.

Clarke, John (1976) 'Style', in Stuart Hall and Tony Jefferson (eds), *Resistance Through Ritual*. London: Hutchinson.

Clarke, John, Hall, Stuart, Jefferson, Tony and Roberts, Brian (1976) 'Subcultures, cultures and class', in Stuart Hall and Tony Jefferson (eds) *Resistance Through Ritual*. London: Hutchinson.

Clegg, S (1989) *Frameworks of Power*. Newbury Park, CA: Sage.

Danto, Arthur (1964) 'The artworld', *Journal of Philosophy*, 61 (4).

Dewhurst, C. Kurt (1984) 'The arts of working: manipulating the urban environment', *Western Folklore*, 43 (2).

Dewhurst, C. Kurt (1988) 'Art at work; in pursuit of aesthetic solutions', in Michael Owen Jones, Michael Moore and Richard Snyder (eds), *Inside Organizations: Understanding the Human Dimension*. Beverly Hills, CA: Sage.

Dorst, John (1989) *The Written Suburb: An American Site, An Ethnographic Dilemma*. Philadelphia, NJ: University of Pennsylvania Press.

Faulkner, Robert R. (1971) *Hollywood Studio Musicians: Their Work and Careers in the Recording Industry*. Chicago: Aldine-Atherton.

Fine, Gary Alan (1996) *Kitchens: The Culture of Restaurant Work*. Berkeley, CA: University of California Press.

Fiske, John (1989) *Understanding Popular Culture*. London: Routledge.

Forrest, John (1988) *Lord I'm Coming Home: Everyday Aesthetics in Tidewater North Carolina*. Ithaca, NY: Cornell University Press.

Gottlieb, George (1916) 'Psychology of the American vaudeville show from the manager's point of view', in Charles Stein (ed.), *American Vaudeville As Seen By Its Contemporaries*. New York: Alfred A. Knopf, 1984.

Greenhill, Pauline (1995) 'Review of *Ordinary Life, Festival Days: Aesthetics in the Midwestern County Fair*', *Canadian Folklore Canadien*, 17 (2).

Hall, Stuart (1981) 'Notes on deconstructing "the popular"' in Raphael Samuel (ed.), *People's History and Socialist Theory*. London: Routledge and Kegan Paul.

Hall, Stuart and Jefferson, Tony (1976) *Resistance Through Ritual*. London: Hutchinson.

Hartley, John (1992) 'Suburbanality (in Cultural Studies)', *Meanjin*, 51 (3).

Hebdige, Dick (1979) *Subcultures: The Meaning of Style*. London: Methuen.

hooks, bell (1990) 'An aesthetic of blackness: strange and oppositional', in *Yearning: Race, Gender and Cultural Politics*. Boston: South End Press.

Hunter, Ian (1992) 'Aesthetics and Cultural Studies', in Lawrence Grossberg, Cary Nelson and Paula Treichler (eds), *Cultural Studies*. London: Routledge.

Jameson, Fredric (1983) 'Postmodernism and consumer society', in Hal Foster (ed.), *The Anti-Aesthetic: Essays on Postmodern Culture*. Port Townsend, WA: Bay Press.

Jenkins, Henry (1992) *What Made Pistachio Nuts? Early Sound Comedy and the Vaudeville Aesthetic*. New York: Columbia University Press.

Jones, Michael Owen (1987a) 'Aesthetic attitude, judgement, and response: definitions and distinctions', in *Exploring Folk Art: Twenty Years of Thought on Craft, Work and Aesthetics*. Logan, UT: Utah State University Press.

Jones, Michael Owen (1987b) 'Aesthetics at work: Art and ambiance in an organization', in *Exploring Folk Art: Twenty Years of Thought on Craft, Work and Aesthetics*. Logan, UT: Utah State University Press.

Jones, Michael Owen (1987c) 'The material culture of corporate life' in *Exploring Folk Art: Twenty Years of Thought on Craft, Work and Aesthetics*. Logan, UT: Utah State University Press.

Keith, B.F. (1898) 'The vogue of vaudeville,' in Charles Stein (ed.), *American Vaudeville As Seen By Its Contemporaries*. New York: Alfred A. Knopf, 1984.

Kuhn, James W. (1996) 'The misfit between organizational theory and processional art: a comment on White and Strati', *Organization*, 3 (2) May.

Leach, E.R. (1954) *Political Systems of Highland Burma: A Study of Kachin Social Structure*. London: Athlone Press.

MacCannell, Dean (1976) *The Tourist: A New Theory of the Leisure Class*. New York: Schocken Books.

McCracken, Grant (1988) *Culture and Consumption*. Bloomington, IN: Indiana University Press.

McLean, Albert F. Jr. (1965) *American Vaudeville as Ritual*. Lexington, KY: University of Kentucky Press.

Morris, Meaghan (1990) 'Banality in Cultural Studies', in Patricia Mellencamp (ed.), *Logics of Television: Essays in Cultural Criticism*. Bloomington, IN: Indiana University Press.

Nasaw, David (1993) *Going Out: The Rise and Fall of Public Amusements*. New York: Basic Books.

Ong, Walter (1982) *Orality and Literacy: The Technologizing of the Word*. New York: Methuen.

Paine, Robert (1967) 'What is gossip about? An alternative hypothesis', *Man*, 2.

Phillipson, Michael (1996) 'Managing "tradition": the plight of aesthetic practices and their analysis in a technoscientific culture', in Chris Jenks (ed.), *Visual Culture*. London: Routledge.

Powdermaker, Hortense (1950) *Hollywood: The Dream Factory*. Boston: Little, Brown & Co.

Prosterman, Leslie (1995) *Ordinary Life, Festival Days: Aesthetics in the Midwestern County Fair*. Washington, DC: Smithsonian Institution Press.

Ramirez, Rafael (1996) 'Wrapping form and organizational beauty', *Organization*, 3 (2) May.

Rose, Frank (1995) *The Agency: William Morris and the Hidden History of Show Business.* New York: Harper Business.

Rusted, Brian (1988) 'Corporate rhetoric versus social action: identifying contradictions in a service organization', in Michael Owen Jones, Michael Moore and Richard Snyder (eds), *Inside Organizations: Understanding the Human Dimension.* Beverly Hills, CA: Sage.

Said, Edward (1983) 'Opponents, audiences, constituencies and community', in Hal Foster (ed.), *The Anti-Aesthetic: Essays on Postmodern Culture.* Seattle, WA: Bay Press.

Silverman, Kaja (1986) 'Fragments of a fashionable discourse', in Tania Modleski (ed.), *Studies in Entertainment: Critical Approaches to Mass Culture.* Bloomington, IN: Indiana University Press.

Slater, Phil (1978) 'The aesthetic theory of the Frankfurt School', in Peter Davison, Rolf Meyersohn and Edward Shils (eds), *Literary Taste, Culture and Mass Communication*, Vol. 1. Cambridge, UK: Chadwyck-Healey.

Snyder, Robert W. (1989) *The Voice of the City: Vaudeville and Popular Culture in New York.* New York: Oxford University Press.

Stebbins, Robert (1968) 'A theory of the jazz community', *The Sociological Quarterly*, summer, reprinted in Charles Nanry (ed.), *American Music: From Storyville to Woodstock.* New Brunswick, NJ: Transaction Books, 1972.

Strati, Antonio (1989) 'Aesthetics and organizational skill' in Barry Turner (ed.), *Organizational Symbolism.* New York: De Gruyter.

Strati, Antonio (1992) 'Aesthetic understanding of organizational life', *Academy of Management Review*, 17 (3).

Strati, Antonio (1995) 'Aesthetics and organizations without walls', *Studies in Cultures, Organizations, and Societies*, 1 (1).

Strati, Antonio (1996) 'Organizations viewed through the lens of aesthetics', *Organization*, 3 (2), May.

White, David (1996) '"It's working beautifully!" Philosophical reflections on aesthetics and organizational theory', *Organization*, 3 (2), May.

Williams, Raymond (1976) *Keywords: A Vocabulary of Culture and Society*, rev. edn 1983. London: Fontana Press.

Willis, Paul (1990) *Common Culture.* Boulder, CO: Westview Press.

Witkin, Robert (1989) 'The collusive manoeuvre: a study of organizational style in work relations', in Barry Turner (ed.), *Organizational Symbolism.* New York: De Gruyter.

Witkin, Robert (1990) 'The aesthetic imperative of rational-technical machinery: A study in organizational control through the design of artifacts', in Pasquale Gagliardi (ed.), *Symbols and Artifacts: Views of the Corporate Landscape.* New York: De Gruyter.

6

Routine Pleasures: The Aesthetics of the Mundane[1]

David Silverman

The aesthetic impulse in organization theory can be located in a genealogy of its metaphors (organizations as machines, organisms, cultures, etc.). However, as Morgan has suggested, such metaphors are not simply means of organizational analysis but practical constructions used in everyday, organizational life. As he puts it: 'Images and metaphors are not just interpretive constructs used in the task of analysis. They are central to the process of *imaginization* through which people enact or 'write' the character of organizational life' (1986: 344).

The heretical implication of Morgan's insight, that theorising is not confined to the ivory towers of academe but is part of the practical activities of everyday actors, had, of course, been foreshadowed by Garfinkel (1967). In place of academic paradigm wars, a whole new, more interesting, field was laid out for organization studies: how organizational members themselves work with images and metaphors to establish the 'whatness' or 'quiddity' of organizations. Jeffcutt catches this movement towards the mundane or 'ordinary': 'organizational analysis turns away from commodifying elite heroics (within both academic and managerial work) and becomes concerned with exploring and representing the extraordinary qualities of the ordinary' (1993: 47).

As Jeffcutt's observation implies, ethnomethodology is not unique in requiring a turn away from heroic or romantic conceptions of 'meaning' towards 'ordinary' practices. Indeed, his concern with practices is also implied by March's work on actual decision-making situations like meetings (see Boden, 1994: 79-107). Moreover, Jeffcutt's depiction of 'the extraordinary qualities of the ordinary' is also wholly consonant with the later Wittgenstein. Time and again, Wittgenstein consciously seeks to reject 'big' questions and global answers in favour of a meticulous examination of apparently unremarkable examples. Rather than shock us with tabloid revelations, he shocks us by reminding us of the complexities of what we know already. As he wrote in his *Philosophical Investigations*:

> What we are supplying are really remarks on the natural history of human beings; we are not contributing curiosities however but observations which no one has doubted, but which have escaped remark only because they are always before our eyes. (1968: para. 415)

What is 'before our eyes' becomes, in Garfinkel's (1967) terms, how indexical expressions are routinely made objective. So ethnomethodology shocks us by pointing to the logical impossibility and yet the routine achievement of a stable, ordered world. Somehow, through methods that await explication, the world-known-in-common is viewed anew as an amazing practical accomplishment.

In this chapter, I explore the aesthetic impulse that lies behind ethnomethodology's focus on the 'whatness' or 'quiddity' of organizations. I begin by attempting to cut away what I view as 'dead wood' blocking our path. In particular, I distinguish such an aesthetics from Romanticism (Gergen, 1992) and vulgar deconstruction (Linstead, 1993). Following Popper and Wittgenstein, I call for a clarity of expression and a focus on the aesthetics of the micro-order. I show how the latter is found in ethnomethodology and conversation analysis and explain how these traditions link up with the focus of some organization theorists upon skills and practices.

As observant readers will note, some of this argument appears to turn against some positions with which I have in the past been associated. In particular, *The Theory of Organizations*' 'Action theory' (Silverman, 1970) can be read as a romantic appeal to hidden 'meanings'. And my later book *Reading Castaneda* (Silverman, 1975) treads very close to the 'vulgar deconstruction' that others have rightly criticised (Linstead, 1993: 54). However, despite the efforts of such classifiers as Donaldson (1985), I refuse to be fully identified with the positions with which I was (sometimes falsely) associated twenty or more years ago. To take textbooks too seriously or, still worse, to cluster together in 'schools' of organization theory advances neither our own thought or its contribution to the community (Reed, 1993). In this context, we would do well to recall the words of Wittgenstein who, in closing his *Tractatus Logico-Philosophicus* tells us:

> My propositions serve as elucidations in the following way: anyone who understands me eventually recognises them as nonsensical, when he has used them – as steps – to climb up beyond them (he must, so to speak, throw away the ladder after he has climbed up it). He must transcend these propositions, and then he will see the world aright. (1971: 6.54)

Romanticism

Reed has correctly suggested that *The Theory of Organizations (TO)* (Silverman, 1970) 'provided an indirect justification for (a) categorization fetish' (1993: 172) associated with paradigm wars. Despite the 30 years that have elapsed since the publication of *TO*, it is dispiriting that many organization theorists are still entranced with the commonsensical opposition between 'society' (as found in Functionalism) and the 'individual' (as found in something that is called 'Interpretivism'). For instance, Aldrich suggests that: 'the various interpretive views have in common their focus on an actor's perspective on life in organizations' (1992: 23). Unfortunately, what Aldrich calls 'the actor's perspective' is a very slippery notion, as Weber (1949) was well aware. As I have noted elsewhere, it can directly lead to a 'romantic' conception of inner meaning (Silverman, 1989). We can see this Romanticism in Aldrich's references to: 'the *expressive* side of participation (which) is as important as the task-related side, as organizations do not operate solely on the basis of a rational economic model' (1992: 25, my emphasis). We might ask Aldrich: why are 'task-related' activities necessarily moulded according to an economic model; why do we have to assume that activities are guided *either* by a 'rational' logic *or* a logic of sentiment? Doesn't this return us not to the 1970s but to the 1930s and the Hawthorne studies?[2] Gergen reveals very clearly the Romanticist auspices of Aldrich's language of 'sides': 'chief contribution of the romanticists to the prevailing concept of the person was their rhetorical creation of *the deep interior* . . . the existence of a repository of capacities or characteristics lying deeply within human consciousness' (1992: 208–9).

Romantic accounts can be seen, as Gergen suggests, as 'forms of language, not in themselves derived from what is the case (and) achieving their impact through rhetorical artifice' (1992: 210).[3] Although Gergen takes this argument in a postmodernist direction, we could use it to support ethnomethodology's focus on the properties of actual language use (e.g. in members' descriptions). Indeed, this is implied in Gergen's discussion of 'representation as a communal artifact' (1992: 214).

Nonetheless, Romanticism lives on in organization theory, usually, as in Aldrich (1992), going under the name of 'Interpretivism'. Even Hassard's (1993) valuable critique of paradigmatic thinking founders when he insists on the existence of an Interpretivist Paradigm, concerned with the 'subjective' bases of social order. Hassard's Interpretivist Paradigm turns out to be based on the experiences and/or the viewpoints of the participants. It appears to leave no space for what people are *doing* as opposed to what they may be thinking or feeling, because its focus is on beliefs or cognitive processes rather than practices.[4]

Similarly, Czarniawska-Joerges (1992) retains a Romantic standpoint, calling for 'an interpretation of organizational processes from the standpoint of the actors involved' (1992: 4).[5] While recognizing the context-boundedness or indexicality of accounts (1992: 123, 136), she still wants to treat accounts as depicting organizational realities: 'actor's accounts are representative . . . (they) reveal a "reality outside" as seen by the speakers' (1992: 136–7).

Vulgar deconstruction

> Unfortunately it is possible to take the idea of freeplay of signifiers as a pretext
> for endless interpretative games, without the necessity to pay regard to
> standards of logic, or ideas of truth. (Linstead, 1993: 54)

If Romanticism reflects a pre-modern, nineteenth-century focus on
'experience' and 'meaning', vulgar deconstruction draws upon the apparent
license of late twentieth-century postmodern thought. Along these lines,
Jeffcutt (1993: 30-1) has argued for a deconstruction of the 'romantic
humanism' present in organizational ethnographies which privilege the
(narrator's account of the) voices of 'the organizationally disadvantaged'
(1993: 30).

Such a focus on the narrative construction of our texts may be an
emancipating activity. This is what I sought to argue in *Reading Castaneda*
(Silverman, 1975). However, when carried on too much or too far, it can
produce what Linstead calls 'the endless interpretive games' that he labels
'vulgar deconstruction'. Linstead cites Derrida (1976: 158) on the need to use
all the instruments of classical description. As Linstead puts it:

> Derrida works with sustained care and meticulous attention to his texts at the
> highest analytical level, and any paradoxical positions he is able to expose are
> invariably hard-won through the rigorous exercise of those tools which created
> the very positions which he overturns. (1993: 55)

Linstead has, in my view, identified a real danger lurking in the appeal of
deconstruction. Cheap linguistic games may be translated as navel-gazing and,
thereby, produce the conditions for a dialogue of the deaf between themselves
and the community (see Silverman, 1993: Ch. 8). For instance, when Jeffcutt,
following Clifford and Marcus (1986) calls for 'experimental writing' in the
narration of organizational ethnographies (1993: 38), he may get more than he
bargains for. In particular, experimental writers need to be reminded of
Kafka's caution about the modernist experiments in which he participated in
the early years of the twentieth century.

Kafka's (1961) wonderful short story 'Investigations of a Dog' creates a
marvellous image of 'Airdogs' *(Lufthunde)* who, like many European
intellectuals, get above themselves. However, in this case, this is a literal
transcendence – the Airdogs float on cushions above the ground, surveying the
world from on high, yet cut off from any contact with it (so cut off that Kafka's
doggy investigator wonders how they manage to reproduce themselves!).

In the same way, the Land Surveyor called K in Kafka's (1957) novel *The
Castle*, who tries to get direct access to the mysterious castle, only succeeds in
over-reaching himself. As Erich Heller (1974) has pointed out, *hubris* is the
fate of those who get above themselves.[6] As Hammersley puts it: 'The idea that
writing is a means of changing the world directly is a fantasy, one which
reflects intellectuals' characteristic over-estimation of their own socio-

historical significance' (1995: 94-5). In part, my resistance to the reflexive turn is also, inevitably, aesthetic. Many years ago, I remember a research student who used to make visiting speakers flounder by asking them: 'how would you apply your own analysis to the text that you have just presented?' As they wriggled, I wriggled too – but not from intellectual difficulty but rather from distaste for this sort of wordplay which appeared to make a not very articulate student into a profound thinker.

Moreover, this student and the many texts of the 1980s that invited us to peer behind the curtain of social science narratives or even set out to construct new literary forms (Mulkay, 1985; Woolgar, 1988), may not have been so original after all. In the eighteenth century, Denis Diderot was already inventing a novel (*Jacques le Fataliste*) precisely directed at deconstructing the tropes of author, character and plot. And, of course, the dialogic form of Socrates anticipated contemporary social science by more than two millennia.[7]

This is not to deny that sometimes it is useful to draw from historical precedents. However, a less than thoughtful repetition of past ploys is hardly to be viewed as the latest breakthrough in social science. Moreover, when it comes to certain rhetorical moves – for instance, not just the construction of social science texts as dialogues but as, say, poetry (e.g. Richardson, 1994) – am I alone in experiencing distaste and even despair?[8]

Clarity

It is worth underlining the kind of 'meticulous attention' to texts that Linstead finds in Derrida. So, in Linstead's reading, we must not treat the crisis of representation as meaning that 'anything goes'. Analytic rigour and expressive clarity are not, therefore, to be dismissed as modernist hangovers (see also Hammersley, 1995: 19).

By contrast to the grand claims of experimental writing, a more modest form of social science seeks to convince the reader on the basis of its evidence rather than on rhetorical flourishes. As some contemporary organization theorists have suggested, such a move need not be backward looking. For instance, note the critique of relativism and incommensurability by Reed (1993: 179-81) and Parker's (1993: 208)[9] neo-Popperian support for 'a dialogue based on mutual respect and the willingness to have one's views altered'.[10]

Like Kafka, another product of Habsburg Europe, Ludwig Wittgenstein, provides the appropriate cautionary message. Wittgenstein was engaged in a passionate search for clarity. His *Tractatus Logico-Philosophicus* was a delicate attempt to establish the bounds of sense by distinguishing what could be said sensibly from what could not. As he wrote in his preface to the *Tractatus*: 'The whole sense of the book might be summed up in the following words: what can be said at all can be said clearly, and what we cannot talk about we must pass over in silence' (1971: 3). This 'minimalist' aesthetic is reflected in the building he designed for his sister which, like the *Tractatus*, was, on the surface, unadorned and purely functional (see Monk, 1990). Although Wittgenstein was later to abandon the pursuit of a crystal clear propositional language, 'clarity' remained his continuing watchword. In his later writings, Wittgenstein pursued clarity through what he referred to as a rigorous intellectual 'hygiene'. This involved asking a very precise set of questions about a preconceived set of phenomena:

> We feel as if we had to *penetrate* phenomena: our investigation, however, is directed not towards phenomena, but, as one might say, towards the '*possibilities*' of phenomena. We remind ourselves, that is to say, of the *kind of statement* that we make about phenomena. (1968: para. 90)

Wittgenstein's new 'phenomena' were grounded in everyday language rather than 'logic' but the pursuit of clarity remained his aim. In all his work, that clarity was to be found by a form of self-restraint which rejected both flamboyant style and the appeal of unanswerable questions (or questions which could only be answered by how one lived).

Of course, as Janik and Toulmin (1973) and Monk (1990) remind us, Wittgenstein was writing in the context of a particular cultural and political constellation. His dislike for the uneconomical use of concepts paralleled the distaste of many contemporary Viennese intellectuals for the baroque and mystifying linguistic forms of the disintegrating Habsburg Empire of the early 1900s. After the First World War, Karl Popper pursued the fight for clarity of expression within the German-speaking world. In this context, Popper had little time for the convoluted Hegelianism of the Frankfurt School. As he writes:

> Some of the famous leaders of German sociology who do their intellectual best . . . are nevertheless, I believe, simply talking trivialities in high-sounding language, as they were taught. They teach this to their students, who are dissatisfied, yet do the same. (1976: 296)

Popper demonstrates this critique by providing a passage of Adorno which, *à la* Wright Mills, he then reduces to a few lines. For Popper, the intellectual's pursuit of what he calls 'critical reason' demands clarity: 'One has to train oneself constantly to write and to speak in a clear and simple language. Every thought should be formulated as clearly and simply as possible. This can only be achieved by hard work' (1976: 292).

But Wittgenstein's project (for clarity, against *kitsch*) finds echoes in many thinkers who, unlike Popper, are very detached from turn of the century Vienna. In the middle of the nineteenth century, Gustave Flaubert was also attacking *kitsch* through his critique of the political pretensions and flowery style of the contemporary novel and his demand for a novel of aesthetic forms.[11] Neither Wittgenstein, nor Popper or Flaubert exemplify the dry, narrow persona of the caricatured 'Positivist'. Instead, in my view, they point towards an aesthetic in which one passionately commits oneself to both beauty and truth. As Polyani notes, although all acts of understanding involve the personal participation of the knower: 'this does not make our understanding *subjective*. Comprehension is neither an arbitrary act nor a passive experience, but a responsible act claiming universal validity' (1964: xiii). Polyani tells us that a passion and responsibility is involved in all scientific endeavours. Science pursues an aesthetics of beauty found in its commitment to clarity. At the same time, clarity advances side by side with the search for truth, constrained by the cautious pursuit of validation. Such caution implies a minimalist aesthetic for organizational studies. As against the flamboyant but unoriginal 'experiments' of new literary forms, I suggest we treat the propositional language of science not as a straitjacket but as the basis of a dialogue with each other and the wider community. Clarity in our writing and economy in our use of concepts does not indicate, *contra* Barthes (1968), a tacit commitment to a specific bourgeois order. Rather, following Polyani, it expresses a timeless, passionate commitment to beauty and truth.[12]

The aesthetics of the micro order

Wittgenstein's German-speaking contemporary, Walter Benjamin, seems to have been fascinated by differences between apparently minor objects. Hannah Arendt tells us that:

> Benjamin had a passion for small, even minute things. For him the size of an object was in an inverse ratio to its significance . . . The smaller the object, the more likely it seemed that it could contain in the most concentrated form everything else. (1970: 11-12)

Apparently, Benjamin carried around with him notebooks containing quotations from daily living which he regarded as 'pearls' or 'coral': 'On occasion he read from them aloud, showed them around like items from a choice and precious collection' (Arendt, 1970: 45).[13]

Organizational ethnographers face a temptation to ignore Benjamin's 'pearls' and 'coral'. 'So what did you find out?' we are asked. And, if we are not careful, we recount the moving or shocking story told to us by an interviewee or observed in the 'field'. The danger is that such an answer mistakes what is immediately newsworthy for what is important. Indeed, its very sense of newsworthiness reflects the priorities not of science but of the mass media or of interpersonal gossip. So we succumb to the appeal of the trite and neglect the profound. Journalists, gossips or poets all have their functions. But can't we do better, or at least differently, as organization theorists?

The kind of temperament required to take pleasure and find reward in such an organization theory must separate itself off from many of the messages that are all around us in the world narrated to us by the mass media. That world demands immediate gratification in the form of simple narratives containing exciting 'incidents'. It has no time to gaze around, no desire to take pleasure in the unremarkable, no ability to view without background sounds or to listen without distracting images.

Today, two writers seem to me to pursue Benjamin's and Flaubert's aesthetic. Milan Kundera has attempted to unpick the modern world's version of 'authentic' experience in the stirring parades of Soviet Eastern Europe and the 'revealing' biography or chat-show interview of the contemporary media. For Kundera, East and West offer two versions of kitsch dressed up in different clothes (see Atkinson and Silverman, 1997).

Like Wittgenstein and Kundera, Nicholson Baker has refused to accept the prevailing version of the 'big' question. Baker's (1996) essays on apparently tiny topics from the history of punctuation to the aesthetics of nail-clippings may infuriate some readers. However, behind such seeming trivia lies what I take to be a serious intent – to seek clarity in place of our often empty accounts of bigger, more spectacular issues. A reviewer of Baker's book writes that 'the ordinary, in Baker's world, is easily strange enough' (Winder, 1996). This catches the Wittgensteinian thrust of Baker's project, underlined by his injunction to us to 'pursue truth, not rarity. The atypical can fend for itself' ('Rarity', in Baker, 1996). Baker's essays refuse to take a great analytic sweep, collecting together many phenomena under a single head. Rather beauty and truth can be found in a project which carefully notes apparently minor differences. As Wittgenstein once remarked to a student:

> No, I don't think I would get on with Hegel. Hegel seems to me to be always wanting to say that things which look different are really the same. Whereas my interest is in showing that things which look the same are really different. I was thinking of using as a motto for my book a quotation from *King Lear*: 'I'll teach you differences'. (Drury, 1984: 157)

A counter-aesthetic also occasionally surfaces in movies. I love the kind of cinema with the absence of narrative thrust and the attention to detail that we find, for instance, in Rohmer's *Claire's Knee*. Or the positively ethnographic pursuit of the 'boring' features of the world in Tavernier's *L327*, a police story almost without arrests or car chases but with a strong focus on the routines of police work as we see Parisian drug cops spending most of the time sitting in their offices, 'cooking' their official reports.[14]

Such movies require a certain discipline from their audience just as scientific work is, in a dual sense, disciplinary. So the organization theorist, like the moviegoer at a Tavernier or a Rohmer film, must forgo the temptation to seek the instant gratifications trumpeted all around. But this does not mean that such a theorist is reduced to a mere technician. Rosen (1976) tells us that classical composers at the end of the eighteenth century were able to develop their own identities and surprise their audiences by both respecting and playing with musical form. Similarly, we owe it to our audiences to surprise them by inviting them, with great clarity, to look anew at the world they already know.

And we owe it to ourselves to respect the discipline (in both senses) as well as the power of social science.

The aesthetics of the mundane

Following Schutz (1962) and Wittgenstein (1968), ethnomethodology and conversation analysis can properly claim to be the major contemporary social science traditions oriented to what I would call the aesthetics of the mundane. Unfortunately, the reception of these traditions by organization theory has been somewhat spotty. The dialogue has not been helped by Garfinkel's (1967) daunting prose or by misunderstandings of ethnomethodology by some writers on organizations.[15]

The beginnings of a helpful mutual dialogue is fortunately available in a recent text (Boden, 1994). As Boden shows, ethnomethodology shares with some organization theory a focus on unearthing everyday skills. Following Turner: 'much of human life is pursued, not by the application of logic, but through the acquisition and application of *skills*' (1992: 59; my emphasis). As Turner implies, the most useful opposition to rational models is not the Romanticist focus on 'deep interiors' but on the skills of organizational practices. By means of a focus on these skills, including (dare we say) their institutional 'functions', the prevailing view of paradigmatic oppositions is threatened and a space cleared for a fruitful dialogue with practitioners (see Silverman, 1996: Chs 1 and 10).

Heritage's standard text shows how conversation analysis offers a method for identifying such skills (1984: 241-4). The method involves three assumptions:

1   *The structural organization of talk*: talk exhibits stable, organized patterns, demonstrably oriented to by the participants. These patterns 'stand independently of the psychological or other characteristics of particular speakers' (Heritage, 1984: 241). This has two important implications. First, it is illegitimate and unnecessary to explain that organization by appealing to the presumed psychological or other characteristics of particular speakers. Second, nonetheless, to understand organizations in action, it is always necessary to examine the local activities through which speakers assemble the 'here and now' meaning of their talk (as both 'context-dependent' and 'context-renewing'). So, while a concern with the social organization of talk rules out analysts' speculations about mental phenomena like 'minds', 'intentions' and 'motives', it demands an analysis of how members attend to these and other matters.

2   *Sequential organization:* 'a speaker's action is *context-shaped* in that its contribution to an on-going sequence of actions cannot adequately be understood except by reference to its context . . . in which it participates' (Heritage, 1984: 242). However, this context is addressed by CA largely in

terms of the preceding sequence of talk: 'in this sense, the context of a next action is repeatedly renewed with every current action' (Heritage, 1984: 242).

3   *The empirical grounding of analysis*: the first two properties need to be identified in precise analyses of detailed transcripts. It is therefore necessary to avoid premature theory-construction and the 'idealization' of research material which uses only general, non-detailed characterizations.

Heritage sums up these assumptions as follows:

> Specifically, analysis is strongly 'data-driven' – developed from phenomena which are in various ways evidenced in the data of interaction. Correspondingly, there is a strong bias against *a priori* speculation about the orientations and motives of speakers and in favour of detailed examination of conversationalists' actual actions. Thus the empirical conduct of speakers is treated as the central resource out of which analysis may develop. (1984: 243)

In practice, Heritage adds, this means that it must be demonstrated that the regularities described 'are produced and oriented to by the participants as normatively oriented-to grounds for inference and action' (1984: 244). Further, deviant cases, in which such regularities are absent must be identified and analyzed.[16]

Consonant with the earlier tone of this chapter, ethnomethodology and CA demand cautious theorising based upon a bottom-up approach. This implies the kind of 'theoretical minimalism' demanded by Gubrium and Holstein:

> Rather than elaborately theorizing the relationship between organizations, interpretive practice and the characterization of self from the top down, we document from the bottom up participants own 'theory work' or practical reasoning (Garfinkel, 1967) about self in the varied settings where this occurs (1994: 686).

What makes an interaction 'organizational'?

Much CA examines ordinary, or casual, conversation. The readers of this book will be mainly concerned with activities occurring in organizational settings. What contribution can CA make to the analysis of such settings?

The first point to note is that CA tells us that what is organizational or institutional about an interaction cannot be taken for granted. As Maynard and Clayman (1991) argue:

> Conversation analysts . . . (are) concerned that using terms such as 'doctor's office', 'courtroom', 'police department', 'school room', and the like, to characterise settings . . . can obscure much of what occurs within those settings . . . For this reason, conversation analysts rarely rely on ethnographic data and

instead examine if and how interactants themselves reveal an orientation to institutional or other contexts. (1991: 406–7)

This means, as Drew and Heritage point out, that, while one can do 'institutional work' on a home telephone, not everything said at work is specifically 'institutional': 'Thus the institutionality of an interaction is not determined by its setting. Rather, interaction is institutional insofar as participants' institutional or professional identities are somehow made relevant to the work activities in which they are engaged' (1992: 3–4).

The question that then arises is how we demonstrate that 'relevance'. Schegloff (1992) has suggested that this is a basic methodological issue. It causes two problems which he calls 'relevance' and 'procedural consequentiality'. These two problems are set out below:

Relevance: 'the problem of showing from the details of the talk or other conduct in the materials that we are analyzing that those aspects of the scene are what the parties are oriented to' (Schegloff, 1992: 110). The problem arises because people can describe themselves and others in multiple ways (Sacks, 1992). This problem, as Schegloff shows, is simply disregarded in social scientific accounts which rely on statistical correlations to 'demonstrate' the relevance of some such description. Instead, we need to demonstrate that participants are currently oriented to such descriptions.

Procedural consequentiality: A demonstration that our descriptions of persons and settings are currently relevant for participants is not enough. We must also show how these features are 'procedurally consequential' for the talk: 'How does the fact that the talk is being conducted in some setting (e.g. 'the hospital') issue in any consequence for the shape, form, trajectory, content, or character of the interaction that the parties conduct? And what is the mechanism by which the context-so-understood has determinate consequences for the talk' (Schegloff, 1992: 111).

Schegloff gives two examples. First, he looks at how a particular laboratory study sought to demonstrate something about how people 'repair' mistakes in talk. He shows that, in this study, only the subject was allowed to talk. Hence many features which arise in whether such repairs should be done by self or other (given that there is a preference for self-repair) were unavailable. Thus it will not do to characterize the context as a 'laboratory setting' because other features (only one person talking) can be shown to have more procedural consequentiality.

Schegloff's second example is taken from an interview between George Bush and Dan Rather in the 1988 US election campaign. The interview became famous because of the apparent 'row' or confrontation between the two men. Schegloff shows that such features were noticeable because Bush refused to co-operate in producing a central feature of 'interviews', i.e. that they consist of question–answer sequences where one party asks the questions and the other holds off speaking until a recognizable question has been posed (Silverman, 1973). The implication is that we cannot describe what went on as occurring in the context of an interview. Instead, interactions only become interviews (and cease to be interviews) through the cooperative activity of the participants.

As Schegloff argues, these examples show that the issue of determining context is not a once-and-for-all affair because parties have to continue to work at co-producing some context. Equally, we cannot explain people's behaviour as a 'response' to some context when that context is actively constructed (and re-constructed). The point is made elegantly by Drew and Heritage (1992):

> CA researchers cannot take 'context' for granted nor may they treat it as determined in advance and independent of the participants' own activities. Instead, 'context' and identity have to be treated as inherently locally produced, incrementally developed and, by extension, as transformable at any moment. Given these constraints, analysts who wish to depict the distinctively 'institutional' character of some stretch of talk cannot be satisfied with showing that institutional talk exhibits aggregates and/or distributions of actions that are distinctive from ordinary conversation. They must rather demonstrate that the participants constructed their conduct over its course – turn by responsive turn – so as progressively to constitute . . . the occasion of their talk, together with their own social roles in it, as having some distinctively institutional character. (1992: 21)

By basing research on tapes of naturally occurring activities, we are in a better position to address Schegloff's two problems because such data can reveal how social contexts are constituted on a turn-by-turn basis.[17] Let me concretize this discussion by showing how organizational members often proceed cautiously upon the process of this constitution.

Cautiousness in organizational talk

In everyday conversation, Maynard (1991) has noted that conversationalists may seek to elicit an opinion from someone else before making their own statement. Maynard gives the example below:

Extract 1 (Maynard, 1991: 459)

1	Bob:	Have you ever heard anything about wire wheels?
2	Al:	They can be a real pain. They you know they go outta line and--
3	Bob:	Yeah the-- if ya get a flat you hafta take it to a special place ta get the
4		flat repaired.
5	Al:	Uh—why's that?

Notice how Bob's report (lines 3–4) is preceded by an earlier sequence. Maynard suggests a number of functions of this 'pre-sequence' (Schegloff,

1980). First, it allows Bob to monitor Al's opinions and knowledge on the topic before delivering his own views. Second, Bob can then modify his statement to take account of Al's opinions or even delay further such a statement by asking further questions of Al. Third, because Bob aligns himself with Al's preferred 'complaint' (about wire wheels), his statement is given in an 'hospitable environment' which implicates Al. Finally, this means that it will be difficult (although not impossible) for Al subsequently to dispute Bob's statement.

Maynard calls such sequences a Perspective Display Sequence (or PDS). The PDS is 'a device by which one party can produce a report or opinion after first soliciting a recipient's perspective' (1991: 464). Typically, a PDS will have three parts: a question from A, an answer by B and a statement by A.

Using data from a paediatric clinic for children referred for developmental difficulties, Maynard (1991) notes how, like Bob, physicians often seek to elicit an opinion from a parent before making their own diagnosis-statement. The extract below is one such example:

Extract 2 (Maynard, 1991: 468)

1	Dr E:	What do you see? as—as his difficulty?
2	Mrs C:	Mainly his uhm-- the fact that he doesn't understand everything and
3		also the fact that his speech is very hard to understand what he's
4		saying, lots of time.
5	Dr E:	Right.
6	Dr E:	Do you have any ideas WHY it is? are you-- do you?
7	Mrs C:	No.
8	Dr E:	Okay I think you know I think we BASICALLY in some ways agree
9		with you, insofar as we think that D's MAIN problem, you know,
10		DOES involve you know LANGuage.

As Maynard points out, doctors are expected to deliver diagnoses. Often, however, when the diagnosis is bad, they may expect some resistance from their patients. This may be particularly true of paediatrics where mothers are accorded special knowledge and competence in assessing their child's condition. The function of the PDS in such an institutional context is that it seeks to align the mother to the upcoming diagnosis. Notice how Dr E's statement on lines 8-10 begins by expressing agreement with Mrs C's perspective but then reformulates it from 'speech' to 'language'. Mrs C has now been implicated in what will turn out to be the announcement of bad news.

Maynard concludes that the PDS has a special function in circumstances requiring *caution*. In ordinary conversations, this may explain why it is seen most frequently in conversations between strangers or acquaintances where the person about to deliver an opinion is unlikely to know about the other person's views.[18]

As Bergmann (1992) suggests, psychiatric intake interviews may also be a site where we can expect expressive caution, foreshadowing 'delicate' matters. Bergmann notes that a recurrent feature of such interviews is that patients are not directly interrogated. Instead, the psychiatrist proceeds by proffering information he has received or impressions he has reached and the patient responds *without having been asked a question*. For instance:

Extract 3 (Bergmann, 1992: 138)

```
1   D:    Doctor Hollman told me something like you were running across the
2         street (not so completely dressed) or something like that
3   P:    (h)yes: that's:– I am a child of God; =
4               = I am his child
```

In Extract 3, notice how D's assertions are very unspecific. By saying 'not so completely dressed' rather than 'naked', Bergmann notes that D makes use of the rhetorical form of 'litotes'. Litotes allows one to speak without specifying what one is talking about. It also serves as an invitation to name or further specify the referred-to object without the doctor having to say why he has topicalised it.

We can see the function of litotes more clearly if we note that 'not so completely dressed' is down-graded twice through D's use of 'something like'. Litotes and down-grades imply what Bergmann calls 'caution' and 'discretion'. Such caution functions to mark an upcoming 'delicate' object.[19]

However, the management of delicacy is not confined to medical encounters. For instance, Clayman (1992) characterizes TV news interviewing as a site for much 'expressive caution' given that news interviewers are supposed to be neutral or objective. Clayman investigates how interviewers shift footing when they come on to relatively controversial opinion statements. Look at the interviewer's utterance in Extract 4, line 4, below:

Extract 4 (Clayman 5) [Meet the Press 12/8/85] (IV = Interviewer)

```
1   IV:   Senator, (0.5) uh: President Reagan's elected thirteen months ago: an
2         enormous landslide.
3         (0.8)
4   IV:   It is s::aid that his programs are in trouble.
```

In lines 1–2, a footing is constructed whereby IV is the author of a factual statement. However, at line 4, the footing shifts to what 'it is said'. As Clayman suggests, such a formulation indicates that IV is no longer the author of the assertion. This serves to mark the item as possibly 'controversial' and to preserve IV's position of 'neutrality' towards such matters. Once more, expressive caution is being used to mark and manage 'delicate' items.

In HIV-test counselling, counsellors (Cs) often receive minimal response from patients (Ps) to detailed information and advice about such topics as the difference between HIV and AIDS, safer sex and the psychological consequences of hearing the test result (see Silverman, 1996). Sometimes, when Ps do offer a response to advice, it is negative (see Extract 7 below).

Given the problems of silence or resistance, the data suggest a number of strategies that professionals can use to stabilise advice-giving. For instance, in Extract 5 below, implied advice can be packaged in the form of a question about a client's personal dispositions:

Extract 5 (US2) [B39 B1]

```
1   C:   now, as far as you're- as far as safer sex is concerned, hh because you have
2        been in a twelve or whatever month relationship with this person, how
3        would you feel about putting the condoms back on?
4   P:   I'd prefer not to actually, um.
5   C:   and how does she feel?
6   P:   well the same way.
7        (0.3)
8   C:   awr:ighdy.
```

The advantage of this strategy is two-fold. First, because questions are part of an adjacency-pair of question and answer (Sacks, Schegloff and Jefferson, 1974), some sort of recognizable answer can be expected. Second, resistance by the answerer to the advice implied in the question need not be threatening to further pursuit of the topic precisely because it is ambiguous whether advice has been given in the first place.

Let me now move on to another interactional solution to the instability of advice-giving. As with framing advice as a question, it plays with the ambiguity of how a minimal client response might be heard. In this case, the issue is advice which is packaged to allow multiple responses to be managed.

As I show elsewhere (Silverman, 1996), personalized advice-giving requires far stronger uptake to stabilize itself than does information-delivery. So, if a set of turns are hearable as perhaps information-delivery, then they can follow one another without any difficulty, given only an occasional response-token from the other party. I refer to this as an Advice as Information Sequence or AIS.

The following data from a British clinic shows how the AIS works. It involves 'advice' about pregnancy to a female client:

Extract 6 (UK1) [SW-2.8A]

```
1   C:   (0.8) Uh:m the other a:spect that I must cover with you as far as the fact
2        that you're fema:le .hhh is: (.) with (.) any females who're having the test
3        if the test is positive .hhh we do tend to advi:se against becoming pregnant.
4        (0.4)
5   P:   Mm [hm.
6   C:   ...[Uh::m having said that (0.8) the statistics are showing about a one in
7        six risk to baby.=t- It depends on whether: that person is an optimist or a
8        pessimist you know as to how they look on that. .hhhh So if a woman
9        really wants a chi:ld (.) then we advise her becoming pregnant sooner (.)
```

10		rather than leaving it.
11		(.)
12	P:	Mm hm=

In Extract 6, C begins by aligning P to the next topic by invoking P's gender, allowing C to appeal to one of the category-bound activities associated with that gender (i.e. 'becoming pregnant', line 5). This activity is embedded in what is hearable as a piece of advice bearing on a fundamental matter ('we do tend to advi:se against becoming pregnant').

However, note P's very limited uptake of the advice. After a 0.4 second pause, she simply produces the utterance 'mm hm'. This sort of response token works only as a continuer; it does not indicate any uptake of the advice. Yet C continues her flow of talk in an undisturbed way, overlapping with P's response token and going on to produce a modified piece of advice on the same topic. Once again, this elicits only a response token from P.

Here is, presumably, an important body of advice. Although it receives very limited acknowledgments, possibly indicating passive resistance (Heritage and Sefi, 1992), no interactional difficulties are observed. How can this be? By contrast, in Extract 7 below, a client's 2.7 second pause after advice is given is treated by C as highly implicative of resistance to advice about condoms:

Extract 7 (US2) [B42A1] (continued)

1	C:	.hhh um (0.7) works >bedder< if you use `em all the ti:me.
2		(2.7)
3	P:	it's the heat of the mo:ment sometimes.=
4	C:	=tch .hh (0.5) n'kay, and then we'll ta:lk about tha:t, too:.

Note here how P's response is followed by C extracting himself from further immediate discussion of the topic by an agenda-statement. Given this, how can advice-giving proceed smoothly with only minimal response-tokens from P in Extract 6?

I suggest that the character of the communication in Extract 6 is hearably much more ambiguous than in Extract 7. First, there is not a complete fit between the categories used in the 'advice' and the advice-recipient. Although P is identified as 'female' (and thus someone who may become pregnant), she has not had her HIV-test yet and, indeed, may not even decide to have one. Thus, when C invokes the category 'the test is positive' (line 4), this links her advice to a category that P does not now (and may never) occupy. This means that it is hearable as the advice C 'would give' if certain things were to happen to the client (i.e. as conditional advice). Such a tentative formulation of a situation which might be appropriate to someone but not necessarily the client has been identified in HIV counselling as a 'proposal of the situation' or POTS device (Kinnell and Maynard, 1996).

Given the implied non-relevance of the 'advice' to P's *present* situation, what C says about pregnancy is hearable not as personalised advice at all but as information-about-the-kind-of-advice-we-give-to-people-in-this-clinic. This way of hearing C's utterance is further strengthened by her preface to it: namely 'we do tend to advi:se', where the use of 'we' and 'tend' imply a general policy rather than recipient-designed, personal advice for this client. So what C says about pregnancy is doubly hearable as information about advice rather than unambiguous personal advice.

This has crucial implications for uptake. Given that what C is saying is hearable as information, P need only offer minimal response tokens to maintain the format. Moreover, apparent 'advice' about a highly sensitive topic can proceed in a way that manages the delicacy of what is being said.

So the AIS works by shielding both C and P from the implications of non-uptake of advice, given that such non-uptake is highly likely where the 'advice' has been delivered without any attempt by C to discover P's perspective about a presumably sensitive matter. In this environment, C's response tokens need *not* be heard as the implicit resistance that Heritage and Sefi (1992) suggest. On the contrary, they are hearable as sustaining information-about-the-kind-of-advice-we-give-to-people-in-this-clinic. Hence, through the AIS, everything can proceed smoothly and C can safely complete her counselling agenda.

The AIS is a powerful device which manages the potentially difficult interactional problems of advice-giving and advice-reception about presumably delicate topics. It constitutes the professional as a mere reporter on the-advice-we-give-in-this-clinic rather than as a potentially intrusive personal advice-giver. It allows the client to be defined as an acceptably passive recipient of information about the kinds of things that other people get told (or that she may get told in future). Finally, and most significantly, it overcomes the potentially damaging local implications of minimal client uptake which would arise if C's could be heard to be giving clear-cut advice.

Finally, it must be stressed that that we have not been concerned here with logical ambiguities of the kind that normative communication textbooks may criticise. Such ambiguities are usually identified without reference to sequential organization with the aim of 'getting language into shape'. Instead, we have followed Sacks' concern with what he calls 'sequential ambiguity'. As he puts it:

> Now when I talk of 'ambiguity', there's some special attention needed to the way I want to use it here. One tends to think about 'ambiguity' that, e.g. a word could mean this or that, or that it could mean this, that, or God only knows what else. The sort of ambiguity that I'm interested in specifically is 'sequentialized ambiguity', where the issue is what sort of thing should go next, turning on what this thing might have been. (1992: 671)

Following Sacks, we have been examining how clients can inspect what an utterance by a professional might mean in order to establish 'what sort of thing should go next'. In addition, we have shown how professionals might monitor that 'next' in producing a further turn. Unlike logicians or philosophers, these practical actors do not usually treat ambiguity as a 'problem' in need of a 'solution' (see Wittgenstein, 1969). This method suggests that both students of communication and practitioners should avoid treating 'ambiguities' as problems in need of solutions. Instead, by playing with ambiguities, both practitioners and clients manage difficult interpersonal relations while displaying considerable interactional skills.

Conclusion

Ethnomethodology and CA possess the capacity to surprise us by making a lot out of a little. As I have suggested, there is an aesthetic here which works hand in hand with a focus on the detail of micro-orders. Part of what seems to be required is the kind of self-restraint we find in the later Wittgenstein, coupled with the detailed attention to the local 'quiddity' of organizational processes found in Garfinkel (1967).

Conversation analysis pursues Garfinkel's path through cumulative observations rather than ironic 'demonstrations'. Of course, Garfinkel's strategy is not the only one available to the organization theorist. Consonant with my commitment to an end of the war between competing paradigms, I suggest that what is called for is a *partnership* between CA and other kinds of organization studies. The terms of this partnership might turn on a division of labour organized around the questions we are seeking to answer. CA is particularly strong in identifying locally organized phenomena through its pursuit of 'how' questions. Once such phenomena have been identified, we are on far more secure ground to pursue 'why' questions. At this *later* stage, we may usefully employ the more familiar strategies of organization research – macro and micro, structural and ethnographic, quantitative and qualitative. Such a modest proposal would seek to establish the pursuit of the aesthetics of the mundane as the *first* but not the *only* step in the analysis of organizations.

Notes

1   Parts of this chapter are revised versions of Silverman (1996 and 1997).
2   Aldrich also makes the common assumption that open-ended interviews are central to all paradigms which reject functionalism: 'to study organizations an analyst must . . . understand its organizations as members do. In practice, this means conducting unstructured interviews, doing fieldwork (and) participant observation' (1992: 25). For further discussion of the limits of the interview method, see Silverman (1993: Ch. 5).
3   Organizational charters provide fruitful data for work on organizational rhetorics (see Dingwall and Strong, 1985; and Meyer and Rowan, 1977).
4   Hassard (1993) attempts to define paradigm spaces through:
    1 *Subject matter*, e.g. social facts, behaviour, definitions.
    2 *Methodology*, e.g. quantitative or qualitative.
    3 *Meta-theory*.

Hassard adapts Burrell and Morgan (1979) to distinguish four schools:

	Order	**Conflict**
Objective	FUNCTIONALIST	RADICAL STRUCTURALIST
Social Organization		
Subjective	INTERPRETIVIST	RADICAL HUMANIST

(adapted from Hassard, 1993: 66).

5   To be fair, she does recognize that actors' 'standpoints' do not speak for themselves but have to be 'collected and retold by a researcher' (Czarniawska-Joerges, 1992: 4).

6   'The German for it (Land Surveyor) is *Landvermesser*, and its verbal associations are manifold . . . (it) alludes to *Vermessenheit* (hubris); to the adjective *vermessen*, audacious; to the verb *sich vermessen*, commit an act of spiritual pride, and also apply the wrong measure, make a mistake in measurement' (Heller, 1974: 123).

7   This is not to claim that all writers who explore new literary forms are unaware of this history. Rather I would argue that they fail to make the case that they can achieve any more than previous scholars.

8   As Paul Acourt (personal correspondence, 1996) has commented about such 'poetry': 'the *motive* may be honourable (to dispel difference and give voice to the Other) but the *result* is typically the establishment of yet another layer of difference in the realm of discourse' (personal correspondence).

9   The debate is carried further into the consideration of agency and structure by Knights (1997) and Reed (1997). Parker's call for dialogue (which echoes rather ironically Lyotard's post-Wittgensteinian (Lyotard, 1984: 63–4) call for a language gaming which retains some idea of justice and eschews the 'terrorism' which allows people to be knocked out of the 'game') has been extended (Parker, 1995a) although his own willingness to have his views altered has been called into question by those who responded to his 'egoistic tantrum' (Carter, 1995; Clegg, 1995; Jackson, 1995; Willmott, 1997).

10   Of course, this is *not* to say that all postmodern ideas necessarily fail the test of clarity and rigour. Indeed, I entirely agree with Linstead's (personal communication) suggestion that ethnomethodology and at least some postmodernists share 'a close attention to detail, a suspicion of romanticism . . . (and) a material concern with technique'.

11   See Flaubert's *Dictionary of Received Ideas*, discussed in Silverman (1989).

12   Of course, Polanyi's position is inevitably not itself scientific but political. Following Popper, I believe that the critical debate of science is our best alternative to violence (Popper, 1976: 292). Equally, one might argue that the examples of Soviet or Aryan 'science' provide a terrible warning of the dangers of introducing what Popper calls 'a sociology of knowledge' approach into our interrogation of science. Ultimately, what should matter is whether a statement is true not who its author is or what interest (s)he 'represents'.

13   Arendt reports Benjamin's admiration for two grains of wheat in a museum on which a kindred soul had inscribed the complete Shema Israel: Benjamin's 'delight that two grains of wheat should contain . . . the very essence of Judaism, tiniest essence appearing on tiniest entity, from which in both cases everything else originates' (1970: 11–12).

14   Arendt reports that, to Walter Benjamin, 'reality manifested itself most directly in the proverbs and idioms of everyday language' (1970: 15).

15 Interestingly enough, both Czarniawska-Joerges and Hassard, while sympathetic to ethnomethodology, appear to misunderstand it. Thus Hassard claims to have completed an 'ethnomethodological' analysis of Fire Service work (1993: 98), but the main source of his data was open-ended interviews, more appropriate to a romanticist project. Czarniawska-Joerges claims that 'organization-specific life differs from everyday life' (1992: 120), arguing that organizational activities are less taken-for-granted, rules are more explicit and understandings more local. But all these claims need to be demonstrated. To demonstrate them, ethnomethodologists would argue that we need detailed studies of everyday interaction to give us a baseline and transcripts of talk in 'organizational' settings to show us continuities and departures from this baseline (see Schegloff, 1991, 1992). Thus the specific contribution of ethnomethodology is *not* to romantic versions of the actor but to the detailed study of organizational practices.

16 See Silverman (1993: Ch. 7) for a further discussion of the role of deviant-case analysis in relation to the validity of field research.

17 Of course, this need not mean that CA cannot be combined with more conventional means like ethnography. Drew and Heritage stress the *complementarity* of such methods, particularly when tape-recording is difficult (1992: 60, fn. 4). Equally, a fruitful division of labour may develop where CA research, which seeks to explore 'how' the context is constituted is followed by a range of other approaches able to answer 'why' questions (see Silverman and Gubrium, 1994).

18 In the paediatric setting discussed, the functions of the PDS are obvious:

> By adducing a display of their recipients' knowledge or beliefs, clinicians can potentially deliver the news in a hospitable conversational environment, confirm the parents' understanding, coimplicate their perspective in the news delivery, and thereby present assessments in a publicly affirmative and nonconflicting manner. (Maynard, 1991: 484)

19 Bergmann notes that one function of such 'indirectness' is that it allows D to catch P 'lying'. Having elicited P's version, D can produce further information which undercuts P's account. Bergmann also refuses to accept that we should assume that certain topics are intrinsically 'delicate' or 'embarrassing'. As Bergmann remarks:

> By describing something with caution and discretion, this 'something' is turned into a matter which is in need of being formulated cautiously and discreetly. Viewed sociologically, there is not first an embarrassing, delicate, morally dubious event . . . instead, the delicate . . . character of an event is constituted by the very act of talking about it cautiously and discreetly. (1992: 154)

References

Aldrich, H.E. (1992) 'Incommensurable paradigms? Vital signs from three perspectives', in M. Reed and M. Hughes (eds), *Rethinking Organization: Directions in Organization Theory and Analysis*. London: Sage. pp. 17–45.

Arendt, H, (1970) 'Walter Benjamin: 1892-1940', in W. Benjamin, *Illuminations*. London: Jonathan Cape. pp. 1–58

Atkinson, P. and Silverman, D. (1997) 'Kundera's *Immortality*: the interview society and the invention of self', *Qualitative Inquiry*, 3 (3) 304–25.

Baker, N. (1996) *The Size of Thoughts*. London: Chatto.

Barthes, R. (1968) *Writing Degree Zero*, trans. Susan Sontag. New York: Hill and Wang.

Bergmann, J. (1992) 'Veiled morality: notes on discretion in psychiatry', in P. Drew and J. Heritage (eds), *Talk at Work*. Cambridge: Cambridge University Press.

Boden, D. (1994) *The Business of Talk: Organizations in Action*. Cambridge: Polity Press.

Burrell, W.G. and Morgan, G. (1979) *Sociological Paradigms and Organizational Analysis*. London: Heinemann.

Carter, P. (1995) 'Writing the wrongs', in *Organization Studies*, 16, (4) 573–5.

Clayman, S.C. (1992) 'Footing in the achievement of neutrality: the case of news-interview discourse', in P. Drew and J. Heritage (eds), *Talk at Work*. Cambridge: Cambridge University Press

Clegg, S. (1995) 'Parker's mood', *Organization Studies*, 16 (4) 565–71.

Clifford, J. and Marcus, G.E. (eds) (1986) *Writing Ethnography: The Poetics and Politics of Ethnography*. Berkeley, CA: University of California Press.

Czarniawska-Joerges, B. (1992) *Exploring Complex Organizations: A Cultural Perspective*. London: Sage.

Derrida, J. (1976) *Of Grammatology*. Baltimore, MA: Johns Hopkins University Press.

Dingwall, R. and Strong P.M. (1985) 'The interactional study of organizations: a critique and a reformulation', *Urban Life*, 14: 205–31.

Donaldson, L. (1985) *In Defence of Organization Theory: A Reply to the Critics*. Cambridge: Cambridge University Press.

Drew, P. and Heritage, J. (1992) 'Analyzing talk at work', in P. Drew and J. Heritage (eds), *Talk at Work*. Cambridge: Cambridge University Press. pp. 3–65.

Drury, M. (1984) 'Conversations with Wittgenstein', in R. Rhees (ed.), *Recollections of Wittgenstein*. Oxford: Oxford University Press.

Garfinkel, H. (1967) *Studies in Ethnomethodology*. Englewood Cliffs, NJ: Prentice-Hall.

Gergen, K. (1992) 'Organization theory in the postmodern era', in M. Reed and M. Hughes (eds), *Rethinking Organization: Directions in Organization Theory and Analysis*. London: Sage. pp. 207–26.

Gubrium, J.F. and Holstein, J.A. (1994) 'Grounding the postmodern self', *Sociological Quarterly*, 35 (4): 685–703.

Hammersley, M. (1995) *The Politics of Social Research*. London: Sage.

Hassard, J. (1993) *Sociology and Organization Theory: Positivism, Paradigms and Postmodernity*. Cambridge: Cambridge University Press.

Hassard, J. and Parker, M. (eds) (1993) *Postmodernism and Organizations*. London: Sage.

Heller, E. (1974) *Kafka*. London: Fontana.

Heritage, J. (1984) *Garfinkel and Ethnomethodology*. Cambridge: Polity Press

Heritage, J. and Sefi, S. (1992) 'Dilemmas of advice: aspects of the delivery and reception of advice in interactions between health visitors and first time mothers', in P. Drew and J. Heritage (eds), *Talk at Work*, Cambridge: Cambridge University Press. pp. 359–417.

Jackson, N. (1995) 'To write or not to right?' *Organization Studies*, 16 (4): 571–3.

Janik, A. and Toulmin, S. (1973) *Wittgenstein's Vienna*. New York: Simon & Schuster.

Jeffcutt, P. (1993) 'From interpretation to representation', in J. Hassard and M. Parker (eds), *Postmodernism and Organizations*. London: Sage. pp. 25–48.

Kafka, F. (1957) *The Castle*. Harmondsworth: Penguin.

Kafka, F. (1961) 'Investigations of a dog', in *Metamorphosis and Other Stories*. Harmondsworth: Penguin.

Kinnell, A.M. and Maynard, D.W. (1996) 'The delivery and receipt of safer sex advice in pre-test counseling sessions for HIV and AIDS', *Journal of Contemporary Ethnography*, 24 (4): 405–37.

Knights, D. (1997) 'Organization theory in the age of deconstruction: dualism, gender and postmodernism revisited', *Organization Studies*, 18 (1): 1–20.

Linstead, S. (1993) 'Deconstruction in the study of organizations', in J. Hassard and M. Parker (eds), *Postmodernism and Organizations*. London: Sage. pp. 49–70.

Lyotard, J-F. (1984) *The Postmodern Condition: A Report on Knowledge*. Manchester: University of Manchester Press.

Maynard, D.W. (1991) 'Interaction and asymmetry in clinical discourse', *American Journal of Sociology*, 97 (2): 448–95.

Maynard, D.W. and Clayman, S. (1991) 'The diversity of ethnomethodology', *Annual Review of Sociology*, 17: 385–418.

Meyer, J.W. and Rowan, B. (1977) 'Institutionalized organizations: formal structures as myth and ceremony' *American Journal of Sociology*, 83: 340–63.

Monk, R. (1990) *Ludwig Wittgenstein: The Duty of Genius*. London: Vintage.

Morgan, G. (1986) *Images of Organization*. Beverly Hills, CA: Sage.

Mulkay, M. (1985) *The Word and the World: Explorations in the Form of Sociological Analysis*. London: George Allen and Unwin.

Parker, M. (1993) 'Life after Jean-Francois', in J. Hassard and M. Parker (eds), *Postmodernism and Organizations*. London: Sage. pp. 204–12.

Parker, M. (1995a) 'Critique in the name of what? Postmodernism and critical approaches to organization', *Organization Studies*, 16 (4) 553–64.

Parker, M. (1995b) 'Response: angry young man has egoistic tantrum', *Organization Studies*, 16 (4): 575–8.

Polyani, M. (1964) *Personal Knowledge: Towards a Post-Critical Philosophy*. New York: Harper and Row.

Popper, K. (1976) 'The logic of the sciences' and 'Reason or revolution', in T.G. Adorno, *The Positivist Dispute in German Sociology*. trans. G. Adey and A. Frisby. London: Heinemann. pp. 87–104, 288–300.

Reed, M. (1992) 'Introduction', in M. Reed and M. Hughes (eds), *Rethinking Organization: Directions in Organization Theory and Analysis*. London: Sage. pp. 1–16.

Reed, M. (1993) 'Organizations and modernity: continuity and discontinuity in organization theory', in J. Hassard and M. Parker (eds), *Postmodernism and Organizations*. London: Sage. pp. 163–82.

Reed, M. (1997) 'In defence of duality and dualism: agency and structure in organizational analysis', *Organization Studies*, 18 (1): 21–42.

Reed, M. and Hughes, M. (eds) (1992) *Rethinking Organization: New Directions in Organization Theory and Analysis*. London: Sage.

Richardson, L. (1994) 'Nine poems: marriage and the family', *Journal of Contemporary Ethnography*, 23 (1): 3–13.

Rorty, R. (1992) 'Cosmopolitanism without emancipation: a response to Lyotard', in S. Lash and J. Friedman, *Modernity and Identity*. Oxford: Blackwell. pp. 57–71.

Rosen, C. (1976) *The Romantic Style: Haydn, Beethoven, Mozart*. London: Faber and Faber.

Sacks, H. (1992) *Lectures on Conversation*, 2 vols, ed. Gail Jefferson with an introduction by Emmanuel Schegloff. Oxford: Blackwell.

Sacks, H., Schegloff, E. and Jefferson, G. (1974) 'A simplest systematics for the organization of turn-taking in conversation', *Language*, 50 (4): 696–735.

Schegloff, E.A. (1980) 'Preliminaries to preliminaries: "can I ask you a question?"', *Sociological Inquiry*, 50 (3/4): 104–52.

Schegloff, E.A. (1991) 'Reflections on talk and social structure', in D. Boden and D. Zimmerman (eds), *Talk and Social Structure: Studies in Ethnomethodology and Conversation Analysis*. Cambridge: Polity Press. pp. 44–70.

Schegloff, E.A. (1992) 'On talk and its institutional occasions', in P. Drew and J. Heritage (eds), *Talk at Work*. Cambridge: Cambridge University Press. pp. 101–36.

Schutz, A. (1962) *Collected Papers I: The Problem of Social Reality*. The Hague: Martinus Nijhoff.

Silverman, D. (1970) *The Theory of Organizations*. London: Heinemann.

Silverman, D. (1973) 'Interview talk: bringing off a research instrument', *Sociology*, 7 (1): 31–48.

Silverman, D. (1975) *Reading Castaneda: A Prologue to the Social Sciences*. London: Routledge.

Silverman, D. (1989) 'The impossible dreams of reformism and romanticism', in J. Gubrium and D. Silverman (eds), *The Politics of Field Research: Sociology Beyond Enlightenment*. London: Sage. pp 30–48.

Silverman, D. (1993) *Interpreting Qualitative Data: Methods for Analyzing Talk, Text and Interaction*. London: Sage.

Silverman, D. (1996) *Discourses of Counselling: HIV Counselling as Social Interaction*. London: Sage.

Silverman, D. (ed.) (1997) *Qualitative Research: Theory, Method and Practice*. London: Sage.

Silverman, D. and Gubrium, J. (1994) 'Competing strategies for analyzing the contexts of social interaction', *Sociological Inquiry*, 64 (2): 179–98.

Turner, B. (1992) 'The symbolic understanding of organizations', in M. Reed and M. Hughes (eds), *Rethinking Organization: Directions in Organization Theory and Analysis*. London: Sage. pp. 46–66.

Weber, M. (1949) *Methodology of the Social Sciences*. New York: Free Press.

Willmott, H. (1997) 'Outing organizational analysts: some reflections upon Parker's tantrum', *Organization*, 4 (2): 255–68.

Winder, R. (1996) 'Swizzles, gruntlings and lumber pie', *San Francisco Chronicle*, 14 April.

Wittgenstein, L. (1968) *Philosophical Investigations*. Oxford: Basil Blackwell.

Wittgenstein, L. (1969) *On Certainty*. trans. D. Paul and G.E.M. Anscombe. New York: Harper and Row.

Wittgenstein, L. (1971) *Tractatus Logico-Philosophicus*. London: Routledge.

Woolgar, S. (ed.) (1988) *Knowledge and Reflexivity*. London: Sage.

Appendix: transcription conventions

The examples printed in this chapter embody an effort to have the spelling of the words roughly indicate how they were produced. Often this involves a departure from standard orthography. Otherwise:

-->   Arrows in the margin point to the lines of transcript relevant to the point being made in the text.

( )	Empty parentheses indicate talk too obscure to transcribe. Words or letters inside such parentheses indicate the transcriber's best estimate of what is being said.
hhh	The letter 'h' is used to indicate hearable aspiration, its length roughly proportional to the number of 'h's. If preceded by a dot, the aspiration is in-breath. Aspiration internal to a word is enclosed in parentheses. Otherwise 'h's may indicate anything from ordinary breathing to sighing to laughing, etc.
[	Left-side brackets indicate where overlapping talk begins.
]	Right-side brackets indicate where overlapping talk ends, or marks alignments within a continuing stream of overlapping talk.
((looks))	Words in double parentheses indicate transcriber's comments, not transcriptions.
(0.8)	Numbers in parentheses indicate periods of silence, in tenths of a second.
:::	Colons indicate a lengthening of the sound just preceding them, proportional to the number of colons.
becau-	A hyphen indicates an abrupt cut-off or self-interruption of the sound in progress indicated by the preceding letter(s) (the example here represents a self-interrupted 'because').
<u>He</u> says	Underlining indicates stress or emphasis.
dr^ink	A 'hat' or circumflex accent symbol indicates a marked pitch rise.
=	Equal signs (ordinarily at the end of one line and the start of an ensuing one) indicate a 'latched' relationship – no silence at all between them.

Fuller glossaries may be found in Sacks, Schegloff and Jefferson (1974: 731–4).

PART 4

CRAFTING AN AESTHETIC

7

Observer Versus Audience

Hugo Letiche

Proximal perceptions – 1

This is a chapter about *dancing* and *writing*, about *perception* and the rendering of perception. The aesthetic is approached here as ontic, an exploration of being, through ethnography and as a phenomenological theme. Specifically, I have asked myself what sort of text can result from looking at the Nederlands Dans Theatre (NDT) in such a way? Because this is not a positivist text, other questions such as: 'How did the NDT organize the researcher's vision – how did "they" determine what the "eye" saw?' and 'What did the authorial subject – "I"- make of the NDT and why?' are important.

To begin with another question: why the choice of the NDT? To some degree the answer is to be found in the dance group's myth(s). In a nation characterized by order and neatness – translated by Shell into highly successful planning via business 'scenarios' and by Unilever into long-term effectiveness – the NDT is a rebel. The NDT supposedly favours risk above certainty, personality above conformity, the unknown above the safe, experiment before predictability. The NDT is both successful – having conquered (and lost?) New York several times – and aesthetic. In the NDT we can see a certain myth of The Netherlands embodied: individualistic, creative, stylish, international, different. Intellectually speaking, the NDT can be seen to symbolize a principal humanist ambition: the dancers' (virtually) unadorned bodies (can be thought to) reveal basic definitions of human-ness. Dance can be construed to be anthropologically revelatory, as if a proximal demonstration of human-ness is being given via the body. Dancers' bodies can be voluptuous or taut, tightly or loosely controlled, light or earthy, ethereal or primal, proximate or distant, sexy or cold. For some '. . . culture wreaks utter tyranny on individual bodies. Bodies . . . are disciplined, molded and rearranged by dominant powers, which simultaneously promote the illusion that people are 'free' to construct their own bodies' (Bordo, 1991); and for others the body is 'protean, capable of slipping out of any fixed role or voice, entering . . . into a flux of endless complication and creative movement' (Suleiman, 1986).

The body can be interpreted to be a site of resistance where dancers and their audiences are directly or vicariously empowered; where they create their own social identities by manipulating and reworking the oppressive body images produced by the dominant ideology. Or else the body can be conceptualized as a mere reflection of prevailing cultural modelling, slavishly displaying current attitudes to the male/female relationship, to work and/or to freedom. What, then, were the characteristics of the dancers as I saw them, as they were shown to me, as I am able to represent them? Assuming that bodies are ensembles of social meaning, what statements were corporeally being made? What are the NDT's espoused definitions of physicality? What portrayal of bodily human-ness can I identify?

My encounter with the NDT took place in the studios and theatre of the dance group in The Hague. In the studios I observed the two house choreographers: Hans van Manen was creating a new dance, *Polish Pieces*, (1995) and Jiri Kylian was rehearsing the troupe. I also saw instances of the dancers working on their own on various projects. Furthermore, I saw all three NDT groups perform in the theatre, as well as the dancers' annual Workshop, wherein they show off their own choreographies. Ethnography, based on *participant* observation, was not possible: I am too old and too overweight to be mistaken by anyone for a dancer. A combination of observing and interviewing had to suffice. The normal problem of translating such fieldwork notes into text is all the more acute in the case of dance. Dance just does not translate easily into text. Choreographers don't even use text to record their work, they simply video everything. Descriptions which appear very literal are possible:

> The stage is well-lighted when seven women enter. Some of the women are wearing white walking shorts with kneesocks, others are in white pants, and all are wearing white tops. Across the width and depth of the stage dancers take random positions, paces away from one another. They face the audience looking straight ahead, arms at their sides – a group of women simply being themselves. A car being started is heard; the car moves away, then there is a crash, followed by police and ambulance sirens. When the sound of sirens dies in the distance, the women begin speaking and moving, the stage is awash in words and gestures. Over the sweeping view of the stage the dancers turn and pivot, some take steps, all of them talk, gesture, but none leave the given spheres in which they began . . . (Barr, 1979)

But these are not very revealing. There is no clear unambiguous language in which to record dancers' movement. As Sally Banes states: 'Dance is unlike verbal language, for it usually creates meaning only vaguely' (1994: 28). Description of dance quickly becomes interpretative, if not downright evaluative. Hans van Manen (NDT house choreographer) argues: 'Dance expresses dance, and nothing further.' But for him 'knitting steps together' into dances, is a matter of erotica, (non-)literary intentions, creativity, risk taking, human-ness, the priority of form above content (van Manen, 1992). Thus, writing about dance is a passport to associative interpreting. Through a vocabulary of movement, dancers make use of their bodies to create aesthetic experiences. Metalevel writing about choreography may prioritize being above meaning and experience above narrative, but most texts are (wildly) associative. A lot of literature emphasizes choreographers' personal quests to define their own style(s) of movement (Banes, 1977; Banes, 1994; Brown, 1979; Sorell, 1992). Dance is an oral, visual and kinetic experience which is multi-interpretable. From (new) expressionism to formalism, 'the purpose of making dances (may) be simply to make a framework within which we look at movement for its own sake' (Banes, 1977: 15). Thus in writing about dance the connotative takes precedence above the denotative. Text about dance has, I believe, as its purpose the contextualization of performance. One doesn't talk about what actually happens (passes or steps, props or lighting), but one does try to interpret what dance is saying about bodily (physical) being. Dance criticism is, thus, radically proximal, with virtually no distal structure (Cooper and Law, 1995).

In an intellectual tradition, such as ours, which is overwhelmingly distal, objective, abstract, keeping the world at arms length, dance is some kind of 'freak' which is not, and cannot be, absorbed easily into the dominant intellectual discourse. Dance is too direct, the lack of tools and technology too radical, the conceptualizations and concepts far too weak to permit a rational discourse of dance to replace tactical, immediate perception. Dance is an intellectual scandal because it can only be approached experientially. Dance is a concrete physical form of *dasein*: a way of being-in-the-world formed by dancers, space, light and music. Witnessing dance confronts one directly with the Other in relationship to a context. Writing about dance tries to capture this relationship between the Other and the context.

What limits should I place on my effort to convey dance experience in language? Not wanting to pre-judge the connotative context of dance any more than necessary, I have not wanted to make a priori choices about the appropriateness of the one, or the other, prose form. But rejecting the convention of writing in specialist (philosophical, social science) vocabulary, poses the threat of not belonging to any recognizable actor network: i.e. I may produce a reflection on the *dasein* of (NDT) dance, which I cannot legitimate within any intellectual hierarchy. Writing about dance provokes a radical deconstruction of the writer – there are too few cognitive traditions, too little theory, insufficient conventions, to be able to produce a distal text. Either one has to write about the proximal experience of dance, or one has to keep quiet. But the writer, in order to write, has to create a grammar of description: what is worth mentioning, which statements belong in the text, which do not. I developed my criteria in a co-research process with the dancers. Text which made common sense to us both was deemed (potentially) appropriate. My goal was to write about the Other as revealed in dance. Working towards that goal, I have discovered that my experience of Otherness varied strongly between when I observed the dancers in the studio and when I saw them perform (even the same works) in the theatre. Observing dance-being-created was very different from sitting (during a performance) in the audience. Thus, by means of ethnographic research, I was able to explore the differences in the discovery of the Other as perceived in dance, during rehearsals and when in the audience.

Organizing ethnography

I have also made use of (my interpretation of) John Law's formulation of ethnographic methodology to inform my research (Law, 1994). The relationship I draw between the seen and the see-er was guided by Law's criteria for rendering 'organizing' and 'ordering'. On the first level this is appropriate because dance is the 'ordering' and 'organizing' of relationships to the Other via the basic bodily manifestation of presence by the dancer(s) on the basis of (some sort of) choreography. On the second level, the chosen point of view is justified because writing about dance orders and organizes, in language, a relationship to an Other. On both levels, investigation is a communicative process. Dance is immediate interaction; writing about dance renders the immanent nature of that interaction. I believe that the study of dance as an object is exceptionally worthwhile because it forces the writer to abandon *langue du bois* and to wrestle with expression of circumstance.

John Law outlines five criteria for ethnography (Law, 1994). Research is to be symmetrical, non-reductionist, recursive, process oriented and reflexive. By symmetrical, it is meant that all facets of the perceived are treated equally. No facet is 'cause or effect'; nothing is prioritized above anything else. Choreographers, dancers, music, technique (especially lighting and staging), props, costumes, sets and audience, all are determinants. No privileged categories are assumed: any aspect of dance may determine any other. For instance van Manen says that his dance *Squares* (1969) was motivated by constructionist art (Ad Dekkers, Peter Struycken and Bob Nieuwenhuis) translated into a decor enjoining a neon balk square within which everything occurs. The decor, which encloses the ten dancers in a space six by six metres square, is crucial. For van Manen *Squares* begins with a 'sense-less fact': one dancer stands up, holds another back and then lies down. Two dancers sit up, look at each other and lie down again. Likewise, it is a 'sense-less fact' that the two dancers, who lie on a black plateau and glide off it when the plateau is risen from the horizontal to the vertical, always make a bet which one will manage to not fall the longest. The drama of who will fall, and of the dancers staying put longer than the audience would expect, has no meaning but it displays an absolutely necessary exuberance and playfulness that has to be thought-up if dance is to work (van Manen, 1992). No one factor determines the success or the failure of a piece. The constructivist neon square, as well as the square plateau, were successes incorporated in dance to music by Satie. This dance investigated *inter alia*: (i) severely limited space, (ii) the exceptional situation of not having a horizontal floor and (iii) Satie's *blageur* world of irony and nonsense. Satie characterized his own works as *'pieces froides'* and *'avant dernières pensées'*; Cocteau claimed that Satie's 'limpid cadences evoke visions of nude boy dancers silhouetted on a Grecian urn'. Satie's ironical, 'inimitable limpid and melodic style with unconventional harmonies, no meter (no barlines), and irregular rhythm' are a crucial element to the dances (Satie n.d.).

I have assumed no privileged cause: any aspect, to organizing the dance, can be crucial. When van Manen creates a new dance, he has an idea for the start and end points; and has chosen the music. But the actual dance is generated in interaction with the dancers. Van Manen displays a possible beginning for the action; the dancers pick that up and mirror it back again. The dance develops on the basis of what the dancers do with the raw forms with which they are presented. Good dancers never just imitate the choreographer's moves; they internalize what has been indicated, and render it in a personal interpretation which displays individual character. Each dancer has a different build; the choreography is adapted to their individual bodily form. A dance group such as the NDT has a training regime which plays a formative role in the dancers' physical abilities. The NDT combines ballet acuity with modern dance technique. The dancers enact modern dance on the basis of having mastered traditional techniques. Their language of movement is modern dance, but in the dancers' posture and physical form there is an echo of classical dance. The dances are moulded by the special physical quality of the troupe's training. Choreography and the dancers' preferences play a big role; but the dancers' training prefigures anything they attempt at the NDT. All factors operate in relationship with all others, and form a complex pattern of interaction without privileging any one factor.

Secondly, following Law, investigation is to be non-reductionist. Every reductionism assumes the priority of one factor; i.e. it asserts that 'in the last analysis dance really is . . .' Reductionism divides reality into first causes and secondary factors; the former are prioritized and the latter repressed. Thus, the non-symmetry of reductionism leads to dualism. Everything from management's commercial considerations to love relations between dancers can determine event. The success of choreographers can be maximalized via competition – during the late sixties NDT had three house choreographers competing to get their work produced. But choreographer effectiveness can also depend on one dominant figure, as is now the case. Jiri Kylian has, in his twenty years with NDT, produced three distinct very successful idioms:

1   the large ensemble dances of *Sinfonietta* (1977) or *Soldiers Mass* (1980) wherein emotion is conveyed via highly graceful movement and the impact is grounded in shared feelings;

2   the extremely dexterous and aesthetic dances inspired by Australian Aborigine dance (*Stamping Ground*, 1983); and

3   the 'Black and White' dances such as *Silent Cries* (1986), *No More Pay/Petite Mort/Sarabande/Falling Angels/Whereabouts Unknown* (1990s) which are minimalist, not decorative and highly confronting.

Are these changes the product of changing social conditions? The first, perhaps, a reflection of Czech group sentiment, replaced by cosmopolitanism and the celebration of pure movement, only to be superseded by an over-lit stage peopled by dancers dressed in black or white costumes, who strain against the odds to maintain their human-ness, while caught-up in the play of cynical humour. Or perhaps the dancers are more important – the dancer population has shifted dramatically. At present there are virtually no American dancers; the troupe has radically Europeanized. Positions at the NDT are very willed; dancers are willing to adapt to whatever the choreographers want. But, on another level, the NDT achieved in 1987 its dream of having its own theatre, whereby a much larger podium and a variety of new lighting possibilities have broadened the expressive possibilities.

Thirdly, investigation needs to be recursive. What it describes on the individual level, it must also invoke on the group and social levels. Every event must imply (all) others – explanation may seize on a small manageable piece of the whole, but understanding depends on relating the particular to an unending process of events, all of which mirror one another. Dance, thus, is the medium and the outcome of the NDT, the process and the result. Dance creates dance, movement refers to movement. The NDT re-creates constantly an ever altering NDT. Each element of movement implies the identity of the NDT and the troupe's gestalt is an unending series of movements. I aspire to writing a text which is part of the unending links of the dance's rationale – dance is to be translated into language and reflected conceptually, but nonetheless to remain a form of 'dance'. The same process which drives the dance forward is the motor of the research. Just as NDT is dynamic and constantly has to recreate itself the ideas should move rapidly on, from one point to the other, trying to achieve the momentum of dance's logic. Dance is the constant organizing of bodies, movement, decor, music. Dance's ambition is to seize its audience's attention, and to draw it further and further into interaction. The relationship between the researched and researcher needs to be like two mirrors set face to face, which endlessly reflect images back and forth on a variety of different levels.

Next, Law argues that ethnography has to be process oriented – it needs to stress 'verbs' and not 'nouns'. Action and movement, processes and transformations are sought after. At issue is how the NDT makes dance, not static evaluations or judgements. Dancing is more interesting than newspaper reviews telling you 'who danced well' or 'what you should see'. Thus we need to focus, for instance, on van Manen making *Polish Pieces*, and avoid reifying his dance. Dances are actions and process, movement and sound: they are never objects. Dancers transform the movements indicated by the choreographer into event and interaction. Our challenge is to capture the organizing dynamism in our analysis. I experienced dance on an interpretative level; as a play of images and interactions. No text can be made of action (verbs) alone – something or someone has to move in a concrete context for action to exist. 'Verb-ness' captures the vitalism of process. 'Noun-ness' threatens understanding with categorization and rationalization. I have tried to preserve dance as movement, and not let it be debased into so many conceptualizations.

Finally, according to Law, the researcher needs to be reflexive, to reveal his/her involvement in the ethnographic process. As already revealed, the NDT is a mythic organization. It tries to keep matters that way. The NDT wants to project a democratic, cohesive, productive image of itself. I wanted to do research with the NDT because I thought that (i) the dancer/choreographer relationship was more complementary than most other work relationships, (ii) the NDT symbolizes the individualist and nonconformist side to the Dutch culture and (iii) the challenge of abandoning organizational vocabulary for the instability of trying to express myself on dance, was a useful challenge. The question I wanted answered was: is dance an alternative form of interaction, which reveals possibilities of organizing not seen in other situations?

An ethnographic essay on the NDT

'Post' post-histories

As George Marcus notes, all ethnography makes use of the cognitive techniques of Modernism: it focuses on reflexivity, produces a collage of collected materials, is a montage of observations, and is a result of dialogism (informant – researcher, as well as, researcher – reader) (Marcus, 1994). Without these techniques, which are in large measure derived from surrealism, ethnographic prose is impossible. A 'messy' text – for instance polyphonous or parodying 'ethnographic authority' is possible; but ultimately, one either chooses for some form of ethnographic representation or has to abandon the goal of trying to describe any object of study. Since the NDT's dancing reflects what Marcus calls the post-'post' period, modernist text devices are probably appropriate. It may be possible, in ethnographic prose, to reveal postmodern condition(s); but not (on a sustained level) to enact them. The return via reflexivity to consciousness, and the 'subject' in the post-'post' period, makes ethnography (once again) possible. Dance can be divided into classical ballet, modern, postmodern and 'post-postmodern' dance. The NDT's principal choreographer, Jiri Kylian, dismisses the corpus of classical ballet as 'museum exhibits' whose 'art is bad' because it does not 'risk . . . necks and be responsible for the history of the future' (in Conlogue, 1994). Modern dances (such as Cunningham and Balanchine) 'propose that the formal qualities of dance might be reason enough for choreography, and that the purpose of making dances might be simply to make a framework within which we look at movement for its own sake' (Banes, 1977: 15).

When the NDT was formed in 1959 it was not on the basis of a conscious choice for Modern dance. The NDT was born of a dancer rebellion at the Nederlands Ballet (supported by Benjamin Harkarvy, interim artistic director, and Carel Birnie, business director), against the extremely authoritarian leadership of the artistic director (Sonia Gaskell). Sixteen dancers broke away to form the NDT. Resistance and rebellion, idealism and daring characterized the effort. Despite government opposition (unlike the competition, the NDT initially got no subsidies) and sabotage from the established ballet critics, the troupe survived. The goal was to 'dance in freedom'. In 1960 Anna Sokolow, a pupil of Martha Graham, was contracted to come to the help of the NDT by rehearsing two of her dances. One of them, Sokolow's *Rooms* (1955), is a classic in American modern dance. One of the dancers (Jaap Flier) recollects:

> She explained to us that *Rooms* was about people in New York, people that lived in rooms which they almost never left. The loneliness of the big city. I found that so impressive. When you heard such an amazingly inspirational woman in our cold, ice cold [rehearsal space in a] church. The sphere fit her. She found she needed to suffer to make art. You had to believe for the full hundred percent in what you did. In those weeks really amazing things happened. We were enormously influenced via the confrontation with a new style of dance. Suddenly we discovered what it was we were searching for. Don't forget that our plan was merely not to work any more for the Nederlands Ballet. The breach was personal. And the repertoire we had ourselves was really terribly light weight. (in Versteeg, 1987: 29)

Anna Sokolow was a happy choice. Her personal vision fitted what the NDT was to become: 'I hate fixed ideas of what a thing should be, of how it should be done. I don't like imposing rules, because the person, the artist, must do what he feels is right, what he as an individual – feels he must do' (Sokolow, 1979). She defines modern dance in terms of rebellion: 'Do what you feel you are, not what you think you ought to be. Go ahead and be a bastard. Then you can be an artist.' She pushed the dancers to face themselves and admonished the choreographers to know who they were and what they felt. Her visit sparked the first breakthrough for modern dance in Holland. 'Modern dance' had started in America as a breakaway movement but by the late 1950s it had developed styles and theories of its own:

> It used stylized movements and energy levels in legible structures (theme and variations, ABA, and so on) to convey feeling tones and social messages. The choreography was buttressed by expressive elements of theatre such as music, props, special lighting and costumes. The aspirations of modern dance, anti-

academic from the first, were simultaneously primitivist and modernist. Gravity, dissonance, and a potent horizontality of the body were means to describe the stridency of modern life, as choreographers kept one eye on the future while casting the other to the ritual dances of non-Western culture. (Banes, 1977: xiii)

The NDT was committed to the modern dance vocabulary, and to the accompanying quest for an organic language of movement which strives to make authentic personal statements. Modernism had triumphed. In 1962 Glen Tetley joined the NDT, to form with Hans van Manen a modernist choreographic duo, who would (with the help of guest choreographers) determine the NDT's identity up to 1970. During the 1969–70 season the two house choreographers, Glen Tetley and Hans van Manen, became a warring artistic duo. The business manager Carel Birnie took care of everything practical, while the choreographers fought one another to see who would get what performed. Birnie flirted with disaster when he asked his two choreographers to make something together (*Mutations*, 1970) for the annual Holland Festival. To avoid conflict, van Manen and Tetley agreed to divide their efforts; van Manen (who was very interested in film) would film three (new) *pas de deuxs* and Tetley would provide the choreography for the live performance. The combination of naked, filmed *pas de deuxs* from van Manen, and then a parallel sequence (choreography Tetley) performed on stage, created a theatrical spectacle which provoked a world-wide scandal and became an enormous crowd drawer. When performed by the NDT in London, glass fibres were thrown on stage in order to sabotage the performance; in St Louis heavy police protection was needed because the dancers were threatened with death. Gerard Lemaitre on the naked *pas de deuxs*:

> Now such a dance would be old fashioned, but then it was the right thing for NDT to do. I danced three years in *Mutations*; three years every night in my naked ass, but if you are at the top of your success three years isn't long. When we went to America, Anja and I had in each city to rush from the airport to the TV studios to be interviewed. It was fantastic. (Versteeg, 1987: 76)

The conflict between Glen Tetley and Hans van Manen boiled over and both left the NDT. During the 1970s, the democratization movement spread like wildfire through Dutch society, provoking at least some dancers to question the authority of the choreographers. Who were choreographers to determine what should be danced? A new artistic line was born: everything was 'research'. From 1970 to 1975, the NDT tried analytic postmodern dance. The term 'postmodern' dance had emerged in America during the 1960s:

> In the theory of post-modern dance, the choreographer does not apply visual standards to the work. The view is an interior one: movement is not pre-selected for its characteristics but results from certain decisions, goals, plans, schemes, rules, concepts, or problems. Whatever actual movement occurs

during the performance is acceptable as long as the limiting and controlling principles are adhered to. (Kirby, 1975: 3)

According to Kirby, postmodern dance rejects musicality, meaning, characterization, mood and atmosphere; it uses costume, lighting, and objects in purely functional ways (Banes, 1977: xiv). Jaap Flier was the new artistic leader who tried to lead NDT into postmodernism. Lemaitre commented on that period: 'Conversations with Jaap were so strange; things like "I do not drink coffee because coffee is black and black has a bad influence on me" ' (Versteeg, 1987: 78). Flier wrote in a newspaper article on the same period:

> The troupe has now enormous national and international success, but it now faces a crucial choice: to continue along the old lines or to choose for a new path. I think that we need to abandon the classical dance techniques which are still part and parcel of the troupe's know-how, totally to concentrate ourselves on new developments and aesthetics. (Versteeg, 1987: 80)

The 'artistic committee', where dancers consulted with the artistic direction on policy, became the forum for contention. But most of the dancers did not want to abandon their classical dance training, for the *avant garde* adventure. Jaap Flier couldn't convince the dancers to follow him to where he wanted to go. Carel Birnie tried to reassert artistic authority by proposing that teams, composed of a choreographer, composer and designer, would work together as equals to stage productions in light, sound and movement. The dancers responded to the proposal by rebelling, and demanding the restoration of recognizable choreography and programming. Postmodernism was a short-lived interlude, to which Jiri Kylian was hired (1975) to put a stop. Kylian was brought to The Hague as full-time choreographer to rebuild the NDT. Thus (analytic-)postmodern dance came and went. It is remembered as a chaotic interlude between the successes of 1964–70 and those of 1978–95. This is a sample of Kylian's way of thinking:

> . . . for the most part [I] insist on the artist's persuasive ability to create his own world. There's a lot of aggression in [some] dance. A lot of slapping people around the walls because the world is like that. It's a feeble excuse. . . . I am not a child. I know terrible things are being done in Yugoslavia and that knowledge works on my imagination. But there is no need to pass it on in raw or literal form. . . . I think any movement the human body can make is valid . . . you watch, and then you add your fantasy. After that, it is up to the audience. (in Conlogue, 1994)

Kylian's 'post'-postmodernism can also be called postmodern if the definition is based more on Charles Jencks's architectural terminology than on American dance criticism (Jencks, 1987). What Kylian and van Manen are now making for the NDT is 'hybrid, doubly coded, based on fundamental dualities', that is, the dances copy, comment on and negate modern dance (Jencks, 1987: 5).

Sometimes [postmodernism] stems from juxtaposition of new and old . . .
sometimes it is based on the amusing inversion of the old . . . and nearly always
it has something strange about it. In short a highly developed taste for paradox
is characteristic of our time and sensibility. (Jencks, 1987: 6)

Comparing choreography/choreographers

The NDT produces dance, and Hans van Manen has been one of the most
important originators of their material. By comparing what van Manen made
in his modernist period (late 1960s/early 1970s), such as *Squares* (1969) and
Situations (1970), with what he now makes during his 'post' post-period, e.g.
Polish Pieces (1995), the difference in styles can be clarified. As already noted,
Squares can be construed to be based on a couple of constructivist givens: a
(slanted) black square platform and a neon baulk barrier which circumscribes
the platform, define a restricted and unorthodox space for dance. *Situations* is
also based on an unconventional premise: the decor encloses the dancers in an
area eight metres broad, six metres deep and four metres high. This space is
decorated with wallpaper resembling giant graph paper, with a door to the
right of the stage and a large (metric) clock hung high on the back wall. Since
the stage was twelve metres broad, when a dancer came on stage you saw
him/her walk to the decor, open the door and enter. When the door was
opened, a red light went on. Sound was provided by a collage of sound effects
(warfare – bombs, shots, etc. – water, aeroplanes, footsteps and a mosquito). In
Situations, the ten dancers begin together and, thereafter, perform five duos
(man–woman, man–man, man–woman, woman–woman, man–woman). The
dance ends when the man from the last duo opens the door and almost leaves;
five times he almost leaves but returns each time, each time displaying a
different emotion. Van Manen's vocabulary of movement was *Alltagsbewegug*:
that is, based on everyday movement and not dance conventions. Each duo
showed another facet of relationships: power and aggression, sarcasm and
vulnerability, two persons coldly examining one another. One duo is composed
of two solos, the persons have nothing to do with one another: the man is self-
absorbed and the woman aggressive. There's also a duo of 'yes–no–yes–no–
yes–no'. The male homosexual duo ends with one dancer opening the 'fly' of
the other. The dance is based on the juxtaposition of constructivist space
(modern, scientific, rational, linear) and the dancers' efforts at relationships.
The red light and the clock serve as reminders of the technological society. The
inclusion of homosexuality, alienated interaction, incertitude in relationships
(does the man stay or leave, and with what feelings?), all reflect the (then)
growing doubts about norms for interaction. Van Manen created 'clean',
'modern' space, filled with social disquietude and personal restlessness. The
dance displays a growing crisis of the 'individual': how does the 'self' draw
identity from its surroundings when those surroundings are claustrophobic,
sterile, depersonalized? What contact can the pairs achieve, and maintain, in
this environment?

Contrastingly, *Polish Pieces* (1995) takes place in a world 'post' all these questions. The twelve dancers are dressed in virtually luminous tight fitting jump suits; each couple wearing the same colour. Very bright colours were chosen: yellow, blue, purple, green, orange, red. *Polish Pieces* can be broken down into two dances, both performed to the music of Gorecki. The first is very rhythmic and characterized by exceedingly dramatic arm actions generated by the dancers responding to the beat of the music (*Concert for Piano & Chamber Orchestra*, opus 40, 1980). When van Manen was developing the dance with the troupe he would thrust his arms to the left, to the right and then upwards, with all his force and much verve, to show what he wanted. His movements were jerky and assertive. Sometimes van Manen would develop the dance for a while, without the music; just playing with the motions. Then he'd put the tape on again and integrate the movements with the music. The dancers followed van Manen, 'marking' the development of the dance – " 'marking' is what dancers do in rehearsal when they do not want to expend the full amount of energy required for the execution of [the] movement' (Rainer, 1979: 146)]. Van Manen was expressive and powerful in

7.1 *Hans van Manen*

his motions; the dancers hesitant and exploratory. The dancers first have to understand the structure of the movement being proposed, then they internalize the choreography and render the dance as kinesthesia. The choreography has to become sensed motion and movement; bodily action and flow. *Polish Pieces* centres on falling and rising, balance and unbalance, stasis and movement. In *Polish Pieces* the dancers are not just tracing geometric lines in space, they assert active, emphatic, energetic movement. When van Manen develops a new dance (like *Polish Pieces*) with the troupe, the dancers do not know what comes next. He works on the dance bit by bit, only going on to the following few movements when he's satisfied with the previous ones. In the first half of *Polish Pieces* the dancers are depersonalized. They are blotches of dynamic colour and movement, communicating energy and unity. The flow of gestures is dramatic and repetitive; a strong, single motional effect is achieved. The second 'piece' revolves around two *pas de deuxs*. Two couples are in the foreground and four form a background. The couples move past one another, creating a brightly coloured visual effect reminiscent of 'interactive pictures' (stereograms). The second half of the dance tends towards sentimentality. The movement of the two couples is only of limited aesthetic interest; nothing dramatic or deeply involving happens. I see no emotional motivation to their actions. The dance vocabulary is flaccid and decorative. While the costumes and use of colour are high tech, the 'arty' music and feel to the dance remind me of Fred Astaire and Ginger Rogers. But the dancers are neither clearly caricaturing romantic sentimentalism, nor are their movements affectively genuine or powerful. Van Manen's romantic pastiche – the music is Gorecki's *Three Pieces in Old Style for Chamber Orchestra* (1963) – makes me uncomfortable. Is it self-consciously or unintentionally kitsch? Of course van Manen has every right to make his audience uncomfortable, but was this really the intention?

Furthermore, the two halves seem to lack a dramatically evident necessary third movement, which would somehow synthesize the two existing unbalanced portions into a 'whole'. The rhythmic first portion offers a headlong surge of reckless activity, which erases individuality in collective movement and offers a powerful assertion of group cohesion. The second movement appears to be a series of quotes about being 'graceful' – coupled to the visual effects of the brightly coloured costumes, gliding along one another, without coalescing into a clear image or sentiment. Taken together the two halves are so many elements searching for a context.

In contrast, Jiri Kylian's work confronts one with very different stylistic issues. His choreography debut was in 1970 with the Stuttgart Ballet; van Manen had already made *Feestgericht* in 1956 for the Ballet van de Nederlandse Opera. Kylian's *Stoolgame* (1974) comes as close to a constructivist work as anything he's ever done. In it, the stools form a central given; the dancers dance with and around them. But dance and dancers predominate; they master the prop. For instance, the dancers form together a human stool and hold the real stools up in the air. Geometric forms, or objects, are never a basic point of departure for Kylian's choreography. Neither is 'sexual liberation' an important theme. Kylian dates from a different generation from van Manen. Henny Bouman, a member of NDT's artistic/teaching staff during 1961–78 describes how Kylian took charge of the NDT:

The arrival of Jiri was a source of relief. He made the people into dancers again. I saw immediately that he had talent. When I came to work with NDT in 1961 it was a purely classical troupe with a small modern element from Harkarvy and the jazzy ballets from Hans van Manen, who slowly developed more and more towards Modern dance. Of course the troupe was open to new developments, but the basis was clearly classical and there was a lot of dance on ballet slippers. . . . With real modern dance I am not so at home. I was classically trained and could follow the work of Harkarvy and van Manen, but Glen Tetley [an American choreographer who worked with NDT during 1963–70 and had a purely modern dance style] was 'too far gone' for me. I saw his dances and I thought: someone else had better do that, let me stick to the classical basics. I understood that renewal was necessary. NDT wanted to speak its own language and then you have to search for things that others do not have. But it was really difficult for me. Slowly the troupe developed in the direction of Modern dance . . . When the [analytic Postmodern choreographies] came . . . I functioned purely as a teacher for [they] needed technical prowess, to achieve the broad scala of movement they sought without falling on their heads. Thus normal ballet lessons went on. And there were things where the rows had to perform parallel and the movements had to fit precisely in the music. But the [pure postmodern] was something which I couldn't be associated with, I had no idea what to do with it. I gave up, I couldn't help with that. . . . I was happy when Jiri Kylian came. I could finally follow someone. He made it quickly clear

7.2 *Jiri Kylian*

that he was an artistic director who said what he thought. The dancers knew what he wanted of them, thanks to him discipline was reinstated. We'd had a period where the dancers determined what happened and the [artistic] direction accepted it as well. But Jiri accepted no trouble making. His 'yes' was 'yes' and his 'no' was 'no'. You got the feeling that you were really building up something. (Henny Bouman in Versteeg, 1987: 88–9)

Likewise Carel Birnie (Business Director of NDT during 1959–92) observes:

Thanks to Kylian, the dancers want, again, to be masters of the classical technique. The dancers had been shaken up by all the people who had used NDT as their field for experiment – now they wanted to have lessons on ballet shoes again. . . . We're more interested in production than reproduction. The troupe has always accepted that. Only the dancers wanted to retain their roots in classical techniques. (Birnie in de Wal, 1987)

Kylian has never been a constructivist or an *avant garde* postmodernist. His early works for the NDT are aesthetic celebrations of shared meaning. These dances value community, and are clearly modernist in their social optimism. Evidently, solidarity and belonging are possible; the relationship between humans and society can be complementary. This optimist social philosophy, is embodied in *Sinfonietta* (1978), *Psalmensynfonie* (1978), *Soldatenmis* (1980) and *Svadebka* (1982). In all these works the individual exists as member of the group. Each dancer may have his/her specific characteristics of bodily expression, but group expression predominates. In Kylian's ballets, expression is manifest in group action. Often he makes use of the 'canon' effect: first one pair sets off with a movement, then the next, and then the next. There is individuality, but contained within group structure. Kylian's vocabulary of movement is very graceful, a sort of modern romanticism. The arm movements are fluid and dramatic, making strong use of the dancers' hands and arms entangled in one another, placed (for instance) on each other's shoulders with their palms held up open to one another. The movement is often choreographed to take up lots of space; as if human emotion filled the stage. The themes are optimistic – such as in the traditional Russian marriage of *Svadebka*; or take an optimistic turn as in the *Soldatenmis* where Kylian seems to single-handedly reverse the Czech defeats of 1948 and 1968 and to assert the victorious dignity of his countrymen.

The second period in Kylian's work was short lived: *Nomaden* (1981), *Stamping Ground* (1983), *Dreamtime* (1983) and the much later *Whereabouts Unknown* (1993). These dances are even more exuberant than what preceded them. They are linked to Kylian's visit to the Australian Aborigines. In them dancers' movements are freer and even more expansive than in the previous work. Instead of a humanity clutching and holding on to one another (however much solidarity such movement implies, it also hints at sorrow and loneliness), we are confronted with half-human, half-animal forms which spring into altogether unexpected positions. In these dances, Kylian abandoned traditional social expression and opted for insect-like poses and animal-like leaps. His previous dances all played themselves off in European social space; those of the second phase are choreographed for a radically different sort of space. Once again the group and not the individual is the unit of existence, but it's a group where dancers jump over one another and take on poses foreign to normal movement. The social boundaries to gestures of affection, sentiment, and expression which were maintained in the previous work were now replaced by animist experimentation:

> *Whereabouts Unknown* [is] visually and kinetically arresting, it seems a dream picture of man and his philosophical landscape. Set to a variety of music – the spareness of Anton Webern, Steve Reich's percussion, the wispy questioning of Charles Ives – it shows men and women shifting in space with elemental grace and dignity. In the foreground a man draws figures in the sand while the measured dancing of the tribe suggests the formal waves and patterns of nature. It is movement that cuts to the root. (Barnes, 1994)

In 1981–3 this style predominated; then it disappeared, to reappear only once, in 1993. Was it too strongly linked to the Aboriginal inspiration? Did the death of one of the dancers (Karen Tims) shatter Kylian's sense of creative joy? Had the tempo of creative work been too demanding? In any event the style of *Stamping Grounds* wasn't sustained.

A new third period of black–white dances began with *Silent Cries* (1986). 'The virtuoso soft and lyrical partnering' of the earlier period is replaced by themes of death, separation and anguish (Berman, 1994).

> Kylian's style has changed. The peasant earthliness that gave his dancers so much weight has been replaced by spidery silhouettes and a wiry dynamic. There is less lyricism or fluidity within the phrasing of the movement . . . Kylian is more interested today in positions than in flow, and the sunlight in the literal sense has been banished from works where . . . (the) essential and magnificent lighting now creates a world of black and gray. Light intrudes here more than it reveals. (Kisselgoff, 1994)

Silent Cries is based on an extremely intense emotional and physical cohesion between the dancer, Sabine Kupferberg (Kylian's wife), and the music/choreography. The dance is framed around a single prop: a slab of glass, approximately 1.80m high by 1.00m wide, which is partially smeared with white powder. The dancer hangs, moves, rotates around the glass; she wipes arcs of powder clean, becoming more visible to the audience. It is a dance of unusual intensity, about the difficulties of communication.

> The new pieces are very Spartan – stark, very little costuming, very little colour. In fact, I went back to the essentials; music, dance, light and space, which is very complicated. All [of the essentials] are very complicated. But it's actually only dealing with the essential things you need. All the unnecessary things were chucked out. I refer to those works as like those children's

drawings which give you the outlines and you fill in the colouring. I call my [new] ballets 'colouring books'. I expect the public to put in their own colours. I give them basically the outlines. I'm talking about their understanding, their emotional colouring. In that way, I expect a lot of active participation of the audience. (Kylian in Pasles, 1994)

The black and white dances demand precision and concentration. For instance, *As If Never Been* (1992) begins with an apple, let loose on one side of the stage, which moves (on a wire) in a straight line across the stage to strike a dancer on the other side. Costumes, decor and lighting are all black and white; the (green) apples provide the only colour. The dancers dance with the apples between their knees, between their heads and while giving the apples from the one to the other. Kylian made use of surrealist images of apples, such as a large container of apples, dumped onto a ramp, which roll down towards the stage. For me, the effort at symbolism is too strained. This is not dance for dance's sake. While there is humour, there is also overwrought seriousness. For me the philosophical pretensions and the danger of becoming too 'wordy' (literary) dominate. These dances are alternately overblown, in that they try to convey too many ideas, and too understated, in that there's too little dancing. These dances can be seen to be excessively schematic and insufficiently passionate; characterized by too much rationalization and too little drama or emotion. It is the difference between empty motions and rich gestures. In short, are the black and white dances an expressionist success, or a formalist false step? Have the dancers been reduced to a depersonalized resource – resplendent in their technique, but robbed of their own human 'voices'? When I see Kylian in rehearsal, I fear the worst. The balance between creative leadership and *terreur* seems to me to be slanted to the latter. While Kylian likes to stress (in interviews) the 'democracy' of the NDT – there are no soloists, all the dancers are equal – is this 'democracy' based on individuality or levelling? While van Manen's rehearsals are spontaneous and emotional, Kylian's are disciplined and appear (to me, as well as to the dancers) 'pent up'. Kylian's 'perfect posture' – he walks as if his back was absolutely straight – and overly deliberate/mannered gestures make him appear unnatural. There's none of the 'messiness' of van Manen, here. The dancers have to strain to hear what Kylian says and to react to his words. He speaks very quietly and over-politely, giving lots of compliments. He almost never loses his temper, but a mood of anxiety and tension pervades the studio as soon as he takes over. New dancers are in awe of his choreographic brilliance, but after having worked several years with him, dancers discover their inability to relate to him. They cannot find the person Jiri Kylian; they do not know him at all well. Working with him means following his direction. In the black and white dances he has reduced the expressive freedom of the dancers to a minimum. When the black and white dances succeed, such as in *Petite Mort* (1991), they are conceptually ravenous. *Petite Mort* is a dance for six men, six women and six foils (i.e. six eighteenth-century dresses standing on their own).

It deals with those who can grasp the rules and learn to play. It shows the world as a place where brutality and love are equally present. As the curtain opens, each of the six men balances on a rapier, which he skilfully manipulates. He then substitutes a partner for the sword, handling her with equal zeal, but here it is mingled with harmony and tenderness. (Malashenko, 1994)

Petite Mort (to two of Mozart's most famous piano concertos) was sexy and sensual, a *pas de trois* for man, woman and fencing foil. The men were equally enamoured with the foils and the women. It was a completely contemporary critique. (Bleiberg, 1994)

Even the men and women in corsets who throw themselves into the sexually tinged athletics of *Petite Mort* (the title is a French literary term for orgasm) emerge from a shadowy world. It is filled with suspended or free standing hoop skirts, remnants perhaps of dead infantas. (Kisselgoff, 1994)

Petite Mort resembles a complex shell game; wherein it is unclear what is hidden or where. Individual gestures are taboo; the total construction of the movement is what counts. Kylian has denied the dancers their individuality in order to achieve the desired effect. The dance is dynamic, abstract, bodily sculpture. The dancers are elements in a choreographer's complex reflective process of questioning. At the beginning of his rehearsal, Kylian welcomes the dancers, and at the end he thanks them. At no point in between do they possess an independent 'voice'.

Dancers in charge

Text about dance does not have to be choreographer centred. Van Manen and Kylian can be put between brackets and NDT can be seen without them. Once a year the troupe puts on the Dancers' Choreography Workshop without them.[1] The dancers take the theatre over for an evening and produce whatever they can make themselves. In 1995 the Business Manager opened the evening stressing the 'big happy family' of the NDT, which led, he claimed, to the dancers' intense motivation and to the high quality of the evening. Actually, a dance career is short; and choreography is one of the few avenues open to dancers to extend it. Thus, choreography may well meet the expressive needs of the dancer by opening up new artistic possibilities; but it is also one of the few possibilities the dancer has to achieve in dance a sustainable career. Furthermore, limited studio space had led, backstage, more to conflict and tension than to positive feelings. But the auditorium was sold out, and sixteen new short works were put on display. The dance varied from chaotic and pretentious, to good fun and insight.

There was a joyously flippant dance called *Sans Réponse* (choreography Patrick Delcroix), where two male dancers in toga, carrying large empty plastic distilled water bottles shouted 'oui' and 'non' to one another. The dancers exchanged farcical 'blows' with their plastic bottles and used them as percussion instruments, generating a mood of humorous disagreement. *Time an Angel* (choreography by Johan Inger and danced by Jorma Elo and Lisa Brake) opened with a male dancer alone waking up on stage, a bit uncoordinated, to do his morning toilette. A second dancer is thrown over a curtain (centre stage), into the arms of her just 'awakened' friend. He, proud, struts about the stage with her in his arms. But while the 'new day' begins with the pair in agreement, they soon start to disagree. They then move wildly, with very active steps, about the stage. The day (evidently) passes and the woman (literally) closes the curtain. *Wet Horses* (choreography by Jorma Elo, danced by Johan Inger and Elke Schepers) revealed a pair jumping and rolling over one another. Acceptance and conflict is rambunctious; the pair close to animist, physical primitivism. One dance took a prop as an essential given – *Stabat* (choreography by Fabrice Mazliah) centred around dancers who appear and disappear by crawling in and out of washing machines. These were dances centering on the theme of relationships, with lots of expressivity and verve. More profound evocations of emotion were rare – only Ramon Reis's short dance *Renacser* (born again), wherein he danced alone, achieved the sort of intensity needed to sustain serious attention. While Kylian's technique, wherein the dancers move in an expressive but very controlled manner, was evident, the complexity of thematization wasn't. Kylian's both witty and serious humour is epitomized by *Sechs Tanze* (1986) in which a conflict between the sexes is rendered farcical by outrageous movements, and in the context of the Mozart music the satire seems to be directed towards the Baroque itself. When we realize that Kylian 'feel(s) we are the children of the baroque, our real roots are in the baroque time' (Kylian in Pasles, 1994), one senses the deeper cultural criticism implied in the piece. The freshness and spontaneity of the Workshop is its strength and weakness. The dances were convincing in their authenticity and directness, but lacked the cultural echoes and meanings which sustain one's interest in Kylian's work. Dance demands more than mere surface meanings. Kylian's successes are all, at least, double coded: behind the surface textures there are other associations and meanings. This layered structure, when it works, sustains the viewers' interest, and keeps the audience wrestling with what it has seen. The Workshop dances were too straightforward to retain an audience's attention for long.

Another strategy for achieving dancer-led performance is to let experienced dancers take (more) responsibility for their own performances. In addition to NDT-1, the main group comprising 32 dancers, and NDT-2, a younger group approximately half as large, aged from 17 to 21, which are both very choreographer led, there is NDT-3 which is both the newest and the oldest group. NDT-3 was founded in 1991 for dancers older than forty. The history:

> You have to say goodbye to dancers you have loved because they no longer have the required physicality (for your work). But these are sometimes dancers who have a wonderful library of experience. Imagine actors in a similar position, having to stop at 40! The idea of doing something with these dancers came to me one weekend while writing answers to a written interview in which the last

question of all was 'Have you anything else to say?' I liked that question. So the same evening I thought of an ad hoc program with four choreographers and four older dancers personally tied to those choreographers. There was William Forsythe and his ex-wife Alida Chase, myself and my wife [Sabine Kupferberg], Hans van Manen and his long-time friend Gérard Lemaitre and Mats Ek and his brother Niklas. By Monday I had it all organized. Forsythe said it was beginning to seem like Dynasty. (Kylian in Littler, 1994)

The most memorable experience I had while observing the NDT, was watching Gérard Lemaitre of NDT-3 in rehearsal, working on *The Politician/Peeling the Onion* (1993), with choreography by Jennifer Muller. This is a solo work made for Lemaitre. In it, he plays a politician who communicates with showman-like gestures. Progressively he ages, retires, loses importance and becomes more and more insecure. The politician peels off his long coat to reveal a uniform, which he peels off to reveal his golf outfit, which, in turn, he peels off to reveal a black *maillot*, etc. This is the physical element to the 'onion' theme, i.e. of peeling off layer after layer of coverings. The dance starts with the politician behind a speaker's rostrum addressing the 'masses'. Since the dais wasn't available, Lemaitre actually worked from behind one of the Workshop washing machines. In the rehearsal, the changes of clothes were only mimed. The score – music and intermittent 'quotes' from prominent US politicians (Nixon, Reagan, etc.) – came from a video of an earlier performance. Martine van Hamel (also of NDT-3) was there to run the video and make comments, while Gérard Lemaitre danced and I observed. Some points in the choreography have to be timed the same every time – such as when Lemaitre smashes his fist on the rostrum at a crescendo. But most of the time, the dancer slows down or speeds up, depending on how he chooses to emphasize different aspects of the part. Lemaitre's force of personality – the fantastic play of imitating a politician's gestures, whereby the motions are at once 'real' and 'simulated', 'evoked' and 'deconstructed' was riveting. It was a masterpiece of meaning and anti-meaning – suggestion and denial. The typical breaks in rehearsing, to question how one could best do something, did not interfere with the flow but affirmed the complexity of the performer's identity. Being in the studio at rehearsal is comparable to being on stage with the dancer during performance: it re-invoked the spirit of the happening of the sixties. When I later saw *The Politician* in the theatre, I witnessed a successful performance without the layers of complexity and changing identity I had seen at rehearsal. In the theatre, the dance was two-dimensional – a good portrayal 'up there before the audience' in a 'there and then' mode, without the 'here and now' impact of the rehearsal. The intimacy of rehearsal, where the dancer explicitly chose different rhythms and interpretations, was lost. Lemaitre sees the dancer's task as being to perform what the choreographer makes for him/her. He makes no claim for dancer-driven performance. *The Politician* was made for him, it makes marvellous use of his abilities as a mimic, and he obviously identifies with the work: 'I'd kill anyone else who danced it' (personal communication). Dance seen from a mature dancer's perspective is a universe of possibilities, with myriad interpretations, conceivable movements and bodily experiments. Dance can be conceived of as *différance*, unlike bodies, disparate emotions, diverse tempos, dissimilar significances, varying audiences. Or dance can be reified, in a rush for performativity. Normally, the dance audience is supposed to see an illusion of effortlessness, and not dancers at work. *Différance* is subsumed to the myth: 'order', 'truth' and 'purpose' take over, dancer individuality disappears.

7.3 *Polish Pieces*

Van Manen comments:

> Kylian's dancers are too often faceless and nameless. Kylian argues 'dancers should be like an empty vase wherein you can put the most beautiful flowers. Or even better like buds from which every flower in the world can open out. . . . When you work the presence of dancers can brake your creativity, your spirit and ideas are often far further than theirs. Sometimes you hit the right note. There are performers whose breadth is unbound; but who need someone else to let them be expressive.' (Versteeg, 1987: 121)

Van Manen has rejoined the NDT (1988) and now faces the constant challenge of producing new dances. While there was some cynicism amongst dancers and reviewers, in the late 1980s/early 1990s, that van Manen was an extraordinarily sympathetic 'has-been', he fooled them all and came back, in the late 1990s, with some very strong work. In fact, *Polish Pieces* was a triumph. Kylian has gone from the American success of *Sinfonietta* (1978), which established him as a name to be reckoned with, to being damned as 'Eurotrash' when he returned to New York in 1987 with dances like *Silent Cries*. But in 1994, Kylian brought NDT back to New York to BAM (the Brooklyn Academy of Music – an *avant garde* address). His 'black and white' programme was enthusiastically welcomed. He had triumphed again. NDT-2 and NDT-3 performances were very well received. Kylian was back – his work reaffirmed as belonging to the world's very best.

The manager

The NDT exists because Carel Birnie (the NDT's Business Manager from 1959 to 1992) led a group of dancers into rebellion against the arbitrary and authoritarian regime of Sonia Gaskell, the 'lady' of Dutch ballet. Dutch politicians tried to destroy the NDT because they wanted to merge the Dutch ballet groups to make them less expensive, more efficient and easier to administer. Newspaper reviewers, especially from Amsterdam, tried to write the troupe to death with negative commentary because it had 'broken the rules'. NDT was born of a late 1950s rebellion against a political and media elite which wanted to control the arts as it saw fit. Thanks to Carel Birnie's stubbornness, charm and sympathetic brilliance the NDT survived, but it almost didn't, more or less going broke in 1961. But Birnie always came up with a foreign tour, a sponsor or an audience-winning project to keep NDT afloat. Nonetheless, Carel Birnie almost didn't survive at the NDT. In 1975, at the height of the conflict around the NDT's artistic future – the fight about what 'post'-post was going to be – Birnie was fired by the Board of Directors. He'd argued for a two-person artistic leadership, on the model of van Manen and Tetley, composed of Jiri Kylian and Jennifer Muller. The dancers were opposed; they and Kylian wanted 'one-man artistic leadership'. Innumerable meetings, countless conflicts and one emotional explosion too many led the Board to fire Birnie. Public opinion forced the Board to reverse itself. Birnie returned to the NDT but Kylian got (virtually) exclusive power over artistic matters (Versteeg, 1987). Birnie had his job back, but had nothing to do:

> After they'd beheaded me in 1975 I felt, of course, that my wings had been clipped. A different artistic policy had come which I didn't really agree with. But I wanted to stay with NDT. I was bored to death. There was little risk-taking then, no adventure (Versteeg, 1987: 93).

Birnie found a challenge to keep him busy – funding and building a theatre uniquely for (NDT) dance. And Birnie filled the new auditorium with his commercial acumen:

> A ballet troupe dances in two ways: in the first place on stage, for the spectators of the art form – and in the second place back stage. . . . For the first sort of dancing you need a different sort of people than for the second. The first sort you find at auditions, at ballet schools, you hire them overseas, . . . Really good dancers are few and far between, but the supply out of which you have to choose the best is enormous. . . . The second sort is even in shorter supply. Really they aren't to be found; but they can suddenly appear. The business manager of NDT Carel Birnie is such a 'devil's magician'. Of course he didn't create NDT all on his own . . . but without his stubborn commitment NDT would have closed down long ago. (de Wal, 1987: 8)

Birnie produced friction; he generated tension for adventure and risk taking. He brought creative people together and conjured up the conditions for them to work together. His spirit of rebellion, creativity and business success was crucial to NDT's identity and development.

Proximal perceptions – 2

Is the NDT the story of repression's victory and rebellion's loss? I began the research with some very different ideas. I thought that the dancers negotiated meaning with the choreographers and music; I thought that dance was a product of artistic community. The NDT has always tried to let its audience believe this. The NDT's current business manager (who succeeded Birnie) repeated these ideas when he welcomed a full hall to the 1995 Workshop. But in Kylian's triumph, there is little or no room for (almost) anyone else. His dances, when effective, are powerfully focused emotional statements where emotion is portrayed by dancers who are doing what they are told to do. One dancer commented to me that he had learned more about Kylian's ideas by reading the newspaper interviews in America than he'd ever learned directly from him (personal communication). Van Manen's expressive creativity appeals much more to me than does Kylian's discipline. But Kylian has made many more successful dances during the last fifteen years than has van Manen. I'd estimate Kylian's success rate at approximately one third of his output. He makes boring work, which I find pointless, pretentious and shallow – my personal hates are *L'Enfant et les Sortileges* (1984) and *L'Histoire du Soldat* (1986). But his successes are brilliant: riveting moments of theatre where one's attention never wavers and where his vocabulary of movement takes possession of one's consciousness.

What effect did the principles I took on board to guide the ethnography have on the research? I have tried to problematize the success and failure of the dances without assuming the primacy of choreography, music, dancers, management, props, lighting, decor. The NDT's present success depends on combining all these elements into outstanding productions. Van Manen chooses to follow a loose regime, where the choreographer, composer, dancer, decor designer, costume maker and lighting director all have an independent role. Kylian follows a tighter strategy, wherein all elements are obviously subsumed to his will. But how much you should see Kylian as the real author of the choreographies and how much the cultural environment is the key determinant is ambiguous. Kylian's black and white dances: do they merely reflect the power of technology (made manifest in the lighting) to overwhelm the human, or do they add a commentary? His retreat into fleeting figures, who run from one brightly lit spot on stage to another, without getting anywhere or achieving anything: what do they convey? The abandonment of group sentiment and community, the stress on the frantic, crazed individual: isn't this a typical product of the *zeitgeist*? Does Kylian's identification of our times with the Baroque deny all of the modernisms lying between the Baroque and ourselves? Kylian doesn't discuss any of this openly, neither with his dancers nor with us. But is van Manen's nostalgia for modernism a real alternative? Can it do more than muster up a few moments of visually gratifying and kinesthetically pleasurable experience?

I tried to avoid reductionism, never to give the impression that dance is merely one thing or another. Dance encompasses all sorts of work and aesthetic relations. I centred more on dance than on dancers. I know that Kylian's choreography is fast and intricate, as well as fiendishly difficult. Kylian tries to achieve an effect where 'the dancers just look like water flowing through a pipe (in the way they move). It's sort of totally seamless' (Booker, 1994). Classical ballet was fascinated by the myth of weightlessness; Kylian's dance seems, at present, to want to provide the outlines of pictures. In both cases the body is asked to create an illusion: then of flight, and now of minimalism. But Kylian's dances are not just minimalist; they're hued in all sorts of textural nuances and can be very satirical, dramatic and startling. My text is recursive, in so far as the myriad levels of experiencing the NDT mirror one another, in an endless relationship of confrontation and commentary. Dance is a process, a vocabulary of movement which needs to remain in motion. Dance may demand connotative description, but it must not be reified. The power of motion and movement has to be preserved if we are to stay loyal to the phenomena. I have tried to achieve such an effect. But the primacy of choreography has eaten away at my intentions. I set out to find interaction, participation and joint-authorship. I thought dance was carnivalesque and discovered that much of the NDT's current success wasn't.

Finally, ethnography is reflexive. This article is about rebellion and repression. It is about participation and control. Without spontaneity, and the will to take risks, the NDT would never have existed; without innovation, creativity and determination it would never have persisted. But what characterizes its *modus operandi*? Ethnography has led me to pose, once again, the question: what really comes after modernism? Kylian's *oeuvre* indicates certain dilemmas. He conveys feelings of emotional loss and loneliness; he is often very good at displaying the frisson of contemporary society. His way of being effective is at the cost of never being open or revealing himself. He withdraws behind his 'colouring books' (i.e. his 'works of art'), leaving the audience(s) to fill in whatever is lacking. Through dance, the experience of dancers and audience can be choreographed. I clamour to be admitted to the recursive process, to become a witness to the dynamics of *différance*. Kylian wants to shut me out. I want to be an observer of the artistic activity, to be let into the risk taking, cognitive experimentation and creative tension. But Kylian only makes room for choreography and audience not for organizing and observing.[2]

Notes

1   Actually some of the year's workshop is sometimes repeated in Amsterdam.
2   I have drawn on the following sources for general background information on NDT which the reader may find of interest: Cohen (1992), Jonkers et al. (1992), Lanz (1995) and Reyniers (1994).

References

Banes, Sally (1977*) Terpsichore in Sneakers.* Hanover: Wesleyan University Press.
Banes, Sally (1994) *Writing Dancing.* Hanover: Wesleyan University Press.
Barnes, Clive (1994) 'A Dutch master at work', *New York Post,* 24 October.
Barr, Burt (1979) 'David Gordon's what happened', *The Drama Review,* 23 September: 33–4.
Berman, Janice (1994) 'Kylian Sets a Breakneck Pace', *New York Newsday,* 24 October.
Bleiberg, Laura (1994) 'Exhilarating Netherlands gives audience its fill', *Orange County Register,* 31 October.
Booker, Zane (1994) in 'Multinational troupe features three from US', *Orange County Register,* 22 October.
Bordo, Susan (1991) 'Material girl', in L. Goldstein (ed.), *The Female Body: Figures, Styles, Speculations.* Ann Arbor, MI: University of Michigan Press.
Brown, Jean Morrison (1979) *The Vision of Modern Dance.* Princeton, NJ: Princeton Book Company.
Cohen, Selma Jeanne (1992) *Dance as a Theatre Art,* 2nd edn. Princeton, NJ: Dance Horizons Book.
Conlogue, Ray (1994) 'Sweeping away the past', *Globe and Mail,* Toronto, 31 October.
Cooper, Robert and Law, John (1995) 'Organization: distal and proximal views', in Samuel Bacharach (ed.), *Research in the Sociology of Organizations,* Vol. 13. Greenwich, CT: JAI Press. pp. 237–74.
Jencks, Charles (1987) *The Language of Post-Modern Architecture,* 5th edn. London: Academy Editions.
Jonkers, M., Kottman, P., Lamoree, J. and Stavenuiter, D. (eds) (1992) *Hans van Manen foto's-feiten-meiningen.* Amsterdam: Nederlands Instituut voor de Dans.

Kirby, Michael (1975) 'Introduction' *The Drama Review*, 19 (March): 3.

Kisselgoff, Anna (1994) 'From the Netherlands, probing questions about existence and death', *New York Times*, 22 October.

Lanz, Isabelle (1995) *Een tuin met duizand bloemen, Jiri Kylian 20 jaar NDT*. The Hague: Theatre Institute Netherlands.

Law, John (1994) *Organizing Modernity*. Oxford: Blackwell.

Littler, William (1994) 'Yes, there's dance life after 40', *The Toronto Star*, 29 October.

McFee, Graham (1992) *Understanding Dance*. London: Routledge.

Manen, Hans van (1992) *Tot U Spreekt* Amsterdam: Nederlands Instituut voor de Dans.

Marcus, George (1994) 'What comes (just) after post', in N. Denzin and Y. Lincoln (eds), *Handbook of Qualitative Research*. London: Sage.

Malashenko, Camilla (1994) 'Nederlands Dans Dazzles', *The Montreal Gazette*, 15 October.

Pasles, Chris (1994) 'Kylian pares his view of dance to the essentials', *Los Angeles Times*, 25 October.

Rainer, Yvonne (1979) 'The mind is a muscle', in Jean Morrison Brown (ed.), *The Vision of Modern Dance*. Princeton, NJ: Princeton Book Company.

Reyniers, Johan (1994) *Het dansende lichaam*. Leuven: Kritak.

Satie, Erik (n. d.) anonymous sleeve notes to *The Piano Music of Erik Satie played by Frank Glazer*. New York: VOX.

Sokolow, Anna (1979) 'The rebel and the bourgeois', in Jean Morrison Brown (ed.), *The Vision of Modern Dance*. Princeton, NJ: Princeton Book Company.

Sorell, Walter (1992) *The Dance Has Many Faces*, 3rd edn. Chicago: Cappella Books.

Suleiman, Susan R (1986) '(Re)writing the body', in Susan Suleiman (ed.), *The Female Body in Western Culture*. Cambridge, MA: Harvard University Press.

Versteeg, Coos (1987) *Nederlands Dans Theater: Een revolutionaire geschiedenis*. Amsterdam: Balans.

Wal, Nico de (1987) 'Groots Avontuur in nieuwe fase', *Opening Programme*, NDT Theatre aan 't Spui.

8

An-aesthetics

Pippa Carter and Norman Jackson

This chapter takes as its theme a definition of 'aesthetic' which locates it as a function of perception – the emotional response to a perceived stimulus (*Oxford English Dictionary* (*OED*)) – and argues that all organization(s) produce(s) an aesthetic which is 'designed' to elicit positive responses from all those with whom transactions, of whatever kind, take place. It is argued that the creation of such an aesthetic is distinct from the creation of organizational image or of legitimation, though both of these may be a part of it; that the aesthetic varies in terms of the audience; and that it is produced by varied means, both positive and negative, and ranging from seduction to coercion. The chapter takes as an example an organization which very deliberately sets out to create an aesthetic, the Commonwealth War Graves Commission (CWGC), and argues that an important element of the creation of an aesthetic is a process of masking and denial of the experienced reality of organization, which operates to provide a comforting sense of security and, at the same time, to defer action which may threaten the status quo. This, it is suggested, is the function of aesthetics of organization.

Aesthetics as the property of an object, or of a person

It is necessary to distinguish between two senses of 'aesthetic': one which refers to judgements about taste, where the aesthetics are a property of some object and thus are external to the individual; and the other which refers to the emotional response experienced by an individual in relation to some externality, where the aesthetics are a property of the individual rather than the externality.[1]

The concept of aesthetics as the study of what is properly beautiful, etc. – what the *OED* describes as 'the "criticism of taste" considered as a science or philosophy' – is a relatively recent sense, thought to have arisen in Germany and imported into English in the nineteenth century. This has become the most common referent of the concept. Its most obvious arena of application is in the arts, and is rooted in the claim that it is possible to establish rules to define what constitutes good art, good poetry, good architecture, etc., thence to apply these rules to judge whether an object can be considered aesthetic. It is noteworthy that, in this sense, 'aesthetic' is synonymous with 'good', and is only used positively. The judgement of aesthetic value is both different to and superior to ordinary responses to such objects and depends on possession of expertise and skill.

The domain of aesthetics in this sense is always objects which are, broadly speaking, artefacts, which are the outcome of the process of organization – it is not a judgement which is applied to natural 'formations', even though these may be the source for development of rules and criteria which become part of aesthetics, as in the case of the aesthetics proposed by, for example, Morris or Ruskin. Thus aesthetics in this sense is inextricably linked to design. In the contemporary world the superordinacy of design as a characteristic of artefacts, whatever they may be, is institutionalized in bodies such as The Design Council in the UK, the strong version of whose ideal might be that the population in general should inhabit a world which conforms to standards of good taste, whether we talk about houses, gardens, cars, clothes, food, washing machines, etc., not to mention art, cinema, theatre, literature and so on. Function can no longer be considered independent of form. That some object should conform to the precepts of good taste is often apparently more important than consideration of the consequences of any particular form. Ideally, we should live surrounded by perfection – though ourselves imperfect[2] – and everything we touch should embody these characteristics of good taste – if we can afford it – though, of course, good taste is a meaningless judgement if it cannot be compared to examples of bad taste.

That this understanding of aesthetics, as the science of good taste, is profoundly normative is evidenced by the awareness that there is never universal agreement about what constitutes good taste, that tastes change over time and that either the rules or the way they are applied is subject to fashion. Such changes are not just refinements of the model of good taste, but often represent total reversal or negation, so that what in one epoch is deemed frightful, in another can be the epitome of good taste. Whether or not aesthetics in this sense is merely, as dismissively described by Raymond Williams, the repository of bourgeois values, certainly the scientific-ness of the basis of judgement can be seen as spurious. Rather, what is involved here is, at least, a process of attenuation in the service of order creation, and order creation both derives from, and has as its object, control. The sense of aesthetics as a science of criticism reveals itself as less the enshrinement of universal precepts of beauty than the manipulation of taste by opinion leaders (these days called 'style experts'), less the domain of expertise than the domain of power. Perhaps, given that the objects of this aesthetics are inescapably and by definition the outcomes of processes of organization, this conclusion is hardly surprising.

In its other sense aesthetics may be seen as less the prerogative of art and design than that of psychology. Here, aesthetics are a function of perception. Both etymologically and philosophically, the prior meaning of aesthetic is 'of or pertaining to things perceptible to the senses' (*OED*), and refers to the emotional response to a perceived stimulus.[3] In this formulation aesthetics relates to emotional reactions which are broadly either positive or negative, and lies in the pleasure/pain domain. Given the fundamental distinction on the basis of perceptions of pleasure and perceptions of pain (see, for example, Freud's Pleasure Principle), then, generally speaking, we try to organize our lives to maximize our relation to what we consider pleasurable and to minimize our relation to what we consider painful. This understanding, thus, puts this sense of aesthetic at a different order to that of the previous sense, since it suggests that all 'taste' is aesthetic and the only meaningful distinction is in terms of a positive aesthetic or a negative one. The absence of aesthetic is anaesthetic – insensate. The other significant difference between the two senses of aesthetic is that in the latter case what is positively or negatively aesthetic is, fundamentally, a response of the individual. It is not possible to establish, externally and a priori, rules or principles of what is pleasurable and what is painful, even though individuals *may* broadly agree on the general aesthetics of some stimuli. It *might* be posited – very warily – that the pursuit of pleasure and the avoidance of pain could be seen as 'innate', but this is not to say that what constitutes pleasure or pain is also innate – in any case, such judgements are obviously manipulable through, for example, vanity, insecurity, socialization, acculturation, fashion, brain-washing, and so on.

The project, initiated by the nineteenth century, of attempting to establish rules of 'beauty', etc., moved aesthetics from the arena of philosophy/ psychology to that of science and, as such, is very much part of the legacy of the Enlightenment and the rise of modernism. The shift of aesthetics from being a property of individuals to being a property of objects resonates deeply with emergent beliefs in the ability of science to resolve all mysteries and the concomitant shift of attention away from the apparently accidental and unquantifiable towards the putatively causal and quantifiable. As part of the 'modernist project', this understanding of aesthetics has been vulnerable to the loss of faith in the rational which characterizes postmodernism. Aesthetics as a set of objective characteristics has come to be seen less as a set of rules and more as the designation of opinion leaders. Like other examples which would now be called pseudo-science, such as phrenology, astrology and eugenics, aesthetics in this incarnation has been recognized as unsustainable as science and has moved into the arena of ideology as a tool of consumer capitalism (though for an example of the complexity of the analysis of aesthetics see the work of the Konstanz School, e.g. Jauss, 1982). To some extent, it can thus be adduced as an exemplar of the 'detraditionalization thesis', with so-called style gurus becoming one of the contemporary forms of authority which have displaced traditional forms, such as the church, the family and the school, and whose dicta now become part of the specification of the organization of structural power relationships. But, whilst traditional sources of authority have usually been identified with some particular goal such as moral well-being or social order, aesthetics as embodied in style have become detached from the formal specification of rules of beauty and are simply the dogmatic opinions of those who claim the authority to judge. Such opinions are merely self-referential, and thus object-aesthetics has achieved the status of the hyper-real.

However, the sense of aesthetic as a function of perception, although of a different order to the sense of aesthetic as 'rules of form', does not invalidate or destroy the latter, since both are rooted in perceptions of what is pleasing and both are related to, and responses to, the outcomes of the process of organization – though at different levels of magnitude. The significance of the distinction between the two usages, however, is profound, in its relation to the *locus* of the aesthetic. Aesthetics as a science locates the aesthetic as a property of the object to which we respond – and, should we find unaesthetic an object designated as aesthetic or vice versa, this is a 'mis-perception' of the observer. Aesthetics as a function of perception, however, locates the aesthetic in the individual, and so judgements about the correctness of the perception are simply irrelevant, or can be seen as a 'problem' of the 'object'. The use of the term aesthetics in this context is, thus, intended to emphasize its referent of being a positive or negative quality of the emotional response to stimuli, amongst which are physical objects – the sense of aesthetics as 'the rules of good taste', or 'rules of form', is rejected. In that aesthetics is about the emotional response to sense data, there are two necessary components: the stimulus and the response – and it is hardly meaningful to speak of one in isolation from the other. Our intention in usage of the concept of aesthetics, hereinafter, is to stress not only the stimulus *and* the response, but also the relationship between them.

The Commonwealth War Graves Commission

Our argument here is that not only is an aesthetic always a reaction to processes of organization but also that all organization(s) produce(s) an aesthetic. To illustrate this point, we will refer to what is, undoubtedly, in some ways an extreme example, but which is an organization which has a deliberate intention to produce something aesthetically pleasing in the sense of eliciting a positive emotional response: The Commonwealth War Graves Commission.

To place this organization in its historical context, it is important to note that World War I (WWI) established a fundamentally new attitude to memorialization of military war dead. Prior to 1914, such commemoration on an individual basis was virtually unknown, such recognition as there was tending to be ad hoc, on a regimental basis, typically to be found in cathedrals and large churches associated with particular regiments. Common, if not exclusive, practice was to identify by name the officers who died, but only by gross numbers the common soldiery. Although there were graves of dead soldiers abroad, these had little permanence. Ironically, the sheer size of the problem in WWI, together with a concern to fulfil the longstanding, but rarely deemed possible, requirement on the military (enshrined in Army Regulations) to clear up battlefields, remove the bodies of the dead and properly dispose of them (Gibson and Ward, 1989), was a major factor animating this profound change. Another major factor was the change in the nature and scale of warfare represented by WWI. Prior to this, battles, and even whole wars, had tended to be set pieces, of short duration and in limited locations (Keegan, 1991). In 1415 the Battle of Agincourt lasted a few hours, occupied a front of 200 yards, with 400 English and 8,000 French killed. Four centuries later the Battle of Waterloo, in 1815, lasted 3 days on a front half a mile wide, with a total of 27,100 casualties. A mere century after that the Battle of the Somme, in 1916, lasted 4.5 months, on a front 5 miles wide, and resulted in 126,200 casualties (Perrett, 1992). At least up to the end of the American Civil War (1865), battlefields were so contained that civilians would have a day out to spectate the combat in relative safety. In WWI, particularly as a result of advances in artillery and the development of aerial warfare, battles were no longer local events, major tracts of land were littered with previously unimaginable numbers of dead and battles continued to rage around them.

As an organization the Commonwealth War Graves Commission has had a very complex history of development. It started as a private initiative of Fabian Ware, under the auspices of the Red Cross, to register graves of those killed in battle, which practice was formally recognized in March 1915, with the commitment to establish, care for and maintain the graves being formulated in January 1916. The Imperial War Graves Commission was formally constituted in May 1917, and did not become the Commonwealth War Graves Commission until April 1960.[4] The CWGC is in many ways an extraordinary and fascinating organization but, in this context, it is our intention to address only those aspects which are directly relevant to the production of a particular aesthetic. It must also be stressed that our discussion is in no way meant as criticism of the work of this organization, which represents a profoundly humane and honorable function and which fulfils this function with remarkable sensitivity and success. It is clearly not part of the function of the organization to comment, directly and intentionally, on the rights and wrongs of war.

The main function of the CWGC is the provision, care and maintenance of cemeteries and memorials for military war dead:

> . . . the Commission records the place of burial or commemoration of all members of the Commonwealth armed forces who died, *no matter where and no matter what the cause,* during the periods of the 1914-1918 and 1939-1945 Wars. For Commission purposes the period of the 1914-1918 War is 4th August 1914 to 31st August 1921 . . . For the 1939-1945 War the dates are 3rd September 1939 to 31st December 1947 . . . inclusive. (Gibson and Ward, 1989: 64; emphasis in original)

It has chosen to do this in a particular way, 'to give *a feeling* of solace and peace and not of depression' (Gibson and Ward, 1989: 55; emphasis added). A primary motivating force was to provide a physical site where the bereaved could come to mourn, or of which they could have a photograph if they were unable to make the journey. The designation of an ambiance was, therefore, very significant. There was additionally the intention to represent the gratitude of the state to all those who died, irrespective of whether a body existed. The result is what Kipling called the 'Silent Cities' (Hurst, 1993), more recently described as 'endless, awesome rows of beautifully designed white headstones'

8.1 *World War 1 grave marker. Of note: the rank and age of the victim, and the stone is grey granite, rather than the usual white. Chanterlands (Municipal) Cemetery, Hull, UK, (from the authors' collection).*

8.2 *Cross of Sacrifice. Ryes War Cemetery, Normandy, France, (from the authors' collection).*

8.3   *Stone of Remembrance. Bayeux War Cemetery, France, (from the authors' collection).*

8.4 *General view of the War Cemetery at Ryes, Normandy, France, (from the authors' collection).*

8.5 *Grave marker showing typical features as specified by CWGC. Of note: the victim died in 1947 and was 61 years old. Chanterlands (Municipal) Cemetery, Hull, UK, (from the authors' collection).*

(Pearce, 1995). The process by which this production is made possible is defined by an extremely detailed set of rules which strictly describe the form and the content of both the function and the ambiance. (Some of these rules can be seen as realizing an aesthetic of taste –as per our first definition– which was dominant in the epoch of WWI and which has survived even to the commemorations of much more recent conflicts.)[5]

Broadly speaking, the elements of the process can be distinguished in terms of principles and structures. Examples of the principles are equality of treatment in memorialization, non-repatriation of the dead and avoidance of reburial. Equality of treatment is defined in very specific rules. For example: each plot is the same size, each headstone is of identical size and design, the layout is non-hierarchical, strict specification is made of allowable decorations and inscriptions and the numbers of letters (60) available for personalized messages in the case of gravestones. Non-specification of the cause of death is another factor, which presumes that all people who died, died because they were there, in service to their country. Nonetheless, this laudable principle of equality is subject to different treatment in specified circumstances. For example, in hospital, rather than battlefield, cemeteries, officers (and nurses) are generally grouped separately to other ranks – and sometimes some ethnic or religious groups, such as Muslims, are buried together – and on major memorials such as the Menin Gate there is a hierarchy of status within regiments and of status between regiments. The strict rule of non-repatriation of bodies can also be seen partly in terms of the principle of equality, in that it overtly recognized that ability to repatriate bodies was a function of wealth (cf. Gibson and Ward, 1989). This particular principle, however, almost exponentially increased the complexity of the CWGC's operations, since graves, cemeteries and memorials are maintained all over the world, and access to the sites had to become an issue covered by specific rules and definitions, though in many cases, as in France and Belgium, the land occupied by the sites has been given in perpetuity to Britain. It is also worthy of note that the principle of equality, once established, is not a matter of choice but is legally enforced (for example, it is illegal to repatriate war dead). Another principle with direct bearing on the aesthetic (in both senses) is that bodies once buried should not be moved (unless the site is for some reason 'unmaintainable'), particularly not for the sake of neatness. This is why it is not unusual to see, amongst the serried rows of neat, symmetrical headstones, a few which seem poignantly out of order, set at odd angles, different.

The rules about structures are particularly illustrative of the process of production of an aesthetic, i.e. the production of a particular emotional response desired on the part of the producer. The headstones are instantly recognizable. Apart from a few exceptions, usually to do with local geological conditions, they are of a standard pattern and found all over the world, and uniquely distinguishable from the war graves of other countries. Two other items of furniture are widely found, the Cross of Sacrifice and the Stone of Remembrance, both of which are of identical design (though not necessarily size) in virtually all cases. The former represents a metal sword superimposed on a stone cross. The latter, weighing ten tons, was designed by Lutyens and was described by him thus:

A great fair stone of fine proportions, 12 feet in length, lying raised upon three steps . . . all its horizontal surfaces and planes are spherical and parts of parallel spheres, 1,801 feet, 8 inches in diameter, and all its vertical lines converging upwards to a point some 1,801 feet, 8 inches, above the centre of these spheres. (cited in Gibson and Ward, 1989: 54)

This is a nice example of the specificity of the rules.[6] Then, the 'gardens':

From the start, the cemeteries were planted under the advice of Captain (later Sir) Arthur Hill, Director of the Royal Botanic Gardens at Kew. Trees and bushes were planted to avoid monotony and headstone flower beds laid out to counter any harshness caused by too many headstones . . . (I)nitial work included the planting of 63 miles of hedges, and the seeding to grass of 540 acres to *produce turf resembling English lawns.* (Gibson and Ward, 1989: 55; emphasis added)

Nothing, however, can minimize the harshness of the great memorials to those who have no known grave, so rather the aesthetic is one of simple grandeur.

Aesthetics and denial

The argument of this chapter has two principal elements. First, that in producing an aesthetic what an organization does, intentionally and/or unintentionally, is to structure both form and content in such a way as to elicit a positive response from all those with whom it has any transaction. Secondly, that the way in which this is done generally involves a profound denial of the reality of organization(s). Both these elements are aptly illustrated by the example of the CWGC. It is that the CWGC deliberately and explicitly seeks to elicit a desired emotional response – 'a feeling of solace and peace and not of depression' (Gibson and Ward, 1989: 55) – which designates its function as a production process, analogous to any other production process, rather than one which simply seeks, for example, to represent the dead. The denial is accomplished, one might say, by the imposition of order on chaos, in the case of the CWGC symbolized by the neatness and precision of the cemeteries and memorials themselves and of the rules of their production, compared to the utter chaos of warfare.

The technology of warfare is, essentially, about killing people (for figures from 'crucial conflicts' over the last 3,000 years, see Perrett, 1992). The CWGC commemorates almost 2 million deaths in 23,175 burial grounds (including specific war grave sites, war graves in municipal cemeteries, etc.), from all conflicts in which Commonwealth members have been involved since 1914 – and this *is* only Commonwealth military dead, not including other, non-Commonwealth, military dead, or those who were killed but who were civilians. Each of these deaths is a unique and individual experience which can be accomplished in many ways – an instant event about which the individual knows nothing or a long lingering death from wounds or disease; intentional or accidental; as combatant or as support; from enemy action or from 'friendly fire'; glorious or farcical. Death itself can be, and in WWI often was, preceded by conditions of extraordinary hardship: life at the front was frequently characterized by hunger, thirst, wetness, filth, exhaustion and terror. All too often people did not know why they were there, sometimes even where 'there' was. Oral histories of experiences at the front (see, for instance, the series by Lyn Macdonald, e.g. Macdonald, 1987) reflect a pervasive and profound sense – amongst all ranks – of powerlessness and futility, with no control over their own survival and the impossibility (legally) of questioning what was happening to them. All this variety is represented by these neat, repetitive, gravestones and memorials.

In that states of war require the acculturation of combatants to a total inversion of the rules of normal socialized existence, the war graves serve to perpetuate that acculturation, promising everlasting glory and immortality – 'Their Name Liveth For Evermore' – and, implicitly and explicitly, the CWGC understands its function as to make death in war acceptable and tolerable to those left behind (Gibson and Ward, 1989). One effect of this is to make it possible that it can happen again. (Memorialization of the dead of WWI was not even completed by the time that WW2 started – in particular, stonemasons were still at work on the Menin Gate when the Germans invaded Belgium in 1940 (Gilbert, 1994).) An especially poignant case of this process of denial is seen in the kindly intentioned lying of officers writing to relatives about the death of their loved ones, which often deliberately sought to protect families from knowledge of the actual circumstances, but at the same time substantiated the culture of glorious death. *Dulce et decorum est* ... When memorials speak of the lost or those who have no known grave – just under 800,000, and about 200,000 graves whose occupants were unidentifiable – what they mean is that these people's bodies were probably so fragmented that there was nothing to bury, so ground into the earth that they were never discovered, so 'disappeared' that nothing could be known about the how and the why of the death. This is the sort of knowledge from which the CWGC protects us, generously but not entirely in our own interest. The principle of equality requires that, even on the gravestones of those 'known', there is nothing about the death except the date it occurred, where that is known – there is a deliberate non-specification of the cause of death which intentionally sanitizes it all. You could be shot by a sniper, decapitated by a shell, be the victim of 'friendly fire', succumb to the horrors of mustard gas, die from a minor wound complicated by gas gangrene, die unwounded drowning in a shell hole, die overloaded with kit because you fell down in the mud, die of hunger, thirst, disease, be shot at dawn, die from any of these reasons because your orders showed no awareness on the part of the Command of the conditions in which you were fighting – it was a moot point whether you were most in danger from the enemy or from your own side. The average rate of death in WWI was 1 per 15 seconds throughout its duration. It has been said that a Book of Remembrance of military war dead which gave one page to each person would be one mile deep between its covers.

The point of all this is that the CWGC deliberately seeks to deny the experienced reality which is commemorated in its work, and explicitly seeks to evoke a positive response from those who visit its sites, for whatever reason. A glance at the Visitors' Book of any CWGC site is instructive in this respect. As time passes and people who visit the sites do so less probably to seek out the grave of someone known to them, and more probably for other more general reasons, the comments reflect a very positive response to the organization but a negative response to war. Nonetheless, there are frequent comments about the aesthetic created, about how beautiful, colourful, peaceful, etc. the sites are.

Not-the-Commonwealth War Graves Commission

In an interestingly apposite passage, Baudrillard (1993: 39) talks about labour in terms of 'death deferred':

Labour is slow death. This is generally understood in the sense of physical exhaustion. But it must be understood in another sense. Labour is not opposed, like a sort of death, to the 'fulfilment of life', which is the idealist view; labour is opposed *as a slow death* to a violent death ... Labour is opposed as deferred death to the immediate death of sacrifice. (emphasis in original)

In some ways, as we previously noted, the CWGC is an extreme case, but in other ways it is just one example among many possibilities. It is our contention that all organization(s) perform(s) this act of repression and denial in order to evoke a positive emotional response from its 'audience' – seek(s) to produce a positive aesthetic – though, one might suggest, with considerably less justification than the CWGC. All organization(s) seek(s) to present itself/themselves, to both public and participants, as beautiful, orderly, humane, eminently positive. It is, however, necessary to distinguish this aesthetic production from both the corporate image and the construction of legitimacy, although both these may be implied and involved in the production of the aesthetic – the image as a deliberate, constructed, message which may seek to evoke, in a variety of ways, a sense of the organization itself and of its products, and the construction of legitimacy as the evocation of a dominant aesthetic to do with the desirability of order, symmetry, etc. Each of these may have a role to play in the production of an aesthetic, but the aesthetic itself is much more profound in both its production and its applications. These aspects involve the fundamental denial of the disorder, indifference to welfare, 'organized chaos' and asymmetry which characterize the general normal experience of organizational life. The difference between the aesthetic and both image and legitimation activities is that the latter can be seen as intentional projection of a desired perception of the organization, but the former always involves *also* a masking of experienced reality, a denial of the experience of the senses.

Whilst the process of denial/masking always characterizes the process of production of an organizational aesthetic, however, the particular forms taken will obviously be varied, both within and between organizations: different constituencies will necessitate different kinds of denial. Thus the experienced conditions of producing a product are rarely an aspect of its marketing to potential customers, but that form would be inappropriate vis à vis the workforce who participate in the production process. The promised pleasures offered by car manufacturers in marketing cars are unlikely to include reference to the pains of production, the isolation, alienation and dehumanization of production line systems. The marketing of fashion does not include reference to sweat shops or child labour, of nuclear power include reference to issues of disposing of waste which will be dangerous to people for longer than our knowledge of history so far, of meat include reference to the conditions under which animals are kept and slaughtered. On the contrary, the implication is often there that the experience of the producers is nothing but positive, or that such issues are trivial compared to the benefits accruing to the individual purchaser. Likewise, the practices of, for example, Total Quality Management and Human Resources Management, with their central concepts of excellence and empowerment designed to convince organizational participants of their value to the organization and of their contribution to it, are usually (though not always[7]) inappropriate when appealing to the purchasing public.

Whilst potential customers are influenced by, for example, cost, production workers know well what the impact of cost-cutting is likely to be – indeed, we all know what the impacts are in our own organizations, but, apparently, are able to ignore that when buying the products of other organizations. While the deleterious effects – physically, socially and psychologically – of organizations generally and of production systems in particular are well known, the products of these systems, and the portrayal of the organization which produces them, are isolated from that knowledge, sanitized, depicted as benign and universally beneficial. The consuming public knows about the dysfunctions, knows that they are being denied and yet accepts and sustains the denial. Desire for the products of the system persistently represses the recognition of self, or mutual, interest to be served by repudiating the mask (Deleuze and Guattari, 1984). As Deleuze and Guattari show, this is a complex and multi-faceted process of denial and repression which forms the aesthetic of capitalism, itself in a mutually structuring relationship with the aesthetic produced by individual organizations within the system.

Generic dysfunctions for individual participants in organizations are also well known. The validity of concepts such as 'the iron law of oligarchy' (Michels, 1968), 'the psychic prison' (Morgan, 1986), 'the deskilling thesis' (Braverman, 1974), 'the iron cage of bureaucracy' (Weber, 1948) and 'panoptical surveillance' (Foucault, 1979) is now quite commonly recognized in both the literature on, and the practice of, organization. People who work in organizations have a certain commonality of experience of being subjected to an Orwellian newspeak, a hyper-real managerial language which can tell us that we are the organization's greatest asset at the same time as we are being made redundant, which can call redundancy empowerment, which can tell us that appraisal is a positive instrument for self and career development at the same time as it is being used to control us and blame us for our perceived inadequacies. The rhetoric which constantly clothes every aspect of organizational process in a benign language of benefit to the participant denies the maxims of economic efficiency which actually produce it. It is an attempt to evoke a positive response to experience which is, for many, profoundly negative.

Aesthetics, power and control

The need to elicit positive responses, and the need to do this through denial, are simply explained. Open recognition of the negative consequences of organization would be seriously problematic in terms of both legitimacy and maintenance of the status quo. Typical organizational practice and process do not sit well with the principles of liberal democracy and humanitarian values which are supposed to be the guiding precepts of the societies in which they operate. Such contradictions, if clearly acknowledged, would threaten crisis. It is noteworthy in this context that, while the 'productions' of the CWGC deny the processes of death and the chaos of war, memorializations of the Holocaust, such as those in Père-Lachaise Cemetery in Paris, are in stark contrast, emphasizing its horror. This is seen as necessary to prevent any such events reoccurring – and this is, presumably, also why in some countries it is literally illegal to deny the Holocaust. It is clear that there is an acknowledgement that once such processes are widely recognized the public sense of revulsion can be harnessed to produce change. A much more mundane example of the same process is to be found in the relatively successful activities of widely based pressure groups against the veal trade. Thus, the attempt to prevent negative experience of organization being foregrounded in the public domain is fundamental to preservation of the status quo. And the production and communication of an aesthetic which operates to restrain such foregrounding in general is sufficiently powerful to create the conviction that it is 'wrong' to criticize organization(s) more often than it creates the conviction that it might be 'right' to do so.

Nevertheless the aesthetic produces dissonance. By its constant reinforcement the denial of experience is encouraged, in favour of the 'received wisdom'. But the negative psychological impact of voluntary denial of subjective experience is, obviously, serious, and, once we deny our ability to assess a situation, we have to abdicate that responsibility in favour of others. Abdication of our own judgement thus increases our dependence on the judgement of others. So the aesthetic acts to induce, sustain and reward *compliance*, what Marcuse (1986: 79) calls 'happy consciousness' which 'reflects the belief that the real is rational, and that the established system, in spite of everything, delivers the goods'. Baudrillard takes this somewhat further. Referring to Lyotard's hypothesis (see, e.g., Lyotard, 1993: 111) about 'the intensity of the exploited's enjoyment ['jouissance'] in their very abjection', he adds, epigrammatically, 'The enjoyment of powerlessness . . . will never abolish power' (Baudrillard, 1993: 41).

The aesthetic that the CWGC chose to represent its desire to produce sites which conveyed feelings 'of solace and peace and not of depression' was not an arbitary choice – it is not *an* aesthetic but *the* aesthetic, and, moreover, the same aesthetic which can be seen as dominant in relation to most organization. This aesthetic is symbolized by order, neatness, simplicity: function, purpose and rationality in a harmony of symmetry. Both implicitly and explicitly, the beauty of the aesthetic is not visual or otherwise sensual, but psychological. But order and symmetry are not inherently positive as aesthetics. They are preferred to the chaos and disorder associated with asymmetry which promote uncertainty, which itself stimulates anxiety. The desire to minimize anxiety produces what Wilden (1980) calls the 'paranoia of symmetry'. But, whereas we seek a comforting uniformity in order to escape the anxiety of chaos, at the same time we desire to believe in our own uniqueness. This sense of the unique is fuelled by emphasizing trivial, even meaningless, differences – the 'narcissism of minor difference'. These complementary demands are profoundly implicated in the production of the aesthetic of organization(s). It is the '"narcissism of minor difference" which results in the "paranoia of symmetry" by which the Oppressor projects his own desire onto those he oppresses' (Wilden 1980: 486). By this token, disorder can be argued to have emancipatory potential. On the one hand, disorder within a system itself escapes from control and, at the same time, diminishes the extent to which the system as a whole can be controlled. On the other hand, disorder represents a nexus at which change can occur. Thus order facilitates restraints on freedom. Yet organizations are disordered, are random, are irrational. The aesthetic which is produced by organization, the evocation of a positive emotional response, appeals to the perceived threat which disorder represents to individuals and, at the same moment, acts to repress the emancipatory potential of disorder. The role of the aesthetic is to appear to minimize the perceived sense of threat, but the resulting sense of security merely masks the extent to which 'stakeholders' are at threat: it does not eliminate the threat, it merely denies it. If it is successful the organizational aesthetic operates to defer action, since, if we believe that everything is benign and beneficial, that all is as it should be, then there is no need to act, other than in compliance. But our sense of security is, thereby, inescapably retained in the gift of the powerful. This is what is at stake in the production of an organizational aesthetic.

An-aesthetics

It is not unusual to find war graves from WWI cheek by jowl with those from WW2, both in war grave cemeteries and in municipal cemeteries. This poignant phenomenon might suggest that the creation of 'a feeling of peace' was perhaps less than successful, given the alacrity with which the world engaged in another global conflict. One of the most moving sights is the existence today of what are known as 'honourable scars' (Gibson and Ward, 1989) on a number of, especially, Western Front headstones and memorials. These are areas of damage on WWI monuments created by WW2 bullets, shells, etc., and which are deliberately not repaired by the CWGC, unless the stone is replaced due to more general deterioration. Clearly, at the end of WWI there was not generally an expectation that, within a generation, there would be another such conflict. Memorialization of WWI dead undoubtedly reflected the conviction that WWI was indeed 'the war to end war'. Yet, that wars continue to provide work for the CWGC does not detract from the 'feeling of solace and peace and not of depression' for the modern-day visitor to war grave cemeteries, whatever the motive for their visit.

In terms of semiotics it can readily be understood that the memorialization of war dead is a text to be read uniquely by each person. While the 'authors' of the text can produce signifiers intended to have particular significations, they cannot specify the actual significations. These signifiers provoke a potentially infinite variety of responses, ranging, perhaps, from complete indifference to reflections on the meaning of existence. However, what Keegan (1991: 280) refers to as 'the beautiful garden cemeteries' undoubtedly furnish a context which is widely accessible and recognized, part of the collective cultural common language of the construct of an English garden.

We would suggest that this is how the creation of an aesthetic works, if it works: by appealing to, or referring to, the 'shared language' of a community, the perhaps unconscious responses, intersubjective recognitions, that constitute a particular culture. However, semiotics also points out that there is always what can be called a surplus signification, unique to each individual. The success of the creation of an aesthetic depends crucially on the balance between these two elements which is evoked by the symbols. The creation of an aesthetic is always directed to the shared language of a community (however defined), and the intention is to manipulate the signifiers to such an extent that the possibility of responding other than in the desired ways is minimized. At best, it aims at the suspension of disbelief, at worst we could say that we are told what to think. Success in such manipulation is, as always, a function of the exercise of power. The extent to which the process is successful, to which we accept the created aesthetic as a definition of the appropriate response to (an) organization, is also the extent to which we abdicate or deny our *own* ability to formulate a response. Acceptance, intentional or unintentional, means that, as individuals, we accept anaesthetization.

We chose the CWGC as an example of our argument because it is an organization which clearly intends to create an aesthetic. The aesthetic of 'solace and peace and not of depression' was, and is, intended to dull the pain of premature loss, often in horrific circumstances, caused by war. This objective is laudable, honourable and benign and, indeed, the 'product' undoubtedly achieves that objective. However, we have described a process that is common to all organizations, including those with less universal benefit, more partial interests, acceptance of whose created aesthetic may even be detrimental to a significant portion of the intended audience. To accept unquestioningly the organizational aesthetic in these cases is to dull awareness, not least of experience and of self-interest. Ironically, organizational aesthetics an-aesthetize.

Notes

1   We must note here our indebtedness to Harry Jamieson who, in many discussions and in giving us access to his work-in-progress, contributed greatly to our appreciation of this distinction. He, of course, is in no way responsible for what follows.

2   Though, in American parlance, an aesthetician is a beauty therapist.

3   A similar understanding can be found in the work of Foucault (e.g. 1984), where aesthetics is seen as a central theme in the (re-)invention of the self which 'occurs at the points where language and, therefore, identity break down' (McNay, 1994: 146).

4   We became interested in this organization as one effect of visiting war cemeteries in France and Belgium, and being drawn to explore how such an organization functioned. It is interesting that, when talking to others about this, one of two distinct (aesthetic) reactions prevail: one on the part of those who never want to

visit these sites, the other on the part of those who do so as a matter of course when in Continental Europe and who seem drawn by the aesthetic produced, which seems to reflect some very personal commitment to what is represented. Also of relevance is that, no matter when or where one visits a war graves cemetery, it is extremely rare to find that it has not been visited by others on the same day or very recently – as witnessed by the Visitors' Book.

5   For the sake of convenience we are not distinguishing between the various incarnations of this organization, but refer to it generically in its current form. It should also be noted that, at the end of the twentieth century, the *main* function of CWGC is to reproduce and maintain this already defined aesthetic, rather than to produce it.

6   Winter (1995) attributes these measurements to Lutyens's involvement in theosophy. If so, such mysticism creates an interesting irony, in that war grave cemeteries generally have a profoundly Christian ethos.

7   For example, the Marriott hotel chain recently ran a series of advertisements emphasizing the benefits of 'buying their product' by depicting the avoidance of various disasters to guests due to the actions of, generally, low-status employees whom the company had 'empowered'.

References

Baudrillard, J. (1993) *Symbolic Exchange and Death*, trans. I. H. Grant. London: Sage.

Braverman, H. (1974) *Labor and Monopoly Capital*. New York: Monthly Review Press.

Deleuze, G. and Guattari, F. (1984) *Anti-Oedipus*, trans. R. Hurley, M. Seem and H. R. Lane. London: Athlone.

Foucault, M. (1979) *Discipline and Punish*, trans. A. Sheridan. Harmondsworth: Penguin.

Foucault, M. (1984) 'On the genealogy of ethics', in P. Rabinow (ed.), *The Foucault Reader*. London: Penguin.

Gibson, T.A.E. and Ward, G.K. (1989) *Courage Remembered*. London: HMSO.

Gilbert, M. (1994) *First World War*. London: Weidenfeld and Nicholson.

Hurst, S.C. (1993) *The Silent Cities*. London: The Naval and Military Press (1st edn 1929).

Jauss, H.R. (1982) *Towards an Aesthetic of Reception*, trans. T. Bahti. London: Harvester.

Keegan, J. (1991) *The Face of Battle*. London: Pimlico (1st edn 1976).

Lyotard, J.-F. (1993) *Libidinal Economy*, trans. I. H. Grant. London: Athlone.

Macdonald, L. (1987) *1914 – The Days of Hope*. London: Penguin.

Marcuse, H. (1986) *One Dimensional Man*. London: Ark.

McNay, L. (1994) *Foucault: A Critical Introduction*. Cambridge: Polity.

Michels, R. (1968) *Political Parties*, trans. E. and C. Paul. London: Jarrold (1st edn 1911).

Morgan, G. (1986) *Images of Organization*. London: Sage.

Pearce, E. (1995) 'The bloody pride of Norman's barmy army', *Guardian*, 18 February.

Perrett, B. (1992) *The Battle Book*. London: Cassell.

Weber, M. (1948) *From Max Weber: Essays in Sociology*, trans. T. Parsons and A.M. Henderson. New York: Free Press.

Wilden, A. (1980) *System and Structure*, 2nd edn. London: Tavistock.

Winter, J. (1995) *Sites of Memory, Sites of Mourning*. Cambridge: Cambridge University Press.

PART 5

AESTHETICS, ETHICS AND IDENTITY

9

'Suaviter in modo, fortiter in re': Appearance, Reality and the Early Jesuits

Harro Höpfl

Introduction

Self-presentation – the cultivation of appearances, even a certain theatricality – as a key constituent of organizational success is not a recent invention. This chapter offers some reflections on organizational appearance, reality and rhetoric by reference to the Society of Jesus – the Jesuits – a spectacularly successful organization – and its enemies.

In the Jesuits' analysis, falsehood and heresy had triumphed in the world because of presentation. The successful Catholic response (the Society's mission) would therefore have to present the truth just as persuasively and attractively. This chapter explores the Society's acute sensitivity to its public face, the impression it was creating: its elaborate procedures for recruiting, training and positioning its members, to ensure that the Society's 'embodiments' were presentable and persuasive; and the systematic publicity, high-profile activities, the visibility and elegance of Jesuit edifices and emblems, as the Society's corporate self-representation. Fundamental to all else was the Society's cultivation of rhetoric: the art and science of persuasive discourse, demanding both mastery of the moral substance of truth and its persuasive presentation: *'suaviter in modo, fortiter in re'*.

The deliberate cultivation of appearances, however, invites a cynical, 'unmasking' response. That response was to 'unmask' appearances as mere facade; reality is what is hidden behind it. The Jesuits' many enemies 'unmasked' the power to control opinion, represented by Jesuits as merely a means to their spiritual ends, as in fact their real end. The ends Jesuits professed, conversely, were mere manipulations of appearances. But ironically, unmasking was, as so often, counterproductive: to 'unmask' the power behind the suave facade was to affirm and confirm its reality. In Thomas Hobbes's aphorism: 'Reputation of power is power'.

'Suaviter in modo, fortiter in re': appearance and reality and the early Jesuits

In a persuasive analysis of the notion of the immortality of the firm, Sievers has argued that in earlier days the Church, and in particular the Roman Church, 'was the predominant organizational representation of our collective Western belief in immortality'; and has suggested that modern corporations have taken over the spiritual and cultural function of the 'collective symbolification of survival, eternity and immortality' (1994: 116). Again, Turner (1992) has argued that the appearance of things has come to exercise a profound influence on the regulation of corporate life, and Anthony (1994) has given critical attention to the influence of corporate imagery in the management of corporate culture. Höpfl and Linstead (1993) have examined the use of evangelical metaphors, salvationist rhetoric and quasi-religious symbolism as devices for the regulation of corporate behaviour, which operate through rhetorical and hierophantic imagery in the service of secular ends. More broadly, organizational theorists have in recent years dwelt increasingly on the relationship between the symbolic and its aesthetic construction, and with ethics and metaphysics insofar as they support such construction (Featherstone, 1995: 37–43; Gagliardi, 1986; Guillet de Monthoux, in this volume; Harju, 1996; Höpfl, 1996; Strati, in this volume).

Such concerns serve as the context for this chapter, which suggests that the rhetoric and self-presentation of the early Jesuits may be profitably compared with their use in contemporary organizational forms. Indeed the motto 'suaviter in modo, fortiter in re' ('agreeable in manner, strong in substance'), always attributed to the Jesuits, commended itself to all sorts of people, even those to whom the Society was anathema, such as Communists. The motto, which was until recently proverbial, derives from a dictum of the Jesuit Superior General Aquaviva of 1606 (Aquaviva, 1606). Aquaviva's point was specific, but the motto fits the Jesuits' *modus agendi* well enough. The counsel it embodied is congruent with many concerns central to the Society of Jesus, which was founded in 1540 and established as the leading and most controversial of the Catholic religious orders by the early seventeenth century.

The contemporary concerns of the Jesuits here were common to the political thinking of early modern Europe in general.

One of the early Jesuits' principal preoccupations was also one of Machiavelli's: the paramount concern with appearances, most notoriously in Chapter XVIII of his *Il Principe* (*The Prince*) (1988: 62–3), where he wrote that

> a prince must take great care to appear, to all who see and hear him, to be all clemency, good faith, integrity, humanity and religion. And there is no quality that is more necessary for him to appear to have than the last-mentioned, piety. People in general judge more with their eyes than with their hands . . . Everyone can see what you appear to be, but few have direct experience of what you really are. And those few will not dare to oppose the opinion of the many . . . And in the actions of all men, but especially princes . . . people judge by the outcome.

Now ironically Jesuits were among Machiavelli's most incisive critics (Bireley, 1990, Ch. 2). They had the relevant qualifications for the role, as fellow-professionals in diplomacy and bureaucracy, but with vastly wider experience and contacts. But Jesuits were themselves accused of duplicity, intrigue, power-seeking, of putting into practice the belief that the end justifies the means and, in short, of being Machiavellians of the deepest hue, as we shall see.

Machiavelli was not alone in his concern with appearances; on the contrary one of the great themes in the political reflection and practice of the sixteenth and seventeenth centuries is *riputazzione*. Jesuits never criticized Machiavelli for urging princes to be concerned about their reputation; they merely argued that Machiavellian techniques for creating and maintaining appearances were doomed to failure if there was no substance. But they and the princes they mostly supported took it as read that one of the salient princely virtues was magnificence (see Bellarmine, 1619, Bk I, Ch. XIV: 'Of the Magnificence which is necessary for a Prince to rule his people'). Magnificence demanded conspicuous displays: extraordinarily lavish and costly garments and accoutrements, the elaborate ritual of the princely courts, patronage of whatever was splendid, and the familiar round of royal progresses and *joyeuses entrées*. The worst thing a prince could do was to lock himself up in his palace. The point was to be seen and to be affable, and yet unapproachable – an idea nicely caught in the obsolete sense of the word condescension, to descend from the heights and be *with*, but of course not *of*, the lowly. Inseparable from the statecraft of princes, that is to say autocrats, is a certain theatricality: princes are in every sense public persons. Of course this theatricality and publicity inevitably generated an interest in what goes on behind the scenes, behind the facade, an interest in the private, the secret, the *arcana imperii* (the secrets of rule) and the 'mysteries of kingship'. It is not a very long step from such a fascination with what is not seen, what is hidden and secret, to the emergence of some kind of conspiracy theory, and the notion that the real is precisely and always what remains hidden from view and does not appear; in short, that appearance and 'reality' are quite different things. This in many ways was precisely Machiavelli's view of things.

But in the political thought of this period there was another motif which runs entirely counter to such a crass distinction between appearance and reality, and this motif is rather more important to the argument this essay seeks to develop. Among Thomas Hobbes's many striking aphorisms, the assertion that 'Reputation of power is power' is by no means the least (Hobbes, 1651, Ch.10: 62). The most familiar characteristic of the Hobbesian sovereign is that he holds the Sword, the symbol of coercion. But in fact Hobbes's preoccupation throughout *Leviathan* was with the control of men's opinions, the 'empire of opinion' as it was later called: 'for the actions of men proceed from their opinions, and in the well governing of opinions consisteth the well governing of men's actions' (Hobbes, 1651, Ch.18: 124). The Hobbesian sovereign therefore would be the fount of public 'honour'. He would control the printing presses, the pulpit and (more important) the universities which provided the personnel for the pulpits, the bishops' palaces, the law-courts and the printing presses. Thus, if there were to be a Hobbesian sovereign, he would control not merely the expression of opinion, but those who form opinions. He would do so, not by excluding people from hearing wrong opinions (which Hobbes thought was impossible in the case of the universities), but because true opinions are advantageous to people generally, and if properly presented (as they are in his *Leviathan*), will prevail.

Opinions in the last resort cannot be controlled, for thought is free, as Hobbes also said. What can however be done is to maintain the credibility of those responsible for the guardianship of public opinion, which demands that they themselves should be disinterested, upright and convinced (Hobbes, 1651, Ch.12: 83–6). Significantly, Hobbes did not believe, any more than the Jesuits, that falsehood could be maintained indefinitely merely by clever presentation.

The point about the 'empire of opinion', then, is that opinion creates and maintains a reality: things are precisely as people think they are, because the only world human beings can ever act in and respond to is the world as they perceive it to be. Reality is a matter of opinion, so to speak: not *merely* a matter of opinion, but *inevitably* a matter of opinion.

To sum up so far, Platonists may think that reality is inherently something other than appearances, and that opinion is one thing, and substance or essence quite another. But Jesuits were good Aristotelians, and as The Philosopher says: 'everything is what it is and not some other thing'. Whatever they might have thought about what went on behind closed doors (and as confessors and increasingly confessors of princes, Jesuits may be supposed to have known a bit about that), they never thought that appearance is somehow equivalent to a lack of reality.

Now the Society of Jesus was not an organization which could insist on people even listening to it, let along obeying it. And no one at all can enforce belief. But the Jesuits' *métier* was belief – faith – and faith is precisely 'the substance of things to be hoped for, and the evidence of things that appear not', as the Epistle to the Hebrews (11.1) says. Faith cannot be compelled, and arguably it is destroyed by any attempt at compulsion. Nevertheless it depends on human communication, notably but by no means exclusively the voice and the printed page. 'Faith comes by hearing', as Scripture also says (Romans, 10.19), but its messengers (such as the Society of Jesus) cannot compel anyone to listen to them. They must first gather and then keep an audience. In this respect, they are comparable to merchants seeking customers, a metaphor that Jesuits used about themselves, or to a company of stage-players trying to secure an audience, a metaphor which understandably they never used. The merchant metaphor incidentally in part accounts for the title the Jesuits gave their association: Societas, Compagnia, Companie, Gesellschaft are all terms in law for corporations of merchants, as well as for guilds of artisans, charitable societies, or associations formally incorporated in some way, including of course 'companies' of soldiers.

But apart from the mercantile metaphor, a much more instructive indication of how the Society from the beginning regarded itself is its self-conscious and elaborate programme of recruitment and professional training for its members. All Jesuits trained in Latin and cases of conscience, as well as religious doctrine; since they were almost all priests or studying for the priesthood, they obviously *needed* Latin, religious education and cases of conscience. But they didn't need the Greek they were increasingly required to study – Greek was certainly useful for theology and philosophy, but for pastoral and missionary work Jesuits would have been better off learning German (which the Jesuits from the Romance countries seem to have found rather more difficult than Chinese or the language of Paraguay, Guarani). As Jesuits became increasingly preoccupied with the war against heresy, studying the theological issues at the heart of the dispute with the Protestants should have been a principal concern. In fact, however, the Society was up and running forty or fifty years before it started producing anything specialized in that line. In fact, the emphasis on Greek as well as Latin was in large part because these were instruments of *rhetoric*. An increasing number of Jesuits became theologians and philosophers, and increasingly Jesuits taught Catholic Europe (Fumaroli, 1980). But all Jesuits were taught rhetoric.

Rhetoric is the art and science of persuasive discourse, whether (as originally) speech or, increasingly since Roman times, writing. It is 'that faculty by which we understandt what will serve our turn concerning any subject, to win belief in the hearer', to quote Hobbes's digest of Artistotle's *Rhetoric* (Aristotle, 1934: 80). Rhetoric was learnt by practice, but a practice informed by the study of exemplars and treatises on the subject, especially those of Aristotle, Cicero and Quinctilian. One of the first Jesuit publications for the general public was Cyprian Soarez's *Three Books on the Art of Rhetoric*, taken principally from Aristotle, Cicero and Quinctilian. The book was endlessly reprinted and no wonder, since it is a masterpiece (Soarez, 1573). The study of rhetoric was by no means the study of a mere method or technique divorced from substance; on the contrary, the exemplars from which the techniques were abstracted were philosophers, theologians, moralists, historians, lawyers and statesmen. And one of the first requirements of rhetoric is precisely not technique, but facility with a set of materials appropriate to any topic at hand, whether it be forensic, deliberative or ceremonial. This was called *inventio* (hence 'inventory'), and the materials to be learnt and kept in the head so that they would be ready for instant use were called *loci communes*, common-places. That word has everywhere acquired the pejorative sense of the cliché, the worn-out, the trite, but of course the skilled rhetorician precisely avoids that because his store is richer and his understanding of his audience more acute. Equally, part of the professional equipment of the rhetorician since Aristotle's *Rhetoric* had been both an understanding of logic, and some understanding of how to analyze the soul, that is, the personality and motivation. Rhetoric inevitably attempts to engage the whole person of the hearer, and thus a competence at verbal pyrotechnics and logical gymnastics is not nearly enough – the point is to move. The person trained in rhetoric, in short, is not merely a master of a technique, but also the possessor of a moral substance: *suaviter in modo, fortiter in re*.

In this sense rhetoric is, or ought to be, the servant of truth and wisdom. But thanks to Plato and his disciples, it has always on the contrary been regarded as the art of making things appear other than they are, especially by representing the false as the true and the evil as the good. The Greek word for a teacher of rhetoric, the *sophist* (from the Greek word for knowledge, truth or wisdom), has become a synonym for a practitioner of specious, deceptive and captious discourse. Nor has it helped that rhetoric has been associated with politicians, and (still more contemptibly) lawyers. It is certainly true that there is no inseparable connection between moral substance and mastery of rhetorical technique – there is nothing in the technique itself to guarantee that it will be efficacious only when employed for virtuous purposes.

Jesuits were obviously aware of the ambiguous reputation of rhetoric, but as far as they were concerned it was neither here nor there. For the true faith to enter or re-enter souls, it had first to get a hearing. What is more, and more central, the Jesuits increasingly became the sharp end of the Roman Church's battle against heresy. As Jesuits readily admitted, heresy had first spread (like a disease, as they habitually said) simply by persuasion, the spoken and written word, even if it was subsequently consolidated by force, intimidation and persecution. Now, for an Aristotelian, no one ever believes what is completely false, just as no one ever pursues anything that is not in some sense good. If heresy as a doctrine and as a way of life had managed to insinuate itself by the spoken and written word, then it must have in some way resembled the truth, either in its content, or in the way it was presented, or both. Heresy ultimately emanates from Satan, the Prince of Lies, but lies, to be credible, must have some resemblance to the truth, and persuasive speakers of lies must outwardly resemble witnesses to the truth – apostles. In fact both had been the case. For if heresy had never incorporated any Catholic truth at all, it would never have got a hearing in the first place: no one swallows poison unless it is concealed in something that is in itself agreeable and is administered by apparently agreeable people. Strangely enough, although poison was another favourite metaphor for heresy, and the idea of the well-presented truth as its antidote was equally common, no Jesuit to the best of this author's knowledge ever employed an image of Plato's which would have been strikingly appropriate here: rhetoric as a *pharmakon*, that is to say something which is both a cure and a poison; or of representation as hollow and indeterminate, simultaneously good and evil, a *pharmakon*, the antidote to which is *episteme*, knowledge (Derrida, 1981: 138–40).

The difference between heresy and Catholic truth, then, was that heresy was entirely a matter of presentation, and when that collapsed, there was nothing left except those fragments of Catholic truth that the purveyors of heresy had necessarily incorporated. Catholic truth, by contrast, is a matter of presentation and substance. When the presentation collapses, as it clearly had done in the sixteenth century, thanks largely in the Jesuits' view to the ignorance and bad example of the Catholic clergy, the substance remained there, merely waiting for someone to re-present it convincingly. It was one of the most profound articles of Jesuit faith that truth (like goodness) is irresistible when properly presented in due form.

In short, the success of heresy had depended on its appearance, its presentation, and so would the success of the Catholic *reconquista*, or reformation. The problem had been the real learning and eloquence of the reformers (as compared to the incompetence of most Catholics) and the specious piety of their persons. It had to be specious, because it was an article of faith of the whole Counter-Reformation that the heresiarchs, the Luthers, Calvins, Zwinglis, Butzers, and so forth, were monsters of pride and arrogance, voluptuaries, drunkards (if Germans) and probably pederasts as well (at least in the case of Calvin).

Thus both the past and the future depended on presentation, and the possession of the substance of truth is a necessary, but by no means a sufficient, condition for success: the Catholic Church had always had the substance of truth, and yet had effectively collapsed in much of Europe because its personnel were incapable of presenting it effectively when the crunch came. From this understanding of what had happened in the world, and what needed to be done to restore it, springs the concern with appearances that is such a striking feature of the Society of Jesus. That concern is conspicuous in the care the Society collectively and individually took both about how it presented itself to the world and whom particularly to win over.

Thus the Society was extremely selective in whom it recruited and retained as members. It insisted on academic and intellectual aptitude and attainments. (Indeed the only titles used in the Society were academic titles; otherwise everyone including Ignatius was either just first names, or later 'Father'.) Such aptitudes were unusual enough, given the stunning ignorance of the average Catholic priest and monk of the time. The Society also insisted on the most exacting standards of poverty, chastity and obedience. But more than this, it looked for qualities of judgement, discretion and prudence in all its members, but especially those who were to hold any office in the Society. Beyond even this, it looked in candidates to the Society for a pleasing manner of speech and verbal facility, and also good appearance in the absence of any notable ugliness, disfigurement or deformity. The point here was that the Society's members should not gratuitously put the public off. For the same reason, other qualities which might commend its members to the world at large, such as distinguished parentage or outstanding talents or accomplishments, were also more than welcome. Of the first five superiors general, the founder was a Basque nobleman, the third was a former viceroy of Catalunya and the fifth was of the Neapolitan nobility; to compensate, the second was of Spanish Jewish descent (albeit a Paris MA and a Doctor of Theology), and the fourth was a Belgian of inconspicuous birth. A candidate for membership might be accepted although he lacked one or more of these attributes, but only if he compensated for the lack in some other way; the only purely optional attribute was some coat of arms, for lack of it could not prejudice admission. All this is written into the very Constitutions of the Society, its articles of association, composed by St Ignatius himself although not ratified until after his death (Ganss, 1970, especially ss 151, 157–8, 161–2, 178, 183, 185–6). By contrast, and as an aside, in the matter of admitting persons of Jewish and Muslim descent, the Society held out for fifty years in admitting candidates with such origins; Ignatius himself insisted on their admissibility and some of its most prominent members came from there. In 1593, they were finally excluded, partly because of anti-semitism in the Society itself, but more because of rampant anti-semitism in society at large, especially Hispanic society (O'Malley, 1993: 188–92).

The same concern was exhibited over the deportment and dress of members of the Society. Thus no distinctive dress at all was prescribed for them; they were simply to dress like respectable priests in their locality, or academics if that was appropriate. Of course Jesuits wore no habit: the Society was always careful to distinguish itself from monastic orders, originally because the very name of 'monk' had fallen into such popular disrepute that it would prejudice people against the 'Society' and its work. This is in part also why the Society called itself that, and not a 'religious order'. In the course of time (as with any organization), a style of dress did become standard, but it was merely the gown (the ancestor of the *soutane*), whether buttoned or not, and the white ruff (the ancestor of the clerical collar?), and this was simply an austere version of a style of dress familiar even amongst the laity and not unfashionable. It could be laid aside without hesitation. The Portuguese Jesuit and founder of the colony of Macau, Matteo Ricci, appeared at the Chinese Imperial Court and elsewhere dressed as a Mandarin; given his astonishing scholarship in science (including maths, astronomy, watchmaking and cosmography), humanities and Chinese, no Chinese ever queried his right to do so. This incidentally was after he had made a gaffe induced by personal modesty and cultural crossed lines: he first dressed as an ambassador, which of course he was in a sense, only to learn that

Chinese society regarded ambassadors as a kind of messenger-boy, of no standing at all (Spence, 1988). The Jesuit Antonio Nobili in India dressed in the robes of a Brahmin.

Equally Jesuits were to avoid giving offence or occasion for scandal and this was one reason why they were ordinarily required to go out in public in twos. They were to be exceptionally cautious in their dealings with women. Their personal decorum and manners were to be above reproach and Ignatius himself set the tone with his exquisite *hidalgo* manners. Approachability and compassion were to characterize the conduct of Jesuits, notably their confessors. For this reason too they were explicitly counselled by their founder to avoid controverted and inflammatory topics generally, and indeed even the teaching of certain doctrines (such as predestination) which were true but were bound to lead to misinterpretation (Loyola, 1865: 200, Rule 15). Accommodation, and stressing points of agreement as well as charity and modesty, wins people over; confrontation does not. St Ignatius was fond of the Spanish proverb, 'We go in through their door and bring them out through ours' (Loyola, 1959: 51). All this is somewhat ironic, in view of the fact that the Jesuits became the foremost controversialists in Europe, and provided the whole of Catholic Europe with its anti-heretical war-machines from the 1590s onwards. But then not even the most consummate rhetorician can please all possible audiences simultaneously.

Again, Jesuits were under no circumstances to accept any state office, except offices in universities, still less to seek them, or to commend each other for them; the only ecclesiastical office they might hold was that of bishop in the foreign missions (which was not a dignity but a crown of thorns), or if specifically directed to accept an ecclesiastical office by the Papacy. All this was not only for reasons of asceticism, but because nothing destroys credibility so much as any suspicion of self-interest or ambition. And for the same reasons, Jesuits under no circumstances accepted remuneration for any priestly, charitable or academic work; they of course accepted and solicited resources of all kinds for the Society, and often with enormous success. They were not a mendicant order – as schoolteachers and academics they could hardly be out begging for their livelihoods and those of their pupils.

The appearance, deportment, conduct and style of individual members were part and parcel of the public face of the Society, its collective self-presentation. The two could not finally be separated: the Society was intended to be exemplary, and part of that was the exemplary character and accomplishments of those who composed it. It did not work in private or secret, unless circumstances (as in Britain and Ireland or the United Provinces (The Netherlands)) compelled it. On the contrary, visibility and prominence were as inseparable from the Society's mission as doing good by stealth. Thus not only did the Society have a very public 'mission statement', so to speak, of exemplary brevity and freedom from jargon, the Institute (see Aldama, 1990), one of the best corporate logos of all time and the very best motto (AMDG, *Ad Maiorem Dei Gloriam* – For the Greater Glory of God), but its churches, colleges and residences were built to be seen, in their location (ideally centrally in central cities), their style (Jesuit colleges and churches were highly elegant as well as functional, wherever funds permitted) and their size, for, wherever possible, Jesuits built on a grand scale. Although the Society did not sing the 'offices', unlike monks, and Ignatius wanted music banned from Jesuit churches, it rapidly became something they cultivated: it was what fashion and the customers wanted. The Jesuits also developed an entire theatre of their own, to bring together town and gown as well as being an educational technique. Unlike Protestants, they never underestimated the power of the eye and the visual imagination.

It is important not to overstate here. Most Jesuits spent their lives in obscurity. The Society never forgot its beginnings working with children, the poor, orphans, prostitutes, prisoners, the sick and the dying. Nor did the Society hesitate to send large numbers of its best members to die of fevers amongst the pagans, or to risk torture and martyrdom in the parts of the heretics and infidels, or worse still to be entirely ignored by supercilious non-Christian high cultures. Nevertheless, it was necessary to decide about where to concentrate its efforts. Thus it was a matter of dispute whether the Society was better advised to send its scarce personnel to waste and die in the Indies, China and Japan, or whether they would be better employed meeting the insatiable manpower needs of the Holy Roman Empire, central and eastern Europe and the Americas. But wherever they went, one of the chief addressees of their work of persuasion were rulers. Good example is more persuasive than any number of words, and the example of princes (as well as their administrative, legislative and punitive interventions on behalf of Catholic orthodoxy) weighs more with their subjects than anything else, as the consolidation of the heretical English Reformation demonstrated. The cultivation of the great was a standard part of the Jesuits' *modus agendi*, written into the Constitutions themselves (Ganss, 1970: ss. 622e, 823, 824).

Another chief addressee of the Jesuits' efforts were opinion-formers, both clerical and lay. It is partly in virtue of this concern that, just as the Society came to concentrate on the refutation of heresy and the reconversion of Europe from heresy, although this was not its original mission, so also it became the foremost academic and teaching order, although this was no part of its original mission either. This was to kill several birds with one stone, for in establishing colleges, universities and seminaries the Society was not only doing the work of the Church and securing a hold over the opinion-formers, rulers and administrators of the future (including not infrequently teaching the sons of heretics), but it was also attending to its own future recruitment and training. All this was of course only possible if the Society did its educational work exceptionally well, since the funding that was needed could only come from voluntary donations and endowments, and recruitment of able new members presupposed a pool of able existing members.

And so, although the Society never neglected the work of parishes, domestic and foreign missions, and the care of the uneducated and the helpless, it prided itself on its ability to field a vast and growing number of public preachers, teachers, academics, confessors and, last but by no means least, writers of publications for every occasion and in every language. Although the Society's own language of instruction and communication, like that of Europe generally, was still Latin, the fact was that the market demanded vernacular publications, and by the early seventeenth century the Jesuits were writing in every language from Japanese to Guarani. Its members were amongst the foremost stylists in Europe, and the teachers of both sacred and secular eloquence to the whole of Catholic Europe (Fumaroli, 1980). The first principle of rhetoric is that the audience and not the speaker determines the manner of communication, as well as its starting-point. If the audience demanded the vernacular (as it did), and a racy, silver-tongued, entertaining and disputatious mode of public oratory and sermons (then one of the most popular forms of mass-entertainment, so to speak), then it was up to the Society to provide it, if it wanted a hearing. The Society did, and what is more it provided manuals on how to do it, as it provided manuals on every other art and science.

Thus not only did the Society persistently engage in high-profile activities, and with conspicuous success, but it also took care to ensure that its own achievements would not lack advertisement, and its legions of denigrators would not go unanswered. This could no doubt be dismissed as mere 'image-management', and certainly composing defences of the Society and recruiting defenders to speak up for it was a regular industry. To celebrate its virtues, triumphs and martyrs all over the world, there was even an annual publication, spiced up with all sorts of fascinating detail: the famous *Annual Letters* of every province of the Society. A Belgian Jesuit was able to issue in 1606 a second edition of *Amphitheatre of Honour*, a not insubstantial volume of writings by Jesuit writers, orators, martyrs and other high achievers (Scribani, 1606). A considerably longer work, an augmented second edition of the (annotated) *Catalogue of Jesuit Writers*, was issued in 1613 (Ribadeneira, 1613). In 1640 the Society gave to the world an enormous, beautifully produced and illustrated folio *Image of the First Century of the Society of Jesus* (*Imago primi saeculi Societatis Iesu*) to mark the centenary of the Society's foundation.

Now all this, as far as the Society was concerned, was no more than to present the substance and truth of the Faith, the Church and the Society itself (and of course also the substance and truth about the enemies of all three) in a form which that truth deserved and which would not gratuitously alienate anyone as yet unpersuaded of that truth. There was therefore no conflict between rhetoric and truth, or appearance and reality.

But of course, and here's the rub, the very success of the Jesuit enterprise made the Society innumerable enemies, not only among Protestants of all kinds, but also among Catholics, as well as politiques, sceptics, conformists and unbelievers of every kind. And inevitably these persons would not share the Jesuits' belief in the intimate and indissoluble unity of Jesuit presentation and substantial truth. From a hostile point of view, the explanation of the Jesuit enterprise and Jesuit successes would be the same as the explanation Jesuits had given of the initial successes of the heretics, and Jesuits therefore found such explanations turned against them.

What happens here is simply that in order to get at the truth (as opponents saw it), means and ends signs must be systematically reversed. So what Jesuits pretended were mere means were presented as in fact the ends they aimed at: wealth, esteem, prestige, influence over the great, elegance, smoothness, display and, indeed, sharp practice of all kinds. Conversely the ends Jesuits claimed for themselves (service to God and neighbours, the practice of humility, obedience and all the virtues and the triumph of Catholic truth) are in fact merely means to the self-aggrandizement of the Society and its members. Duplicity is thus the Jesuits' principal characteristic (Duhr, 1981).

So appearance once again becomes facade; the Jesuits' 'sacred eloquence' (as they termed rhetoric in the service of truth; see Fumaroli, 1980) is merely sophistry and rhetoric in the old sense of specious plausibility; the Jesuits' benign and accommodating approach to all manner of persons is a stratagem or ploy to win influence. Conversely, whatever is not public, visible, apparent, presented, and especially what is secret, becomes the truth, the real. The great thing about really deep secrets is that the absence of evidence is proof of how well hidden the secrets are, and how clever, duplicitous and conspiratorial the organization is that can keep such secrets and practice such abominations in secret; and equally, of course, how astute and dedicated to truth are those who ferret such secrets out. After that, anything can become evidence. Thus the Jesuits were held to practise and incite the murder of rulers and the mass-murder of Protestants – the evidence was there in the fact that their writings endorsed 'tyrannicide' (see Lewy, 1960, Ch. 9) and the *exterminatio* (banishment, but it might mean execution, at a pinch) of obstinate heresiarchs. Jesuits were equally accused of torture, fornication and (as a natural consequence) infanticide on a grand scale. One such monster of depravity was the Jesuit Cardinal Robert Bellarmine, to whom all this and more was attributed in a pamphlet which also announced that he had died cursing God. He was however still very much alive and was thus able to offer an early version of the 'reports of my death have been much exaggerated' quip.

There is nothing like a good conspiracy theory, and in the anti-Jesuit rhetoric the Society becomes the paradigm of a conspiratorial society. There are any number of such writings; a standard English example would be Thomas Bell's *The Anatomie of Popish Tyrannie* of 1603, which is in fact largely an anatomy of Jesuit tyranny (Bell, 1603, e.g. Bk. I: 2, 9). It is no wonder that the greatest of the anti-Jesuit libels (still being published in this century and vastly superior in quality to more famous hack-work like *The Protocols of the Elders of Zion*, which was amongst Hitler's favourite reading) was entitled *The Secret Instructions of the Jesuits* (Monita Secreta), first published in 1614. The peroration of that work (which being the work of a renegade Jesuit, was not only in the authentic Latin, style and vocabulary of actual Jesuit documents, but was also well structured and did not voice the more egregious accusations against Jesuits about murders and poisoning, and only gave the game away because of its obsession with rich widows, which the author foisted on to the Society) was a paraphrase of an authentically Machiavellian maxim: 'Those who do not love the Society should at least be made to fear it'. The composer of this libel obviously expected his readers to get the point: the ostentatious Jesuit campaign against Machiavelli and reason of state was merely a defence-in-depth of the authentic Machiavellianism of the Society of Jesus.

In sum, then, the Society of Jesus understood the substance of its enterprise as literally a matter of (eternal) life and death; but the enterprise also demanded a condign form, or presentation, for that substance. Presentation in turn demanded the recruitment and motivation of a personnel capable of persuading the addressees of its message: a mastery of rhetorical technique in oral and printed form, but also and especially its visual complements. The very success at presentation, and at controlling the resources necessary for successful presentation, however, invited an 'unmasking' response, an inverting interpretation which treated the Jesuits' control of resources (or power) as the 'real' end at which Jesuits end, and the religious and moral substance of the 'message' as merely a means to that end.

In terms of organizational aesthetics, then, the account of the Jesuits offered here may serve as a paradigm and illustration of what is now termed *production aesthetics*; it was an intuitive understanding of this that underpinned the Jesuits' cultivation of appearances. What is striking about the Jesuits in this respect is their acute sensitivity to the visual as a reinforcement of the verbal. A ready parallel to this kind of aesthetic sensibility is to be found in the way that contemporary organizations have sought to achieve a continuous aesthetic in presentation, text and style, so much so that corporate presenters can appear to be an extension of their texts.

There are of course any number of parallels between what has been discussed here and the current practice of organizations in respect of, for example, the conscious and explicit use of rhetoric in marketing the products and images of organizations, the construction of statements, strategies and structures designed to achieve organizational objectives and the deliberate use of mythopoeic imagery and narratives to support the construction of organizational histories. At bottom, cultivation of appearances has to do with the relationship between style (*modus agendi*) and desired outcome, which for the Jesuits was the glory of God, the saving of their own souls and those of their neighbours, and for modern organizations is the veneration of corporate identity and corporate 'survival, eternity and immortality' (Sievers, 1994: 116). The organization as a site of meaning and the production of imagery requires that its representatives and representations (images and texts) are accepted as convincing by its various audiences. Recent years have seen the elaboration of corporate rhetoric directed towards employees in the pursuit of greater commitment and in the construction of ornate narratives and organizational 'performances'. In the pursuit of these objectives, there has been an increasing emphasis on the manipulation of spiritual experience and of the heroic sentiment.

This, however, brings us to one respect in which the parallel is necessarily imperfect. The Society of Jesus could claim to represent the highest good of and for its members; it could therefore demand from them unlimited commitment and sacrifice as the quid pro quo. Modern secular organizations, having no reward of remotely equivalent value to bestow, have no right to demand such a quid pro quo from their members. If they do so, nevertheless, they simply incur ridicule the moment that disbelief is no longer voluntarily suspended. And in this they positively invite an unwillingness to suspend it: an 'unmasking' response to their spiritual and heroic pretensions.

But the reality of appearances here ironically has the last word. The unmasking approach to organization is likely in many respects to prove as counterproductive as that adopted by the Jesuits' opponents. For the revelation of what is ostensibly behind the constructed facade or appearance, whether it be the enormous might of the Jesuits or the force of corporate ideology, does not abolish that appearance – it merely confirms its reality. Reputation of power is power.

References

Aldama, Antonio M. de (1990) *The Formula of the Institute.* St Louis, MI: Institute of Jesuit Sources. pp. 2–23 (1539 and 1550 versions).

Anthony, Peter (1994) *Managing Culture.* Buckingham: Open University Press.

Aquaviva (or Acquaviva), Claudio (1606) *Industriae ad curandos Animae Morbos,* 11.1 cited in (1958) *Stevenson's Book of Quotations, Ancient and Modern,* 7th edn: 'fortes in fine consequendo, et suaves in modo'. London: Cassell,

Aristotle (1934) *Poetics of Aristotle; On Style, by Demetrius; and Aristotle's Rhetoric with Hobbes' Digest; and Ars Petica by Horace,* ed. T.A. Moxon. London: J.M.Dent.

Bell, Thomas (1603) *The Anatomie of Popish Tyrannie,* repr. Amsterdam: Theatrum Orbis Terrarum, 1975.

Bellarmine, Robert (Cardinal) (1619) *De Officio Principis Christiani Libri Tres,* Cologne: B. Gualter.

Bireley, Robert (1990) *The Counter-Reformation Prince: Anti-Machiavellianism or Catholic Statecraft in Early Modern Europe.* Chapel Hill, NC and London: University of North Carolina Press.

Derrida, Jacques (1981) *Dissemination.* London: Athlone Press.

Duhr, Bernhard (1891) *Jesuiten-Fabeln.* Freiburg i. B.: Herder. Ch. 4.

Featherstone, Michael (1995) *Undoing Culture.* London: Sage.

Fumaroli, Marc (1980) *L'Age del'Eloquence.* Geneva: Droz.

Gagliardi, Pasquale (1986) 'The creation and change of organizational cultures: a conceptual framework', *Organization Studies,* 7 (2): 117–34.

Ganss, G.E. (1970) *The Constitutions of the Society of Jesus.* St Louis, MI: Institute of Jesuit Sources.

Harju, Klaus (1999) 'Protext: the morphoses of identity, heterogeneity and synolon', in S. Linstead (ed.), *The Textuality of Organization, Studies in Cultures, Organizations and Societies*, 5 (1): 131–50.

Hobbes, Thomas (1651) *Leviathan*, cited according to the Richard Tuck edn, Cambridge: Cambridge University Press, 1991.

Höpfl, Heather J. (1996) 'Angelus in Los Angeles', paper presented to Standing Conference on Organizational Symbolism, UCLA.

Höpfl, Heather J. and Linstead, Stephen (1993) 'Passion and performance: suffering and the carrying of organizational roles', in S. Fineman (ed.), *Emotion in Organizations*. London: Sage.

Lewy, Guenther (1960) *Constitutionalism and Statecraft during the Golden Age of Spain* Geneva: Droz.

Loyola, Saint Ignatius (1865) *Regulae Aliquot Servandae ut cum orthodoxa Ecclesia sentiamus. An addendum to the Exercitia Spiritualia*, cited according to the Paris: Goupy version. 197–202.

Loyola, Saint Ignatius (1959) *Letters of St Ignatius of Loyola*, trans. W.J. Young. Chicago: Loyola University Press.

Machiavelli, Niccolo (1532) *The Prince*, written 1513; the translation is a slightly modified version of that of the edition of Quentin Skinner and Russell Price, Cambridge: Cambridge University Press, 1988.

Monita Secreta (1614) first appeared anonymously in Cracow, with false date and imprint. (The scores of editions and translations it enjoyed were variously entitled *Monita Privata, Instructio Secretissima, Cabinet, Geheime Vorschriften, Mystäres, Secrets*, etc.)

O'Malley, John W. (1993) *The First Jesuits*. Cambridge, MA: Harvard University Press.

Ribadeneira, Pedro de (1613) *Catalogus Scriptorum Religionis Societatis Iesu*, augmented posthumous 2nd edn. Antwerp: Plantin-Moretus.

Scribani, Karel [under pseudonym and anagram Clarus Bonarscius] (1606) *Amphiteatrum Honoris*. Paleopolis Aduaticorum: A. Verheyden.

Sievers, Burkard (1994) *Work, Death and Life Itself.* Berlin: De Gruyter.

Spence, Jonathan D. (1988) *The Memory Palace of Matteo Ricci*. London: Faber and Faber.

Soarez, Cyprianus (1573) *De Arte Rhetorica Libri Tres, ex Aristotele, Cicerone et Quintiliano praecipue deprompi*. Paris: T. Brummenius.

Turner, Barry (1992) 'The symbolic understanding of organizations', in M. Reed and M. Hughes (eds), *Rethinking Organizations*. London: Sage.

10

Resurfacing an Aesthetics of Existence as an Alternative to Business Ethics

Stephen Cummings

If one looks far enough two approaches to ethics may be discerned: *codes of behaviour* and *forms of subjectification* (Johnson, 1996: 30; Thacker, 1993). Codes of behaviour refer to collective rules of conduct that exist over and above individual bodies in the world. They can be used to legitimate, or prove right or wrong, independent actions. Forms of subjectification refer to individuals constituting themselves as subjects of moral conduct through the development of relationships with the self: relationships for self-reflection, self-examination or self-aesthetics, relationships for the decipherment of the self by oneself. Systems of morality comprise both elements, but in some societies the emphasis is on the former, in others on the latter. The emphasis in the West, in the modern age, has been on developing codes with the 'systematicity, . . . richness, . . . [and the] capacity to adjust to every possible case and to embrace every area of behaviour' (Foucault, 1984: 29; Thacker, 1993: 14). Forms of subjectification have been sadly neglected.

The past two decades have witnessed a growing appreciation that organizational activity and managerial work involves ethical issues and dilemmas (De George, 1986; Donaldson, 1982). This appreciation has fuelled a new field of study: 'business ethics'.[1] This field, emerging as something of a subset of the modern world's system of morality, brings with it the same emphasis and neglect mentioned above. As a new field seeking to establish itself, its level of privilege may even be more extreme. Business ethics has emerged as an 'industry . . . largely devoted to codifying what is "ethical"', and narrowly focused upon 'the development and elaboration of codes of conduct' (Kjonstad and Willmott, 1995: 445, 449).

Interestingly, the rise of a literature concerned with business ethics has been paralleled by a literature devoted to outlining the nature of the currently changing state of the Western world, a state described by Jean-Francois Lyotard as 'the postmodern condition', characterized by 'an incredulity towards meta-narratives of legitimation' (Lyotard, 1984: xv). A 'meta-narrative' is any universal schema claiming to exist over and above actions in the world, and grounding and legitimating particular developments. Examples include Marxism, Hegelianism, the model of scientific rationalism, Christianity, a Freudian emphasis on the dominance of the unconscious mind, or collective codes of behaviour. Since Lyotard's definition, hundreds of articles and books have described the postmodern environment, within which most organizations must now act, as characterized by a privileging of heterogeneity and difference above essential commonalities; pluralism, pragmatism and pastiche; paradox, fragmentation and indeterminacy; and a scepticism toward, and distrust of, meta-narratives of any sort (Cummings, 1996; Harvey, 1990).

The juxtaposition of a snapshot of the state of business ethics against one of the postmodern condition brings into view an interesting tension. Organizations waking up to the importance of ethics, but constrained by boundaries that conceive of ethics as primarily about collective codes, may well be promoting a form of business ethics ill suited to current conditions. Perhaps this is why many now regard the current codes, that constitute people's appreciation of what business ethics amounts to, as so general as to be meaningless as a guide to practical action in a fast-changing world characterized by unique situations; why ethics is of little use in the development of a company's strategy, other than in a restrictive sense; and why many see business ethics as only being cynically or instrumentally adhered to on an 'as needed' basis. Perhaps this is why some commentators implore that it is 'necessary to move beyond a preoccupation with the development and implementation of codes of conduct if the theory and practice of business ethics is not to be brought into disrepute' (Kjonstad and Willmott, 1995: 461).

This chapter seeks to move beyond the preoccupation with codes by drawing upon the last histories of Michel Foucault to resurface an ethical understanding that operates with a greater awareness of self-subjectification. Aware that societies other than our own conceived of ethics differently, Foucault explored the subjectification of the self in ancient Greek and Roman societies, finding an approach he termed an 'aesthetics of existence', or 'self-aesthetics' (1984: 12). This approach may provide an alternative to the code-dominated view of business ethics, one that offers a more useful means of guiding an organization's strategic development in postmodern environments. In order to better understand the different nature of this alternative, the emergence of the tension described above is firstly outlined in more detail.

Modern ethics, modern tensions, postmodern conditions

The word 'moral' is commonly used in relation to what is right and what is wrong, what is good conduct and what is bad. 'Ethics' is generally defined as the science, study, or philosophy of morals. In our time ethics is not about developing relationships with the self to discover how one should act. Indeed we are told that individuals cannot 'create their morality by making their own rules' (Beauchamp and Bowie, 1988). Ethics is rather 'about how we ought to live' (Singer, 1994: 2), the emphasis being on the collective 'we'.

The dozens of definitions that have already emerged as to what constitutes business ethics typically take it to be the above understanding of ethics, simply applied to the realm of business. *The Economist*, a good barometer of the Western managerial *zeitgeist*, claims ethics to be '[t]he vexed question of what is right and wrong in everyday behaviour' and business ethics, subsequently, 'the codes of behaviour over and above this that professional and business people agree among themselves constitute the proper way to deal with the general public and each other' (*The Economist*, 1994).

Business ethics, in step with modern ethics in general, has come to be about the study and development of collective charters and codes of conduct that provide rules, enforceable by 'independent' bodies, for individual business people, organizations, industries and professions, to live by. The intent of such codes is usually to reassure existing or prospective suppliers, customers, employees and regulators that they are dealing with an 'ethical' company that can be 'trusted' (Robertson and Schlegelmilch, 1993; Waters et al., 1986). This approach has dovetailed with other recent strategic initiatives that stress the importance of companies improving themselves by looking outwards. In particular, one may note the primacy afforded a marketing focus which puts the 'customer first' and 'stakeholder approaches' to strategic development. Ethical codes in modern organizations are seen as having important legal functions, identifying and protecting the rights and duties of corporations, managers and employees, and providing routinized means of rationalizing and managing that which has identified itself as potentially problematic. In short, business ethics has come to be about rules, obligations, and instructions. About seeking guidance from others rather than from 'within'. A 'restrictive' rather than an 'empowering' form of ethics (Kjonstad and Willmott, 1995).

This type of ethics is based upon three very modern assumptions: humanism, Cartesianism and liberal individualism. These are the assumptions upon which the Enlightenment and modernity are largely based, and an understanding of each, and the relationships between them, describes both the nature of the modern view of ethics, and the tensions that have now emerged between it and postmodern conditions.

The combination of the humanistic belief, that all humans share a common essence (and thus common norms) and a Cartesian splitting of mind and external matter (including human bodies) that exists objectively 'out there', that places primacy of action in matter, makes it possible to see human beings as subject to the principles of the traditional empirical sciences (physics, chemistry, biology). This possibility emerged in the seventeenth century. The Enlightenment 'project' that followed turned this possibility into a programme that would enable individuals to break out of the vagaries of nature and chance, by making life more understandable, and thus more 'manageable'. It invested fields of human inquiry with a desire, and a necessity, to be based upon the models of the empirical sciences (Foucault, 1970).

The case of the transformation of medicine in the seventeenth and eighteenth centuries is exemplary. Here we find the emergence of the modern human science 'medical science' and its counterpart, the well-disciplined and ordered 'modern hospital', enabling the establishment of one another. As medicine sought to become more like physics or chemistry or biology in taking its references not so much from various author-authorities but from an objective object ('Man') it required a domain of such objects to be perpetually offered up for examination to create a 'back catalogue'. This enabled a collective code of normality, incorporating categories of measurement and bands of normality within these measures, to be established. In order for the hospital to become a medically useful space in the modern age, it must provide the conditions that enable the emergence of these norms and provide an examination space where individuals can be charted and their characteristics monitored against standard criteria: type of illness/symptoms (i.e. abnormality), pulse, temperature, colour, blood count. Thus, the hospital provides a sterilized table or 'tableau', a standard backdrop or normative order, against which the individual can be codified and treated objectively. This in turn reinforces the norms against which one should be measured, or how the individual should be known. While the modern hospital is often seen as a consequence of medical science, it is difficult to imagine how one could have existed without the other (Visker, 1995: 64). The modern hospital provides the 'laboratory' in which medical science can isolate, observe, and codify its object. The mental asylum performs the same role for the establishment of psychiatry.

One may view the rise of the modern penal system in the late eighteenth century in the same light. The late eighteenth century, the height of the Enlightenment, witnessed the almost simultaneous abolishment of old laws and customs and establishment of new penal codes, in societies as disparate as Russia (1769), Prussia (1780), Tuscany (1786), Pennsylvania (1786), Austria (1788) and France (1791) (Foucault, 1977: 7). The emergence of modern prisons in this same period fulfils the same function as the modern hospital for medical science. Standardized all-encompassing laws and guidelines for punishment enabled each person (or, more correctly, 'case') to be tried as an individual against the catalogue of crimes (manifestations of abnormality), incarcerated for the appropriate length of time, and monitored accordingly, further reinforcing norms regarding suitable forms of treatment.

In the modern West, unlike in most other societies, the tabling of individuals against an objective backdrop that is believed to be independent of those individuals, and have real objective meaning, not only becomes acceptable, but accepted and encouraged as the way forward. Modernity thus 'solved' the problem of 'the entry of the individual [not just 'species' or community] into the field of knowledge' (Foucault, 1977: 191), and made 'sciences of the individual', that Aristotle warned against, a possibility (Flynn, 1993: 43). It did so by seeing humans as susceptible to all-encompassing criteria, and then separating out individual characteristics that cannot be tabled (personality, culture, relationships, etc.), judging these to be irrelevant (or at best secondary) to the decision-making process and treatment. The object, or 'matter', of the individual that comes before the surgeon or the judge is what matters, not his or her non-material context.

It is easy to see Cartesianism and humanism manifest in the establishment of the modern hospital/medical science and prison/legal system, the modern quest for objective collective tableaux which can be used to code individuals. However, the impact of the Enlightenment belief in 'liberal individualism' is also crucial to the development of the modern predilection for equating ethics with collective codes of behaviour. The new 'sciences of the individual' can in some respects be seen as adding to the cause of liberal individualism (by enabling emancipatory knowledge), but there is at once an obvious tension between analytical frameworks based on objective human norms, and a liberal belief in an individual's right to be different. Ethical codes were implemented to order the tension created by the juxtaposition of Cartesianism and humanism against liberal individualism to ensure the latter, given the former.

Codes emerged outlining patients rights, doctors responsibilities, criminals rights, and so forth, all designed to protect individuals rights now that backdrops of universal objective frameworks, against which each individual could be plotted, had become a given. Also, the emphasis on codes was influenced by the problems of order that emerge when liberal individualism, in the form of democracy, usurps traditional charismatic and hereditary forms of authority. Following Weber's analysis, a modern order must be based on a rational/legal authority (Morgan, 1986), and there is no more appropriate vessel for this than the ethical code. The provision of ethical codes founded upon secular rational grounds and independent of individual biases, that could be used as an objective backdrop against which individual ethical problems and happenings could be judged, became an important linchpin for the Enlightenment project.

Modern ethics, like modern medical studies and legal systems, set out to develop itself as an objectively valid empirical science. Alasdair MacIntyre has described modern ethics' vain attempt to make itself so, describing his work in this regard as an attempt to outline 'at once the outcome and epitaph of the Enlightenment's systematic attempt to uncover a rational justification for morality' (MacIntyre, 1981: 38). MacIntyre illustrates this quest through reference to nineteenth-century moralist Henry Sidgwick's manifesto for a 'new ethical science'. One must, according to Sidgwick, pursue ethics, and indeed all knowledge, with 'the same disinterested curiosity to which we chiefly owe the great discoveries of physics' (MacIntyre, 1990: 181). Modern ethics sought something akin to Newton's universal laws.

Despite his grand aims, Sidgwick came to despair that such an ethical science was beyond reach, announcing, sadly, that where he had looked for cosmos he found only chaos (MacIntyre, 1981: 65). But in the chaos Sidgwick portrayed as failure, G.E. Moore, around the turn of this century, found an enlightening and liberating general law: 'emotivism', the view that all moral judgements, for all people in all cultures at all times, are 'nothing but expressions of preference, expressions of attitude or feeling' (MacIntyre, 1981: 11). On this view moral judgements can neither be true or false, and moral belief and moral knowledge are not possible, because while there may be rational justifications for actions, real rational 'un-emotional' justifications do not exist (Audi, 1995: 222–3). The general universal modern moral law is that people do what they feel first, they then, after the fact, may rationalize their behaviour into a moral schema. People of all persuasions today act as if this were the case, hence the increased emphasis upon psychology, relative to ethics, over the last century.

We find a two-fisted outcome-epitaph: on the one hand, Sidgwick's despair that a general ethical theory cannot be achieved; on the other, Moore's optimistic view that it can, resulting in a law that disproves the existence of morality. As such, MacIntyre's analysis suggests that the Enlightenment project's failure in this regard is relatable to the culture created by the tensions brought about by its founding assumptions. He outlines this tension by describing this culture as 'bureaucratic individualism', bringing organizational issues back into focus.

Bureaucratic individualism's emergence can be related back to the tension created by the Enlightenment's emphasis on liberal individualism and democracy. The major problem with this emphasis is that it tends to produce societies which are difficult and inefficient to control and steer as a whole, thus hindering the development of mankind's 'rational' progress in terms of the provision of objective frameworks, and also, crucially, in terms of enabling large predictable capital gains – also key elements of modernity. So, while modernity spawns individualism, at the same time, bureaucracy emerges as *the* mode of organization. This leads MacIntyre to conclude that

> there are only two alternative modes of social life open to us, one in which the free and arbitrary choices of individuals are sovereign and one in which the bureaucracy is sovereign, precisely so that it may limit the free and arbitrary choice of individuals. Given this . . . it is unsurprising that the politics of modern societies oscillate between a freedom which is nothing but a lack of regulation of individual behaviour and forms of collectivist control designed only to limit the anarchy of self-interest. (1981: 33)

One can see this view manifest in business ethics today, with its emphasis on the provision of codes as forms of collectivist control designed to limit what is regarded as humans' natural selfish interest. Whereas medical science found(ed) the tableau upon which it could erect itself in the modern hospital, and the modern legal system drew on the modern prison, the modern bureaucracy would have provided the perfect trellis upon which a science of business ethics, focused on the provision of codes, could bloom. The classic modern bureaucracy might have provided a handy replication of the empirical scientist's laboratory, where individual behaviour could be isolated, and judged, against general procedures. The only problem was that by the time business ethics came to be on the agenda, the bureaucratic form was on the wane. Its composition was ill suited to postmodern environments characterized by the embracing of multicultural perspectives, rapid and unpredictable change, an acceptance that human behaviour is non-generalizable and a demand for 'tailor-made' products and services.

Broadening out the debate again, MacIntyre claims that the general outcome of the tension created by the rise of modernity, and between postmodern times and modern mindsets, is that we now cling to 'simulacra of morality'. Despite the epitaph described earlier, we continue to talk and act as though we have recourse to a framework for thinking about and resolving moral issues objectively and rationally, but our moral debates can find no terminus. Subsequently, there is no way of securing moral agreement in our culture. Rival moral premises are such that we possess no rational way of weighing the claims of one against the other, but we continue to ask general questions, for example 'is abortion right?', 'are nuclear weapons a necessary deterrent?' and 'is the primary purpose of a business to maximize profit?', above and beyond particular contexts, in a way that suggests objective answers exist. Our moral debates still appeal to a type of consideration that is independent of the relationship between speaker and hearer, and presupposes the existence of impersonal criteria, despite conditions to the contrary (MacIntyre, 1981: 9).

To recap, business ethics has emerged as a subset of modern ethics, an approach that due to its modern heritage generally takes ethics to be about the provision of collective codes of behaviour. This heritage prompted a desire for ethics to become a science, like physics or medicine. This desire might have been fulfilled in a world where we could conceive of isolating social interactions, or business activities, in laboratory type institutions, like an extreme form of bureaucracy: perhaps such a conception was held at one point in time. Such institutions would have enabled the development of standard codes of normal ethical behaviour, against which individual acts could be plotted to determine whether they were ethical or not, and describe how those that were not could be treated. While we may still speak as if recourse to such codes is a possibility, current conditions, described here as postmodern, at once speak of the impossibility of such normative codes existing objectively over and above individual behaviour, and bearing any relation to today's environment. Consequently we have a situation where business ethics as it is currently conceived is ill suited to the business environment as it is currently conceived. What of the alternatives?

Foucault and an aesthetics of existence

Fredrich Nietzsche saw the epitaph that MacIntyre describes as inevitable over a century ago, finding the first fateful steps towards such a predicament in Christianity's setting in stone of the Socratic/Platonic assumption that an 'ideal world' must exist, if *this* world was to make any sense. The Christian notion of 'providence', emphasizing the idea of history as the history of salvation and a development towards such an ideal, changed the way in which the West conceived of time, creating an emphasis on the future. Some things change as modernity emerges. We find laws such as the English Act of Toleration (1689) founded in an attempt to quell post-Reformation factional conflict, and with a 'confidence in the ability of the Truth to vindicate itself without the instrument of state coercion' (Clements in Lyon, 1994: 62). Modernity sought to overcome systems based upon traditional belief, to remove the influence of religion on the affairs of state, and promote a tolerance of plurality, sure in the knowledge that objective truths with regard to human affairs were within its grasp. At the same time, modernity retained key elements of its Christian heritage, but developed them in strictly worldly and secular terms. Crucially, history as a temporal movement towards an ideal was retained, as the Christian belief in 'providence' became the modern belief in 'progress' (Compagnon, 1994: xiii; Lyon, 1994).

In traditional Christian societies, the quest for the future was underwritten by clear, particular ends promoted by the Scriptures. However, once these traditional ends were problematized, in the quest for pure secular objectivity, all that remained was the means. Uncoupled from tradition, the ideal of progress became a hollow one, since its ultimate value could only be to create conditions in which further progress is possible in a guise that is always new. By removing the presence of the past, or tradition, from the equation, and by depriving progress of a final destination (a destination only gains its meaning from the acceptance of some past tradition), modern secularization dissolves the very notion of progress, as there can be no agreement as to what it is towards which we might be progressing (Vattimo, 1988: 4-9).

Nietzsche observed that the modern age of 'abstract mores, abstract law, abstract government . . . a culture without any fixed and consecrated place of origin . . . [with] . . . the random vagaries of the artistic imagination unchanneled by any native myth' would in this way be 'condemned to exhaust all possibilities and feed miserably and parasitically on every culture under the sun . . . the result of a Socratism bent on the extermination of myth' (Nietzsche, 1967: XXIII). Modernity's quest to discover essential laws that override local tradition ironically opened the door to a hyper-plurality where anything goes. Such foresight led to Nietzsche being regarded (with Martin Heidegger) as the original philosopher of postmodernism (Arac, 1987; Compagnon, 1994; Vattimo, 1988).

Foucault regarded Nietzsche's thought as a well-spring throughout his career (Foucault, 1989). In his last works he sought to use a Nietzschean-style construction of an opposition between aesthetic forms of subjectification and an emphasis on general moral codes, as a means of outlining the contours of two distinct understandings of patterns of ethical constitution retrievable today. Believing the modern 'search for a form of morality acceptable to everybody, in the sense that everybody should submit to it', as 'catastrophic' (Foucault, 1991), Foucault wondered whether an emphasis upon a 'stylization of existence' or an 'aesthetics of life', might offer an alternative (Johnson, 1996: 30).

'What strikes me,' wrote Foucault, 'is the fact that in our society, art has become something which is related only to objects and not to individuals, or to life. That art is something which is specialized or which is done by experts who are artists.' But, he wondered, 'Couldn't everyone's life become a work of art? Why should the lamp or the house be an art object, but not our life?' Foucault believed that the idea that an essential self may not be given to us (an idea characteristic of the postmodern condition), left open 'only one practical consequence: we have to create ourselves as a work of art' (Foucault in Rabinow, 1986: 350). In contrast to an approach to ethics that provokes the self to define itself in terms of a system of rules posited as universal, Foucault saw an aesthetic attitude as one which enjoins a commitment to the elaboration of a 'beautiful life', one which permits the self to treat the harmonious development of a unique personality as the telos[2] of its own individual existence (Johnson, 1996: 30).

The Greek 'discovery' of the 'aesthetic existence' – the doubling or relation with oneself and the invention and nurturing of this relationship (Deleuze, 1988: 101–2), a discovery that modernity for the most part spurned – was obviously a crucial moment for Foucault. His last two books, *The Use of Pleasure* (1984) and *The Care of the Self* (1985), sought to explore the thought of the ancient Greeks and Romans who had, after this discovery and before the Christian beginnings of the path to modernity, worked with a moral predilection towards the 'care of the self', elaborating their own personal regimens of truth to bring a measure of proportion to their existence.

Beyond the ancient Greek aphorism 'know thyself', the most pervasive of all Greek maxims, Foucault outlined this predilection via a number of examples. He cites Epicurus' view that it was never too early, or too late, to occupy oneself with one's self, for this is what philosophizing should be (for the Epicureans teaching about everyday life was organized around taking care of one's self in order to help every member of the group with the mutual work of salvation); and points to an Alexandrian text which refers to an enigmatic group called the Therapeutae, whose practices revolved around their principle task: 'the concern for oneself'. In addition, Foucault notes Socrates' defence of himself, in Plato's *Apology* (29e), via the claim that his city prosecutors were 'not ashamed to care for the acquisition of wealth and for reputation and honour', but did not concern themselves with themselves, that is the 'wisdom, truth and the perfection' of one's self. Socrates, on the other hand, claimed one of his central tasks as a philosopher was to make sure that citizens occupied themselves with themselves, a concern that would at once lead them to concern themselves with their city as a whole by making them conceive of the way their self related to the city (Foucault, 1988: 20–1).

Foucault was interested in the ways in which these ancient schools of thought promoted individuals setting rules of conduct for themselves, whilst seeking transformation 'in their singular being'. Thus they made 'their life into an oeuvre that carries certain aesthetic values and meets certain stylistic criteria' by 'bringing into play between themselves and themselves a certain relationship that allowed them to discover the "truth of their being"' (Foucault, 1984: 10–11, 5). The manner by which this was achieved with an aesthetic slant can be seen in the ancients' approach to the 'folds of subjectification'. Gilles Deleuze, perhaps the most astute reviewer of Foucault's philosophy, summarizes the outlook that emerged from Foucault's investigation into forms of subjectification, as four folds flowing into the self 'like the rivers of the inferno' (Deleuze, 1988).

The first fold concerns the *material part of ourselves* which is to be surrounded and enfolded: for the Greeks this was the body and its pleasures, the 'aphrodisia'; but for Christians it became the flesh and its desires, or desire itself, a completely different substantial modality. Next is the fold of the *relation between forces*, or the rules that one chooses to follow; for it is always according to a particular rule that the relation between forces is bent back in order to become a relation to oneself. It makes a difference whether one's rules are natural, divine or scientifically rational, or aesthetic, as it did for many of the Greek schools. The third fold is the *fold of knowledge*, or the fold of truth insofar as it constitutes the relation of truth to our being, and of our being to truth. This serves as the formal condition for any kind of knowledge: a subjectivation of knowledge that is always different, whether in the Stoics, the Epicureans, the Christians, Plato, Descartes, or Kant. The fourth fold, the ultimate fold, is the *fold of the outside* itself. It is this that constitutes an 'interiority of expectation' from which the subject, in different ways, hopes for immortality, eternity, salvation, freedom or detachment. For the Greeks this was likely to have provoked a striving for a happy, unique, well proportioned and aesthetically pleasing life story, rather than the adherence to a collective normative code.

Beyond the ancients' appreciation of, and aesthetic orientation towards, these folds, Foucault believed that the emphasis on the aesthetic self and the un-pervasiveness of 'normalizing' rule-codes in ancient times were clearly linked. He wrote of the Stoics: 'I don't think one can find any normalization in [their] ethics [because] the principal aim [of their] kind of ethics was an aesthetic one. First, this kind of ethics was only a problem of personal choice ... [and t]he reason for making this choice was the will to live a beautiful life ... to leave to others memories of a beautiful existence. I don't think we can say that this kind of ethics was an attempt to normalize the population.' Of the Cynics he noted that for them a 'person is nothing else but his relation to truth' and that the truth takes 'shape or is given form' only in an individual's 'own life'. The true life could only be embodied – never be handed down in the form of commandment, prohibition, or law (Foucault in Miller, 1993: 345, 360-1).

MacIntyre similarly admires the lack of universal normative codes in ancient Greek culture, noting that 'the most obvious and astonishing absence from Aristotle's thought for any modern reader [is that] there is relatively little mention of rules anywhere in the *Ethics*' (MacIntyre, 1981: 141). MacIntyre's reasoning for this absence is that vice, for the ancient Athenians, could not be adequately specified independent of circumstances. Consequently, 'judgement', for the Athenians, had 'an indispensable role in the life of the virtuous man which it does not and could not have in, for example, the life of the merely law-abiding or rule-abiding man' (MacIntyre, 1981: 144). Indeed the only way out of modernity's moral predicament was, MacIntyre believed, a return to an Aristotelian ethics.

Aristotle's ethics was shaped by a teleological world-view, its moral schema involving three elements: untutored human nature, individuals-as-they-could-be-if-they-realized-their-*telos* and the moral precepts that allow us to pass from one to the other. For Aristotle, once one was aware of one's *telos* (an awareness that could only come from self-reflection on one's tradition and place in one's world), 'is' could imply 'ought' and moral statements could be statements of fact. For example, to say 'he/she is a good sea captain' would imply that that individual, for a fact, does certain things that sea captains do. By the same token, 'knowing thyself', would enable one to know not just what one ought to do, but what one must and will do in order to be true to one's self. On this view, each individual must fill a unique combination of roles: the member of a family, citizen, soldier, philosopher, servant of God, and so forth; each of which has its own point and purpose, and each unique combination of which, that constitutes each individual, amounts to each individual's *telos*. Of course, all of these things, which hinge upon the second of the three Aristotelian elements, are individualistic, culture bound and set by tradition, precisely the things that the modern human sciences sought to be above.

Instead of modernity's '"double-bind" of individualization and totalization' (Visker, 1995: 101), or a Christian/modern approach that 'separates the individual [and] breaks his links with others' (Foucault, 1983: 211), the ancients took for granted a view of the self not as something pre-given, as in the Christian conception of soul or a modern material object, but constituted by one's developing community of relationships. The self did not, and could not, exist apart from these, detached or separate. Hence to focus on one's self was not be to be 'selfish' in the modern sense, but was to at once focus on one's community and traditions.

MacIntyre subsequently places great emphasis on the importance of narrative reasoning to the ancients' aesthetic approach to life and ethics. Every life was conceived of as a narrative, an epic, or a story. The story, considered a somewhat childish genre in modernity, was for the Greeks the only way of conceptualizing individual lives and the life of the community as a whole (Tsoukas and Cummings, 1997). One's life-task was to make his or her story, through the everyday act of living, as good or as aesthetically pleasing as it could be, in order to enable, eventually, a good and proper ending. Such a story would be woven into the development of the stories that made up the fabric of one's community.

Foucault, like Nietzsche, came to believe that '[o]ne thing is needful – to "give style" to one's character – a great and rare art. It is practiced by those who survey all the strengths and weaknesses of their nature and fit them into an artistic plan until every one of them appears as art and reason, and even weakness delights the eye . . . through long practice and daily work at it' (Foucault in Rabinow, 1986: 342; see also Nietzsche, 1974: 232). This art came more easily to the ancients than it does to us because of their lesser belief in, and subsequent lack of, normalizing codes of behaviour.

The 'arts of existence' lost importance as they were assimilated into the exercise of priestly power in early Christianity, and, beyond this, into modern medical, psychological, and educative, types of practices (Foucault, 1984: 12). Modernity, underpinned by the remnants of Christian morality and scientific rationalism, emphasizing the renunciation of the self, and the importance of 'detachment' from individual points of view, split the community-relational view, creating a conception of the individual alone within vast impersonal backdrops. Self-aesthetics in such an environment could only be equated with self-absorption, self-centredness, selfishness and irrationality. Consequently, an aesthetics of existence has been neglected as a possibility in the modern West. Foucault envisaged his study as part of an emerging struggle for subjectivity, the right to difference, variation and metamorphosis. By reevaluating a neglected aspect of history, he sought to free modern ethical thought from what it silently assumes, and 'enable it to think differently' (Foucault, 1984: 9). This chapter now seeks to apply his thought to think differently about business ethics.

Organizational strategy based on an aesthetics of existence

Foucault's resurfacing of an ethics as an aesthetics of existence enables us, in this context, to ask: why should the lamp or the house be an art object, but not an organization? why should we not seek to 'give style' to our organizations, surveying all the strengths and weaknesses of their nature and fitting these into an artistic plan until every one of them appears as art and reason? and, further, could these conceptions not act as ethical basis for organizational strategy? It is argued here that the predicament that MacIntyre and Nietzsche described, combined with the way that ethics is still for the most part perceived, has led to manifestations of business ethics (mission and vision statements, charters, codes of conduct), that are often so bland, general and devoid of meaning to the particular organizational community that they are supposed to refer as to be of little use in guiding strategy. This is particularly so in rapidly changing environments where flexibility is key. A turn towards forms of subjectification, with an aesthetic emphasis, is put forward here as a possible alternative.

This alternative would at the outset require the acceptance of a human individual as a metaphor for organization, not an unproblematic assumption in that it does seem to imply that an organization has a unitary whole (Morgan, 1986, Ch. 3). However, this is negated somewhat if one works without the modern view of an individual having an essential and logically consistent core. Either way, it is important to note at the outset that we are operating in a metaphorical sense here. Beyond this metaphorical assumption what else would an aesthetics of existence approach to organizational ethics entail?

A characteristic of the modern West is its emphasis on turning to detached and objective experts to get to know what one ought to be and do: the scientist, the doctor, the lawyer, the therapist, the financial advisor, the councilor, and so on. In the process, individual self-knowledge tends to be diminished. Modern organizations turn to detached and objective external consultants for the same sort of advice. These consultants are considered expert because they have performed similar tasks across a large number of wide-ranging organizations. This leads to a normalization which is manifest, for example, in mission statements in which an organization's name is sandwiched into a coating of well-meaning axioms that could apply to just about any organization.

A self-aesthetic approach must, by contrast, begin with a desire for the organization to 'know thyself', not by bringing in external objective parties to consider external 'stakeholders'. An understanding of the self's relationship with its crucial 'stakeholders' will then emerge secondarily, and in a more clearly defined way. This requires the organization, or a representative group of employees, to ask questions of their organization's self. Such a group might invoke the folds of subjectivity, for example, asking of the first fold questions like: what is the material organization? and what is its pleasure? Of the second: to what rules of living do we wish to relate? Of the third: what do we do to learn about our being? and what exterior relationships are of particular importance to us in this regard? And of the last: how will we be detached from and connected to others, different and free from others? what is our place relative to significant others? what is our *telos*? how do we want to be remembered? or, in Nietzsche's words, what is this organization's *style*?

What would emerge is, in effect, a 'personality profile' of the organization in question. Perhaps the most suitable way to record this would be through a set of organizational anecdotes that reflect the organization's self, as opposed to a general code or mission statement. Nietzsche once remarked, drawing on the anecdotal lore of the Cynic Diogenes, that 'what is truly irrefutable' in any philosophy is what is 'personal', adding that 'with three anecdotes, it is possible to convey the image of any individual' (Nietzsche in Miller, 1993: 366).

This aesthetic approach would encourage organizations to base action not on a series of ethical questions like: what is expected of us?; how can we conform? and how do we act in accord?; but rather who are we? and, how/why are we different? Questions that, once answered, will imply certain actions as situations emerge. Organizations on this view may replace 'being a good corporate citizen' and slogans like 'we care because you do' and 'everything we do we do it for you', which are greeted with increasing scepticism in postmodern times, with 'we do what we do because we are this, which is different from something else'. Perhaps this is a more realistic view of things. Perhaps organizations in postmodern environments who try and satisfy everyone end up satisfying nobody. In any case, it is argued here that this approach would allow an organization to develop an ethical view of itself which is far more able to guide strategic decision making than received models. This is particularly the case in an environment where people have increasingly less faith in there being objective 'best practices' and general theories, plans that can satisfy all potential stakeholders at once, general rules that can account for the richness of every possible case as the future unfolds, and where it is recognized that every plan must exclude some point of view, and thus 'must be partially immoral' (Churchman, 1971: 256).

A 'personality profile' of an organization could work in much the same way as an author's preliminary sketch of a character, incorporating that character's key historical relationships with other characters. Such sketches enable an author to begin a narrative with a knowledge of the range of reactions a character could plausibly have to situations that emerge as a narrative unfolds. This analogy emphasizes that characters are not static, but will be changed by the situations they encounter. Thus, a character's profile will develop from the original conception over time.

This analogy brings us back to a narrative understanding of life, and, at once, is in keeping with recent approaches to strategy that suggest that strategy is emergent rather than about deliberate and detached forward planning

(Mintzberg, 1987, 1994; Weick, 1987). It also connects with Heidegger's philosophy. Being, for Heidegger, is a temporal unfolding. As such, no human activity can be understood without a conception of being-into-the-future (being-unto-*telos*), or 'thrownness'. Humans and organizations are 'thrown' by the past into the world, unfolding into the future in unique and historically determined directions. It is this historically directed unfolding that gives every individual a unique point of view. This recognition should lead us to be cautious of seeking to transplant approaches from one organization to another, and encourages those engaged in strategy to know the unique traditions of the organization they are seeking to re-direct.

While this may seem to indicate that organizations are prisoners of their pasts, Heidegger's philosophy may enable strategists greater freedom. Recognizing that it is only our thrown-ness, our own historically shaped aesthetic view of the world, rather than any foundational basis, that directs our actions, enables questions to be asked about often unquestioned assumptions. We are encouraged to question the way in which historical events have thrown ourselves, and supposedly natural modes of being-in-the-world. This does not, however, mean that anything goes. Our tradition-directed unfolding makes certain decisions and paths for the future unlikely or impossible. But we do achieve some sense of liberation in recognizing why this is so, and in this way broaden our horizons to re-orient things to an extent, 'even if only within the limitations of thrownness', by sticking something of a rudder in the torrent, instead of being thwarted by the flow and unaware of why this is so (Heidegger, 1962: 366; Cummings and Brocklesby, 1997).

A self-aesthetic-based approach to the ethical development of strategy would therefore be empowering as well as restrictive. To paraphrase Foucault's own view of his purpose as a philosopher, one must make an effort to think one's own history, in order to free one's present thinking from what it silently assumes to be necessary, and so enable it to think differently, but realistically, for the future (Foucault, 1984: 9). This view of ethics forces an organization to recognize the past in order to know one's self in the present, in order to develop an aesthetically pleasing future for itself. We find ourselves back to an Aristotelian understanding of ethics, where one's ethics are concerned with one's *telos*, which is intimately connected with an understanding of the particulars of one's past.

It must be stressed, in conclusion, that this work does not mean to dismiss the role played by ethical codes, but rather to provide a further approach to organizational ethics – one which may be particularly useful as a strategic guide for companies operating in postmodern environments. There will be some organizations who will find it more useful than others. For companies whose competitive advantage is based upon standardized products, and creating islands of environmental stability that override the chaotic elements of a postmodern sea, it may not seem particularly relevant. At the same time it must be stressed that this chapter is only an introduction to a *possibility*, and as such it leaves much on which to expand. However, there are many organizations who could benefit from beginning to develop and promote 'their legitimate strangeness' (to appropriate one of Foucault's favourite poets, Rene Char – cf. Eribon, 1991) as an ethical approach to doing business.

Notes

1   While it is appreciated that 'organizational ethics' would be a more inclusive term, 'business ethics' is used in this chapter to replicate the name of the field as it is commonly referred to.
2   *Telos* translates from the Greek to mean, at once, 'completion', 'end' and 'purpose' (Peters, 1967). One might equate it with *raison d'être*, for want of a better English translation.

References

Arac, J. (1987) *Critical Genealogies – Historical Situations for Postmodern Literary Studies.* New York: Columbia University Press.

Audi, R. (1995) *The Cambridge Dictionary of Philosophy.* Cambridge: Cambridge University Press.

Beauchamp, T.L. and Bowie, N.E. (1988) *Ethical Theory and Business.* Englewood Cliffs, NJ: Prentice Hall.

Churchman, C.W. (1971) *The Design of Inquiring Systems: Basic Concepts of Systems and Organization.* New York: Basic Books.

Compagnon, A. (1994) *The 5 Paradoxes of Modernity.* New York: Columbia University Press.

Cummings, S. (1996) 'Back to the oracle: post-modern organization theory as a resurfacing of pre-modern wisdom', *Organization*, 3 (2): 249–66.

Cummings, S. and Brocklesby, J. (1997) 'Towards demokratia – myth and the management of organizational change in ancient Athens', *Journal of Organizational Change Management*, 10 (1): 71-95.

De George, R.T. (1986) *The Limits of Authority.* Lawrence, KA: University Press of Kansas.

Deleuze, G. (1988) *Foucault,* trans. S. Hand. London: Athlone.

Donaldson, T. (1982) *Corporations and Morality.* Englewood Cliffs, NJ: Prentice Hall.

Economist, The (1994) *Pocket Strategy.* Harmondsworth: Penguin.

Eribon, D. (1991) *Michel Foucault.* Cambridge, MA: Harvard University Press.

Flynn, T. (1993) 'Foucault's mapping of history', in G. Gutting (ed.), *The Cambridge Companion to Foucault.* Cambridge: Cambridge University Press. pp. 28–46.

Foucault, M. (1970) *The Order of Things: An Archaeology of the Human Sciences* trans. A. Sheridan. London: Tavistock.

Foucault, M. (1977) *Discipline and Punish: The Birth of the Prison,* trans. A. Sheridan. London: Allen Lane.

Foucault, M. (1983) 'The subject and power', in H.L. Dreyfus and P. Rabinow (eds), *Michel Foucault: Beyond Structuralism and Hermeneutics.* Chicago: University of Chicago Press. pp. 214–32.

Foucault, M. (1984) *The Use of Pleasure – The History of Sexuality: Volume Two,* trans. R. Hurley. London: Penguin.

Foucault, M. (1985) *The Care of the Self – The History of Sexuality: Volume Three,* trans. R. Hurley. London: Penguin.

Foucault, M. (1988) 'Technologies of the self', in L.H. Martin, H. Gutman and P.H. Hutton (eds), *Technologies of the Self: A Seminar With Michel Foucault*. London: Tavistock. pp. 16–49.

Foucault, M. (1989) *Foucault Live: Interviews, 1966-1984*, edited by S. Lotringer. New York: Semiotext(e).

Foucault, M. (1991) 'The ethic of the care for the self as a practice of freedom' (trans. J.D. Gauthier), in J. Bernauer and D. Rasmussen (eds), *The Final Foucault*. Cambridge, MA: MIT Press. pp. 1–21.

Harvey, D. (1990) *The Condition of Postmodernity*. Oxford: Blackwell.

Heidegger, M. (1962) *Being and Time*, trans. J. Macquarrie and E. Robertson. Oxford: Blackwell.

Johnson, P. (1996) 'Nietzsche's reception today', *Radical Philosophy*, November/December: 24–33.

Kjonstad, B. and Willmott, H. (1995) 'Business ethics: restrictive or empowering?' *Journal of Business Ethics*, 14: 445–64.

Lyon, D. (1994) *Postmodernity*. Buckingham: Open University Press.

Lyotard, J.-F. (1984) *The Postmodern Condition – A Report on Knowledge*, trans. G. Bennington and B. Massumi. Manchester: Manchester University Press.

MacIntyre, A. (1981) *After Virtue – A Study in Moral Theory*. London: Duckworth.

MacIntyre, A. (1988) *Whose Justice? Which Rationality?* London: Duckworth.

MacIntyre, A. (1999) *Three Rival Versions of Moral Enquiry: Encyclopedia, Genealogy and Tradition*. Notre Dame, IA: University of Notre Dame Press.

Miller, J. (1993) *The Passion of Michel Foucault*. London: HarperCollins.

Mintzberg, H. (1987) 'Crafting strategy', *Harvard Business Review*, July/August: 66–75.

Mintzberg, H. (1994) *The Rise and Fall of Strategic Planning*. New York: Free Press/Prentice-Hall.

Morgan, G. (1986) *Images of Organization*. Beverley Hills, CA: Sage.

Nietzsche, F. (1967) *The Birth of Tragedy*, trans. W. Kaufman. New York: Random House.

Nietzsche, F. (1974) *The Gay Science*, trans. W. Kaufman. New York: Vintage Books.

Peters, F.E. (1967) *Greek Philosophical Terms – A Historical Lexicon*. New York: New York University Press.

Rabinow, P. (1986) *The Foucault Reader*. Harmondsworth: Penguin.

Robertson, D. and Schlegelmilch, B. (1993) 'Corporate institutionalization of ethics in the United States and Great Britain', *Journal of Business Ethics*, 12: 301–12.

Singer, P. (1994) *Ethics*. Oxford: Oxford University Press.

Thacker, A. (1993) 'Foucault's aesthetics of existence', *Radical Philosophy*, 63 (Spring): 13–21.

Tsoukas, H. and Cummings, S. (1997) 'Marginalization and recovery: the emergence of Aristotelian themes in organization studies', *Organization Studies*, 18 (4): 655-83.

Vattimo, G. (1988) *The End of Modernity: Nihilism and Hermeneutics in Post-modern Culture*, trans. J.R. Snyder. Cambridge: Polity Press.

Visker, R. (1995) *Michel Foucault – Genealogy as Critique*, trans. C. Turner. London: Verso.

Waters, J., Bird, F. and Chant, P. (1986) 'Everyday moral issues experienced by managers', *Journal of Business Ethics*, 11: 445–59.

Weick, K. (1987) 'Substitutes for strategy', in J. Teece (ed.), *The Competitive Challenge – Strategies for Industrial Innovation and Renewal*. Cambridge, MA: Ballinger. pp. 221–33.

PART 6

RADICAL AESTHETICS AND CHANGE

11

Cultivating an Aesthetic of Unfolding: Jazz Improvisation as a Self-organizing System

Frank J. Barrett

In the last two decades the natural sciences have been experiencing a fascinating revolution. The consequences of this revolution are still reverberating, but already we can see that it strikes at the very heart of the rational, empirical assumptions that have dominated 'normal' science since the Enlightenment. First introduced in physics and biology, this new science, known as complexity theory, claims that systems are so complex and interdependent that linear, reductionist thinking is inappropriate. Complexity theorists claim that dividing up and analyzing a system's parts cannot lead to prediction of their behavior or control over their activity. Linear thinking and reductionism fail to notice that systems have self-organizing principles that transcend the properties of their parts; that small changes can have large outcomes; and that knowledge about such systems is a matter of active co-participation rather than detached observation.

Although complexity theory cannot predict with any sense of empirical accuracy the consequences of small actions, it does claim to know something about the conditions of possibility that lead to creativity and system transformation. Perhaps what is most interesting, for present purposes, has been the discovery of those dynamic properties of systems that are highly creative and adaptive. Complexity theory proposes that systems are most creative when they operate with a combination of order and chaos. When systems are at the edge of chaos they are most able to abandon inappropriate or undesirable behaviors and structures and discover new patterns that are more appropriate to changing circumstances.

With the migration of these scientific concepts into the social sciences, organizations are encouraged to value diversity, change and transformation rather than predictability, standardization and uniformity. Executives are encouraged to notice instability, disorder, novelty, emergence and self-organization for their innovative potential rather than as something to be avoided, eliminated or controlled. A new vocabulary that highlights fragmentation and marginality encourages a more positive attitude toward those elements that were once considered inconsistent with the goals of organized, goal-directed activity. These suggestions, whilst provocative, have often been prescriptive rather than descriptive, and we have few actual models of a human system living at the edge of chaos, making creative things happen.

The emergence of complexity theory within the social sciences coincides with the call to discuss the aesthetics of organizing (Strati, 1992, 1999). This new science suggests that analytic reasoning and rationality may be limited guides in helping us grasp the dynamic tension between chaos and order that complex systems exhibit; that a detached, rational, cognitive way of knowing cannot capture the dynamics of complex systems (Chia, 1998; Chia and King, 1998). Some go so far as to suggest that the search for certainty and predictability, ideals consistent with an Enlightenment view of knowledge, may actually prohibit the innovative potential of organizations. If rational ways of knowing are inadequate, are there any alternatives beyond a blind groping or random guessing? A core assumption of this chapter is that to understand social complexity requires cultivating an appreciative way of knowing, an aesthetic that values surrender and wonderment over certainty, affirmative sense making over problem solving, listening and attunement over individual isolation.

In order to explore a few of these ideas I will consider a concrete application of a self-organized, complex system. Specifically I will discuss jazz improvisation as a collective activity that exhibits many of the characteristics of a system that borders on the edge of chaos and order. After briefly exploring a few of the characteristics of complexity and improvisation, I will explore the unique appreciative way of knowing that makes improvisation possible, the paradox of learning to improvise, and the aesthetic practices and structures which allow jazz bands to self-organize.

Jazz improvisation as a complex system: minimal structures that guide autonomous contributions

I will begin by briefly exploring jazz improvisation as a prototype of an organization that values novelty and emergence. Jazz bands consist of diverse specialists living in turbulent environments, interpreting vague cues, processing large chunks of information, formulating and implementing strategy simultaneously, extemporaneously inventing responses without well-thought-out plans and without a guarantee of outcomes, discovering the future that their action creates as it unfolds. Jazz bands, in short, embody many of the characteristics of post-industrial, post-bureaucratic organizing that complexity theorists extol. Jazz bands have minimal hierarchy, decision-making is dispersed, they are designed to maximize flexibility, responsiveness, innovation and fast processing of information. It is a form of social organization that produces order with little or no blueprint, organized from the bottom up: individuals have personal freedom to take initiative and operate on their own authority (their musical imaginations), guided by the constraints of the task, the conventions of practice and the enactments of other players.

Complexity theory suggests that human groups are capable of self-transformation when they enter a transitional phase that contain elements of stability and instability, when there is a minimal structure that keeps agents richly connected as they respond to one another in non-linear ways (Chia and King, 1998; Stacey, 1996). Jazz improvisation is an activity that cultivates these very elements. Information flows freely yet is restrained, members are diverse yet conform, members are richly connected, constraints are minimal and feedback is non-linear (i.e. there are many possible responses to a given stimulus and these responses can themselves stimulate unexpected behaviour). Such a system is a good candidate for the development of novelty: tiny changes can amplify and alter the state of the system, escalating into qualitatively different patterns (Stacey, 1996). Tension between these forces are continually rearranged, keeping the system in a state of fluctuation and dynamic instability.

What keeps jazz improvisation at this transitional edge without disintegrating into chaos is a minimal structure that limits and guides what the soloists can play. This framework that provides the necessary backdrop to coordinate action and organize choice of notes is the song. Songs are 'cognitively held rules for musical innovation' (Bastien and Hostagier, 1988: 585). Songs are made up of chords and corresponding scales that provide the conventions that guide note and harmonic choice. So, for example, a standard jazz song based on the popular standard song, 'Whispering', is made up of a series of chord changes in the standard key of E-flat. There are agreed-upon chords over each of the 24 bars. When the chorus ends, the song 'turns around' and repeats as the soloist 'plays over the changes'. This structure is minimal enough that it encourages considerable variation and autonomous expression, so that a musician playing this same song in a different performance will introduce considerable variation.

These ongoing chord structures are tacit rules that allow players to coordinate action whilst inviting autonomous expression, diversity and extemporaneous responsiveness to one another's gestures. The song acts as a temporal structure, a minimal set of rules (Eisenberg, 1990). Routinized patterns of chords provide enough background regularity that action can be coordinated, yet not overly constrained. It is significant that these minimal constraints are temporal structures of coordination – they are continuous throughout the life of the song. Players do not have to stop to negotiate their position and orientation as they proceed: everyone knows where they are supposed to be and assumes others will orient themselves accordingly. Chord changes signal shifts in contexts that provide the constraints and materials that invite transformations and embellishment. Given this orientation, there is an enormous amount of latitude and individual autonomy permitted. It is the mutual recognition of shared rules that allows the players to coordinate activity.

Implications of an aesthetic way of knowing

In the previous section I discussed how jazz improvisation relies on minimally-shared agreements that encourage diverse and multiple contributions. While these structural conditions make the system a good candidate for self-organizing processes, there is another dimension of emergent systems that deserves exploration, namely how agents view knowledge creation. In this section I will discuss how jazz musicians approach their unusual task with an *aesthetic sensibility*, one that prepares them to be spontaneous and encourages them to be mutually responsive to what emerges.

It is appropriate that an exploration of aesthetic ways of knowing begins with Giambattista Vico. Born 16 years after the death of René Descartes, Vico challenged the dualistic assumptions of a rational, detached way of knowing that Descartes had helped to introduce. Vico argued that Cartesian ideas concerning the quest for certainty were constrained by a reduction of human capacity, a disembodied conception of mind. The mind and body, for Vico, were inseparable: awareness is not only abstract, but also something felt and imagined, what he called 'poetic wisdom'. To say that humans are capable of a poetic wisdom is to claim that humans are not passive recipients of sense impressions or mirrors reflecting the external world. Rather we are active, sensing, feeling and thinking participants in creating knowledge. Whereas rational knowing involves a detached approach to the world, eliminating any pre-judgements or feelings, poetic wisdom involves intuiting glimpses of immediacy and fluidity, experiences of awe, reverence and wonder, much like the ancient Greeks 'whose minds were not in the least abstract, refined or spiritualized, because they were entirely immersed in the senses, buffeted by the passions, buried in the body' (Vico, 1966: 118). What makes this kind of poetic wisdom possible is an absence of certainty and a fresh perception of the ordinary world: 'for ignorance, the mother of wonder, made everything wonderful to men' (Vico, 1966: 116).

The valuing of innocent wonder and ignorance is certainly at odds with the Enlightenment values of certainty, analytic reasoning and the reliance on predictable responses. But is it possible to re-create this innocent wonder, to suspend stock responses? By unpacking what happens when jazz musicians improvise, we can see that improvisation involves an aesthetic that attempts to be sensitive to the dynamics of emergence and surprise, building up knowledge and skills, only to surrender these stock responses in order to awaken fresh perception, novel action and the capacity to respond instantaneously to other human actors who themselves are attempting novel contributions. It is a world of intuitive, empathic connection rather than detached, planned and strategic intent. Following from Vico's notion of the pursuit of poetic wisdom, we might expect jazz musicians to talk about their activity not from a detached perspective but with a language of feeling, wonder and joy of discovery.

The nature of improvisation

To say that jazz music is improvised means that jazz music is spontaneous, unrehearsed and not written down beforehand. By definition, improvisation involves an openness to emergent possibilities. The word 'improvisation' originates from the Latin 'improvisus', meaning 'not seen ahead of time'. Improvising involves 'playing extemporaneously . . . composing on the spur of the moment' (Schuller, 1989: 378). Berliner defines it thus: 'Improvisation involves reworking precomposed material and designs in relation to unanticipated ideas conceived, shaped, and transformed under the special conditions of performance, thereby adding unique features to every creation' (Berliner, 1994: 241).

In a recent review article, improvisation was defined as the degree to which execution and composition converge in time (Moorman and Miner, 1998). This definition emphasizes the temporal order, the degree of simultaneity between composition and implementation, between the formulation of strategy and its implementation. In this sense improvisation is similar to Schön's notion of reflective practice. Schön defines it as 'on the spot surfacing, criticizing, restructuring, and testing of intuitive understanding of experienced phenomena' (1983: 147). Weick defines it as the simultaneous unfolding of thinking and doing (1996: 19).

Since the music is composed and performed simultaneously, and there is no guarantee of where one's queries will lead, there is an inherent risk in improvising. Saxophonist Paul Desmond described what he does when improvising: '(I) crawl out on a limb, set one line against another and try to match them, bring them closer together' (quoted in Gioia, 1988: 92). Or consider the way that jazz saxophonist Steve Lacy compares improvisation to exploring on the edge of the unknown:

> There is a freshness, a certain quality, which can only be obtained by improvisation, something you cannot possibly get from writing. It is something to do with the 'edge'. Always being on the brink of the unknown and being prepared for the leap. And when you go out there you have all your years of preparation and all your sensibilities and your prepared means but it is a leap into the unknown. (Quoted in Bailey, 1992: 57)

Unlike classical musicians who rely on pre-scripted music, jazz players face an unpredictable future, fraught with instability and anxiety as they 'leap into the unknown'. Jazz critic Ted Gioia describes the challenge of improvisation by comparing it to the creative processes of other art forms:

> Imagine T.S. Eliot giving nightly poetry readings at which, rather than reciting set pieces, he was expected to create impromptu poems – different ones each night, sometimes recited at a fast clip; imagine giving Hitchcock or Fellini a handheld motion picture camera and asking them to film something, anything – at that very moment, without the benefits of script, crew, editing, or scoring . . . (Gioia, 1988: 52)

When improvising, one journeys into the unknown and is expected to create coherent musical ideas that are novel and unpredictable. Jazz musicians find themselves perilously 'out on a limb', at the edge of their comfort level, seeking to create coherent, original statements out of disparate, evolving musical material, often in the presence of an audience. Introducing such instability increases anxiety, the fear of failure and a temptation to play what is comfortable and has proven successful in the past. For this reason, there is often a temptation to rely on well-learned stock phrases. Musicians who repeat their solos or who play flawless patterns are not regarded highly by the jazz community. Musicians often make it a priority to guard against over-relying on successful routines. As Keith Jarrett speaks of this challenge: 'You're never in a secure position. You're never at a point where you have it all sewn up. You have to choose to be secure like a stone, or insecure but able to flow' (in Palmer, 1974). In the next section I would like to explore how musicians cultivate the unique mindset that welcomes what some might regard as perilous and risky activity.

Cultivating an aesthetic of surrender: embracing risk and letting go of the familiar

How is it possible that great jazz musicians are able to create such novelty? How can we account for master players like Charlie Parker 'Bird', for example, who was able to improvise fast tempos, weaving diverse themes together, suddenly quoting a phrase from an unrelated tune that seemed to 'pop' into his mind? There is a romantic notion that jazz musicians are natural geniuses or that they are simply picking notes out of thin air. In fact, jazz musicians prepare to be spontaneous in the way that they practise: they attempt to get beyond the necessary stage of rote learning to create conditions that challenge the boundaries of their capacity.

Jazz musicians practise their art form in a unique way. Like all expert skills, there is a stage of rote learning and practise necessary. They learn to be creative by first imitating others. Students of jazz learn the motifs and phrases of previous masters, practise them repeatedly until they become somewhat automatic. They study the masters' solos, learn the overall strategy and choice of notes, how they harmonized certain phrases and matched phrases to chord changes. These phrases, or what they call 'licks', become part of the players personal repertoire. According to trumpeter Benny Bailey, 'You just have to keep on doing it [practising phrases] over and over until it comes automatically' (Berliner, 1994: 165).

After mastering others' phrases and styles, musicians begin to combine them with previously unrelated material, introducing incremental alterations. They add grace notes, dissonant passing notes, repeat and extend parts of a familiar pattern, substitute a similar phrase over a down-beat rather than an up beat, alter the harmonic extensions of the basic chord progression. Miles Davis captured this paradox: 'Sometimes you have to play a long time in order to play like yourself' (1986). These incremental alterations and unique combination of the disparate materials begin to point to the development of one's unique style. At some point, the player begins to add, re-combine, vary the patterns that have become automatic by sheer repetition. Players export, borrow material from different contexts, combine unrelated modes, apply familiar phrases to seemingly unrelated chord changes.

Once players have mastered a repertoire of 'licks', they engage in practices that guard against over-reliance on these same skills. Musicians *cultivate surrender* by:

1   exploring and monitoring the edge of competence;
2   developing provocative learning relationships that simultaneously support and challenge;
3   creating incremental disruptions that demand opening up to unexplored paths.

I will briefly explore each of these below.

Exploring the edges of competence

Players must resist the temptation to play what is within their comfortable reach. They often develop a self-reflexive capacity, challenging themselves to explore the very edge of their comfort level, to stretch their learning into new and different areas. Jazz musicians often take steps to guard against over-relying on playing 'certain stock phrases which have proven themselves effective in past performance (rather than) push themselves to create fresh improvisations' (Gioia, 1988: 53). Pianist Bill Evans continually practised musical passages he did not quite understand and, once mastered, took on other difficult passages (Evans, 1991). Saxophonist John Coltrane learned songs in the most difficult, rarely played keys.

Musicians monitor the edges of their competence and deliberately explore the limits of their capacity. They throw themselves into actual playing situations 'over their heads', stretching themselves to play in challenging contexts. Musicians must also do other things to 'trick' their automatic responses so that they do not continue to play well-worn phrases that are predictable and comfortable. Saxophonist Ken Peplowski describes how musicians welcome surprise and willingly abdicate control. He says that

> we have to risk sounding stupid in order to learn something . . . We are always deliberately painting ourselves in corners just in order to get out of them. Sometimes you consciously pick a bad note and try to find a way to get out of it. The essence of jazz is to try to put three to eight people together while they're *all* trying to do this at the same time. (Peplowski, 1998: 560)

Developing provocative learning relationships

Jazz musicians develop provocative learning relationships that simultaneously support and challenge learned habits by stretching them to take risks. One classic learning situation is the 'jam session'. Here musicians often throw themselves in over their heads, improvising with other more competent players. The young Miles Davis discovered from earlier masters that learning to improvise jazz is a treacherous, if exhilarating, adventure. He recalled the terror he felt when he replaced Dizzie Gillespie in Charlie Parker's band in the 1940s. Parker would deliberately play difficult tunes at very fast tempos, beyond Davis's facility with the instrument:

> Sometimes I just couldn't play what Dizzy played. He played so fast I just wanted to quit every night. He would leave the stand and leave me up there. I thought 'shit'. . . so I finally learned how to play that fast and feel comfortable. (Davis in Berliner, 1994)

Feelings of terror aside, most jazz musicians would agree with Davis's conclusion that such 'stretches' are necessary for a musician's growth. Many veterans tell stories of suffering through anxious situations that in retrospect motivated them to new discoveries. Part of cultivating an aesthetic of surrender is appreciating that such difficult moments might lead to wonderful discoveries.

In addition to self-challenge, musicians often cultivate learning relationships in which they stretch and support one another to achieve new discoveries, going after what is not quite at hand. These are often described with a certain admiration and fondness. Local communities of practice developed in the early 1950s around metropolitan areas such as Detroit, Chicago and especially New York: players would 'hang out' and learn from each other. Trombonist Kurtis Fuller recalls how peers challenged and sustained one another through collaborative discoveries, attempting difficult technical passages or importing other kinds of music:

> I stayed at 101st street, and Coltrane was at 103rd street and every day I could just take my horn and walk around there – stay over there all day. We'd have tea and we'd sit and talk, and we'd laugh and put on records. Coltrane would say, 'Hey Curtis, try to play this on the trombone'. And I would try to run something down. I'd struggle with it and he'd say, 'You're getting it' and so on and so on. Paul Chambers lived all the way in Brooklyn, and he would get in the subway and, gig or no gig, he would come over to practise. He got this thing – a Polonaise in D minor – and he'd say 'Hey Curtis, let's play this one'. It wasn't written as a duet, but we would run that down together for three or four hours. A couple of days later, we'd come back and play it again. The whole thing was just so beautiful. (Berliner, 1994: 39)

A special fraternity often develops among jazz musicians as they guide each other through obstacles and challenges that lead to new learning experiences.

Jazz musicians talk about provocative learning relationships that model surrendering to possibility rather than defending enactments. Trumpeter Wynton Marsalis grew up under the tutelage of a master pianist who happened to be his father, Ellis Marsalis. On one of Wynton's recordings, he asked his father to play piano. In jazz vernacular, this role is often referred to as 'sideman' – a term that emphasizes the accompanying or supporting role. According to Wynton:

My father's so much hipper than me and knows so much more, but I can tell
him, 'I don't like what you played on that', and he'll just stop and say, 'Well,
damn, what do you want?' Then I'll say, 'Why don't you do this?' and he'll try
it. That's my father, man, . . . If I said I didn't like it, he'd change it and at least
look for something else, because he's a sensitive musician. The more I get away
from him, man the more I know how much I learned from him just by looking
and watching. I grew up with one of the greatest examples. (Berliner, 1994: 41)

This exchange is an interesting microcosm of a provocative learning
relationship that nurtures an aesthetic of openness and surprise. In this situation,
Wynton apparently has musical insight that he thinks is harmonically more
appropriate than the chords the pianist (the father) was playing. Upon hearing
the band leader's (Wynton's) suggestions, the sideman (Ellis) does not defend
the correctness of his musical ideas, or generate rationales to explain his choice,
but immediately respects the son's suggestions. There is an irony in this
exchange. Who is the learner here? Ellis appears to be the one learning to try
different musical ideas, but upon further inspection, there appears to be another
kind of learning happening as well: he is teaching the son something about non-
defensive, open approach to inquiry. Wynton seems to walk away with a lasting
insight, admiring his father's approach to and immersion in music, an openness
to learning and commitment to creative invention. What he taught him
apparently is to avoid becoming too attached to what is comfortable and secure,
to be open to exploring new pathways, to avoid defensive routines. The young
Wynton was learning that even established, competent musicians must be
willing to abandon comfortable practices and to abdicate postures of established
status that block the emergence of good ideas.

Creating incremental disruptions that demand openness to what unfolds

Miles Davis found a provocative way to disrupt secure habitual ways of
responding in hope of awakening fresh responses and exploring the edge of his
capacity. In a famous 1959 recording session, the musicians arrived in the
studio and were presented with sketches of songs – some only partially
complete – written in unconventional modal forms. One song, 'Blue in Green',
contained 10 bars instead of the more familiar 8- or 12-bar form that
characterized American popular music. Never having seen this music before,
and unfamiliar with these odd forms, the musicians had no rehearsal. The album
that resulted – *Kind of Blue* – consists entirely of 'first takes' so that what we
hear when listening to this music is these musicians discovering the new music
at the very moment they are inventing it. Miles Davis nurtured an aesthetic of
surprise: he introduced incremental disruption that handicapped routines and
made it impossible for the players to rely on rote learning and habitual
responses (see Barrett, 1998). This is how pianist Bill Evans describes this
famous session in the original sleeve notes:

There is a Japanese visual art in which the artist is forced to be spontaneous. He
must paint on a thin stretched parchment with a special brush and black water

paint in such a way that an unnatural or interrupted stroke will destroy the line or break through the parchment. Erasures or changes are impossible. These artists must practise a particular discipline, that of allowing the idea to express itself in communication with their hands in such a direct way that deliberation cannot interfere. The resulting pictures lack the complex composition and textures of ordinary painting, but it is said that those who see will find something captured that escapes explanation. This conviction that direct deed is the most meaningful reflection, I believe, has prompted the evolution of the extremely severe and unique disciplines of the jazz or improvising musician.

This passage poetically articulates the aesthetic of surrender, the deliberate attempt to suspend deliberation, embracing the 'direct deed' in the hopes of catching the glimpse of fleeting, transient relations. By taking familiar structures away, musicians are hoping to notice the mobile, flowing configurations, the fragments and dispersed collages that are seeds for potential exploration and development.

In sum, musicians employ deliberate, conscious attention in their practise, but at the moment when they are called upon to play this conscious striving becomes an obstacle. Too much regulation and control restricts the emergence of fresh ideas. Musicians must *surrender* their conscious striving. They prepare to be spontaneous by practising, mastering and then letting go: by deliberately facing unfamiliar challenges, by developing provocative learning relationships and by creating incremental disruptions that demand experimentation and risk. As saxophonist Ken Peplowski said: 'You carry along all the scales and all the chords you learned, and then you take an intuitive leap into the music. Once you take that leap you forget all about those tools. (Peplowski, 1998: 561)

Cultivating an aesthetic of surrender involves a special preparation: exploring the edge of competence, developing relationships that challenge learning, creating incremental disruptions that demand opening up to the unexpected. Each of these practices attempts to dislodge linear, predictable responses. Cultivating an aesthetic of surrender invites openness and wonderment to what unfolds, enhancing the self-organizing potential of the system by preparing players to respond in unpredictable, novel ways. When each of the musicians adopts an aesthetic of surrender to what unfolds, there is an increased likelihood that small actions amplify into large consequences, qualitatively different patterns emerge and complex systems achieve creative breakthroughs.

An aesthetic of appreciation: the art of affirmative engagement

Since players must compose responses on the spot, there seems to be limited foresight and control at one's disposal. That such a precarious situation does not lead to anarchy speaks to the subtle and tacit aesthetic that is sensitive to the dynamics of unfolding while envisioning future paths. The aesthetic that gives coherence to the music is an affirmative sense-making. Simply put, improvisation requires a mindset of appreciation. Since jazz players cannot prescribe where the music is going to lead beforehand, they are left to making

sense of what has already happened and making guesses and approximations
that project what is likely to happen next:

> The improviser may be unable to look ahead at what he is going to play, but he
> can look behind at what he has just played; thus each new musical phrase can be
> shaped with relation to what has gone before. He creates his form
> *retrospectively*. (Gioia, 1988: 61)

The musician looks back on what is emerging – the various chord progressions,
melodic fragments, rhythmic patterns – and jumps into the morass. An
appreciative sense-making involves attending closely to what is happening,
seeing the potential for embellishing on motifs, linking familiar with new
utterances, adjusting to unanticipated musical cues that reframe previous
material. In a continual dialogical exchange, each of these interpretations has
implications for where one can proceed, as this excerpt illustrates:

> After you initiate the solo, one phrase determines what the next is going to be.
> From the first note that you hear, you are responding to what you've just played:
> you just said this on your instrument, and now that's a constant. What follows
> from that? And then the next phrase is a constant. What follows from that? And
> so on and so forth. And finally, let's wrap it up so that everybody understands
> that that's what you're doing. It's like language: you're talking, you're speaking,
> you're responding to yourself. When I play, it's like having a conversation with
> myself. (Max Roach cited in Berliner, 1994: 192)

Improvisation involves continually attending to cues, retaining some part of the
past, variation on other parts so that one can look back on what has happened
and extend it.

Weick (1993) compares the jazz improviser to Lévi-Strauss's concept of
bricolage, the art of making use of whatever material is at hand (see also
Linstead and Grafton Small, 1990). *Bricoleurs*, like jazz musicians, are
pragmatists: they learn by continual experimentation, by playing with
possibilities, by tinkering with systems while noticing emerging patterns and
configurations. He cites the example of a junk collector in upper-state New
York who built a tractor from a huge collection of unrelated junk and diverse
parts he had accumulated in his front yard. The jazz musician, like the junk
collector, looks over the material that is available at that moment, the various
chord progressions and rhythmic patterns, and leaps into the morass assuming
that whatever he is about to play will fit in somewhere. Like the *bricoleur* who
assumes that there must be a tractor somewhere in that pile of junk, the
improviser assumes that there is a melody to be worked out from the quandary
of rhythms and chord changes. Sense-making occurs appreciatively and
retrospectively: as new phrases or chord changes are introduced, the improviser
makes connections between the old and new material and adds to the unfolding
scheme with the assumption that what is happening will appear purposeful,
coherent and inevitable.

Appreciating the affirmative potential in every musical utterance becomes a
self-fulfilling prophecy for improvising musicians, especially when dealing
with errors. Jazz improvisation is marked by a restless adventurousness, an

eagerness to travel into unexplored territory. There are hazards, risks, gambles, chances, speculation, doubts. Jazz is an expressive art form that encourages players to explore the edge of the unknown, and if improvisation legitimizes risk taking, it is inevitable that there will be discrepancies, miscues and 'mistakes'. Jazz musicians often turn these unexpected moments into something sensible, or perhaps even innovative. Errors are often integrated into the musical landscape, an occasion for further exploration that might just lead to new pathways that otherwise might not have been possible. Herbie Hancock recalls that Miles Davis heard him play a wrong chord, but simply played his solo around the 'wrong' notes so that they sounded correct, intentional and sensible in retrospect. Jazz musicians assume that 'you can take any bad situation and make it into a good situation. It's what you do with the notes that counts' (Barrett and Peplowski, 1998: 559).

Rather than treat an unintended enactment as a mistake to be avoided, often jazz musicians treat these gestures as another theme. They do not stop to analyze the error, problem solve and set up controls to prevent its recurrence. Rather, they repeat it, amplify it and develop it further until it becomes a new pattern. When pianist Don Friedman listened to a recording he made with trumpeter Brooker Little, he realized that he had played the wrong chord. Little, however, brilliantly shaped his solo around the alleged 'wrong notes':

> Little apparently realized the discrepancy during his solo's initial chorus, when he arrived at this segment and selected the minor third of the chord for one of the opening pitches of a phrase. Hearing it clash with the pianist's part, Little improvised a rapid save by leaping to another pitch and resting, stopping the progress of his performance. To disguise the error further, he repeated the entire phrase fragment as if he had initially intended it as a motive [*sic*], before extending it into a graceful, ascending melodic arch. From that point on, Little guided his solo according to a revised map of the ballad. 'Even when Brooker played the melody at the end of the take', observed Friedman with admiration, he varied it in ways 'that fit the chord I was playing'. (Berliner, 1994: 383)

Little does not seek to fix blame or search for causes of the mistake but simply accommodates it as material to be queried for possible direction. Such a move is affirmative as well as forgiving: his utterances contain fragments of Friedman's, making the 'error' sound intentional in retrospect. Such reflection grants validity to the other's offering and leads to transformation, re-direction and unprecedented turns. Jazz improvisation assumes that there is affirmative potential waiting to be discovered from virtually any utterance (Barrett, 1995). Within the morass of dynamic instability that characterizes improvised settings, an appreciative mindset provides a guiding, retrospective focus that enhances the self-organizing potential of the entire system.

An aesthetic of attunement: hitting the groove

Perhaps the most striking characteristic of jazz improvisation and the source of its novelty and unpredictability is that it is an ongoing collaborative art form.

Jazz improvisation involves ongoing social negotiation between players. In order for jazz to work, players must be actively listening and responding to one another, attuned to the unfolding world that they are simultaneously creating and discovering. From the moment a performance begins, the improviser enters an ongoing stream of musical activity that is constantly changing and evolving: drum accents, harmonic alterations, segmented bass lines, fragmentary melodies intermingling through temporal structure of the song. Players enter this undulating flow, constantly interpreting the musical material before them, merging their own ideas with others', attempting to create a coherent statement. They are constantly anticipating one another's intentions, making guesses and predictions. Players are committed to stay engaged with one another, to listen to emerging ideas and to pay attention to cues that can point to an unexpected trajectory.

Jazz improvisation is often likened to a conversation between players: like a good dialogical exchange, participants strive for attunement by listening, anticipating and responding. They are engaged with continual streams of activity: interpreting others' playing, anticipating based on harmonic patterns and rhythmic conventions, while simultaneously attempting to shape their own creations and relate them to what they have heard. In some sense, attunement is built into jazz performance by the practice of turn taking. Through iterative patterns of exchange, each person takes a turn developing a musical idea. While one person is developing an idea, others take on a support role by accompanying, or 'comping'. The task of those 'comping' is to focus on helping the other develop his or her emerging idea, to empathize with the soloist and to anticipate the direction of the phrases so as to blend, encourage and augment.

Cultivating an aesthetic of attunement suggests that when members are richly connected they are able to respond to one another's utterances. Such a context may provide a 'holding environment' a safe context allowing one another to explore, develop, grow. Musicians often refer to this as a 'groove'. When they strike a groove, the players successfully negotiate a shared sense of the beat and the music seems to take on a life of its own. Players talk about these moments in sacred terms, as if they are experiencing something out of ordinary time:

> When the rhythm section is floating, I'll float too, and I'll get a wonderful feeling in my stomach. If this rhythm section is really swinging, it's such a great feeling, you just want to laugh. (Emily Remeler in Berliner, 1994: 389)

The attunement that they achieve pulls them to new heights, they speak of playing beyond their capacity. They speak in metaphors that relay a sense of ecstasy and joy: waves, surges, sailing, gliding.

> The first time I got the feeling of what it was to strike a groove, it was very similar to how your body is left after an orgasm; you really lose control. I remember that I was playing and grooving and it felt so good, I just started grinning and giggling. (Jazz drummer in Berliner, 1994: 389)

When you're really listening to each other and you're performing together, it's like everyone is talking to each other through music. When groups like Dave Brubeck's or Miles Davis's or Art Blakey's play, they have good conversations, group conversations. When that's really happening in a band, the cohesiveness is unbelievable. Those are the special, cherished moments. When those special moments occur, to me, it's like ecstasy. It's like a beautiful thing. It's like when things blossom. When it's happening, it really makes it, man. (Curtis Fuller cited in Berliner, 1994: 389)

Relating fully to every sound that everyone is making not only keeps the improvising spirit going, but makes the experience complete. To hear it all simultaneously is one of the most divine experiences that you can have. (Lee Konitz cited in Berliner, 1994: 389)

The lucid apprehension of groove is not the understanding of the cognitive mind; rather the musicians feel and sense this connection in their bodies, an awareness that supports Vico's notion of poetic wisdom. The openness, receptivity and fluid coordination that occurs when musicians strike a groove point to a paradox that is implicit in the quotes above: good improvisers must be thinking creatively and avoiding over-learned habits, but when they strike a groove they are *not* consciously thinking, reflecting or deciding on what notes to play. They seem to aim for a surrender of control, a suspension of rational planning that allows them to open up to a deeper synergistic connection. Further, when this occurs, they seem to be able to play beyond their previously learned capacities.

Summary: toward an aesthetic of unfolding

This chapter follows Chia's (1998) contentions that a rational, cognitive orientation cannot capture the dynamics of complex systems, that propositional knowledge is reductionist and that 'intellect is incapable of establishing sympathy with the fluid living nature' (1998: 366). Jazz musicians are immersed in a fluid social world in which changing ensembles of relations are continuously transforming themselves. Conventional analytic methods of problem solving, as Chia implied, are not up to the task. Indeed groups who are improvising, producing without a blueprint or plan are hindered if they assume that their activity is clearly differentiated, isolatable, locatable within some pre-existing system of classification. Jazz improvisers cultivate an aesthetic that senses the dynamic unfolding of creative human action and appreciates the emergent, incomplete, mistake-ridden nature of human activity that often in retrospect leads to coherent, creative production. I am suggesting here that what is appropriate for grasping social complexity is an aesthetic of the dynamics of unfolding, an aesthetic that values surrender, appreciation, trust and attunement as seeds that sprout dynamic, novel social action.

When I say that complexity calls for an aesthetic way of knowing it may be useful to revisit the meaning of the word 'aesthetic'. It originates from the Greek 'athetisch', meaning 'pertaining to perception by the senses'. Perhaps the closest meaning that remains in our vocabulary is its opposite, 'anaesthesia', which refers to the deadening of the physical senses, the *in*ability to feel or perceive things (see Carter and Jackson, Chapter 8 in this volume). A doctor applies an anaesthetic when she wants the patient to feel nothing. If the opposite of aesthetic is numbness, an aesthetic awareness is one that is *open to the immediacy of wonderment*. When pianist Bill Evans describes eliminating prior deliberation in the creation of art, he is pointing to the suspension – the surrender if you will – of conventional problem solving and routine ways of knowing so as to be open to what emerges in the moment. These habits of deliberation need to be abandoned because sheer repetition and reliance on pre-existing categories creates a disembodied experience – an anaesthesia. When Wynton Marsalis's father continues searching for ideas that blend rather than defending his enactments, he chooses a stance of attunement to what is unfolding. Holding on to routines and stock responses obstructs immersion in the immediacy. To be open to the aesthetics of unfolding is to be vulnerable in the face of the unknown – and indeed there is something quite touching about vulnerable human beings exploring the further reaches of their comfortable grasp, testing the limits of their understanding. The surrender of deliberation, the commitment to appreciate the potential of preceding enactments and to build on whatever emerges, the attunement to the inevitable surprises, might serve as catalysts for recapturing the innocent ignorance and poetic wisdom that Vico envisioned.

Jazz musicians cultivate an aesthetic of surrender. They learn to embrace risk and let go of the familiar. They engage in a rigorous method to prepare themselves for such precarious and potentially wonderful moments, to catch glimpses of fleeing transient configurations of relationships. They practise by building up their memory of repertoires that helps them recognize emergent patterns; these very skills, however, lend themselves to building stock responses which are the enemy of improvisation. To guard against habitual playing, they continually challenge themselves to stretch beyond comfortable limits; they deliberately create incremental disruptions and surprises that provoke fresh rather than stock responses. Most importantly, they are careful not to become too linked to comfortable habits that have worked in the past. At the moment of performance, they leap in and make the most of the resources they have at their disposal, continually synthesizing fleeing images into something coherent.

Noticing the potentials rather than the obstacles that one faces necessitates an affirmative aesthetic, the assumption that there is a latent, positive possibility to be noticed and appreciated (Barrett, 1995). In order for jazz to work, the improviser must assume that whatever has happened will make sense, that prior note selections must be leading somewhere and that there must be some order in the disparate material waiting to be enticed and queried. Rather than engaging in fault finding or holding one another responsible for inevitable errors that happen when one is experimenting on the edge of one's familiarity, each player is committed to sustaining the ongoing dialogue. To do this, musicians assume that there is an affirmative potential direction in every interaction and every utterance. They assume that everything that is happening – even the most blatant 'errors' – makes sense and can be a possible springboard for an inspired musical idea.

Finally, musicians cultivate an aesthetics of attunement, a willingness to respond to one another's enactments, a hope that others are responding in turn, and a common yearning for a shared sense of the rhythm and creation of a groove. When musicians are listening attentively, they have an enormous amount of influence over the direction of one another's playing. At any given moment, the music can go off into an unanticipated direction: a solo line might suggest unique sets of chord voicings that in turn might lead to expanding the harmonic extensions that a melody can explore. It is a recursive process in which every player has the potential to alter the fabric of the musical landscape, depending on what he or she hears and how they respond. When players are relating and responding well, the jazz band achieves a state of dynamic synchronization.

Jazz improvisation is a complex system that cultivates an aesthetics of unfolding, one that allows players to quickly notice and respond to unanticipated cues, abandon what doesn't work and create novelty that takes the system in a new direction. They grapple with the constrictions of patterns and structures, strive to listen to what is happening around them and respond coherently. At the same time they try to break out of these constrictions and patterned structures to create something new with the awareness that committing to either path entails a risk.

Conclusion

Considering organizations as complex systems is a metaphorical construction, just as imagining organizations as machines or organisms is a suggestive metaphor. The value of the metaphor of chaos and complexity is that it suggests a new language, a new way to talk about a familiar project. This chapter pushes us imaginatively one step further by imagining jazz as a concrete enactment of self-organizing processes.

Traditional approaches suggest that the purpose of organizing is to simplify complexity, to reduce chaos by creating order and control. One outcome of cultivating an aesthetic sensibility in relation to non-linear feedback systems is that organizing looks more complex, if not messier. We begin to see various tensions and paradoxes: the need to build up skills and competencies only to surrender these familiar responses at the moment of enactment; the need to jump in, take risks and focus on innovative contributions while amending these as we respond to the enactments of others. When we look closely at organizations as networks capable of continuous variety and novelty, we can appreciate that tiny utterances and fluxes can escalate into qualitatively different patterns. In one sense, appreciating the complexity of self-organized systems is an appreciation of the sheer boundlessness of human action. We are radically interdependent in a social world that is at once recalcitrant to our dreams of control and prediction while also responsive to the tiniest perturbations.

If Wheatley (1992) and others are correct, that the new logic for organizing in the twenty-first century requires an appreciation of chaos and complexity, then certainly the way we approach organizing needs to change. It would seem that our cognitively embedded, familiar routines are fiercely parochial in the vastness of an unfolding complexity. For now, with the jazz metaphor playing in the background, one can only pose a question: what would our organizations look like if managers and executives were encouraged to recapture a poetic wisdom, to be suspicious of comfortable routines, to create provocative learning relationships, to see appreciation and affirmative engagement as a core task and to value wonder over suspicion, surrender over defensiveness and listening and attunement over self-promotion?

References

Bailey, D. (1992) *Improvisation*. New York: Da Capo Press.
Barrett, F.J. (1995) 'Creating appreciative learning cultures', *Organization Dynamics*, 24 (1): 36–49.
Barrett, F.J. (1998) 'Creativity and improvisation in jazz and organizations: implications for organizational learning', *Organization Science*, 9 (5): 605–22.
Barrett, F.J. and Peplowski, K. (1998) 'Minimal structures within a song: an analysis of "All of Me" ', *Organization Science*, 9 (5): 558–60.
Bastien, D. and Hostagier, T. (1988) 'Jazz as a process of organizational innovation', *Journal of Communication Research*, 15 (5): 582–602.
Berliner, P. (1994) *Thinking in Jazz*. Chicago: University of Chicago Press.
Chia, R. (1998) 'From complexity science to complex thinking: organization as simple location', *Organization*, 5 (3): 341–69.
Chia, R. and King, I. (1998) 'The organizational structuring of novelty', *Organization*, 5 (4): 461–78.
Eisenberg, E. (1990) 'Jamming: transcendence through organizing', *Communication Research*, 17 (2): 139–64.
Evans, B. (1991) *The Universal Mind of Bill Evans* (video). New York: Rhapsody Films.
Gioia, T. (1988) *The Imperfect Art*. New York: Oxford University Press.
Linstead, S.A. and Grafton Small, R. (1990) 'Organizational bricolage', in B.A.Turner (ed.), *Organizational Symbolism*. Berlin and New York: Walter de Gruyter. pp. 291-309.
Moorman, C. and Miner, A. (1998) 'Organizational improvisation and organizational memory', *Academy of Management Review*, 23 (4): 698–723.
Obenhaus, M. and Smith, Y. (1986) *Miles Ahead: The Music of Miles Davis* (video). London: WNET/Thirteen and Obenhaus Films, Inc.
Palmer, B. (1974) 'The inner octaves of Keith Jarret', *Down Beat*, October.
Peplowski, K. (1998) 'The process of improvisation', *Organization Studies*, 9 (5): 560–2.
Schuler, G. (1989) *The Swing Era*. New York: Oxford University Press.
Stacey, R. (1996) *Complexity and Creativity in Organizations*. San Francisco: Berrett-Koehler.
Strati, A. (1992) 'Aesthetic understanding of organizational life', *Academy of Management Review*, 17 (3): 568–81.
Strati, A. (1999) *Organization and Aesthetics*. London: Sage.
Vico, G. (1968/1774) *The New Science of Giambattista Vico*. Ithaca, NY: Cornell University Press.
Weick, K. (1993) 'Organizational redesign as improvisation', in G. Huber and W. Glick, (eds), *Mastering Organizational Change*. New York: Oxford University Press. pp. 346–79.

Weick, K. (1996) 'Drop your tools: an allegory for organizational studies', *Administrative Science Quarterly*, 41: 301–13.

Wheatley, M.J. (1992) *Leadership and the New Science*. San Francisco: Berrett-Koehler.

12

The Rhythm of the Saints: Cultural Resistance, Popular Music and Collectivist Organization in Salvador, Bahia in Brazil[1]

Stewart Clegg

Introduction

The primary point of departure for this chapter was research done for the Karpin Commission of Inquiry into the 'Leadership and Management Needs of Australian Industry for the Twenty-First Century', published in 1995 as *Enterprising Nation*. The research task consisted of defining what an embryonic industry was, and then researching its leadership and management needs for the future. (A fuller account of the research may be found in Clegg et al., 1996.) The definition that we came up with said:

> Embryonic industry is new and emerging. Its novelty lies in the application of distinctive practices to production, service or problem resolution in ways that are discontinuous with existing technologies, values and knowledge. The root metaphor is that of an 'embryo'. If there is not something that is new and discontinuous then there would be no new conception, nothing in embryo. At the core are innovation in products and processes. Innovation is not just technical; it is also organizational and managerial. Effective innovation harnesses technical innovation in products and processes to social systems that can manage, organize and deliver them to markets effectively. (Clegg et al., 1996: 268)

All research involves complex stories. Not just *a* story, because, over time and between different perspectives and participants, including the readers, the story changes sufficiently to become several, perhaps even many, stories, sometimes shifting subtly, sometimes abruptly. Initially, one thought that one knew the narrative possibilities for this research. It seemed simple. Identify the industry structure of Australia at the present; look at the global scene; identify the gaps; spot the comparative advantages; and advocate clairvoyance premised upon plugging the gaps. The task proved not to be as simple as this. For one thing, existing gaps are not merely holes waiting to be filled, even where comparative advantage suggests itself. If this were the case the sheep's back would have ended up more often as a fine worsted or suiting in Australia rather than as a fleece steaming away to foreign shores. There is a global structure of trade, unequal exchanges and historical practice to contend with. These are not immutable, of course. Yet they do have consequences. Gaps are not necessarily just a matter of accident or oversight. They are not innocent of these larger matters. Often, an absence may be symptomatic of other factors which are present – and not necessarily where one is looking.

A simple proposition might suffice to make the point that there are other sources of innovation than technology. If one were to sample the best-selling cookbooks in Australia for every decade since Federation or if one sampled the generic style of restaurants available in the major capital cities over the same period (by using a combination of *Yellow Pages* and licensing records, one could do this easily), then one would find a profound and culturally conditioned shift. In this instance, the shift would be from less to more variety, contingent on a massively expanded cultural reservoir of immigration. Culture, in the sense that social scientists have of it as the fabric within which everyday lives are tailored, is both a great source for embryonic industry and one that is systematically neglected both in policy and in the literature of innovation. Think of the pizza. It implies a cultural revolution not only in eating, but in distribution through home deliveries, in the manufacture of equipment for making it, in the cultivation of sensibilities attuned to different forms of experience associated with its consumption. One thinks, for instance, of the delights of short black, flat white, caffe latté and coffees macchiato, sun-dried tomatoes, olive oil, Frascati. Not only these tastes: one thinks also of the consumption of different kinds of instructional manuals for the preparation of food – hence the proliferation of new kinds of recipes to conquer new markets. Market innovation feeds on cultural innovation.

Cultural innovation

Culture entered the story in a number of ways. First, it entered the interpretative schema in the very obvious sense of ethnically diverse cultures. Also, it entered through the emergence of new cultural demands, norms and values that can shape market opportunities to which entrepreneurs might respond. Often, these are more abstract and unfocused, less market segmented, than the more easily identifiable markers of ethnic cultures, such as foodstuffs, music, ritual, clothes, styles and custom, that tend to relate to residential districts, as in contemporary Australian multiculturalism.

It is not only multiculturalism that generates different cultural values and value in the city. The Gay and Lesbian Mardi Gras occurs annually in Sydney. It turns over more than $50 million in the New South Wales economy, centred on Sydney's gay and lesbian districts. These function similarly to the famed industrial districts that support the enterprise of Emilia-Romagna in Italy. That is, they are distinct precincts or areas of the city in which the cultivation of a particular aesthetic is the passport to commercial success widely based on networks of people closely connected not by ethnicity, religiosity or class, but by lifestyle aesthetics.

An idea began to form, one that suggested that the notion of a cultural district may be analogous in many ways to that of an industrial district, one frequently used by geographers, economists and sociologists, as well as some management scholars. The notion of cultural districts did not emerge from a stroll down Oxford Street, centre of Sydney's gay aesthetic, however. Nor did it emerge from the realization of the culturally innovative impact that ethnically based residential districts might have in terms of cultural innovation. In fact, it didn't even emerge in respect to Australia at all.

In 1994, after having completed the 'embryonic industries' project, I went to Brazil to present some of the research findings concerning the role of business networks, complexes, incubators and chains in generating innovation. Whilst travelling there, serendipitously I found an almost perfect example of culture generating embryonic industry, in the capital city, Salvador, of the north-east state of Bahia.

The Rhythm of the Saints

The Rhythm of the Saints was the title of a best-selling record released by Paul Simon in 1990. The opening track introduced a new sound to many ears – recorded in historic Pelourinho Square, the heart of Salvador, Bahia, the original colonial capital of Brazil – the sounds of Olodum. A martial, insistent, hypnotically rhythmic beat, the sound of a troupe of drums, percussive and shuffling, behind a typical Paul Simon lyric, 'The Obvious Child'. The name of the troupe of drummers was *Grupo Olodum*.

Olodum means *The God of Gods* or *The Supreme God* in the West African language of Yorubá, and formed on 25 April 1979. Although world music fans may know Olodum as a band, they are, in fact, much more than that. They are a social and a cultural movement. Inspired by the profound example of Bob Marley for black consciousness they began as a movement of cultural resistance, of the outcast, the dispossessed and the despised, drawn from the ranks of the *droguistas* and *prostitutas* (or, for the latter, more disparagingly known as *putas*), who congregated in Pelourinho, the then decaying heart of Salvador, Bahia. While the voice was inspired in part by the reggae music of

Marley and the Bahiano traditions of *tropicalismo*, to be found in Caetano Veloso, Gilberto Gil, Gal Costa and Maria Bethânia, to name only the most famous Bahiano artists, it also drew nourishment from the surrounding culture of syncretic religion, the blend of African animism and Catholic rite that is institutionalized as the church in Bahia. Paul Simon popularized the music of Olodum, but the influences that shaped that percussive rhythm initially were far from the internationally commercial context that he added, as one can hear when one listens to Olodum, proper, in their own terms.

Samba is the music of the people of Brazil, the people brought from Africa as slaves to work the sugar plantations and the latifundia economy of imperial Portugal in the New World. Forced to adopt the religion of their oppressors, the people infused it with a parallel system of beliefs, deities and saints, in the *Macumba* and *Candomblé* which preserved and re-created the animism of traditional belief-systems in Africa.[2] Olodum built on this heritage, taking it further to create an imagined community (Anderson, 1983) through its imagery of Africa, especially in the re-creation of the Ashanti rhythms of Ghanaian music. Moreover, it had a particular liminal space in which to develop – the traditions of Bahiano *Carnaval*.

Carnival has common characteristics wherever we encounter it: theatricality; being, however briefly, what ordinarily you are not; a zone and a space in which one can try out various masks, sometimes literally, sometimes, more metaphorically, as identities which define sensibility. Traditionally, carnival reversed social orders and sanctioned transgression – a space of release prior to Lent, a space of pleasure prior to a period of denial. (It is noteworthy that the Gay and Lesbian Mardi Gras in Sydney is in this respect not a traditional carnival, its timing is not prior to Lent, but during Lent, a date that is more accidental than purposefully contingent.)

In Bahia, since about 1950, *Carnaval* has been synonymous with the *trios eléctricos*. Evolved from a simple old 1929 Mustang, with a loudspeaker transmitting the music of Dodô and Osmar, musicians from Recife, the *trios* are now a spectacular procession of articulated trucks, with musicians and dancers on top of a revolving platform, itself built over a massive bank of speakers, flanking each side of the truck. The amplification is loud, the music pulsating, the costumes colourful and the dancing marvellous. The *trios* are today predominantly the voice of the *Afro-blocos*, the black Bahiano version of the *escolas de samba*, that, starting historically with the *Filhos de Ghandy*[3] in the 1940s, first imagined, and thus created, a space in the Latin *Carnaval* in which black people could parade with dignity and without fear.

There are exceptions – some *trios* are more commercial and often somewhat paler in complexion, but in the music of the *trios*, and especially in the *blocos* such as Olodum and Ilê Aiyê, is to be found the heart of Bahiano Carnaval. And the heart of *Carnaval* in Salvador comes from the old quarter of Pelourinho.

Salvador was founded in 1549 by Tomé de Souza, first Governor-General of Brazil, on a hill overlooking the Bay of Bahia, in a strong defensive position. At the centre of the settlement was a plaza, known since 1807 as Pelourinho, named thus when the authorities established there the pillory at which slaves were whipped. The old historical district of Salvador takes its name, Pelourinho, from that instrument of torture once located in its heart. In times past, at the dawn of the eighteenth century, Pelourinho housed the elite and the aristocracy of Brazilian society. They lived in large mansions and townhouses, built from fortunes amassed from the profits of the *Recôncavo* sugar plantations, the expropriation of slave labour. In and amongst their homes were many beautiful churches, ornate in the Portuguese way, testament to the economic surplus extractable from slaves, sugar and surveillance reinforced by the whip.

By the nineteenth century sugar was not the staple that it had been. New colonists in the Caribbean had realized the profitable combination of black bodies, green fields and white expropriation, and the profits accruing to the prime movers lessened greatly. By the end of the nineteenth century the old elite were down at heel. New bourgeoisie took their place: businessmen and bankers – capitalists – who, influenced by the prevailing positivist philosophies of progress, sought a space outside the unhealthy, crowded and unsewered historic city. Slowly Pelourinho changed. No longer the social magnet of this city, its population shifted as the wealthy formed homes elsewhere. Not all abandoned Pelourinho but seepage produced a net outflow.

The 1930s saw the complexion of the district rapidly change. Many Syrian, Lebanese and Italian migrants had moved there, and then, in 1932, the police moved the prostitution district into Maciel, adjacent to Pelourinho. From this era date the picaresque novels of Jorge Amado. The area declined rapidly, into a largely 'ungovernable' space of drug addicts and prostitutes in which few people ventured easily at night, in which many people lived illicit lives, the old town houses being subject to multiple occupancy, often by squatters, who practised lifestyles far removed from those of the rich and famous who had once lived there. Fires, started by unsafe and illegal tapping into the electricity supply, decay and dereliction threatened to wipe out the legacy that imperial settlement had bequeathed to the world in Salvador – the finest collection of Portuguese baroque colonial architecture in the Americas. By 1990, when I first saw Pelourinho, the area was nearly derelict, with over thirty buildings a year collapsing, despite it having been placed on the World Heritage Registry of UNESCO in 1984, after an initial report on the district in the 1960s.

By the time of a return visit in 1994 the picture had been reversed totally. Some of the changes are evident in the built environment. Others are less obvious than the glossy photographs of the official handbooks: more present in their absence, one might be tempted to say. About 500 squatters were obliged to move, many into the surrounding districts. To ensure that order is maintained in the new Pelourinho 'A special battalion of military police has been created for the area to dispel its old reputation of violence' (Lamb, 1994: 46). They are quite menacing when one sees them on the streets. Some residents have incorporated themselves into the renewed entrepreneurship of the district; others remain as 'outsiders', a dangerous, riotous possibility in the crowds that mass and seethe through the streets, especially when Olodum present one of their free street concerts. It is better not to walk alone to Pelourinho at night if you do not know the way or the people of the street. Like any place else, Pelourinho has a context, an environment, a hinterland, and its reality should not be glossed. Let us now enter the historic streets, safely deposited there by taxi or car, seduced by the sounds of samba, already catching the scent of the night on the breeze. What will we see?

Today the whole district has been sewered, repaired, refurbished and repainted in the vibrant pinks, blues and yellows of the colonial stucco that fronted the buildings. It is a magnificent spectacle of restoration. The initiative was taken by the state government in 1991 to commit the funds necessary to save Pelourinho before it was too late. Why, in 1991, after the need had been evident for many years, did the project start? Many explanations have been advanced – a popular explanation in governmental periodicals is that the state governor, newly embarked on a third term, had intimations of mortality and wanted to have done one really big, good thing while he still had opportunity to do so. Undoubtedly, without political will the restoration would never have occurred. Yet, the project had been on the cards (or on the back burner) since the mid-1960s. What made the difference?

One contributory factor, as the musician Caetano Veloso (1994: 83) acknowledges, was undoubtedly the organizational basis provided by the cultural resistance that Olodum, and other *blocos* like them, generated. Additionally, the Minister for Culture in Bahia was Gilberto Gil, a popular musician, composer and singer of *tropicalismo*. To say that he is a popular musician hardly does him justice. He is far more than that, as popular musicians can be in Brazil. Gilberto Gil was one of several Brazilian musicians who kept alive the spirit of revolt against the military dictatorship through the songs that he wrote in exile in Europe. As such, he has enormous popular legitimacy as truly a poet of the people. The conjuncture was thus unusually favourable.

Long before the governor committed the funds, the people who lived in Salvador had already begun their own self-managed revitalization, through the drum schools, the cultural *blocos* and the arts and crafts associated with these, of which Olodum is the most famous. A base had been built already in a successful street-based social movement. According to Ireland (1996: 3) it was the change of name from the 'Olodum Carnival Club' to the 'Olodum Cultural Group' in 1984 that signalled a transition in objectives:

> to include both the development of black pride and identity, and leadership in the struggle for better living conditions for the residents of the Maciel-Pelourinho area of Salvador where Olodum, along with several older Afro Carnival clubs, have their headquarters. Linking those broad concerns were several more specific preoccupations: with the right of young blacks to study, to go to school and proceed to tertiary education; with the right to vote and put forward candidates committed to the black struggle. (Ireland, 1996: 3)

The music spawned the social movement; the social movement created a distinctive, unique music; the music became part of Paul Simon's *bricolage*; the world saw a glimpse of Salvador in the accompanying video; and the state government saw an opportunity to capitalize before it was too late. No one factor was sufficient; all proved necessary, in a highly contingent process that began in a movement of resistance by young Afro-Brazilians premised on their blackness.

Today, in the renewed Salvador, through the cultural innovations associated with the *blocos*, Salvador became revalorized from a space that was declining and dangerous to one that became considerably entrepreneurial.[4] Salvador provides an object lesson in how cultural innovation can seed and produce embryonic industry, even in the least likely circumstances. Moreover, it stands as a case of an authentic and glamorous postmodernism emerging from a space previously bleak and borderline, a place of darkness and dangerous desires, as judged by the 'normal' hierarchies of taste or cannons of innovation. Pelourinho, as its social mobility went inexorably downward, became the authentic heart of darkness in Bahia. Yet, from an eighteenth-century slave market, through a nineteenth-century pillory, to the twentieth-century revival, it had always had an Afro-Brazilian connection. In Bahia it is impossible not to have this. But the recent revival would have been almost unimaginable without the efforts of the black cultural movements, like Olodum, to positively valorize the cultures of colour in Bahia through (re)imagining Africa in Brazil. The various *Afro-blocos* and *Candomblé* religious groups to be found in Pelourinho create both new identities for the people of Bahia and re-create old ones. Undoubtedly the most globally famous cultural entrepreneurs are Olodum.

The headquarters of Olodum, *Casa de Olodum*, were established in 1985 and the social movement that it represents, as well as the thousands who form their *bloco* at *Carnaval*, are what made revitalization possible. Because of the resistance orchestrated by the *blocos*, the *Filhos de Ghandy*, *Olodum* and the many others there was a cultural capital waiting to revalorize the space. They provided a hermeneutic reflexivity, one that inscribed cultural innovation, meaning-making and resistance through the creativity of *carnaval*, that gave Pelourinho its 'postmodern' form.

Postmodernity involves de-differentiation, a breakdown of the distinctiveness of each sphere of life and of the criteria which legislate each vertical dimension. Differences implode, as a result of the pervasive effects of the media and the aestheticization of everyday life. There is a shift from contemplation to consumption as differences between cultural objects and audiences dissolve and the relationship between representations and reality is problematized. This can occur in many ways; it may be a contrived experience, orchestrated as a drama such as the play *Tamara*, that David Boje (1995) describes, where the audience becomes a part of the play, gaining a degree of control over the script that they will follow, or it may occur through a more emergent process, where notions of who or what is, or can be, a performer, and what the relation of performance to audience are, become redefined. The *blocos* are a bit like this in *Carnaval*: part performers, part audience, part of the script, part of the surprise. They are the street theatre, along with the *trios* that they follow.

The *blocos* wear the *Carnaval* costume of the bloc that they follow, literally, down the *Carnaval* route. As a spectator one knows them as a bloc by their signs and images. (One might as well say as a tourist, for that is what an outsider becomes at *Carnaval* time.) The city population swells at *Carnaval*. When we are tourists we consume visual signs, even when, like myself in Salvador, we are supposedly, sophisticatedly, not acting as tourists at all, but as ethnographic researchers (Lash and Urry, 1994: 272). Actually, it is not only visual signs; other senses come into play as well. Notably, olfactory senses: *Carnaval* has a pungent odour, that of beer, spirits, sugar cane and urine mingled together in the detritus that pollutes the city streets as people, mostly men, relieve themselves where they stand. (The sugar cane is pulped by small machines along the street to extract the pure cane sugar, a pick-me-up after a night of revelry.) In part men use the street for bladder relief because of the *Carnaval* fervour and the laxity of rules that accompanies it; in part it is a necessity. There are few official or public convenience places that one can use. The streets are lined with makeshift bars, erected on carts, cardboard or wooden boxes, and the opportunities for liquid ingestion far outnumber the formal provision for its disposal in other than the form of sweat.

Carnaval helped the rebirth of Pelourinho, but what has been reborn is not just a space that is momentarily colonized and then goes back to its everyday business. (In Hong Kong such momentary colonization is routine: it occurs with far greater frequency than the once-a-year colonization of *Carnaval*. Indeed, it has a weekly frequency. Every Sunday, the 131,165 officially registered maids, nearly all of whom are from the Philippines, have their day off. As they usually occupy very little personal space in the apartments in which they sleep, surplus to sleeping, they head for the streets. In an extraordinary and vibrant colonization, they take over the whole of the city centre from the Star Ferry terminal through and under the Hong Kong Bank, and all around the surrounding streets, now blocked off to traffic as the authorities surrender to the popular ritual. The architectural and postmodern conviviality of the famous Hong Kong Bank Building, with its open but sheltered plaza at ground level, and its hollowed-out interior reaching upwards, hums to a very different sound of commerce to that of the masters of business who frequent it during the week. The Filipinas trade, cook, eat, perform various kinds of body work, like massage, make-up, hair cutting and styling, exchange gossip, news from home, local information, pictures, jobs, accommodation, mail and parcels; Catholic church services are provided in the open air; and a huge, temporally and ethnically specific informal market in just about every aspect of their everyday existence creates itself every Sunday. But come Monday morning there is no sign of it all.)

Pelourinho has become a specific and permanent site of postmodernity, more than just a carnivalesque moment. It joins architecturally odd company. One might say that the famous sites of North American postmodernity, such as the West Edmonton Shopping Mall in Alberta, represent a carnivalization of everyday life in a specifically fabricated environment, built to encapsulate, to entertain, to contain, to distract and attract, as a place of simulacra, of virtual rather than real things. They were specifically designed to be this way. Pelourinho is not like that.

Carnaval is both a time and a moment that occurs somewhere specific in space. Yet, in Pelourinho, *Carnaval* has escaped its liminal space, seeped out into the streets of every day life, and transformed a baroque masterpiece into a postmodern, spectacular space, one in which, with surprising ease, one can see the postmodern not only in the premodern carnival form but in the way that these forms have reshaped a baroque space into one that, for the moment at least, remains authentic.

The buildings may be the re-creation of premodernity but the cultural activities and spaces that they house are the postmodern context that valorizes Pelourinho. The physical context is also a symbolic and semiotic context. The place that is Pelourinho is marketing less the image of a dead colonial past and more a lively Afro-Brazilian present and presence. Its creation as such can be said to begin from the 1930s, with the picaresque novels of Jorge Amado. However, it is through the popular music of the more recent past that the contemporary inhabitants of Pelourinho found their identity.

It should be understood that this identity, one here labelled postmodern, was never consciously contrived as such from the outset. Perhaps, one might wonder, it is a form of authentic postmodernity? Instead, it was a form of resistance to the rationalizing tendencies of modernity, that marginalized certain spaces and the people who occupied them, as premodern, as almost anti-modern, in their resistance to the disciplines of modernity. In the case of Bahia as a whole, its blackness, its Africanness, marked it out as different to the southern industrial cities, notably São Paulo. Pelourinho, special home of those excluded or expelled from civil society, was clearly the most marginal and least colonized zone, a wild space where the rhythms that disciplined every day of modernity barely registered. Pelourinho's rhythms were resistant. While they were resistant of the labels attached to the marginalized space occupied, their resistance was orchestrated not just against discipline but through discipline – the discipline of the drum school. Olodum was formed by the despised, those whom Paulo Freire referred to as the 'wretched of the earth', in terms of the social hierarchies that prevailed in Salvador. It was a project that sought to find pride and a place in *Carnaval* through black consciousness reimagining Africa from its traces in Bahia. The disciplines were new, the consciousness new, the music new. Tradition was being invented.

The identity of Pelourinho is, above all, symptomatic of racial resistance creating a centre of consumption grown from black consciousness. Olodum's project began in April 1979, to restore dignity to those outcasts who, from the

1930s, had moved into Pelourinho; dignity built through collectivist organization (Fischer et al., 1992). Here, collectively orchestrated, the experience of participation provided a crucible for cultural revivification through an imaginary Africa, signified in part through colour. In Pelourinho, Olodum's imaginative use of symbols expresses itself most symbolically in its colours of green, red, yellow, black and white. Each colour has a symbolic significance: green represents the rain forests of Africa; the deep red is symbolic of the blood of the people, shed in so many centuries of suffering, from the slavery days to the present; golden yellow represents the colours of gold, for prosperity; black is for the colour and the pride of the people; while white is symbolic of world peace. Together, these colours are symbolic of the African diaspora, 'the movement of Jah people', as Bob Marley (1977) once put it.

The vision that Olodum developed latched on to the dereliction of what had been *the* architectural heritage of the Americas. The *blocos* aesthetic interest in projecting a positive image of Africa, and of negritude of, for and to the dispossessed, created not only a counter-hegemonic project that became, in its own space, hegemonic, but one that also became a space for a cultural entrepreneurship that *The Rhythm of the Saints* broadcast globally.

The local project of cultural hegemony, plus the resources that the state government brought to the restoration of Pelourinho, produced a conjuncture that mirrors almost exactly that which Lash and Urry (1994: 216–17) propose as the scenario of a successful postmodern, consumption and tourist based place-image.

Born from resistance, matured through a type of collectivist organization, and articulated in accord with other, more official, projects, the relation of Olodum and Pelourinho is a perfect example of an embryonic industry forged from cultural innovation. Today, Salvador, the city in which Pelourinho exists, is the second most-visited tourist spot in Brazil (Lamb, 1994: 42). Just four years previously it was only the eighth most visited. Today, many bars, restaurants, museums, arts and crafts shops, workshops, cultural troupes and schools occupy space that previously was virtually ungovernable, non-taxable and uncivil. Few spaces can combine the elements for marketing place-image as successfully as Pelourinho, but, it is worth recalling, just four years previously it existed as such a place-image hardly at all. It appeared, to all intents and purposes, an ungovernable space, peopled by an underclass. Today the areas surrounding Maciel-Pelourinho are still dangerous for a white person, such as myself, to tread alone, because, as everywhere, despair and poverty often produce forms of local resistance no less creative in extracting surplus from outsiders, but which offer rather less pleasure than do the entrepreneurs of 'Pelo'.

In one sense, Pelourinho is a peculiar space in some familiar ways. I grew up in the West Riding of Yorkshire, as it once was called. As I grew into maturity the industry that had sustained my forefathers slipped into extinction. The mills of the 1950s, whose hooters and steam whistles competed with the church bells to mark the rhythms of the day, slowly were silenced. Most mill towns declined with the mills, their younger people, particularly those from overseas who had been imported into the textile labour process in the post-war days, being condemned either to a semi-permanent underclass or to lives of exhausting street-level entrepreneurship. But not all towns suffered this fate.

One unusual conjuncture occurred in Haworth: mills at the bottom of the hill, near the railway station (itself a hallmark of cultural innovation, preserved by enthusiasts as a stop on the Worth Valley steam train line, as a refusal to accept extinction), a long cobbled street up the hill and, at the top, the parsonage, church, and pubs associated with the Brontës. A literary connection remade the town into kitsch. Regency architectural details, such as small paned and bottle glass windows, flourished on solid Victorian terraces; gift shops, sweet shops, cafes, restaurants, bookshops, all claiming a Brontë connection, invaded the steep street like a plague, along with the coach loads of tourists who flocked there. Of course, it was a very successful colonization – at least in business terms. Haworth did not suffer the same decline that occurred in many other mill towns. Yet, it is undoubtedly kitsch. It is cultural opportunism, fuelled by small business opportunism. Like a number of other place-marketed sites in the UK, such as 'Shakespeare's Stratford-upon-Avon', or 'Jane Austen's Hampshire', it is inauthentic and culturally anchorless, clinging to a void that once was filled with an industry far removed from the present-day business of 'recreation'.

Can Pelourinho be different? Can it escape kitsch? Has it already succumbed? At present, I think not. The *blocos* remain genuine cultural movements, they draw on a large pool of committed and creative supporters, and the identity of their icons, such as Olodum, are sufficiently fluid in terms of personnel that their fetishization and abstraction away from the street-life that shaped them has not occurred much at all. However, the process may be under way. Olodum's recent music shows a shift to a more North American influenced format than did the earlier work. The re-creation of Ashanti rhythms has a limited value for a market whose turnover is premised on novelty: rap and guitars now blend with the drums.

Pelourinho remains a place in which, as Ireland (1996) makes clear, many communally based entrepreneurs of identity emerge from work done within the cultural associations, *blocos* that are much wider than just the music: they contain arts and crafts, historiography and sociology, cuisine, dance and theatre, as well as music. Perhaps the diversity of cultural forms, as well as their rootedness in popular experience, may ensure the vibrancy of the place. Had the reputation of a restored Pelourinho rested only on the novels of Amado then the future would seem more likely to be scripted towards a museum of kitsch, preserving an already half-remembered and fading past, barely related to the present being re-made on the street on a daily basis. Had Olodum been a singular event, a group waiting to be 'discovered' in a move that, ultimately, would mean them leaving the place that nurtured them for the metropoles of the recording industry, this might have happened. But Olodum are not just a band; they are a *part* of a social movement, and the movement is bigger, more complex and more diverse than Olodum alone. It spills in and out of Pelourinho, invigorates the centre as it draws support from the surrounding streets, and seeps out into the new globalism of world music: Olodum, Ilê Aiyê, Timbalada, – the music that once travelled a few kilometres around the streets of Salvador on the back of a carnival truck now travels the world, inserted into the global marketing of the 'big five' recording companies. Within each community, each *bloco*, Pelourinho is renewed, each *Carnaval*.

The importance of cultural diversity for embryonic industry

Readers may accede that culture can seed embryonic industry, at least in what may seem an exotic Afro-Brazilian example. Yet, crucial to the example is not the exoticness of the culture signified – after all, it is hardly exotic to the people concerned – but the sense of identity that cultural symbols provide. In Brazil, the salience of Africa for the people of Bahia, is unquestionable. Forced migration, expropriation and exploitation through slavery made it so, even many generations after the end of slavery.

Brazil had African slavery as well as European migration contributing to its demographic mix. Australia never shipped slaves from Africa, although it did ship forced indentured labourers from the Pacific islands to the Queensland cane plantations in a trade known as 'blackbirding'. Australia's story is, of course, well known. It began as a disciplinary society by shipping convicts from Britain, and then surplus population from the British Isles and Eire, who, by the end of the nineteenth century, were free to participate in what, because of wealth generated from sheep, gold and wheat, had become the best-paid labour market on earth (Connell and Irving, 1979).

High wages had their price. In Australia the cost included exclusionary policies on the part of labour designed to keep the supply of workers short and their price high in a country largely peopled by migrants and early generation settlers. For many years a so-called White Australia policy effectively excluded broader migration, and it was only in the post-Second World War period that migration began to be welcomed from a wider array of countries than Britain and Northern Europe. A consequence of this is that Australia is now simultaneously the most multicultural *and* least officially hegemonic culture on earth, partly as a result of the development of 'multiculturalism' as an ideology that articulates the lived experience of the many ethnic groups that comprise the country today.

Some would argue that cultural memories from the past underlay the contemporary Australian psyche and its periodic racist irruptions, despite multiculturalism. Bronowski (1992) traces the symbols which Australians have used historically to portray Asia and convincingly argues that Australia's past trade myopia (when it came to Asia) was a consequence of its cultural myopia, one born originally from a tradition of defensive 'labourism' concerned, above all, to minimize competition in a labour market that shortages made more favourable to suppliers, rather than buyers, of labour. Yet today, in Australia, where diversity flourishes, this diversity of cultures offers major sources of value for enterprises.

Socially, innovation comes from cultural diversity just as it comes from a diverse gene pool biologically. The food industry complex is the most evident case in point. Shifts in values that derive from culture create new market opportunities. A second major source of value for industry comes from the diversity of the personnel who comprise it. In selling overseas, whatever the product, whether traditional or innovative, national enterprises in a country such as Australia have a remarkable opportunity to do good business through the serendipity of multiculturalism. Australians who are also competent speakers of a customer's language, because they already know the language as their community language, have a head-start in doing good business in that culture. This is because they already have much of the tacit knowledge and implicit learning that those who are alien can acquire only slowly and painfully. In general, a great deal of learning occurs through making mistakes. In business this can be costly. Multiculturalism presents the possibility of much lower-cost learning. However, diversity requires good management for innovation.

There is a third important attribute of culture in relation to embryonic industries. Recent studies assess and compare cultural attitudes towards technology. Such attitudes mediate the effective use to which technological innovation may be put (Gattiker and Willoughby, 1993; Littek and Heisig, 1991). Public policy clearly is part of a complex that affects the prospects of embryonic industry. Yet, the role for public policy is reserved not merely for technological innovation: the case study of Pelourinho makes this clear as does the policy of the previous Australian Government in launching the 'Creative Nation' initiative, an indication of public policy spending on culture that couples public support of cultural activities with investment in state-of-the-art CD-ROM technologies for the production and dissemination of cultural production. It is less the technological innovations *per se* that are important than the fusion of technology and culture.

The division between 'culture' and 'technology' as sources of innovation is blurring: interestingly, this tips the balance towards the more 'open' societies, because they will blur furthest and fastest in those democracies whose public policies support open communication. To seek to control technologies of open communications as if they were like printing presses that can be closed; broadcasters who can be censored, or print material that can be seized, is not only foolish; it sunders also the culture/technology nexus, and in the twenty-first century increasingly it will be from culture that innovation in content flows, even as it does so through new technological forms.

Good management of the multicultural workforce is vital, but there is more to culture than merely its proliferation across the diversity of employees. There is also the question of cultural identity in the marketplace, the identity of customers and consumers. In all 'postmodern' societies, by definition, these identities will be fragmented, disparate and heterodox. This leads to a final point. Where strong cultures function, they do so more as a mechanism designed to try and create unity where it is usually absent, than as a sign of its inalienable presence. Ordinarily, cultural diversity should be seen as a strength rather than a weakness. Only rarely can strong cultures be achieved by management fiat. Again, the case of Pelourinho makes the point beautifully. Olodum and the other *blocos* did not emerge from an already strong and unitary culture. They forged one. A strong culture exists because they made it. They made it not from a position of strength, of hegemony, of cultural superiority, but as a form of resistance to the ghetto life to which they had been consigned. The strength of Olodum and the other *Afro-blocks* resides in their roots in the local communities. It is from these communities that the subjectivities that are exhibited in, and sustain, the *blocos*, emerge. The revalorization of African roots and, with them, the recolonization of the colonialist architectural heritage of the Americas, by those who had been the most wretched, the most culturally dispossessed, built cultural strength. And it built it from the bottom up, through collectivist organization and self-management, rather than through manipulation of a mass of followers by a leader, or the management of symbols *by* superordinates *for* subordinates. Many of the refurbished houses in Salvador still house the people who were squatting previously, but now they live in houses that the State Government has renovated. This is not gentrification where the workings of the market dispossess previous inhabitants but renovation made possible through a project of cultural revitalization. Only five hundred people were moved out from the many thousands previously resident there. One can join with Linstead (1996: 18) in saying of Pelourinho that

> It is *socially* constructed and negotiated; it is *symbolically* constructed; and it is *historically* constructed through style or genre, and through its place in a *narrative* of the past and future sustained in specific accounts or more distributed discourses in the present.

Pelourinho, as a built environment is thus much more than a place of bricks and stucco; it is a socially constructed place, negotiated out of the emergent and resistant bodies and identities that narrated themselves there. Black bodies, slaves wrenched from Mother Africa found one part of their being in the church and with the spirits of *Candomblé*, some other parts of their being in that space opened up by the *Filhos de Ghandy*. Proud, working black men, stevedores and dockers, men armed with a philosophy of peace and brotherhood, opened a narrative space where myriad ways of historically recollecting and reconstructing being black were born in a style and genre that emerged from the realities of everyday life in the ghetto and release from it in *Carnaval*. And part of this quotidian quality ensures that, if the cultural entrepreneurs of the *blocos* loose their sense of place, displaced into the star-making machinery that stokes the popular song (Mitchell, 1973), others with a stronger sense of being there will re-make it. One sees this already in the conclusions of Ireland (1996: 13) when he notes that the 'successful cultural associations' are those that 'give unflinching priority to maintaining local grassroots ties and commitments'. With him, we may refer to the rivalry between *blocos* such as Ilê Aiyê and Olodum, and the fragmentation between different *blocos* and associations, as a source of strength because it is in the fragments, and the tensions between them, that possible identities emerge into being. Pelourinho, we should conclude, is a place that is much more than it appears to be.

Conclusion

For any organization to survive it must have some distinctive competence (Selznick, 1957), those things that it does especially well when compared with its competitors in a similar environment. It doesn't matter whether this competence is the discipline of a drum school or the presentation of a gay sensibility.

Innovation can be cultural just as much as technological: cultural competencies can generate innovation. Cultural competency refers to the ability to be able to harness and use culturally diverse myths, symbols, rituals, norms and ideational systems creatively to add value to an organization's activities. In the future, in both the core and the periphery of today's world system, value will accrue to those who do so manage. The *Carnaval* of Bahia and the Carnival of Sydney are very different events, staged at roughly the same time, in two very different parts of the world. What each has in common is the way that value is produced from values. In both instances the values were once weak, despised and downtrodden, serving to demonstrate that organizational value may be found in the most unlikely places, from the least likely sources. The flows through Pelourinho were such that it seemed a ghetto, a wasteland, a dangerous place where civility did not tread the street. Yet, with collective organization and a supportive public policy, the situation was transformed. In Australia, the streets might now seem less dangerous but that is because of the opportunities for reflexive cultural innovation that have been generated: both by multiculturalism and by gay and lesbian sensibilities. Although each form of difference was distinct, once upon a time difference was disguised, disfigured, dispirited. The flows are different and the spaces through which they stream differ. In each case analysis suggest a central role for culture, one where culture can valorize a collective identity built out of adversity, affirmed in *Carnaval*, constitutive of organizational innovation that can build embryonic industry.

Every cultural innovation that achieves institutionalization carries the seed of potential demise, if it lapses into kitsch, if its expression ceases to be authentic, if it abandons creativity and improvisation, if it becomes a managed event, or if it is co-opted by elites and looses connections with its roots. Any institutionalized innovation, of any sort, faces the paradox that once institutionalized, it ceases to be innovative but lapses into the repetition of familiar organizational routines.

Between the lines, I want to suggest two things. First, the imaginary journey of this chapter may show more than it says: for finally, how many organizations can ever achieve the creativity of the *blocos* that emerged out of *Carnaval*? Perhaps the ranks are limited only to those that are genuinely democratic and self-managed communities? Perhaps cultural entrepreneurs first have to follow before they can lead? Perhaps the case of Olodum has something to offer, not only to entrepreneurs but also to professors of management and organizations, as well as policy practitioners. Finally, I hope that I have drawn into question some canonical distinctions embedded in the organization of high modernity, those between art and science, between elite and popular culture, between personal biography and scientific narrative, between presentation and representation.

Notes

1 The material for this chapter derives from several sources. First, there are notes I made during field-trips to Pelourinho. Especially, I would like to thank Ericivaldo Veiga, archivist and researcher of the *Casa de Olodum* and Antônia Maria Sampaio des Reis for the opportunity to talk extensively with them on 30 September, 1994, in *Casa de Olodum*. In addition, the work of Marcelo Dantas (1994) was invaluable, as was Nelson Cherqueira's (1994) wonderfully illustrated edited volume *Pelourinho: Historic District of Salvador – Bahia: The Restored Grandeur.* Finally, *Bahia Verão & Folia* (1994), also provided useful background information. After I had written several drafts of this piece I came across Rowan Ireland's (1996) work on Salvador and was intrigued to find a fellow Australian working on the same Brazilian topic. Although our purposes and approaches differ somewhat, there are many points of convergence between our work. I would like to thank Rowan for making the paper 'The dancing spirits of world capitalism' available to me.

2 *Candomblé*, as a basis for resistance and reappropriation, was not only ethnic in its politics: it was also a gendered politics, as women were both numerically and representationally the most powerful actors within *Candomblé*, from its earliest development in the slavery days. It is women who are the privileged site of incorporation as the *filhas dos santos*, dressed in traditional white lace dresses, waiting for deities (*orixás*) to possess them during *Candomblé* rituals, when the spirits are called down, incorporated into the bodies of the devotees, speaking through them (but not of them) to offer advice to those who want or need it. *Candomblé* creates a space which enhances their status as women and offers opportunities for informal networking and power. The gendering associated with *Candomblé* is a complex matter, hardly addressed by the usual binary categories, as Cornwall (1994) makes clear in her fascinating account of Salvador.

3 The 'Sons of Ghandy' were formed from the ranks of waterside workers attracted to the non-violent philosophy of social change promoted by Ghandi. The spelling of '*Filhos de Ghandy*' is one that they adopted. Their costume is blue and white, originally fabricated from old white sheets and blue towels. As they march in majestic procession in *Carnaval* they are an inspiring presence.

4   This is one of several points at which, had it been possible, I would have used photographic data, to display the colourful and folkloric representations that constitute signs of entrepreneurship, literally, in Pelourinho. You will have to see them for yourself, or, if you are able to, consult Cherqueira (1994), which contains many excellent photographs by Bruno Furrer.

References

Anderson, B. (1983) *Imagined Communities: Reflections on the Origins and Spread of Nationalism.* London: Verso.

Boje, D.M. (1995) 'Stories of the storytelling organization: a postmodern analysis of Disney as "*Tamara*-Land" ', *Academy of Management Journal,* 38 (4): 997–1035.

Bronowski, A. (1992) *The Yellow Lady: Australian Impressions of Asia.* Melbourne: Oxford University Press.

Cherqueira, N. (ed.) (1994) *Pelourinho: Historic District of Salvador – Bahia: The Restored Grandeur.* Salvador: Fundacão Culturado Estado da Bahia.

Clegg, S.R., Dwyer, L., Gray, J., Kemp, S. and Marceau, J. (1996) 'Managing as if tomorrow matters: embryonic industries and management in the twenty first century', in G. Palmer and S.R. Clegg (eds), *Constituting Management: Markets, Meanings and Identities.* Berlin: de Gruyter. pp. 267–305.

Connell, R.W. and Irving, T.H. (1980) *Clan Structure in Australian History: Document, Narrative and Argument.* Melbourne: Cambridge University Press.

Cornwall, A. (1994) 'Gendered identities and gender ambiguity among *travestis* in Salvador, Brazil', in A. Cornwall and N. Lindisfarne (eds), *Dislocating Masculinities: Comparative Ethnographies.* London: Routledge. pp. 111–32.

Dantas, M. (1994) *Olodum – de bloco afro a holding cultural.* Salvador: Edicões de Olodum.

Fischer, T.M., Dantas, M., Silva, F.L. and Mendes, V. (1992) 'Olodum – a arte e o negôcio', *Anais de ANDAD,* 6, – Organicaöes, Canela, Set.

Gattiker, U.E. and Willoughby, K. (1993) 'Technological competence, ethics and the global village: cross-national comparisons for organization research', in R.T. Golembiewski (ed.), *Handbook of Organizational Behaviour.* New York: Marcel Dekker. pp. 457–85.

Ireland, R. (1996) 'The dancing spirits of world capitalism: globalization, popular culture and citizenship in Salvador, Bahia', unpublished paper, Department of Sociology, La Trobe University.

Lamb, C. (1994) 'United colours of Pelourinho', in N. Cherqueira (ed.), *Pelourinho Centro histórico de Salvador – Bahia: A Grande Resurada.* Salvador: Fundacão Culturaldo Estado da Bahia. pp. 40–6.

Lash, S. and Urry, J. (1994) *Economies of Signs and Space.* London: Sage.

Linstead, S. (1996) 'Understanding management: critique, culture and change', in S. Linstead, R.G. Small and P. Jeffcut (eds), *Understanding Management.* London: Sage. pp. 10–33.

Littek, W. and Heisig, U. (1991) 'Competence, control and work redesign: *Die Angstell* in the Federal Republic of Germany', *Work and Occupations,* 18: 4–28.

Marley, Bob (1977) 'Exodus', New York: Bob Marley Music/Almo Music Corp. (ASCAP).

Mitchell, Joni (1973) 'Free man in Paris', Hollywood: Warner Bros. Music Ltd.

Selznick, P. (1957) *Leadership in Administration.* New York: Harper and Row.

Veloso, C. (1994) 'Caetano Veloso erudito – fragmentos de entrevista coletiva a imprensa para Gideon Rosa', in N. Cherqueira (ed.), *Pelourinho Centro histórico de Salvador – Bahia: A Grande Resurada*. Salvador: Fundacão Culturaldo Estado da Bahia. pp. 82–4.

Name Index

Subject Index